D1258117

FITZ-JAMES O'BRIEN

A Literary Bohemian
of
The Eighteen-Fifties

FITZ-JAMES O'BRIEN

A Literary Bohemian of The Eighteen-Fifties

By FRANCIS WOLLE

Professor of English Literature

University of Colorado

University of Colorado Studies

Series B. Studies in the Humanities

Vol. 2, No. 2

Boulder, Colorado

May, 1944

Price $2.00

Contents

List of Illustrations

PREFACE

The single authoritative account of the life and writings of Fitz-James O'Brien was published by his friend William Winter in 1881—*The Poems and Stories of Fitz-James O'Brien.* Winter's introductory sketch, with the accompanying letters written to him from other friends of O'Brien, has been almost the sole source of our knowledge, and all the succeeding accounts have made extracts or condensations from it. But Winter both because of lack of space and because of the desire to reveal his friend in the best light possible suppressed many items that he had collected and many facts that he knew. Most of his collection found its way, after the sale of his library in April, 1922, into the hands of Charles Romm, collector and secondhand-book dealer of New York, and through his generosity I was permitted to make copies of the manuscripts and letters. Romm disappeared about 1931, and nothing was heard about him thereafter until his death in 1939. His property was disposed of, and I lost all trace of the O'Brien-Winter manuscripts until February, 1944, when they were listed in catalogue No. 13 by K. Gregory, of 222 East 71st Street, and were immediately purchased by the New York Public Library as a part of the Berg collection. There they have a permanent home, but as the manuscript of this book was already in the hands of the printer when the library made its acquisition, all footnotes still refer to these MSS as in the Romm collection. Five other manuscripts as well as traditions about O'Brien's habits were supplied through the kindness of Alfred F. Goldsmith, bookseller of 42 Lexington Avenue, New York City.

Practically all the material of Chapter I is new; for Winter knew nothing definite about O'Brien's ancestry, about his immediate family, nor about his life as a boy and young man in Ireland and England. Through the interested cooperation of Mr. Vincent Fleming O'Reilly, librarian of the American Irish Historical Society, and the books he made available, O'Brien's earliest poetry in *The Nation* of Dublin was found, and an almost complete account of his maternal ancestry. Afterwards, on a trip to Ireland in September, 1929, I succeeded in tracing his father's family and visited the places Fitz-James knew as a boy. In Dublin through the greatly appreciated courtesy of Dr. Richard I. Best, of the National Library of Ireland, I was granted free access to the stacks, and so was able to discover poems, essays, and stories of O'Brien's in Irish and English periodicals of whose very titles I was unaware.

Of O'Brien's animated share in the social, literary, and Bohemian life of New York City in the days before the Civil War this book presents an almost unbroken record; and it is hoped that the gay but turbulent personality it reveals will prove as interesting to the reader as it has been stimulating to the author. The materials have been brought together from widely separated sources; and, though the ferreting out of the facts has been an arduous task, it has also been a luring one. Many poems and articles have been identified for the first time; autograph letters have been found; files of ephemeral magazines have yielded verses, cartoons, and references; daily and weekly papers of the fifties have supplied dramatic reviews, while those of the sixties, carefully scrutinized, have yielded a nearly complete war record; and visits to his old haunts in New York and Boston, to the scenes of his battle skirmishes at Bloomery Gap, and to his grave in Brooklyn have furnished local color and personal background.

To most readers O'Brien is known only as the author of "The Diamond Lens" and "What Was It?", the two weird tales that continue to find favor with the anthologists. Much of his other work is difficult of access, and, therefore, in the interests of thoroughness, considerable space has been devoted to some poems and sketches which in themselves are relatively unimportant. The main emphasis, however, has been placed upon the stories, the form in which O'Brien made his chief contribution to the development of American literature; yet even here I trust that friendly feeling for the man has not made me blind to the shortcomings of the author.

The concentration of this study upon Fitz-James O'Brien as a man and as a writer may seem to isolate him unduly from the general literary history of the times in which he lived; and it is true that when the manuscript was originally completed in 1933 considerably more space was devoted to the social and literary backgrounds of the decade during which he flourished in America (1852–1862) and to an account of the magazines and papers for which he wrote. Since then, however, three books have appeared which cover these phases so well that this biography as it now stands represents a shortening of the original manuscript by approximately a fourth. *The*

Feminine Fifties (1940) by Fred Lewis Pattee adequately and entertainingly explores the backgrounds, and the excellent volumes of Frank Luther Mott thoroughly and competently survey the journalistic field—especially *A History of American Magazines, 1850–1865* (1938) and *American Journalism* (1941).

The ferreting out of O'Brien's work was begun in 1925 under the stimulus of that excellent scholar and sympathetic guide, William Peterfield Trent, and the finished manuscript was read with meticulous care by Ralph L. Rusk, whose constructively helpful criticisms formed the basis of its first revision. George F. Reynolds, head of the English department of the University of Colorado, also read the manuscript and gave many suggestions for improvement; while the constant encouragement of Arthur Hobson Quinn during seven long years of digging will always be gratefully remembered. Of the many librarians who so kindly aided me I recall especially the infinite patience and hard physical labor of the staff in the newspaper room of the New York Public Library as they brought to my desk all the bound volumes of all New York newspapers from 1852 to 1862, the extraordinary courtesy of the men at the Yale library, and the helpful interest of the custodian of the Historical Society of Pennsylvania.

A great deal of time was consumed in travelling about the country from library to library locating files of the short-lived periodicals to which O'Brien contributed, a labor which would no longer be necessary since the publication of the *Union List of Serials* (1943).

The manuscript was originally prepared to meet the requirements for a doctoral dissertation at Columbia University and was so accepted in 1933, but for the present form of the book, the result of a recent revision, the Columbia committee is to be absolved of responsibility. My colleagues on the faculty of the University of Colorado and my friends in Boulder gave me the help and encouragement necessary to carry the work through. Chief among them are George F. Reynolds, head of the English department; Muriel V. Sibell, head of the Fine Arts department; Waino S. Nyland and Paul V. Thompson of the College of Engineering; Elizabeth Selleck, reference librarian; and especially Mrs. June Waterfield West, whose acute criticisms all along the line were invaluable; and Carter Victor Dorrell, who gave moral support and generous contributions of his time during the arduous task of getting the manuscript ready for the printer.

The greatest stimulus away from home was supplied by Charles I. Glicksberg of New York, who shares my enthusiasm for the period of the 1850's and who gave me valuable hints about places in which to investigate.

I gratefully acknowledge the courtesy of the authors and publishers in granting permission to quote copyright material, as follows:

Acknowledgments

American Book Company for a sentence from *The Short Story* by Brander Matthews, New York, 1907.

The Atlantic Monthly Press for sentences from *The Atlantic Monthly and Its Makers* by M. A. DeWolfe Howe, Boston, 1919.

Columbia University Press for names from *Annals of the New York Stage* by George C. D. Odell, New York, 1931.

Doubleday, Doran and Company, Inc. for "The Two Vaults" by Walt Whitman from *The Uncollected Poetry and Prose of Walt Whitman* by Emory Holloway, Garden City, 1921.

Harper and Brothers for sentences from *The Development of the American Short Story* by Fred Lewis Pattee, New York, 1923.

For sentences from *A History of the American Drama from the Beginning to the Civil War* by Arthur Hobson Quinn, New York, 1923.

For paragraphs from *An Epistle to Posterity* by M. E. W. Sherwood, New York, 1898.

Henry Holt and Company for paragraphs from *The Short Story in English* by Henry Seidel Canby, New York, 1909.

Houghton Mifflin Company for sentences from *The Life of Thomas Bailey Aldrich* by Ferris Greenslet, Boston, 1908.

Mr. M. A. DeWolfe Howe for paragraphs from his *Memories of a Hostess*, Atlantic Monthly Press, Boston, 1922.

Miss Mildred Howells and John Mead Howells for paragraphs from *Literary Friends and Acquaintances* by William Dean Howells, Harper and Brothers, New York, 1911.

Professor Jay B. Hubbell for all of the material and much of the wording of Chapter I, which appeared as an article of mine in *American Literature*, Vol. XIV (November, 1942).

J. B. Lippincott Company for a sentence from *New York, Old and New* by Rufus Rockwell Wilson, Philadelphia, 1909 (Third Edition).

The Macmillan Company for paragraphs from "A Keltic Poe" by Dr. Joseph J. Reilly, originally appearing in *The Catholic World* (reprinted in his book *Dear Prue's Husband*, New York, 1932).

Oxford University Press for paragraphs from *The Cowells in America* by M. Willson Disher, London, 1934.

G. P. Putnam's Sons for sentences from *The Supernatural in Modern English Fiction* by Dorothy Scarborough, New York, 1917.

Burton Egbert Stevenson for a clause from *Poems of American History*, Houghton Mifflin Company, 1910.

Frank Winter for all quotations from the books, letters, and manuscripts of his father, William Winter.

FITZ-JAMES O'BRIEN

From a drawing by Sol Eytinge, Jr.

Chapter I

Beginnings—Fitz-James O'Brien in Ireland and England

(1828–1851)

In the little town of Granby, Connecticut, sat an old man in his comfortable, old-fashioned home, and while the sun lengthened out the golden shadows of the late afternoon he talked of the days of his youth in New York before the Civil War, of the ambitious strivings of his young manhood as he was learning to be an artist, of the staunch friends and jovial comrades with whom he worked and played, of his courtship and wedding—Thomas Bailey Aldrich acting as best man, and Launt Thompson as one of the ushers—and with especial relish he recalled the evenings spent at Pfaff's beer cellar on Broadway just above Bleecker Street. As, on August 20, 1927, this ninety-five-year-old gentleman recalled the days of seventy years before, he grew wistful and tender, and the old comrades crowded before him as he talked; and for two hours I sat enthralled, seeing for the first time with a sense of reality men with whom I had long been familiar only as names. Walt Whitman was there, and Henry Clapp, and Frank Bellew, and Thompson, besides many, many others. But the plainest, the most alive—because they had been "A. D.'s" closest friends and his most lively comrades—were "Tom" and "Fitz." A. D. Shattuck became an artist, picturer of sheep and of the lovely landscape of Connecticut, where he went to make his home; Thomas Bailey Aldrich became, after Longfellow, one of America's most beloved poets, essayists, and storytellers; and Fitz-James O'Brien became—well, nothing very much after 1857, '58, and '59, when he so frequently supped at Pfaff's with Aldrich and Shattuck. He was killed by an enemy's bullet in the Civil War and gradually he faded from memory, until William Winter in 1881 published a book of some of his poems and stories. This renewal of his fame was but temporary, however, and his power as an artist, his place in the development of our American literature, was not recognized until Brander Matthews pointed it out in connection with his study of the short story. Since then the place of O'Brien has been generally admitted, but the facts of his life have remained unknown.

After the vitalizing help of A. D. Shattuck's reminiscences I decided to follow the footsteps of Fitz-James back from their fairly well-marked path through the years in New York City to their entirely untraced beginnings in his native Ireland. So two years later (1929) I landed at his home city of Cork and for the next four months sought through Ireland and England for the evidences of his life there. The search led first through the most beautiful parts of southwestern Ireland, especially the county and city of Cork, to the estates on which the immediate members of the family of Fitz-James O'Brien had lived; then to the home of his step-father in county Limerick on the banks of the Shannon; and finally to Dublin to check records in the various governmental offices and to scour the periodicals in the National Library for the poems he sent to the local magazines and newspapers. From there the trail moved to London, where he squandered his inheritance lavishly and wrote for the journals of his friend R. Kemp Philp.

Until the facts unearthed by this trip were published in *American Literature* for November, 1942, Fitz-James O'Brien had been known only as a gay and brilliant young Irishman who late in December of 1851 arrived in New York City on a sailing vessel from England. From the time of his landing in America, however, he was well known, and the general course of his career was plainly marked, even though many details went unrecorded. He almost immediately became a contributor to American magazines, and during the next ten years was identified with the group of clever young men who, seeking a living by their pens, formed what may be termed New York's first literary Bohemia. Of this crowd, who frequented Pfaff's beer cellar until it became a sort of informal headquarters, none except Walt Whitman and Henry Clapp, Jr., surpassed Fitz-James O'Brien in vividness of personality. His verve carried him through many highly colored episodes, until with a final glorious flash he ended his life fighting for the Union in the Civil War.

To supply his needs he wrote copiously in many forms, but he was reckless and extravagant and he drank excessively. He enjoyed playing practical jokes as much as he enjoyed quarreling, thus making warm friends and bitter enemies; and whatever he did, he did with an intensity which impressed itself on his contemporaries.

Poems, plays, essays, criticisms, satires, and short stories poured from his pen, and a study of them forms an interesting commentary on the production of popular literature as it flourished in the United States during the decade of the fifties. Besides, O'Brien knew and appreciated the work of Edgar Allan Poe, and in trying to imitate Poe's technique of the short story he made his definite contribution to the development of American letters.

I. In Ireland

Michael Fitz-James O'Brien[1] was born sometime between April and December 31, 1828, in Cork,[2] either at the home of his parents in the city or at the country seat of his maternal grandparents at Baltimore House in the southwestern part of the county. The only child of James O'Brien, Esq., one of the county coroners, and of Eliza, his beautiful young wife, he was named Michael in honor of both his grandfathers, and Fitz-James, meaning son of James, in honor of his father. The Michael he seems never to have used.

About his father's family little is known. His paternal grandfather owned Brownstown, a farm of some 246 acres lying on the coast about five miles south of Clonakilty, county Cork; and Brownstown House, which with its farm buildings stood almost in the midst of the not-too-fertile fields, served as the home of the resident farmer.[3] Michael's wife was Catherine Deasy, and their son James was born in 1780.[4] In 1796, upon

[1] O'Brien's middle name occurs in four different forms—Fitzjames, FitzJames, Fitz-James, Fitz James. The first form—as one word with a small *j*—appears in print three times (in Ireland and England) and is the form used in his mother's letter. The second form—as one word, but with a capital *J*—is the way in which it would seem to be necessary to interpret one of the signatures (most often the signature is merely "F. J.") and is the form preferred for names of this type according to good Irish practice of the present time. During O'Brien's life in America the name was printed either with the hyphen or as two separate words, an equal number of times each way. The present general acceptance of the hyphenated form is due to its use by William Winter in his volume of 1881, *The Poems and Stories of Fitz-James O'Brien;* and this usage is confirmed by the fact that it is the form in which, with only three exceptions, the name appeared in the magazines of Ireland and England. Thus, established usage and the young author's own sanction when he was in a position to have his name printed as he wished it are both in favor of the hyphen, and that form is here retained.

[2] The exact date and place of his birth are unknown. The inscription on his coffin plate was, "Died April 6, 1862, Aged 33 years." Winter says he was born in county Limerick, his impression probably arising from the fact that O'Brien's later boyhood was spent in that county. See *The Poems and Stories of Fitz-James O'Brien*, ed. William Winter, Boston, 1881, p. xv. (This volume will hereafter be cited in the notes as Winter, 1881). It seems far more likely that with both sides of the family residing in county Cork he was born there.

[3] See *Guy's Topographical Directory of County Cork*, Cork, 1888, p. 5. The population of Brownstown in 1881 was 39, and the valuation £ 184, 15s.

[4] These facts about his father's family should correct the interesting stories which were circulated after Fitz-James became prominent in America, connecting him with William Smith O'Brien, the Irish patriot, and with the O'Briens who belonged to the Irish aristocracy—Lord Fermoy and Baron Inchiquin, Marquis of Thomond.

arriving at the age of sixteen, James was entered at the King's Inn, Dublin, as a solicitor's apprentice, the affidavit being made by his maternal uncle Richard Deasy, of Clonakilty.[5] By 1810 he was established in the South Mall as an attorney,[6] by 1820 he was voting on the governmental or winning side in an election,[7] and by 1823 he was one of the four county coroners.[8] To obtain the office of coroner he must have had an established position as an attorney and have been an owner of property with means sufficient to carry out the duties of the office with dignity. He lived at 58 South Mall, the most respectable street in the city, and seems to have had his attorney's office in the same building.[9]

After obtaining the office of coroner, James O'Brien married Eliza O'Driscoll, who was some twenty years younger than himself, being then only eighteen or twenty. Eliza was the daughter, the only living child, of Michael and Helena O'Driscoll of Baltimore House, Baltimore.[10]

Baltimore is a small fishing village almost on the southwestern point of Ireland, and was before the time of Queen Elizabeth a flourishing port ruled over by the chief of the clan O'Driscoll, whose castle stronghold, Toberanargid, commanded the town and the harbor. The castle was in ruins, however, long before the time of Michael O'Driscoll, though the title of "The O'Driscoll" by which he was generally known shows that he was regarded as a descendant of the old chief and as head of the ancient clan, which can be traced back historically to 1276 and traditionally to 366 and the Kings of Munster. On his mother's side "The O'Driscoll" traced his descent from the O'Gradys of Kilballyowen, one of the most ancient families of county Limerick.

Baltimore House stands on the shore of Baltimore Harbour in the midst of scenes of picturesque and rugged beauty, the waters of the bay stretching away to the northwest where they are broken into by jutting headlands,

[5] Copy from Admission Paper in King's Inn, Dublin, supplied through the kindness of Thomas U. Sadleir, Registrar, Office of Arms, The Castle, Dublin.

[6] See Will West, *A Directory, and Picture, of Cork and its Environs*, Cork, 1810, p. 93.

[7] See pamphlet, *City of Cork Election*, for 1820, pp. 122 and 128. James O'Brien appears similarly in *Lists of the Freemen and Freeholders Alphabetically arranged, who voted at the Cork Election, December 1826*, p. 96.

[8] See *The Cork Almanack, 1823;* quoted in *Journal of the Cork Historical and Archaeological Society*, II, 201 (Oct., 1893). He is still listed as coroner in *Connor's Cork Directory for the year 1830*, p. 18.

[9] See *Connor's Cork Directory for the year 1830*, pp. 18, 19, and 103.

[10] Michael and Helena had four children—one son, Denis, and three daughters, Helena, Eliza, and Jane. Denis and Jane died at comparatively early ages, and Helena died a spinster in 1826.—See MS. *Index to Prerogative Wills, 1811–1858*, in Public Record Office of Ireland, Dublin.

and interrupted by a number of Carbery's "hundred isles," while in the blue distance, long lines of mountains rise one above the other. To the west and south, on Sherkin Island just across the bay, stand the beautiful ruins of Dunalong Abbey, set off by the vivid green of the protected valley which shelters them, and not far away, conspicuous on a rocky headland, rise the few remaining stones of Dunalong Castle. Behind Baltimore House in the more immediate vicinity, on an eminence at the foot of which cluster the few small cottages of the village, are the ruined walls of Toberanargid; and though its lords, the old O'Driscolls, had generally been engaged in piratical enterprises, tradition has it that once upon a time Sir Fineen O'Driscoll entertained within its walls the officers of Queen Elizabeth's fleet.[11]

Michael's wife Helena did not have to change her name when she married, as her father was Timothy O'Driscoll of Lakeland. Lakeland is one of the most attractive of the many estates lying along the River Lee below Cork, and is situated some three miles out of the city on the banks of Lough Mahon, as the widening of the river at that place is called. Timothy O'Driscoll was a justice of the peace, as was his son, Helena's brother Alexander, who had a seat at Cloverhill about half way between Lakeland and the city; and after Michael had married Helena and had come into possession of her considerable dowry, he too became a justice. He was swept out of this distinction, however, along with other Roman Catholics in the county, by the staunchly Protestant chancellor, Lord Manners, when he was appointed to the office in 1807.[12]

Michael's father, Denis, lived southwest of Cork, at a manor called Creagh Court, about half way between Skibbereen and the coast; so it was only natural that Michael O'Driscoll with his wealthy wife should establish himself at Baltimore House, a place rich in family tradition and within easy riding distance of his nearest kin.

When Michael O'Driscoll died in 1830,[13] he had no male heir other than his infant grandson Fitz-James O'Brien, to whom he left his property, including Baltimore House and perhaps a smaller cottage some three miles away across the hills, on the shores of Lough Hyne. By this salt-water lake

[11] See *Miscellany of the Celtic Society*, ed. John O'Donovan, Dublin, 1849, p. 397. His story was told by Fitz-James years later in "The Lost Room," *Harper's*, XVII, 494–500 (Sept., 1858) q.v.

[12] For confirmation of the above details and a further account of the genealogy of the O'Driscolls, see *ibid.*, pp. 397–398.

[13] See entry in *Index to Prerogative Wills, 1811–1858, loc. cit.* The fact that his will was proved in the Prerogative Court shows that the testator had been a person of considerable property.

of the south coast, with the beauty of its enclosing hills and castle-crowned Bally Island rising from its midst, it is certain that Fitz-James spent many of his childhood days; and so deep an impression did it make on the sensitive boy that before he left his native land he described it in two poems, while a little later he made it the setting for his first short story. In the opening paragraph of the latter, "The Phantom Light," he thus gives the general features of the district:

On the south-western coast of Ireland there is a little nook of country over which impetuous tourists step disdainfully, nor notice the many exquisite beauties that lie there like hidden violets, lovely, but unseen. It is a land of hoary castles, and many a mouldering tradition—a land where the blue sea indents the shore into sweet and sunny bays, seeming as if the ocean loved the earth and sought to steal half-timidly into its arms;—a land where wild and rugged rocks start up by every solitary pathway—strange, uncouth, fantastic in their forms, like nightmares petrified. It is rife, too, with the chronicles of the past; and white-haired Senachies will sit by the bog-wood blaze the long night through, telling of vanished days, and long-forgotten deeds of the old sea-kings of the coast, ruthless, reckless men, who, sitting on the summits of their lofty watch-towers all day long, gazed across the wide Atlantic for some hapless bark whose rich spoils might fill their greedy coffers.[14]

After this, more definitely localizing the place, the author expatiates upon the beauties of Lough Hyne:

One spot in particular seemed to be the especial haunt of all such lore, and truly there never was a meeter dwelling for romance! It was a small and lovely lake. In the midst was set a green island, which the rippling waves clasped as if in very love; while on its emerald turf through which the white rocks peeped, arose an old, grey castle. Above the crumbling top the snowy seagulls gleamed as they floated in the sunshine, and the rabbits played beneath its walls in many a wild and antic gambol. Beyond this island lay a narrow, rocky channel, through which the sea rushed foaming into the lake, and where, on one side, a tall and spectral stone stood up as if to guard the pass. It was the traditioned grave of a famous saint [Saint Bridget], who, the peasants said, might be sometimes seen in the dusk of twilight weeping for a brief while over the sins of a wicked world. Farther still, over the seaward shores of the lake, gleamed the blue ocean, that, like a beauty-bestowing cestus, girdled around that fairy scene. . . .

There was a lofty mountain, too—a sullen, haughty-looking giant, who, with his dark fir-groves that waved like a beard upon his cheek, sat watching jealously the azure lake that sparkled gem-like at his rugged foot. Sometimes, in the

[14] *The Home Companion*, I, 5 (Jan. 3, 1852).

winter time, when the winds whirled around his summit, strange sounds of wrath would be heard afar up his steep declivities, and lightnings would flash around his crown, as if he was engaged in fearful combat with some spirit of the air who sought to steal his treasure from him. Then, again, in the golden summer, when Old Ocean's heart was calm, how gently its billowy bosom throbbed against his rocky base; with what low, sweet sighing, the wind came down the deep defiles, and wantoned with the waves! Then the apple-trees were borne down with fruit, and the storm-cock revelled on the crimson berries of the mountain ash. Flocks of fishing-boats went out each dawn, and in the dusk of night returned; and then, if more than ordinary success had crowned their toils, what revelling there was around each humble hearth! It was a calm, a blessed place—that remote and lonely lake; and many a time and oft its features mingle with my dreams, and make my slumbers happy!

This sentimentalized though accurate description is merely an expansion of a poetic treatment of the same subject, written six years earlier when Fitz-James was but seventeen.

I know a lake
Where the cool waves break,
And softly fall on the silver sand;
And no steps intrude
On that solitude,
And no voice save mine disturbs the strand.

And a mountain bold,
Like a giant of old,
Turned to stone by some magic spell,
Uprears in might
His mighty height,
And his craggy sides are wooded well.

In the midst doth smile
A little isle,
And its verdure shames the emerald's green;
On its grassy side,
In ruined pride
A castle of old is darkly seen.[15]

[15] *The Nation* (Dublin), July 26, 1845. The name is variously spelled—on the Irish Ordnance Survey maps it is always Lough Hyne; in *The Nation* it is Loch Ina; in the next poem—see below—it is Lough Ine; in Hayes it is Ine in the text and Ina in the contents and index, and in a story in *Bolster's Quarterly Magazine,* (Cork) I, 319 (Nov., 1826) it is written Loch Ein.

These simple verses of "Loch Ina" are locally famous. All the school children of Skibbereen learn them by heart at an early age, and throughout the surrounding country they are known by everyone, old and young. Even in Cork the poem is a familiar one. Yet the identity of the author was unknown, and great was the delight of the inhabitants of Skibbereen upon learning that the composer of the lines which so satisfied their local pride had been a boy of their own neighborhood.

The poem appeared anonymously in *The Nation* (Dublin) on July 26, 1845, under the title "Loch Ina, A Beautiful Salt-Water Lake, in the County of Cork, Near Baltimore," but six years later it was reprinted over the author's name in *The Family Friend* (London).[16] That it became popular is due, however, to the fact that in 1855 Edward Hayes included it in his two-volume collection of *The Ballads of Ireland*.[17] After the descriptive stanzas quoted above, the poem contrasts the present use of Cloghan Castle's ruined walls in serving as a sheepfold with their use in bygone days as the hall of a warrior chief and his men; and finally dwells on the beauties of the lake under the soft light of evening. Even though artificial and far from rhythmically perfect, yet the stanzas when recited—as I often heard them—with the slow caressing cadence required by the line arrangement evoke some measure of that wistfulness and faery quality which the English-speaking world regards as typically Irish.

Once more O'Brien made poetic use of Lough Hyne, this time as the setting for a ballad, "Una of Lough-Ine," which deals with the sad fate of his great-great-grandfather, Florence O'Driscoll, the owner of Cloghan Castle situated on the island in the lake. As a rebel chief against the English, Black Florence, or Fineen Dhuv, as he was called, was shot by the redcoats while trying desperately to escape through the whirling tidal rapids of the lake, and Una, his beloved, rushed after him with "maddened shriek" and was drowned there too.[18]

James O'Brien died in 1839 or 1840, when he was close upon sixty years of age, while his son was but eleven or twelve, and his wife Eliza certainly under forty, probably not over thirty-five. This remarkably beautiful widow after a proper interval, though while Fitz-James was still a lad,

[16] *The Family Friend*, IV, 197 (Apr. 1, 1851); spelled "Lough Ine."

[17] *The Ballads of Ireland*, col. and ed., Edward Hayes, 2 v., London, Edinburgh, and Dublin, 1855, I, 21–22. "The Boatmen of Kerry" (I, 15–17) and "Irish Castles" (II, 355–356) were also included in this collection. Reprinted in Boston, 1856.

[18] *The Cork Magazine*, I, 639–640 (Aug., 1848).

married DeCourcy O'Grady, a man of irreproachable ancestry and many generations back from the same stock as his wife, the O'Gradys of Kilballyowen.[19] DeCourcy O'Grady's father, also DeCourcy O'Grady, lived at a beautiful country seat, Carrigmahon, on the narrower part of the Lee estuary about four miles below Lakeland, the home of Eliza's grandfather, Timothy O'Driscoll.

After the marriage O'Grady leased the property of Cloon, conveniently situated at the edge of the village of Castleconnell, county Limerick. In the immediate vicinity were five large estates owned by members of the O'Grady family,[20] all of whom were more or less closely related to DeCourcy, and one of whom figures with vociferous prominence as a character in Lover's *Handy Andy* (1842). Here on the banks of the Shannon at its most beautiful point he established himself with his wife and stepson, and here Fitz-James lived from about his fifteenth year until he came of age.

Just as the village of Baltimore is dominated by the ruined castle of the O'Driscolls, so the village of Castleconnell lies at the foot of a rock-crowned ruin, which was long, long ago the castle of the O'Briens, kings of Munster. The Shannon here is strikingly picturesque, as it sweeps for half a mile in a wide curve, dropping considerably all the way over a rocky bed, and so forming the roaring and foaming white water of the Falls of Shannon, or, as they are generally called, the Rapids of Doonass. On either side of the turbulent river lie beautiful estates, whose green lawns slope up to fine mansion-houses on the hills. Among these lovely and romantic surroundings Fitz-James, who adopted part of his stepfather's name, calling himself Fitz-James DeCourcy O'Brien,[21] shared with the boys and the young men of the neighboring O'Grady families the outdoor life of the place—the typical sporting life of the Irish gentleman. Besides the riding, hunting, and shooting usual in all parts of Ireland, the swimming, boating, and

[19] See Sir Bernard Burke, C. B., LL. D., *A Genealogical and Heraldic History of the Landed Gentry of Ireland*, London, 1912, pp. 530–531.

[20] See Ordnance Survey Maps of Castleconnell, 1845, and *Primary Valuation of Tenements*, 1851, p. 117, the latter in the Valuation Office, Ely Place, Dublin.

[21] It was by this name that Dr. Collins and Dr. R. Shelton Mackenzie knew him in England and by this name that he signed himself in a letter he wrote to Thomas Bailey Aldrich some years after the beginning of their friendship in America. Aldrich in writing of it to William Winter says: "It is the only instance I know of his signing himself Fitz-James *DeCourcy* O'Brien. You know he was Baron Inchquin, or something of the sort. I used to call him Baron Linchpin, when we were merry."—T. B. Aldrich to William Winter, Oct. 20, 1880; quoted in Winter, *Old Friends*, 1909, pp. 101–102.

fishing made possible by the Shannon must have occupied many hours; and to these activities Fitz-James added a particular interest in birds. Later he made frequent allusions to them in his writing—especially to the seagull and the gannet, the bullfinch and the robin—and in "Bird Gossip" (1855), a rambling essay of miscellaneous information about birds, he says:

I have, since boyhood, exercised a singular power over three species of animals, birds, dogs, and horses. My empire over the two latter I attribute to my sporting education, having been at an early age introduced to gun and saddle, but for the control which I have at times possessed over birds I am entirely unable to account. As a lad, I was singularly fond of the fields, and spent many an hour, I hope not unprofitably, in lying under the broad sky watching the birds. I soon attained a singular proficiency in imitating their cries, and I blush to say that my skill in this line was the destruction of many a flock of golden plover and whistling teal.[22]

Following this O'Brien relates two incidents from his hunting experience:

I was prowling one day, gun in hand, round my father's place, ready to sacrifice everything but a robin red-breast or a sky-lark, when I thought I discovered a flock of stone-curlew feeding in the meadows that lined the river. The stone-curlew, in the months of May and June, is a delicious and succulent bird, and this chance was too tempting to forego. In a moment I was racing down the lawn in order to get under shelter of a quick-set hedge, by means of which I could crawl into a trench that drained the lower meadows.

. . .

I once formed one of a shooting party at Adare Manor, the seat of the late Earl of Dunraven. Our main object was the pheasants which abounded in the Earl's splendid preserves, but we were also prepared to be enlivened in the pauses by much rabbit-shooting, that active little animal being wonderfully abundant in the thick fern cover of the upper part. . . . We were all standing in a sort of wild, grassy avenue, about twenty feet wide, bordered on either side by the tall ferns, through which it had been cut in order to give the sportsmen a vista to mark the game. The game-keeper—a tall, handsome fellow, not unlike Tregarva in Charles Kingsley's "Yeast"—sent a lurcher into cover. In a few seconds we heard a sharp yelp, and the next moment a rabbit bolted out of the ferns about fifteen paces from where we stood. He had scarcely broke cover when our game-keeper held out his right hand toward him, and stooping forward, seemed to look earnestly at the little gray fellow, who, to our great amazement, sat up on his haunches

[22] *Harper's New Monthly Magazine*, XI, 824 (Nov., 1855). (This magazine will hereafter be cited in the notes as *Harper's*).

and stared steadily back at the game-keeper. Mr. Wyndham Quin, Lord Dunraven's youngest son, now went slowly up to the rabbit, who permitted him to take him by the neck, but the instant he was grasped commenced kicking violently.

The carefree life of a well-to-do youth living among fine estates along a beautiful river was sharply broken into, however, by the first of the great Irish famines, which occurred in 1845. The counties of Cork, Clare, and Limerick were especially affected, and the papers of the time are full of the awfulness of conditions. In almost every case Skibbereen is mentioned as a place where the destitution had reached its worst stages—the workhouse built to care for 800 was housing 3280; in its infirmary the number in each bed varied from two to six; and even as late as 1852 the town was still referred to as "the charnel-house of Skibbereen."[23] The dire distress resulting from the famines was added to the terrible poverty and political oppression already existing, and death and starvation ran rampant. Seeking relief from such conditions the Irish peasants left their homes by thousands and, flocking to the southern and western ports, crowded across the ocean as fast as the ships could carry them. In the single month of March, 1848, 9,414 Irish emigrants landed in New York, and during the first four months of 1850, 3,613 emigrants sailed from the port of Cork alone;[24] while it is estimated that from 1846 to 1851, both inclusive, 1,174,311 Irishmen emigrated to North America, and that of these 926,306 settled in the United States.[25] The towns of Limerick and Skibbereen lost about twenty thousand inhabitants each, the loss in the latter instance reducing the population by more than a third.[26]

The stricken wretchedness about him so stirred the sixteen-year-old Fitz-James O'Brien that he wrote some verses about it and sent them to *The Nation*, a weekly newspaper edited in Dublin by Charles Gavan Duffy and dedicated to the cause of Irish patriotism. As Duffy was constantly and vigorously agitating for Irish freedom, it is surprising that he printed the poem, even though he used it as the butt of caustic comment against such

[23] See *The Advocate: or, Irish Industrial Journal* (Dublin), Dec. 16, 1848, quoting *The Cork Examiner;* and *The Dublin University Magazine*, XL, 122 (July, 1852).

[24] See *The Limerick Chronicle*, May 13, 1848; and *The Satirist* (London), May 12, 1850.

[25] See W. P. O'Brien, C. B., *The Great Famine in Ireland*, London, 1896, p. 253; and Peter Condon, "The Irish in the United States," in *The Catholic Encyclopedia*, New York, 1910, VIII, 135.

[26] See *Schedule of the Population of each Superintendent Registrar's District or Poor Law Union in 1841, 1851, 1861, 1871, and 1881*, Dublin, 1883.

weak-kneed escape from English tyranny as flight to America. The lines appear, on March 15, 1845, with editorial introduction and conclusion as follows:

This might be called "The Coward's Resource:"—

Oh! Give a Desert Life to Me

Oh! give a desert life to me,
    Where I no tyrant's law need fear;
For there, indeed, I may be free,
    Nor live a slave as I do here—
        For here we're born,
        For England's scorn.
We weep o'er our degraded land—
Or ban the head such curses planned.
Oh! on the pampas wild I'll dwell,
    Amongst Columbia's free born race,
With dog and steed that love me well,
    My flying herds I'll swiftly chase.
Oh! then a desert life for me,
    Dependent I will live no more;
My soul is longing to be free,
    Without the weight of chains it bore—
        But when again
        Old Erin's chain,
Is cleft by freemen's swords in two,
        The sea I'll brave,
        And o'er the wave,
I'll come again, dear land, to you.

FITZJAMES O'BRIEN.

We recommend our friend *not* to come again when the work is over. He will get a cold welcome from the men he left to bear the heat of the harvest.

Although this earliest poem by Fitz-James was imagining a life "amongst Columbia's free born race," when he left for New York seven years later it was neither Irish famine nor English oppression that sent him.

The initial rebuke of *The Nation* did not deter Fitz-James; but he was sufficiently cautious thereafter to submit his contributions without signature. "T. J. O'B." are the initials over which, just two weeks later, *The Nation* printed some trivial lines containing a touch of gallantry and Irish blarney entitled "Epigram on hearing a Young Lady Regret her Eyes being

Bloodshot."[27] Fitz-James was apparently pleased with his cleverness, for after slight revisions each time he had it twice reprinted within the next few years.[28] Indeed, Fitz-James seems to have been an insistent and somewhat obstreperous youth, high-spirited and egotistic, with a belief in his own superior cleverness and refinement of sensibilities and possessed of all the blatant self-assurance of seventeen, fostered rather than held in check by the uncritical admiration of a devoted mother.

To the next poem "Loch Ina"—which has already been quoted from and discussed[29]—there could be no objection; but about two months later, adopting the patriotic pseudonym Heremon,[30] Fitz-James began sending to *The Nation* political verses which the editors considered highly unpatriotic. On October 4 they declined Heremon's "Irish Hurra for Past Heroism"; but the irrepressible author continued to submit it until, more than a month later, they were driven by his effrontery to remark, "whatever Heremon may think to the contrary, we actually do read contributions before we reject them, and we have already declined this piece under as many aliases as belong to a London swell-mob man."[31]

The following week (November 15) they objected to his plea on behalf of Henry de Loundres, the rather highhanded archbishop of Dublin under King John, for a niche in the English House of Parliament, saying, "He has no claims at all upon the veneration of Irishmen." But Heremon was undeterred; and on February 7, 1846, the editors' comment is, "Declined.— . . . 'Heremon' (he is a dangerous fellow; does he forget that amidst the wreck of our national institutions, there is a Queen's Bench left us still?)"

Just a month after this, on the other hand, Fitz-James wins editorial favor by a poem, "The Famine."[32] Stirred by the shocking conditions in his beloved corner of Ireland, he appeals to the rich and powerful to give relief and warns them of the "wild riot" which will result if they do not do so; and the week following in "The Boatmen of Kerry"[33] he again makes use of familiar native material in describing the mass celebrated yearly upon the

[27] *The Nation*, Mar. 29, 1845.

[28] "Impromptu to a Lady, on her Complaining at Breakfast that her Eyes were Blood-shot," *The Cork Magazine*, I, 663 (Sept., 1848); and "Impromptu On Hearing a Young Lady Complain that her Eyes were Bloodshot," *The Parlour Magazine*, I, 215 (June 21, 1851).

[29] *The Nation*, July 26, 1845.

[30] Heremon was a legendary king of Ireland in the twelfth century B. C., the founder of the Milesian dynasty. In America, too, O'Brien occasionally used the name: see pp. 44–46.

[31] *The Nation*, Nov. 8, 1845. See also *ibid.*, Oct. 4, 1845.

[32] *Ibid.*, Mar. 7, 1846.

[33] *Ibid.*, Mar. 14, 1846.

sea by the Kerry fishermen. "Excelsior,"[34] the last of O'Brien's contributions to *The Nation*, is in form a well-handled Shakespearean sonnet, but in story and spirit is an exact duplicate of Longfellow's poem of like name (1841).

These early writings of Fitz-James O'Brien show that he knows the poetry of his time and that in spirit and technique he apes the late romantics—he is enthusiastic about natural scenery which he sentimentalizes, he tells love tales and supernatural stories of the long ago in ballad form, and he utters his cry for individual freedom. At the same time the subject matter is born of his own experience and his Irish environment, and frequently he uses his verse scathingly to attack the political and social evils that come under his ken.

The next poem by Fitz-James did not appear until July, 1848, and what occupied him from the end of his eighteenth year to the beginning of his twentieth is a matter of uncertainty. Most of those who have written letters or newspaper articles about him have accepted his own statement that, being expected to become a lawyer like his father, he was educated at Trinity College, Dublin.[35] There is no record at Trinity, however, of his having matriculated there; and he did not with any consistency claim to have gone through to a degree. It is possible that he went up to Dublin and became a Sizar Candidate; but if so, he failed to obtain the desired appointment, and consequently his name does not appear on the college books. If he attended any college, his career measured by academic standards was probably not a brilliant one; for he seems to have learned little of Latin, Greek, or mathematics. On the other hand, he must have read largely in the general literature and out-of-the-way sciences, and he acquired great proficiency in French. Davis says that "when he knew him during the last few years of his life he habitually read every French play that appeared" and adds "that his learning with reference to many subjects seemed ample and minute, and when he chose to speak of literary affairs he enthralled the listener with his eloquence."[36]

O'Brien's command of French, however, is just as likely to have been

[34] *Ibid.*, Mar. 13, 1847. These last three poems are all signed "Heremon."

[35] See Frank Wood, *The New York Leader*, Apr. 12, 1862; editorial, same paper, same date; *Harper's Weekly*, VI, 267 (Apr. 26, 1862); Wm. H. Merriam, eulogy in *New York Daily Times*, June 21, 1862; Winter, 1881, p. xv; and T. B. Aldrich, Oct. 20, 1880, in Winter, *Old Friends*, p. 101. (*Harper's Weekly* will hereafter be cited in the notes as *H. W.*).

[36] Winter, 1881, p. xxxiv.

acquired by a residence in France as by study in Ireland; for he may easily have traveled to Paris with his parents or a tutor and at intervals have toured the Continent.[37] Still another possible way to account for these two years would be to give credence to the rumor that connects O'Brien with the British army. Stephen Fiske, a fellow journalist, says, "He was an admirable swordsman, and had served in the English army, although he was always reticent as to his history. I have seen several instances of his skill with the pistol."[38]

The O'Grady family holding the position it did, O'Brien would as a matter of course have served as an officer; therefore, the absence of his name from the English army lists makes it almost certain that he did not see regular service, although it does not preclude the possibility of his having held a commission in one of the regiments of Irish militia.[39] But life in the army is not necessary to account for his athletic frame and his skill with sword and pistol; the life at Castleconnell with its riding and shooting would have developed these. On the whole it seems most likely that he was receiving such an education as was deemed fitting for a young gentleman, either by attendance at college or less formally under tutors. Certainly he must have been out of Ireland most of the time, for the break with *The Nation* occurred sharply; and after his reappearance in *The Cork Magazine* for July, 1848, his connection with the journalistic world is practically continuous.

The Cork Magazine, which ran only from November, 1847, to December, 1848, was planned as a distinctly literary journal, and to it O'Brien contributed ten poems in six issues. The first, "An Ode to the Divinest of Liquors," sings of champagne with joyful gusto.[40] Instead of affixing his own signature, however, he signed with the name Fineen Dhuv, which it will be remembered was the sobriquet of Florence O'Driscoll, or Black Florence—the rebel chief who was Fitz-James's ancestor and the owner of

[37] A letter from his mother of Oct. 25, 1861, describes a Continental tour as more or less habitual with the O'Gradys. A. L. S. in the collection of Charles Romm, quoted on p. 218.

[38] Stephen Fiske to William Winter, Oct. 8, 1880, in Winter, 1881, p. liv.

[39] So far as known, the only reference to his military service earlier than Fiske's in 1880 is a one-word hint in the editorial column of *The New York Leader* for April 12, 1862. The statement there is that it was "the intention of his family to prepare him for the bar; but his fondness for literature and arms thwarted the designs of his friends." Winter says simply that "it is remembered that he claimed to have been at one time a soldier in the British service," (Winter, 1881, p. xv) a claim which Stoddard discredits in these words: "That he was ever in the British army, as he claimed to have been, may be doubted." (*N. Y. Tribune*, Mar. 6, 1881).

[40] *The Cork Magazine*, I, 564–565 (July, 1848).

Cloghan Castle in Lough Hyne. The next month he used the old chieftain as the hero of his poem "Una of Lough-Ine,"[41] a typical example of ballad writing according to the romantic school of the eighteen-forties, no better nor much worse than the average, though the meter might easily have been improved. Smoothness of technique and delicacy of touch are, however, manifest in the four stanzas of "My Childhood's Prayer," appearing also in the August number.

The September issue carried three poems—"Impromptu" repeated from *The Nation*, a short "Serenade," and a graceful, imaginative story about "The Loves and the Fate of the Dragon-Fly and the Water-Lily."[42] Although slightly marred by irregularity in execution, these last two poems, delicate and tender, show that Fitz-James was improving in technique and that for the moment he was regarding the writing of poetry as a serious, if not almost a sacred, occupation. Two more appeared in October, "The Fisher's Lay," which though undistinguished is contained and delicate, and "Where Shall We Dwell?", which is simply trite. The last four are all love poems, as is "The Epicurean," which followed in November, with its motto "Our pole star, pleasure, our haven, Love!" But in "The Epicurean" the rhythm flows more easily than it did in the earlier poems; and in "Forest Thoughts,"[43] the last of those written for *The Cork Magazine*, the reader feels for the first time that perhaps Fitz-James did have in him the true poetic spark. Its opening lines are much in the manner of Bryant's "A Forest Hymn" (1825), and the pace of its Spenserian stanzas is varied by skillful use of the caesural pause. When in one stanza the poet grows enthusiastic about the

> music in a wild bird's song,
> That wreathes the soul with strange impassioned spells,
> Making old blood rush youthfully along,

one cannot but believe that O'Brien had himself experienced the thrill of hearing "the lonely robin's liquid song" in the woods at sunset—especially as he twice repeated the idea in verse after he came to America.[44]

A couple of months after Fitz-James O'Brien ceased writing poems on conventional literary subjects for *The Cork Magazine*, "Heremon" sent some

[41] *Ibid.*, I, 639–640 (Aug., 1848).
[42] *Ibid.*, I, 663 (Sept., 1848); I, 653; and I, 681–683.
[43] *Ibid.*, II, 99–100 (Dec., 1848).
[44] See note 89, below.

patriotic verses to *The Irishman*, of Dublin, and the editors printed them with the following introductory remarks: " 'Heremon'—Though young in years is not weak in rhythmic power. We like his movement; it is bold and free."[45] The poem begins with an invocation,

"Say sacred Clarseac—hallowed harp of old,"

and in the three stanzas that follow the author deplores the sad state of Ireland and the fate of her patriotic poets, who are either in prison or driven into exile.

And Freedom bids the few who linger here—
    Our prostrate Isle to fly,
And Hope's glad light, that shone for many a year,
    Seems just about to die.

On this despondent note the writing of Fitz-James O'Brien for the journals of his native island ceased; for in the year 1849 he came of age and inherited whatever fortune was left him by his father, James O'Brien, and by his grandfather, Michael O'Driscoll. That his grandfather left to Fitz-James, his only male descendant, a considerable estate is borne out by the fact that his will was proved in the Prerogative Court. O'Brien himself said it amounted to £8,000;[46] and although he may have been guilty of exaggerating the amount, both in order to appear as a person of importance and to attract to himself the sort of romantic interest that attaches to anyone who has lost a fortune, nevertheless his tastes and desires of a few years later testify to a habit of luxurious living. He had a discriminating appreciation of opera, which he must have acquired in London, and once he so far deviated from his usual reticence as to say that he had heard Herr Formes sing at Covent Garden.[47] He liked to give his friends elaborate and expensive dinners at Delmonico's; and George Arnold, the poet, writing in 1865, says: "When I first knew him, in '56, '57, he had elegant rooms, with a large and valuable library, piles of manuscripts, dressing-cases, decanters, pipes, pictures, a wardrobe of much splendor, and all sorts of knicknackery such as young bachelors love to collect."[48] Stoddard, who was also at one time a

[45] *The Irishman* (Dublin), Feb. 3, 1849.

[46] See obituary notices in *N. Y. Times*, Apr. 10, 1862; in *N. Y. Leader*, Apr. 12, 1862; and in *H. W.*, VI, 267 (Apr. 26, 1862). Aldrich states erroneously that the money ($40,000) came from his father—see Aldrich to Winter, Oct. 20, 1880, quoted in Winter, *Old Friends*, p. 102.

[47] See *The Saturday Press*, Nov. 13, 1858.

[48] *The New York Citizen*, Sept. 30, 1865, reprinted in Winter, 1881, p. 1.

close friend, discounts this statement, but in his contradiction fortifies the impression as to O'Brien's tastes:

The personality of Fitz-James O'Brien must have cast a glamour over the poetic soul of Mr. Arnold, or he would not have magnified his surroundings as he did. The rooms of which he wrote were in no sense elegant, nor did they contain books enough to be called a library, valuable or otherwise. Pictures were there, no doubt, and the pipes, but not the dressing-cases, nor the splendid wardrobe. Fitz-James O'Brien lived very much like other young men who follow literature as a profession. At one time he occupied good apartments; at another, and not very remote time, he occupied indifferent lodgings. If it had rested with himself, he would certainly have been surrounded with elegancies and luxuries.[49]

II. In England

Almost immediately upon coming of age and receiving his inheritance, Fitz-James left Ireland and went up to London; and although he must have lived rather riotously and certainly extravagantly to have run through his money in two and a half years, he nevertheless retained his interest in writing, for only two months after his last appearance in *The Irishman* of Dublin, a poem of his appeared in *The Metropolitan Magazine* in London.[50] It is true that the editors of the latter may merely have copied "Forest Thoughts" from the December number of *The Cork Magazine*, but it is also possible that Fitz-James submitted these his best verses to the London periodical soon after his arrival in the city. Three more months, however, and all doubt vanishes; for with July "F. J. O'B." is found taking part in definition contests conducted by *The Family Friend*, and for some months his initials appear after facetious and punning bits such as are typical of youthful cleverness:

Debt. A pound that human donkeys sometimes get into, and from which it takes many pounds to release them.

Nobody. The man who trained his hop plants to the North Pole, and tied them up with the Equinoctial Line!

Economy. The plumb-line with which we sound our way over life's ocean, and avoid the shoals of extravagance.[51]

[49] *N. Y. Tribune*, Mar. 6, 1881.

[50] *The Metropolitan Magazine*, LIV, 395–396 (Apr., 1849).

[51] *The Family Friend*, I, 207 (July, 1849); I, 208; and II, 147 (Mar. 1, 1850). For complete list see Bibliography.

The Family Friend, which began its career in January, 1849, under the editorship of R. Kemp Philp, provided light but proper reading for the family circle, contained directions concerning household duties, and conducted departments for games and contests. The editor, probably attracted by the numerous squibs submitted by "F. J. O'B.," got in touch with him and before long seems to have engaged him as a regular contributor. The first writing likely to have been done under such an arrangement is a brief essay entitled "Philosophy in Disguise,"[52] which, by means of allegory, suggests what sort of teaching will bring the best results in children. Philp won such great popularity with *The Family Friend* that he changed its original monthly numbers to a fortnightly issue, and finally to a weekly one.[53]

O'Brien became intimately acquainted with Philp, and contributed nine items to *The Family Friend* in addition to those already mentioned, signing some of them with his initials and some with his full name. A little poem, "Lines Addressed to a Young Lady about to Depart for India,"[54] glorifies the constancy of love in an Irish heart and refers to the distressing state of Ireland; and "A Lyric of Life"[55] draws from the unbending conduct of an oak tree the lesson "that man should bear up with a spirit as brave." After this O'Brien turned to prose as the medium for expressing his moral observations, and the only verses that appeared were repetitions of "Loch Ine" and of "The Loves and the Fate of the Dragon-Fly and the Water-Lily."[56] The little homilies that he wrote about the conduct of domestic life were, with their stilted self-consciousness and lack of humor, obviously done to order, and their titles, "Family Conversation," "Home," and "On Ostentation,"[57] sufficiently indicate their content. The exuberance of O'Brien could not be tied down for long, however, by the demand for religious and domestic sentimentality, and in his very next essay the wit and fun natural to his temperament broke forth. He wrote an amusing tirade on "Babies!"[58] and turned his satirical darts upon parents who, at the most inopportune moments, parade their spoiled and petted darlings for bachelor guests to admire. The article gave offence to those too serious to see that it was written in a spirit of mocking humor and entirely without malicious intent,

[52] *Ibid.*, I, 294–295 (Nov., 1849).
[53] For Philp's interesting career see *DNB*, XV, 1111–1112.
[54] *The Family Friend*, III, 45 (July 15, 1850).
[55] *Ibid.*, III, 106 (Aug. 15, 1850).
[56] *Ibid.*, IV, 197 (Apr. 1, 1851) and III, 77 (Aug. 1, 1850).
[57] *Ibid.*, III, 131–134 (Sept. 1, 1850); III, 282–285 (Nov. 15); and IV, 9–11 (Jan. 1, 1851).
[58] *Ibid.*, IV, 73–75 (Feb. 1, 1851).

and protesting letters flooded in upon the editor. To these Philp printed a lengthy and apologetic reply, and O'Brien sought to make amends by a further article, entitled "Children. A Vindication,"[59] in which he insisted on a distinction being made between babies and children and praised the latter for the interest of their infinite variety. The essay included a dream story, the moral of which is somewhat muddled, but the style of which in the prettiness and smoothness of its modulations shows a close approximation to the sentimental best of either Dickens or Leigh Hunt.

In "Babies!" O'Brien had referred to himself as a bachelor in lodgings and had spoken of his friends as "very respectable people" who "live in Cavendish Square, give good dinners and pleasant *soirees*."[60] These autobiographical items were confirmed and supplemented in the editor's reply to "His Friends," in which he sketched O'Brien's life and habits, saying:

> that Bachelor O'B. is a very intelligent and intimate friend of ours; that we have never annoyed him by *our* babies, and that, therefore, he frequently sits at our dining-table, leads the conversation at our *soirees*, turns over the music for the ladies, sometimes rides with us and them in the Park, and often occupies a seat in our Editorial sanctum. The latter fact is a sufficient indication that his influence with us is considerable. He is known to the readers of the *Friend* as a Councillor, and Essayist and Poet. More than once his address has been sought from us; and it is a sober fact that a lady somewhere, having ascertained the initials F. J. O'B. to represent an unmarried gentleman, addresses numerous *billets doux* to him, through our care; and that we have strange suspicions that O'B knows and thinks more of the lady in question than he has ever ventured to confide to us.[61]

O'Brien's contributions to *The Family Friend* were all short, and the writing of them could have interfered very little with the main business of enjoying life. Besides, it will be noticed that it was not until September, 1850, considerably over a year after he came to London, that O'Brien first appeared in the role of hack writer, or, as he would probably have put it, assistant to the editor. In the meantime his money and his connection with the DeCourcy O'Grady family must have given him entree into London society and have enabled him to cut something of a figure in the less rigid circles of the fashionable watering place of Bath.[62]

[59] *Ibid.*, IV, 170–174 (Mar. 15, 1851).
[60] *Ibid.*, IV, 73 (Feb. 1, 1851).
[61] *Ibid.*, IV, Appendix, p. 9 (Feb. 15, or Mar. 1, 1851).
[62] The only autograph of O'Brien's yet found that antedates his arrival in America is on a

In London the year 1851 was marked by the Great Exhibition at the Crystal Palace, and of the three of four periodicals devoted to its interests one was gotten out by Houlston and Stoneman, printers of *The Family Friend*. O'Brien had become a fairly regular contributor to this magazine, was on intimate terms with its editor, and could not have been unknown to its printers. It is, therefore, not surprising to find him represented in the first number of the new magazine, and it is almost certain that he was its editor.[63] It appeared in weekly numbers during the progress of the Exhibition, from May 3 to December 20, and was printed on machines within the Crystal Palace as part of a practical exhibit. It was called *The Parlour Magazine of the Literature of All Nations* and, besides containing translations from various literatures, it gave such information as made it a guide to the different sections of the palace exhibits. Even though its weekly numbers were small, the supplying of material and the preparation of copy must have kept Fitz-James pretty constantly occupied, and he helped fill its columns with a number of his own contributions. To the opening issue he furnished an ode in five stanzas addressed "To a Captive Sea-Gull,"[64] and two weeks later contributed a short apologue in smooth, rhythmical prose, the superscription of which ran, "The Sunbeam, the Dew-Drop, and the Rose. From the Persian, by Fitz-James O'Brien."[65] After this the editor printed three of his earlier poems[66] and added "Our Old Garden Chair,"[67] a new one, which followed the popular trend by dwelling sentimentally on the peace and beauty that come to a husband and wife who have grown old together.

---

note concerned entirely with the formalities of social procedure. The letterhead is a lozenge containing a crown, with the word *Bath* below, and the note runs as follows:

Dr Sir

I had much pleasure in calling on you to-day . . . but found you by mere chance. The address that you gave me was 354 which is at the other end of the street, and is a church. I tried all the 54's down the street and thus found you. I will call again this evening but in the meantime I hope you will do me the favor of dining with me on next Saturday if not otherwise engaged, at half past five P. M.

Yours faithfully
F. J. O'Brien

—A. L. S. in Simon Gratz Collection, Historical Society of Pennsylvania.

[63] See Winter, 1881, p. xvi.

[64] *The Parlour Magazine*, I, 23 (May 3, 1851).

[65] *Ibid.*, I, 94 (May 17, 1851).

[66] *Ibid.*, "Forest Thoughts," I, 95 (May 17, 1851); "An Ode to the Divinest of Liquors," I, 119 (May 24); and "Impromptu," I, 215 (June 21).

[67] *Ibid.*, I, 215 (June 21).

In spite of his editorial activities on *The Parlour Magazine* O'Brien was able to supply Kemp Philp with a story, which the latter used on July 1 as the initial item for the fifth volume of *The Family Friend.* The title, "The Simple History of a Family Friend," was appropriate for an article occupying such a position; and the narrative, which is told in simple, unpretentious style, once more bears witness to O'Brien's interest in birds. He had already written about the robin's song and the captive seagull, and this tells the life story of a pet bullfinch. It probably represents a real incident; for some years later (1855) he repeated the story and, though using less elaboration, he gave the same details about the birth of the bird in its forest home, its tameness as the favorite companion of the author, its recognition of its owner even when deceit and disguise were practised on it, and, finally, its death by a hawk.[68]

The next five of O'Brien's writings were poems that helped fill the pages of *The Parlour Magazine.* In "The Lonely Oak"[69] there is a touch of patriotism, a regret that the steadfast oak must stand and see such deplorable changes as were taking place in the land of Erin. Both this poem and "Dawn,"[70] the one that followed it, are well written, and though they are lacking in distinction, they are almost entirely free from the faults that so often marred O'Brien's verse—faults of rhythm and diction, and especially the fault in taste which led him into sentimentality or melodrama. "Dawn.—A Sonnet" builds a rather ornate description through such smoothly moving lines that later it received the honor of being printed with the author's full signature in *The Dublin University Magazine.*[71]

In the issue of the latter magazine for August, 1851, there was printed a poem dealing with Irish life, which though unsigned is almost certainly O'Brien's. The poem, which is entitled "The Wish; or, the Fall of the Star," is one of a number included in an article composed of miscellaneous verses strung together on a slight thread. Such articles of "choice selections" were a regular feature of *The Dublin University Magazine*, supplied by Jonathan Freke Slingsby. "The Wish" tells how "as Dermot was tending his herds on the mountain" Norah scornfully passed him by; nevertheless, upon the fall of a shooting star he wished for her as his, and a little later won her by rescuing her from a mountain torrent. The last stanza tells of

[68] See "Bird Gossip," *Harper's*, XI, 824–825 (Nov., 1855). A pet bullfinch is also the center of the story "The Bullfinch" in *The Knickerbocker*, LVIII, 29–40 (July, 1861).

[69] *The Parlour Magazine*, I, 287 (July 12, 1851).

[70] *Ibid.*, I, 359 (Aug. 2, 1851).

[71] *The Dublin University Magazine*, XLI, 299 (Mar., 1853).

their domestic bliss, and of the blessing that followed Dermot's "wish on the fall of the star"; and at the conclusion of the poem Slingsby exclaims, "Bravo; a very pretty piece of versification; it illustrates one of our native superstitions."[72]

A sequel to these verses, continuing the story of Dermot and Norah, appeared about a month and a half later (September 20) in *The Parlour Magazine*, which in the meantime had printed two other of its editor's poems. While "To an Infant" is an irritatingly careless performance, "Hateful Spring,"[73] stated to be "From the French of Berenger," is a thoroughly satisfactory rendering of that author's cleverly turned persiflage. With its second volume (September–December) *The Parlour Magazine* modified its policy to include only translations, and it was therefore as if "Translated from the original Irish of a Peasant Bard at Ballingarry" that the second Dermot-Norah poem, "Fortune in the Fire,"[74] was given space. The two young peasants sat before their turf fire dreaming of wealth and ease. "Rain down the chimney soon quenched" the fire, however, and the couple returned sensibly to their work. Later with a new title, "Irish Castles," and an additional stanza showing how Dermot's industry succeeded in earning them a snug mansion, the poem was included by Edward Hayes in *The Ballads of Ireland*.[75] It is highly probable that O'Brien was responsible for a number of the other translations in *The Parlour Magazine*, mainly those from the French, and that he was kept busy supplying material for the presses which operated in full sight of the crowds that visited the Crystal Palace.

When the exhibition ended, the life of the popular little magazine ceased also, and its buyers and subscribers were recommended to patronize a new magazine, *The Home Companion*, as its successor. *The Home Companion* was another of the many ventures of R. Kemp Philp, and according to its subtitle was to be "a Weekly Magazine of the Amusing and the Useful." In anticipation of its early appearance Philp had evidently commissioned O'Brien to write him a story, for beginning in the first number and continuing serially through nine of its weekly issues appeared "The Phantom Light: A Christmas Story. By Fitz-James O'Brien."[76] It is apparently

[72] *Ibid.*, XXXVIII, 141 (Aug., 1851).

[73] *The Parlour Magazine*, I, 431 (Aug. 23, 1851), and I, 449 (Aug. 30).

[74] *Ibid.*, II, 69 (Sept. 20, 1851).

[75] Edward Hayes, *op. cit.*, II, 355–356.

[76] *The Home Companion*, I, 5–6 (Jan. 3, 1852); 21–22 (Jan. 10); 37–39 (Jan. 17); 53–55 (Jan. 24); 68–70 (Jan. 31); 84–85 (Feb. 7); 101–102 (Feb. 14); 117–118 (Feb. 21); 131–133 (Feb. 28).

O'Brien's earliest attempt at a full-length story, and as such has an importance far greater than that due it because of artistic accomplishment. The plot is bad; it rises to no climax, the hints and suggestions it makes as to supernatural interference come to nothing, and it is frequently ridiculously melodramatic or irritatingly homiletic. The style is bad too, being so stilted and unnatural in the dialogue of the principal characters that it entirely prevents them from seeming real. On the other hand, the facts that "The Phantom Light," even in its title, suggests the supernatural, and that throughout its chapters it contains incidents based on peasant superstitions and reports of miraculous occurrences, show that the young O'Brien, brought up in the southwest corner of Ireland, had a mind well saturated with the myth-making habits of the Irish peasantry; and when the peasant characters—Oonagh, the old nurse, Donal, the aged fisherman, the poet's son, and the stable boy—are allowed to speak for themselves, telling in their rich brogue and in half-fearful tones tales about fairies, omens, and unaccountable lights, the story takes on life.

The writing of "The Phantom Light" must have been undertaken by Fitz-James no later than the first of November; for although the first number of *The Home Companion* is dated as of January 3, 1852, it seems to have made its appearance almost a month earlier,[77] and the material for it must have been in the printer's hands almost three weeks previous to that, if one is to believe the editor's statement that it took sixteen days to print the copies required for each issue.[78] It was only by such an arrangement of early issuing and late dating that O'Brien's story was timely; and the last instalment, emphasizing the Christmas spirit of forgiveness, reconciliation, and good-will, and describing the Irish Christmas scene and Christmas customs, was probably written shortly before the holiday itself. The number of *The Home Companion* in which it was printed is dated February 28, 1852; but before that day arrived, Fitz-James O'Brien had left England, had arrived in America, and had had at least one poem accepted and printed in *The Lantern*, a weekly periodical of New York City. Thus O'Brien's last writing before he crossed the ocean was a tribute to his native land and

[77] See *The Parlour Magazine*, "Preface to the Second Volume," which is dated Dec. 20, 1851, and which refers to *The Home Companion* as having "within a few weeks, obtained the enormous circulation of *One Hundred Thousand Copies Weekly*."

[78] See *The Home Companion*, Preface to Volume One.

a sympathetic description of the customs and scenes of his own southwestern corner of it.

Afterwards he mentioned Ireland but seldom, and in only four instances made use of Irish settings. " 'Carrying Weight.' A Reminiscence of the Turf,"[79] printed during his first year in America, is written in a vein of extravagant humor and deals with racecourses and betting, with improvidence, drinking, and debt. O'Brien creates as the narrator of the story an impecunious and drink-loving Irishman, who, in order to arouse sympathy and extort money, pretends to have a sick wife and numerous children. The proceeds of this hoax are used to keep himself supplied with port. "His feuds with his neighbors are very amusing. There is an unhappy village doctor whose bills he never pays, but whose attendance he compels under penalty of being obliged to fight him. Indeed our Irish friend appears to think that the offer of 'satisfaction' ought to liquidate every claim."[80] Although O'Brien recognized this as a humorous aberration in the character of his Irishman, he himself was not free from feeling and acting in much the same way, and records of duelling challenges are not infrequent along the course of his turbulent career.

"Bird Gossip," already quoted from,[81] is the second article that refers to Ireland, and "How a Prima Donna Was Fledged"[82] is the third. The latter, designed as a compliment to the Irish singer Agnes Robertson, tells how a family of blackbirds living in Ireland adopted a fairy child, who was soon able to outsing them. In the fourth one—three paragraphs of the story "The Lost Room"—O'Brien becomes more personal and describes the country where he was born and grew up, the home of his maternal ancestor, Sir Florence O'Driscoll, "a strange old sea-king, who dwelt on the extremest point of the southwestern coast of Ireland." He then tells of O'Driscoll's piracies, of his trip to London to visit Queen Elizabeth, with whom he became a favorite, and of his final return home to find his estates confiscated and himself dispossessed of all except "his castle by the sea and the island of Inniskeiran."[83] The meagreness of these references to Ireland is paralleled by the vague and uncertain statements of O'Brien's American

[79] *The American Whig Review*, XVI, 269–272 (Sept., 1852).
[80] *Ibid.*, XVI, 263.
[81] *Harper's*, XI, 820–825 (Nov., 1855).
[82] "The Man about Town," in *H. W.*, I, 531 (Aug. 22, 1857).
[83] *Harper's*, XVII, 495 (Sept., 1858).

friends, who almost without exception testify to his extreme reticence in regard to his origin and his early life in his native land. He "was absurdly ashamed of his Irish birth,"[84] says Augustus Maverick, one of his associates on the *Times*; and certain it is that he held himself distinctly aloof from the hordes of Irishmen who during the decade of his life in New York crowded into the American ports. In 1852 and 1853 approximately 300,000 arrived, and by 1860 some 600,000 more.[85] The majority of these were poverty-stricken, ignorant, half-starved peasants, and Fitz-James, aristocratically trained and educated, avoided all contact with them.

It is because of his reticence that reports of O'Brien's connection with two other London periodicals have remained only conjecture. William Winter remarks that "it is said that . . . he also wrote for the Leisure Hour;"[86] but this "Family Journal of Instruction and Recreation," beginning publication at the same time as *The Home Companion*, has nothing that can be identified as O'Brien's. The other report, made in the *New York Daily Times* on April 10, 1862, is that O'Brien wrote for Dickens's *Household Words*. Winter and Frank Wood do not mention any such connection, but "L. H. B." writing in *The Round Table* of June 6, 1868, says that "before coming to America, O'Brien contributed several articles to the first two volumes." It has been my privilege to go through the original manuscript office book of *Household Words* wherein are listed the names of the contributors and the sums paid to each,[87] and O'Brien's name is not there. For the year 1851, however, there are three anonymous contributions, any or all of which come easily within the range of O'Brien's capabilities. On November 8 a prose fantasy, under the title "An Arabian Night-Mare," tells jokingly of the frozen spirits of Eblis in a style that imitates the over-ornateness of oriental phrasing. "An Abiding Dream" of a week later[88] is a sentimental ballad of a miller's boy who remains true to his early dream of love. The third piece, a poem of December 13 entitled "A Child's Prayer," I should like to assign definitely to O'Brien. It is the same in its

[84] Augustus Maverick, *Henry J. Raymond and The New York Press, for Thirty Years*, Hartford, Conn., and Chicago, 1870, p. 143.

[85] See P. Condon, *op. cit.*, pp. 135–137, *passim*; and W. P. O'Brien, *op. cit.*, p. 253.

[86] Winter, 1881, p. vi.

[87] Made available through the courtesy of Elkin Matthews Ltd., 33 Conduit Street, London, W. 1.

[88] *Household Words*, IV, 182–183 (Nov. 15, 1851).

subject matter and its sweetly religious mood as the earlier "My Childhood's Prayer," and the reworking of previously successful ideas and styles was a common habit with Fitz-James. The typically O'Brien note, however, is the stanza about the robin's song. Here the bird "sang his evening song to God," and in the other three poems his song thrillingly carries the listener to thoughts of the Divine.[89] Being convinced, therefore, that "A Child's Prayer" is O'Brien's, I see no reason for hesitating to claim as his the other two pieces which come so close to it in time and in method of recording.

All the reports and rumors, whether of O'Brien's education, of his serving in the army, of his squandering his patrimony, of his haunting the theater and the opera, of his making trips to Paris, or of his contributing to *Household Words*, find their culmination in the story of a love affair, which, if true, was responsible for closing the chapter of O'Brien's London days. "He had gained experience in London, where he dissipated his patrimony and underwent a grand passion," says George Arnold;[90] and Stephen Fiske writes that he spoke guardedly of an attachment that had marred his life,—"It was the old story,—trite enough to be almost ludicrous." O'Brien had said to him, "Passion I can feel, but never again shall I know what it is to love. A man who once really loves can love but once. I have loved one woman; for all other women my heart is dead; but my passions, which have no heart in them, are as strong as lions, and they tear me like lions."[91]

The story as Aldrich told it is recorded by Mrs. James T. Fields, wife of the Boston publisher, with whose circle Aldrich became acquainted after leaving New York for Boston. "He [O'Brien] was a handsome fellow, and began his career by running away with the wife of an English officer. The officer was in India, and Fitz-James and the guilty woman had fled to one of the seaports on the south of England in order to take passage for America, when the arrival of the woman's husband was announced to them and

[89] The robin's song is a feature of "Forest Thoughts," *Cork Magazine*, II, 99–100 (Dec., 1848)—reprinted in the *Metropolitan Magazine*, LIV, 395–396 (Apr., 1849), and repeated in the *Parlour Magazine*, I, 95 (May 17, 1851); of "Our Old Garden Chair," *Parlour Magazine*, I, 215 (June 21, 1851); of "A Storm," *New York Times*, July 19, 1853; and of "A Storm in Summer," *H. W.*, I, 419 (July 4, 1857). The robin is also referred to in "Bird Gossip," *Harper's*, XI, 824 (Nov., 1855).

[90] Winter, 1881, p. lii.

[91] Winter, 1881, p. lvii.

O'Brien fled. He concealed himself on board a ship bound for New York."[92] Much the same story is told by Richard Henry Stoddard in his somewhat carping review of William Winter's 1881 volume. Stoddard himself had, under contract with Putnam's, been collecting material for an O'Brien book when Winter's volume appeared. It is, therefore, but natural that he should take delight in pointing out flaws or oversights in Winter. "This romantic episode (which seems to have escaped his biographer)" Stoddard relates as follows:

He was not wholly unknown to an officer belonging to that [the British] Army who was stationed in India, and who had left his wife behind him in England. Returning suddenly one day he found her in a charming establishment near London; but he did not find a young gentleman whom he had expected to meet with her, for he had suddenly gone to Paris. If our irate military friend had waited a little longer, he might still have missed our other young friend, but he would certainly not have missed his old family silver which was just on the point of being sent to him when he concluded to cross the Channel.[93]

The relish of gossip is in these stories; but, whatever the discrepancies as to detail, the main point of the intrigue would be thoroughly in keeping with the life and character of Fitz-James as Aldrich and Stoddard knew him in America. That O'Brien's reputation, however, had not suffered too much by a general circulation of the story is borne out by the following letter of R. Shelton Mackenzie, an editor and journalist of excellent standing:

In 1834–38, I edited a newspaper in Liverpool. Among the friends whom I most highly esteemed there was Dr. Collins, whose brother had been Catholic Bishop of Cloyne, in the south of Ireland. Late in 1851 or early in 1852, Dr. Collins knowing that I had, for several years, been a correspondent of M. M. Noah's *Evening Star* and other New York papers, wrote to me begging that I would send him a letter or two of introduction for Mr. Fitz James DeCourcy O'Brien, a young, talented, and well educated friend of his, who had got into pecuniary trouble, from living somewhat too fast, and had resolved to try his fortune, as a Journalist, in the New World. It was not entirely *en regle* according to

[92] M. A. DeWolfe Howe, *Memories of a Hostess. A Chronicle of Eminent Friendships drawn chiefly from the diaries of Mrs. James T. Fields,* Boston, 1922, p. 227 (entry under date of Nov. 9, 1865).

[93] *N. Y. Tribune,* Mar. 6, 1881.

English habit, to introduce a gentleman whom I had never seen, but Dr. Collins' voucher was so sufficient for me that I sent letters to Major Noah, Geo. P. Morris, and two or three other New Yorkers, whom I knew through many years' correspondence.[94]

With the chance of such associations, then, Fitz-James O'Brien sailed, near the end of the year 1851, from English shores.

[94] R. Shelton Mackenzie to William Winter, Oct. 9, 1880 (MS in Romm collection).

Chapter II

Establishment in New York

(1852)

When Fitz-James O'Brien landed in New York early in 1852, ostensibly to retrieve his fortunes, his first steps in that direction were those of characteristically O'Brien illogicality. "He ran a career of dissipation, landing with only sixty dollars. He went to a first-rate hotel, ordered wines, and left a large bill behind when the time came to run away."[1] While living thus splendidly on sixty dollars and charge accounts, he made use of the introductions with which Dr. Mackenzie had generously furnished him and presented himself to Major M. M. Noah, General George P. Morris, and the other prominent New Yorkers to whom he had letters. At any rate it was not long before "Mr. O'Brien found these introductions of use to him," as Mackenzie puts it;[2] for through them the well-born, well-bred, and accomplished young Irishman secured entree into New York's literary circles. The best social circles also welcomed him. Mrs. M. E. W. Sherwood, who met him at one of Mrs. Botta's receptions, speaks of him as a "fascinating conversationalist, a rather handsome, dashing, well-dressed young Irish gentleman, very much courted in society for a brief hour," and further describes his appearance as

always that of a graceful, well-dressed, clean, well-groomed, and pleasing man. His conversation reminded one of Bulwer's fine lines:

> "Fancy is ever popular; all like
> The sheeted flame that shines, but does not strike—
> Those fine merits above all;
> Point without sting, and satire without gall;
> A courteous irony, so free from scoff,
> The grateful victim felt himself let off.
> St. Stephen takes not from St. Giles his art,
> But is a true, good gentleman at heart."

[1] M. A. DeW. Howe, *op. cit.*, p. 227.

[2] Mackenzie to Winter, Oct. 9, 1880, *loc. cit.*

So whatever were the faults of this genius and poet Fitzjames O'Brien, he was as a dinner-table guest or in a country house most delightful company.[3]

Stoddard finds himself in entire agreement with this picture, which he completes by adding a detail or two: "He was a bright young fellow, of pleasing address, elegant manners, and more than the average amount of intelligence. Everybody liked him. He was a favorite at evening parties, which had not yet been banished by afternoon kettledrums, a favorite at stag parties, where his wit set the table on a roar, and he was a member of a fashionable club."[4]

Membership in a fashionable club, week ends at country houses, or mere attendance at formal dinners and evening parties entail on a young bachelor considerable expense. For, though the meals may be free, the clothes are not; and for the young man who landed with sixty dollars, a regular attendance at such functions, well-groomed as he always was, must rather quickly have become a matter of some financial embarrassment. The numerous stories which he tells of a young man in debt, humorous and withal a bit pathetic, almost invariably show their hero—the author under various disguises—as vexed and troubled by tailors' bills and tailors' duns, and as reduced sometimes to poverty-stricken makeshifts to hide or disguise the meagreness of his wardrobe. One of the last stories on which he was working, left unfinished in manuscript, and entitled "On a Rock,"[5] deals with just such a state of destitution; while as early as the end of July in the initial year of his New York life, he is writing of the expedients to which a poet is put to supply himself with a decent shirt. O'Brien during the rest of his life was always living beyond his means; indeed, he became a typical example of the impecunious Irishman, and when he did receive money for his writings was much more likely to spend it in giving extravagant dinners for his friends than to use it in payment of his debts.

To supply the fashionable wardrobe, or what was even more exigently pressing, to keep himself fed and housed, O'Brien must very soon after landing have sought literary employment. This he obtained under a fellow countryman of his, the well-known actor, John Brougham. On January 10,

[3] Mrs. M. E. W. Sherwood, *An Epistle to Posterity Being Rambling Recollections of Many Years of My Life*. New York and London, 1898, p. 126; and *The New York Times*, July 2, 1898 (Saturday Review of Books and Art), p. 444.

[4] *N. Y. Tribune*, Mar. 6, 1881.

[5] MS in Romm collection.

1852, Brougham began the publication of a comic magazine called *The Lantern*, and in the issue of February 21 appeared what is the first identified writing of Fitz-James O'Brien in America. According to Frank Wood, "Brougham saw that O'Brien was a valuable man to have on the *Lantern* staff, and the young author, before he had time to recover from the surprise his success caused him, was engaged as a regular contributor to the paper."[6]

"A Legend of the Olden Time,"[7] however, would scarcely seem to justify great faith in its author's abilities. A poorly written poem, in all sorts of meters, with constant changes in line length, with forced rhymes, single, double, and triple, it tells the story of the Prince of Squince who, to keep secret the fact that he has asses' ears, kills each month the barber who comes to shave him. His wife learns the secret, tells it to an oak tree, which repeats it to a bard; and so it becomes generally known. From this a humorous moral is drawn. That Brougham considered it valuable material for the magazine is seen by the fact that it was published in two parts, that each part was given space of a page and a half, and that each was illustrated by Frank H. Bellew. This artist and author O'Brien made the acquaintance of "at one of Brougham's weekly dinners, in Windust's old place, near the original Park Theatre,—at which the writers and artists of his *Lantern* were regularly convened, and at which everything but the paper was discussed."[8] Bellew and O'Brien soon became intimate friends, and Bellew's characteristic signature, which won him the name of Triangle, is for the next ten years often seen on illustrations accompanying O'Brien's contributions. In a letter to William Winter, Bellew tells of their being roommates. "The first place he [O'Brien] lodged at was in Leonard St—between B'way and Church St—we lived there together—from there we moved to B'way opposite to where the Metropolitan [Hotel] now stands—over a fashionable confectioners on the site of the afterwards notorious Stanwix Hall—where Bill Poole was murdered."[9] To three others of O'Brien's *Lantern* contributions Bellew supplied the illustrations—"The Gory Gnome," "The Demon Tie," and "The Wonderful Adventures of Mr. Papplewick."

The first of these, "The Gory Gnome: or The Lurid Lamp of the Volcano!

[6] Winter, 1881, p. xxxix.

[7] *The Lantern*, I, 70–71 (Feb. 21, 1852), and I, 90–91 (Mar. 6).

[8] Winter, 1881, p. xvii.

[9] F. H. Bellew to William Winter, Oct. 7, 1880; in Romm collection.

A Model Melo-Drama. In Three Acts,"[10] is a burlesque of the popular spectacular melodrama of the day. Its grand transformation scenes are silly, and something of its style can be gained from the list of the characters: "Flamanfuri, The Gory Gnome; Camphino, the lurid Lamp of the Volcano; Augustus Henry, The despairing Lover; Anna Matilda, The Distressed Heroine."

This early interest of Fitz-James in the theatre was undoubtedly stimulated by his friendship with Brougham. It remained with him always: he became intimately acquainted with New York's leading actors; before the year was out he had a play produced on Broadway; among a number of others which he wrote, one, *A Gentleman from Ireland*, remained successful for years; he was press agent for the famous actress Matilda Heron; and he was dramatic critic for the *New York Saturday Press*. These activities are in complete accord with O'Brien's habit of dramatizing himself; he lived theatrically.

On March 13 *The Lantern* began a serial story, "The Wonderful Adventures of Mr. Papplewick," which ran intermittently until May 8, and then stopped unfinished.[11] The story contains much pure fun, but it is full of extravagant and farfetched incidents. Nevertheless, like "The Phantom Light," even this ridiculous yarn contains examples of the technique upon which O'Brien's fame as a writer of weird tales was to rest—the localization of fantastically unbelievable events in well-known, even prosaic surroundings. Thus he places Papplewick, who has become a human magnet, as one of the new exhibits in Barnum's famous museum.

While "The Wonderful Adventures" was running, seven other contributions appeared in *The Lantern*, the first two of which, "The Ballad of Sir Brown" and "The Demon Tie," are social satires in verse. This is another type of writing in which Fitz-James became especially proficient and with which he attracted the attention of his contemporaries. These first two are undistinguished, but they do show an interest in the local scene and a clear perception of the undue emphasis given to conventional social usage. In them O'Brien was merely, as usual, adapting his sharp wit to the trend of the time and giving the public what it wanted.

The new American plutocracy was going through its first stages of devel-

[10] *The Lantern*, I, 73 (Feb. 28, 1852).

[11] *Ibid.*, I, 94–95 (Mar. 13, 1852); 120–121 (Mar. 27); 133 (Apr. 10); 150–151 (Apr. 17); 163 (May 1); and 180 (May 8).

opment in these years before the Civil War; and those merchants and organizers who were making money, and those who were beginning to take advantage of the enormous possibilities of America's natural resources, could in their social life do no more than imitate certain external features of the life of fashionable and aristocratic European society. The new French Emperor and his court exerted an especial attraction upon the imaginations of the moneyed Americans, and they with their extravagances and foibles very naturally drew upon themselves the attention and the satirical thrusts of the young journalists of the city. The most successful of these was George W. Curtis, who in February, 1853, hit just the right note in "Our Best Society," the first number of his enormously popular *The Potiphar Papers*.[12]

"The Ballad of Sir Brown,"[13] written in ballad form and with much of the usual ballad paraphernalia, tells of how Sir Reginald de Snooke tries to break into the best New York society without first obtaining the sanction of the social arbiter, Sir Brown, by paying to him the customary fees. The description of Sir Brown and his functions is a direct satire on Isaac Brown, sexton of Grace Church, who in addition to his duties in connection with the church was regulator supreme of the world of society. As O'Brien put it:

> Sir Brown, he was a doughty wight,
> And much had he of jaw;
> All thin-legged boys and maidens mild
> Did look on him with awe,
> Because among each "set" of *ton*
> His word was as a law.
>
> . . .
>
> For know, that I am stout Sir Brown,
> And Warden of the Church—
> I am the stone on which the town
> Doth step to Fashion's perch—
> And he who doth not stump it down,
> I leave him in the lurch!

Sir Brown's prestige as wielder of social power continued for some time,[14] and twice later O'Brien returns to the attack: first in a series of prose

[12] This appeared in *Putnam's Magazine*, I, 170–179 (Feb., 1853).
[13] *The Lantern*, I, 99 (Mar. 13, 1852).
[14] See Mrs. Ellet, *The Queens of American Society*, 1868, p. 453.

sketches entitled "Brown Studies,"[15] whose characters belong to the society of Fifth and Madison Avenues over which Mr. Brown still holds sway, and second in a satire "About the Sexton Bumble-Bee," the arbiter of fashion, who controls the entree to Fifth Avenue society, who passes upon invitation lists, who presides over fifty-thousand-dollar weddings, and who "consigns people to the grave with just as much elegant grief as they can afford to pay for."[16] In these sketches the earlier Sir Brown has assumed his proper form of fashionable sexton of a fashionable church—in the first it is Disgrace church, in the second the Church of the Holy Symphony—and as such he might be considered as cooperating in beautiful harmony with a rector like the Reverend Crinkum Crankum, or even with the Reverend Cream Cheese of *The Potiphar Papers*.

The second poem, "The Demon Tie,"[17] in its poor puns and in its forced double and triple rhymes, betrays a youthful attempt at cleverness. In mechanical means the author was rather obviously trying to imitate Lowell's *A Fable for Critics* (1847); but whereas the model gives an effect of easy gaiety, the imitation indicates laborious striving. Nevertheless, "The Demon Tie" in its light and mildly satirical way manages to be an amusing poem about a young dandy whose immaculate choker ties are the despair of all his rivals.

Longfellow had revealed to the world the possibility of dealing tenderly and delicately with the domestic affections and with the joys and particularly the sorrows of undistinguished persons in singing verse of simple metrical patterns. And what a boon this proved to the female versifiers of the fifties! They all wrote tenderly—oh, so tenderly!—and an orgy of mawkish sentimentalism burst loose. But the men were not to be outdone; and, as a number of them like Fitz-James had to make their livings by their pens, they followed the demands of the market and often beat the women at their own game. "An Old Story"[18] tells of the death of a woman of the streets. It is snowing hard, "the wind is laden with cutting sleet," "as a fainting woman goes wandering by." She was lovely once, but now the snow remains "unmelted, upon her marble breast."

[15] See the weekly numbers of *Young America*, Mar. 1, to June 7, 1856.
[16] *H. W.*, I, 130 (Feb. 28, 1857).
[17] *The Lantern*, I, 130–131 (Apr. 3, 1852).
[18] *Ibid.*, I, 143 (Apr. 17, 1852).

And lifeless she falls at the outer gate
Of *him* who has left her desolate!

Though men have spurned her, the snow covers her,

As though GOD, in his mercy, had willed that she
Should die in a garment of purity.

This shows to what extent O'Brien could go in the sentimental vein; but to avoid censuring him too severely it is well to recall that this was the age that first witnessed and participated in the tremendous enthusiasm over the story of Camille, the regeneration of the fallen woman through the power of love. And the best poets, in spite of their maudlin imitators, continued to write in the mood which would excite pity and bring the tear. Longfellow's "Excelsior" appeared as early as 1841 and the volume *Hymns to the Night* in 1847. In the latter year also appeared "The Changeling" by Lowell; but Aldrich's "Babie Bell" came out as late as 1855, Holmes's "The Voiceless" in 1858, and Longfellow continued to be the best and most popular purveyor of delicate sentiment in such poems as "My Lost Youth," "The Children's Hour," "The Haunted Chamber," and "The Cross of Snow" from 1855 almost to the time of his death in 1882.

"To April,"[19] O'Brien's next poem, is a mere trifle, neat and clever; but the two that follow are keyed to the popular reforming spirit of the age. The great crusade against slavery which the publication of *Uncle Tom's Cabin* had just unloosed is not reflected in any of O'Brien's writing, but he gave his hand to sharp attacks in verse on many of the evils which fell under his more immediate observation in the city of New York. *The New-York Daily Times* had on April 14 and April 15 printed articles on the terrible conditions under which the "*sewing* women" of New York must work, and thus had renewed the interest created by such a poem as Hood's "The Song of the Shirt" (1843) and by such novels as Mrs. Gaskell's *Mary Barton* (1848) and Kingsley's *Alton Locke* (1850). So "The Shirt Fiend, A Christian Carol," which appeared in *The Lantern* for April 24, was well timed. It tells the story of a mother who wears herself out sewing shirts to earn her children bread. The Shirt Fiend tears the work and orders it brought back next week properly done.

[19] *Ibid.*, I, 144 (Apr. 17, 1852).

> "Oh, Heaven! my children"—was all she said,
> As she fell at the Shirt Fiend's threshold dead![20]

Fitz-James testifies to the success of this poem by a repetition of its method and subject matter just six weeks later. The first half of "The Spectral Shirt"[21] retells exactly the story of the earlier poem; but, here, before "tottering to the door, she fell and died," the woman gets in a tremendous curse, with the result that the shirt fiend is thenceforward haunted by a visionary shirt which drives him to despair and suicide.

Still later in the summer Fitz-James uses the shirts again, this time in a prose sketch, written apparently to supply space-filling copy demanded by an insistent editor. He resorts to making capital of his own foibles and gives a seriocomic sketch of himself as "the Sentimental Poet." He describes the poet as "of a middle height, with large eyes, large nose, and a head shaped like an isosceles triangle." That these details are characteristic of O'Brien we know from descriptions by his friends—the very small chin, referred to by George Arnold and appearing as a distinguishing feature in the cartoons by Bellew, accounting for the triangularity of the head.[22] The autobiographical account continues:

> If you were to judge of him by his verses, you would imagine that he was continually burning with indignation against the social abuses with which the world is, according to him, overran [*sic*]. In his Street Lyrics he inveighs bitterly against moneyed power, and comes down upon cheap clothes sellers with tremendous energy. Nevertheless he would not refuse a hundred dollars if you were to offer them to him; and when he has to purchase an outfit, does not hesitate to wade down Chatham street in search of "bargains." He published a fierce Poem, entitled "The Shirt Fiend," some weeks back, in which he made an old Jew commit suicide, because he sold shirts too cheap; but what was our astonishment to meet him a few days afterwards coming out of a cheap shirt store, with a brown paper parcel under his arm. "Why," said we, "you surely have not been purchasing shirts from one of those miscreants?" "No, no," said our Poet stammering and blushing, "that is, not exactly; but you see I went into the shop to study character you know, and I was—as it were—forced to purchase some-

[20] *Ibid.*, I, 154 (Apr. 24, 1852).
[21] *Ibid.*, I, 219 (June 5, 1852).
[22] See Winter, 1881, p. xlvii; and illustrations.

thing. Not that I ever intend to wear them—oh! no. Not that I ever intend to wear them!"
Next day he came to our Office in a dollar shirt.[23]

"The Shirt Fiend" was only the first of many poems of social protest to be written by O'Brien. He followed it the next week with the first of a series of three "Street Lyrics," each of which attacks some humanitarian problem. The first, "The Beggar Child,"[24] tells an incident of "a wealthy man and proud" who has been completely incredulous about the stories of dire poverty in the city. The poet, however, takes him out into the cold street, where he meets a child scantily clothed, barefooted, and pinched with lack of nourishment. She leads him "to her wretched home, A cellar damp and cold," where her mother by sewing tries to earn enough to support five children—the father having been killed in the Mexican war. The proud man is humbled, and he wants to use his wealth to help relieve such desperate conditions. This poem and "The Shirt Fiend" initiate a type of writing in which Fitz-James later became especially proficient, stirring his reform-loving contemporaries with rhymed attacks on the finishing school, the prize fight, and the tenement house. When it is recalled that of the poems he wrote in Ireland and England only "The Famine" shows any such interest, all the others treating of safely conventional subjects, the ready adaptability of Fitz-James to the conditions of his new environment and his new market strikes the reader with almost as much force as it did his contemporaries. Perhaps the change in his own circumstances from a position of affluence to one in which he ate only as his pen produced had thus quickly after his arrival in New York forced upon him a sympathetic consciousness of the hard conditions of the poor.

In the next poem, "Wine!",[25] O'Brien contributes his mite to *The Lantern's* campaign against heavy drinking; but even though he himself often drank too much this bit sounds sincere: it describes the joys of overindulgence at night, and then with equal vividness pictures the distresses of a bad hangover in the morning. He returned the next week, however, to the humanitarian theme and in the second of the "Street Lyrics," "The Crossing Sweeper,"[26] practically retells the story of the good Samaritan; but the

[23] *The Lantern*, II, 44 (July 31, 1852)—"Lantern Slides. No. III. The Poet."
[24] *Ibid.*, I, 166 (May 1, 1852).
[25] *Ibid.*, I, 174 (May 8, 1852).
[26] *Ibid.*, I, 186 (May 15, 1852).

victim in this case is a starving girl of "scarce thirteen," while the only one who comes to her aid is a poor old woman who gives half her all. The third of the series, "The Street Monkey,"[27] pleads in an oversentimental way for more kindly treatment of animals.

The only other items in *The Lantern* definitely identified as O'Brien's are the first two numbers of "Lantern Slides."[28] The first satirizes "The Comic Artist," for which Bellew almost certainly posed; the second bewails the irritating idiosyncrasies of various types of "Joke Makers." Five other articles may, without much conjectural doubt, be attributed to O'Brien. The earliest, "The Physiology of Pantomimes Un-'ravelled',"[29] deals with the theatrical fare of the day and thrusts satirically at the popular performances given by the Ravels at Niblo's Garden. The next is a narrative poem of about the same length and in the same spirit as "The Demon Tie," and its hero, Dr. Botts, "considered himself the Fifth Avenue beau," just as did Danby Fitz Green, the hero of the immaculate ties. The friends of the doctor, playing upon his belief in himself as irresistible to the ladies, make him the butt of a practical joke in which Anna Matilda (also in "The Gory Gnome") acts as the bait. Under the general heading "Fifth Avenue Legends," this story of "The Doctor, the Lawyer, and the Lady"[30] cleverly but cruelly pierces the conceited pose of the "perfect" young gentleman, who is willing to meet a lady first at Barnum's museum and then in Washington Square.

"He Writes for Bread"[31] is a poem which, like the sketch of the Sentimental Poet, seems to be largely autobiographical. The young man in his garret at midnight must sit up and write clever bits, cudgeling his brains and forcing himself to keep at it as he looks at the table empty of food. Although everyone else in the publishing business is amply paid, the writer gets not enough to meet his bills. It is a hard lot!

"The Man without a Shadow. A New Version"[32] is a prose sketch and has, as it says, nothing to do with Peter Schlemihl. It is, instead, a parody of Poe's "Shadow: A Parable," which had been published in the *Southern*

[27] *Ibid.*, II, 8 (July 10, 1852).

[28] *Ibid.*, I, 257 (June 26, 1852), and II, 23 (July 17).

[29] *Ibid.*, I, 112 (Mar. 20, 1852).

[30] *Ibid.*, I, 250–251 (June 19, 1852).

[31] *Ibid.*, II, 47 (July 31, 1852). This poem and "Fifth Avenue Legends" were brought to my attention by Charles I. Glicksberg, with whom I concur in assigning them to O'Brien.

[32] *Ibid.*, II, 91 (Sept. 4, 1852); also brought to my attention by Charles I. Glicksberg.

Literary Messenger for September, 1835; and even though it seems to have been written primarily as a humorous piece, it so closely imitates the original which it is burlesquing that it produces an effect of unexplained oddness and unnaturalness. But this grotesque bit, in which Shadow unshakably accompanies the author and does and says identical things (the Poe touch), is set in a perfectly plausible locale (the O'Brien touch), a cheap boarding-house where Shadow by eating and dressing the same as the author irritatingly causes a double expense. Its final affront is that "it put on one of my clean shirts"—shirts seem to be an obsession of O'Brien's during these *Lantern* days—"(as I did myself), and went out with me. At the door it borrowed a five dollar bill, and—vanished. It is the nature of Shadows to vanish. I have since heard that the same Shadow has vanished from more than one boarding house in the most shadowy manner."

O'Brien's other two contributions to *The Lantern* did not appear until almost a year later; so it is probably in reference to these that Thomas Bailey Aldrich, who became an intimate and lifelong friend of Fitz-James, remarked, "When I first knew him, he was trimming the wick of the *Lantern*, which went out shortly afterwards."[33] *The Lantern* printed its last number on June 4, 1853; but September 4, 1852, is the date of the last issue for the year to contain anything by O'Brien. He must therefore about this time have been forming other journalistic connections, the results of which appear shortly afterwards. In the very next month, August, appeared his first contribution to *The American Whig Review;* and before the year was out he was writing for *The New-York Daily Times* as a member of its staff, and appearing as the author of a critical review in the first number of *Putnam's Monthly.* During the next year, 1853, he contributed to the *United States Magazine and Democratic Review*, and *Harper's Monthly* published the first of what was to be a long series of articles, poems, and short stories by him. In 1856 he was writing for the comic sheet *Young America*, and for *The Home Journal*, which under the editorship of Nathaniel Parker Willis and General George P. Morris was for many years the most popular of the weeklies. Upon the advent of *Harper's Weekly* and the *Atlantic Monthly* in 1857, O'Brien's work appeared in their pages; and he wrote spasmodically beginning in 1858 for the *Knickerbocker Magazine*. O'Brien once refers to the latter as the *Knuckleunder Magazine* established on the principle of a mutual

[33] Winter, 1881, p. xvi.

admiration society; and, alluding to its practice of sucking the blood of its contributors (of printing their work without paying for it), he speaks of it as being "edited by that pleasant fellow, Jolly Vampyre."[33a] This is an obvious hit at its well-known editor, Lewis Gaylord Clark. Poems by O'Brien also appeared in *The Household Journal* and *The Continental Monthly*, poems and a story in *The New York Picayune*, a various assortment in *Vanity Fair*, and miscellaneous articles in *The Saturday Press*, *Young America*, *Wilkes' Spirit of the Times*, and in various newspapers.

From the above enumeration it is clear that Fitz-James O'Brien found a ready market for his writing.[34] As *Harper's Weekly* says:

> Permanent and recognized positions in the press were always at his command, and were at different times held on the *Times*, *Putnam's Magazine*, *Harper's Weekly*, and subsequently, and for a still longer period, upon that brilliant but erratic paper, the *Saturday Press*. But for a while it seems pleasanter to write only what and when one pleases, than to be bound by fixed obligations to furnish so much matter, of a certain kind, at a specified time. O'Brien knew that he could always transmute his fancies into current coin; and freedom was so delightful, and he doubtless flattered himself that his leisure would be spent in accumulating stores of observation and experience for the "Great Work," which, like all young writers, he proposed to accomplish at some future day. So he retained these definite positions but for a short time; and the great portion of his literary labors are in the shape of isolated contributions to various periodicals.[35]

The total number of journals and periodicals flourishing in 1852, papers to which O'Brien might contribute and by which he might be paid, was at first not large; but there was during the decade before the Civil War a rapid growth in periodical literature, and even some advance in the scale of prices for contributors.

Besides the periodicals listed as those in which O'Brien's contributions have been found, New York could boast four well-established six-cent newspapers—*The Evening Post*, the oldest, pursuing its dignified and conservative course under the editorship of William Cullen Bryant; *The Courier and*

[33a] "The Man about Town," *H. W.*, I, 195 (Mar. 28, 1857).

[34] The whole subject of American periodicals is competently covered in the excellent volumes by Frank Luther Mott, *A History of American Magazines, 1741–1850*, New York and London, 1930; *1850–1865*, Cambridge, Mass., 1938; *1865–1885*, Cambridge, Mass., 1938; and *American Journalism*, New York, 1941.

[35] *H. W.*, VI, 267 (Apr. 26, 1862).

Enquirer, edited by the fiery Col. J. Watson Webb;[36] the *Commercial Advertiser*; and the *Journal of Commerce*—and three smaller one-cent papers—*The Sun*, controlled by Moses S. Beach; *The Herald*, popular and sensational, owned by James Gordon Bennett; and the *New York Daily Tribune*, crusading for various reforms under the leadership of Horace Greeley. *The World* was established as a moral and religious paper in 1860.[37] Of the weeklies the first real rival to *The Home Journal* was the *New York Ledger*, brought out in March, 1856, by Robert Bonner, who by a series of innovations made it a conspicuous and sensational success.[38] *Frank Leslie's Illustrated Newspaper* began publication in 1855, and during the next fifteen years Leslie launched ten illustrated papers and magazines with varying fortunes. Of the monthlies *Graham's Magazine* rapidly declined after the retirement of its editor in 1853,[39] while *Godey's Lady's Book* continued its popular career. As for the comic magazines, there were so many abortive attempts to establish an American *Punch* that even the names of most of them are lost. O'Brien wrote regularly for four of these weeklies—*The Lantern*, *Young America*, *The New York Picayune*, and *Vanity Fair* (1859–1863); while *Charivari* and *Momus* were perhaps the most noticed of the others. Of humorous monthlies *Cozzens' Wine Press* (1854–1861) seems to have been the most prominent.

That Fitz-James had to write copiously in order to make a living is readily realized when one glances at the low rates which even the better magazines paid for copy. *Graham's Magazine*, which for many years set the standard, paid from three dollars to twelve dollars a page. The latter figure, however, is distinctly referred to by N. P. Willis as a very liberal sum which is paid to only their principal contributors.[40] Three dollars a page was their usual rate,[41] as it was of *Godey's* also. To Poe they had paid four dollars

[36] See Allan Nevins, *The Evening Post, A Century of Journalism*, 1922, Chap. IX, *passim;* and A. Maverick, *op. cit.*, pp. 36–39.

[37] See Frank M. O'Brien, *The Story of* THE SUN, 1918, Chaps. I and VI, *passim;* and Frederic Hudson, *Journalism in the United States from 1690 to 1872*, 1873, Chaps. XXVII and XXXIII, *passim*, and p. 667. For additional facts about these newspapers see also Willard Grosvenor Bleyer, *Main Currents in the History of American Journalism*, Cambridge, Mass., 1927, Chaps. VI–IX; and George Henry Payne, *History of Journalism in the United States*, N. Y. and London, 1926, Chaps. XVIII–XXI.

[38] For details see Hudson, *op. cit.*, pp. 646–649.

[39] See Ellis Paxson Oberholtzer, *The Literary History of Philadelphia*, Philadelphia, 1906, pp. 283 ff.

[40] See *The Prose Works of N. P. Willis*, Philadelphia, 1852, "Ephemera," p. 723.

[41] See Algernon Tassin, *The Magazine in America*, 1916, p. 212.

a page for his critical articles and not much more for his tales.[42] Edmund Clarence Stedman, writing of the period from 1859 to 1863, during which he was having a hard struggle to make ends meet, and calling it "New York's Bohemian Olympiad" says, "There was not much of a literary market at that time. Newspaper salaries were very low. There were few magazines, and scarcely any but *Harper's* and the *Atlantic* paid much of anything."[43] For even these two the rates were not high: the *Atlantic* paid six dollars a page for prose, or ten dollars if the author's name helped; and *Harper's*, seven and a half to ten dollars a page. For a poem the *Atlantic's* price was fifty dollars. *The North American Review* in its conservatism still stuck to a dollar and a half a page; *The Knickerbocker's* rate was three dollars.[44] Comics like *The Lantern* could frequently not afford to pay at all. In an undated letter written at the office of *Putnam's Monthly* O'Brien gives direct evidence as to what he thinks his own stories are worth; but one of the sentences indicates that he is not at all sure the editor will agree:

Office, Putnam's Monthly
Oct 20th

Dear Sir
I cannot let you have the story sooner than the 28th, at least. It will be a modern love story. The scene laid in New York. Will be called "the Artist on Wood," or "My friend the Artist." Will make about five or six pages of your magazine. My price for a story of any length over 5 pages and under ten is fifty dollars. If these terms suit you and the tale will be in time, I shall send it on in case of no reply from you. If however my plan or terms do not suit you, let me know by return post. By the way you never mentioned about my poem, the three Pictures. I am really anxious about it, so pray drop me a line.

Yours tr—
Fitz James O'Brien[45]

The fact that O'Brien's pieces appeared in such a wide variety of short-lived periodicals, complete files of which are difficult to find, makes the establishing of an O'Brien bibliography a real problem; but additional haz-

[42] See E. P. Oberholtzer, *op. cit.*, p. 273.

[43] Laura Stedman and George M. Gould, M. D., *Life and Letters of Edmund Clarence Stedman*, 2 v., 1910, I, 209. For a discussion of prices paid by the periodicals to their contributors see A. Tassin, *op. cit.*, Chap. IX, *passim*, and F. L. Mott, *A History of American Magazines, 1850–1865*, pp. 19–25—"Rates of payment."

[44] See "Literary Pay," (editorial), *The Saturday Press*, Nov. 13, 1858.

[45] A. L. S., Fitz James O'Brien to Dear Sir, Oct. 20th, in Historical Society of Pennsylvania.

ard and uncertainty are added to the task from the continuing practice of the periodicals in concealing the authorship of their contents under the cover of anonymity. Nevertheless, through records of his friends and acquaintances, through personal acknowledgement, and through various references and clues, 295 poems, short stories, critical essays, and miscellaneous articles have been identified as contributions from his facile and erratic pen.[46] In addition to these, five plays of his were produced, and sixteen of his letters have been preserved.

The first poem of O'Brien's after the squibs and verses in *The Lantern* was a page of blank verse called "Madness" printed in the August number of *The American Whig Review.* It is distinctly imitative of Poe in purporting to be the expression of a man who feels himself growing gradually insane, and the phrases and mood of "The Haunted Palace" (1839) keep constantly flashing across the reader's mind. Nevertheless, the poem is poor. The idea itself is an awful one, and as Poe shows both in verse and prose, is capable of awesome treatment; but facility and power in handling blank verse sufficient to create the necessary feeling, O'Brien does not possess. It is the wrong medium, not the wrong subject that he has chosen; for later, in prose, it is about persons in abnormal states of mind that he writes his most effective stories.

"Madness" was followed in September, October, and December by groups of essays, poems, and short stories, held together in a framework, the form of which is sufficiently indicated by the title, "Fragments from an Unpublished Magazine." As authors of the "Fragments" O'Brien invents the "tender, melancholy, and impassioned poet Heremon," whose name it will be recalled was signed to some of the Dublin *Nation* pieces; the "quizzical Pro;" the "wild, half-mad, extravagant, imaginative metaphysician Origen Od;" and "the Irishman, profound, humorous, and pathetic by turns, and terminating every article with an entreaty to advance him five dollars."[47]

An analysis of the six poems and seven prose pieces contributed by this quartet gives interesting indication of O'Brien's personal and literary characteristics. The very fact that "Fragments" is a potpourri of short pieces in a variety of forms and a greater variety of moods shows immediately what is one of the weaknesses and one of the advantages of his method and

[46] This number does not include the twenty-nine poems, two stories, and eleven miscellaneous articles printed in Irish and English periodicals before he came to America, nor the items which remain unlocated or only in MS.

[47] *American Whig Review*, XVI, 263 (Sept., 1852).

product. His talent or such genius as he possessed could best express itself only in short spurts; he was incapable of sustained effort. His friends, Winter and Arnold, have both described him at the work of composition:[48] he could work furiously and concentratedly for a day or two, and then relaxation or dissipation of some kind seemed to be necessary. Not infrequently, therefore, O'Brien is found giving play to his fancy in articles of a mixed nature.[49]

The "Fragments" reveal also O'Brien's faculty of imitation, his use of the manner and material of widely divergent literary forms, and his habit of making critical comments upon his own productions. His interest in Poe is, in the December number, definitely stated—a fact of especial interest, since it is on his success in imitating and modifying the tale of terror that the claims of O'Brien to a place of permanence seem bound to rest. He lacks Poe's power of restraint and artistic condensation; but the Irish nature which denied him this supplied him with a sense of humor, which saves him from certain mistakes of which Poe is guilty. Still O'Brien is a follower and imitator of Poe, and in no way his rival; he lacks his finish, his sense of style, his power over the rich suggestiveness of the right word.

The December "Fragment" which refers to Poe is a poem of four stanzas, entitled "Oinea,"[50] from which, the author says, Poe took hints "as to the mechanical construction of his poetry," just as for "his very powerful sketch of 'The Pit and the Pendulum' " he so obviously plagiarised "from an article which appeared in Blackwood about a year previous to the publication of Mr. Poe's tale." "Oinea" is a subtly versified version of Poe's "Shadow," which O'Brien had three months earlier parodied in "The Man without a Shadow." O'Brien's comment, which follows the poem, gives some light:

This strange poem is intended, we suppose, to typify the confusion of ideas, resulting from an over-indulgence with the bottle. Oinea, the goddess of wine, apparently a sort of female Bacchus, gets decidedly inebriated in the last stanza. . . . The lines,

> "Her heart was in time with the tremulous tread
> Of a mourner in passing the graves of the dead,"

[48] See Winter, 1881, pp. xxi–xxiii, and xlix; and *Old Friends*, pp. 71–72.

[49] See "The Editor at Large," "Bird Gossip," "The Man about Town," "A Paper of All Sorts," "Dramatic Feuilleton," and "Here and There."

[50] *Am. Whig Review*, XVI, 566–567 (Dec., 1852).

are very fine, and quite equal to Poe's finest alliterative lines. There is also in the second stanza an expression,

"The swaying and pendulous leaves of the vine,"

which is perfect word-melody, and expresses the idea in sound as perfectly as syllables can do. If, after the examples we have pointed out, our readers do not see the similarity between our unknown poet and the author of Annabel Lee, we pity their want of discrimination.

As for the rest of the poems all except "Pallida"[51] contain something of the weird or the grotesque, and even this is on the typical Poe subject, the death of a beautiful woman. It is by far the best of the poetic "fragments," being smooth, delicate, and apt. "The Song of the Immortal Gods. Written at their Express Desire,"[52] by Origen Od, a madman, is "reckless and capricious." As the reader's attention is constantly drawn to the trochaics in which the poem is written, he is far more likely to agree with the part of the comment which speaks of the wild, unsatisfactory nature of this poem, than with the part which mentions all its beauties. "The Old Knight's Wassail" and "The Shadow by the Tree"[53] are balladlike poems with medieval setting. The first is lacking in distinction of any kind; the second attempts to be terrifying but, because of its stereotyped and crude expressions, it comes perilously near being ridiculous. It is unfortunate that, as far as poetry is concerned, O'Brien did not live up to the critical commentary with which he accompanies this poem:

We decidedly object as a rule to these tales of terror. They neither benefit society nor the author. We recollect the time when we could not ourselves write a tale without three murders in it, interspersed with a ghost or two. But these days are gone by with us; and henceforward we will stick to nature.

"The Captive Sea-Gull," which had been used in the first number of *The Parlour Magazine*, is here reprinted after some introductory remarks of extravagant praise.[54]

The prose of the "Fragments" is of two kinds—the running comment,

[51] *Ibid.*, XVI, 264 (Sept., 1852).
[52] *Ibid.*, XVI, 268–269.
[53] *Ibid.*, XVI, 272 (Sept.), and XVI, 364–365 (Oct., 1852).
[54] *Ibid.*, XVI, 364.

discursive and critical, connecting the various "contributions," and the set pieces themselves. The first type has been sufficiently indicated by quotations; the second comprises a varied assortment. "A Voyage in My Bed"[55] is a strange story of dream experience, well done in smooth, easy style, though with frequently conventional diction. Reminiscent of DeQuincey, it gives forecasts of O'Brien's power of handling, in telling prose, weird and otherworldly material. "Carrying Weight"[56] has been discussed as one of the few stories in which O'Brien shows anything of the background of his Irish life. Humor is the chief element. Humor is also the distinguishing characteristic in a series of epigrammatic witticisms called "Odds and Ends" by Pro, and in "The Woes of a Literary Partner,"[57] a letter in which Job Mawkins feelingly tells of the perfidiousness of his erstwhile friend Theophilus Toggs (names reminiscent of Dickens), with whom he had been engaged to write a novel in serial numbers, each doing an alternate chapter. Mawkins, jealous of his wife, kicks Toggs out; and thereafter each of the collaborators in his chapter tries to counteract the effect of the preceding chapter of his rival, until Toggs finally wins by having the heroine, Sophonisba, ground up in a sausage machine and sold "at sixpence a pound to a hungry mechanic with a large family."

The two remaining pieces, more pretentious in their scope, are short stories. "One Event,"[58] German in inspiration, is a very uneven production. For the most part it is smoothly told; the atmosphere of brooding romance and melancholy is successfully created; and the conception of the solitary recluse, of his adoption of a ward, and of the gradual change of his character through his growing love for her, though not original, is interestingly handled. But the story forfeits all claim to praise because of the melodrama of its end, and especially because of the bad taste and crude style of a number of its paragraphs.

"The King of Nodland and his Dwarf,"[59] a tale in five chapters, is a curious mixture of a number of moods. The large sections of political and social satire, with discussion and description in the manner of Swift, do not coalesce with the intrigue type of story nor with the tenderness of the idyllic

[55] *Ibid.*, XVI, 264–268 (Sept., 1852).
[56] *Ibid.*, XVI, 269–272.
[57] *Ibid.*, XVI, 272 (Sept.), and XVI, 567–568 (Dec., 1852).
[58] *Ibid.*, XVI, 351–362 (Oct., 1852).
[59] *Ibid.*, XVI, 554–566 (Dec., 1852).

love passages with which they are interspersed. The setting is a mythical island far away in the Pacific Ocean; but the description of Nodland under the reign of King Slumberous and the premiership of Lord Incubus carries satirical thrusts at England, while the state of slavery in which the Cock-Crows are held refers to conditions in the United States. The story, despite its diffuseness and variety of moods, is in itself interesting, and the author included it in a list of twenty of his stories, written down about 1861, "which he thought worthy of preservation."[60]

In the same month of December with a slightly altered title—"From an Unpublished Manuscript"—a discursive essay by Fitz-James appeared in William Cullen Bryant's newspaper *The Evening Post*, where it filled more than one of those long columns, "On Social Manners in America."[61] In a facetious vein it discusses appropriate dress for both men and women—the author dislikes the word *female*,—pokes fun at the customs of conventional mourning, and gives rules for seemly behavior in unseemly social predicaments.

The year 1852 also saw O'Brien form two other interesting connections, another with the world of the newspaper, the second with that of the theatre. The first came through his employment on the regular staff of *The New-York Daily Times*. This paper, first issued by Henry J. Raymond on September 18, 1851, prospered immediately; and the story of its expansion, in so far as it concerns O'Brien, is thus told by Augustus Maverick in his book on *Henry J. Raymond and the New York Press:*

In 1852, the space added to the *Times*, by doubling its size, gave Mr. Raymond ample opportunity to make a good newspaper. Some of the best writers of the day became regular contributors; bright wits sent sparkling papers; new men were introduced into the staff of editors; cost was not counted when a good article was to be secured; and the *Times* became the best family paper ever published in New York. Four writers, whose productions appeared regularly in the columns of the *Times*, in the course of this second year, are now dead; but their effusions live, and, if collected and edited, they would form an interesting volume. One of these contributors was Charles C. B. Seymour,—a young Englishman, who was subsequently the musical and dramatic critic of the *Times*, and died while holding that position. Another was Fitz-James O'Brien, an Irishman who was absurdly

[60] *H. W.*, VI, 267.

[61] *The Evening Post*, Dec. 24, 1852. This item was identified as O'Brien's by Charles I. Glicksberg.

ashamed of his Irish birth, but who was one of the most brilliant of all the brilliant brotherhood of New York at that day.[62]

Others to be employed were Dr. Frank Tuthill, who wrote "quaint papers on rural and domestic topics"; Charles Welden, author of "The City-Hall Bell-Ringer"; and later, Charles F. Briggs, William Henry Hurlburt, E. L. Godkin, William G. Sewell, and R. J. De Cordova.

The writing for the *Times* done by O'Brien consists chiefly of light essays on subjects of general interest, the average length of the articles being about two columns. On November 13 he compares the difficulty of breaking into the literary profession in London with the ease of doing so in America; on November 27 he advocates originality and insurgency in art; and on December 2 he reviews the work of Sir Thomas Browne. Each of these articles is signed "F. J. O'B"; and an editorial in the *Times* for April 7, 1862, states that "his first essays in this City appeared in our own columns, soon after the establishment of the *Times*"; while the issue of April 10 says that "many of his best articles appeared in the *Times*, of which paper he was for many years a valued contributor."

Dr. Mackenzie's letter, part of which has already been quoted, refers not only to O'Brien's early association with the *Times* but also to his initial appearance in the New York theatre:

When I reached New York, a little before Christmas 1852, I found that Dr. Collins ['s] reliance on his young friend's talents was justified by the fact that he was at work on the New York Times, then recently established, and also on several magazines in New York & Boston.

I met him, for the first time, on Christmas-day, 1852, I think, at his rooms in Union Square, in consequence of his having invited me, in a very courteous note, to dine with him that day. Unless I am much mistaken, I also made the acquaintance of Mr. Bellew, there & then, and the party adjourned from the dinner-table to Wallack's Theater (in Broadway near Broome St.) where a bright little comic piece, by Mr. O'B., was then played for the first time.[63]

The bright little piece the opening performance of which on Christmas night Dr. Mackenzie attended in company with the author was *My Christmas Dinner*, "an original farce written for this theater"[64] (Wallack's Lyceum).

[62] Augustus Maverick, *op. cit.*, p. 143. See also Elmer Davis, *History of the New York Times, 1851–1921*, 1921, Chap. I.

[63] Mackenzie to Winter, Oct. 9, 1880.

[64] T. Allston Brown, *A History of the New York Stage, From the First Performance in 1732 to 1901*, 3 v., 1903, I, 479.

The leading part in the play, that of Hunter Savage, was acted by Lester Wallack, who, then on the threshold of his great career, was appearing on the stage as Mr. Lester.[65] During the years that followed, Lester and O'Brien continued the friendship begun at this time, enjoying frequent meetings in the theater and at Pfaff's; while Lester's father, the veteran actor, James W. Wallack, who had formerly been a favorite in Ireland and who was now and for the rest of his life a successful theatrical manager in America, took a great fancy to the young Irish writer, and became his devoted friend. Wallack had come to New York in the spring of 1852, only a few months after O'Brien himself had arrived, had taken over Brougham's Lyceum, and "soon succeeded not only in rivaling, but in a measure superseding Burton's Theater in public esteem. The hand of a master was visible in every production, and the taste, elegance, and propriety displayed about the whole establishment gave it a position of respectability never hitherto enjoyed in New York, except at the old Park Theater. The ascendancy it then secured it has ever since maintained, and for many years it has been the leading theater of the city."[66] The production of his farce at such an establishment as that of Wallack's must have been valuable to O'Brien, not only by putting him in the way to earn money, but by giving him a certain prestige in theatrical circles. His intimacy with the Wallacks is made clear by the following letter, written to William Winter in 1881 after his book had come out:

13 West 30th Street
March 27th

Dear Willie—

Knowing my great fondness for O'Brien—it was like your thoughtful kindness to send me the book—You have wrestled with a great difficulty with wonderful

[65] See Lester Wallack, *Memories of Fifty Years*, 1889, p. 216, and *N. Y. Tribune*, Dec. 28, 1852. The advertisement in *The New York Herald*, Dec. 2, 1852, announces the cast for *My Christmas Dinner* as:

"Mr. Iceberg....................Mr. Hale Miss Iceberg....................Mrs. Cramer
Mr. Echo....................Mr. Rea Amy Iceberg....................Mrs. Rea"

George C. D. Odell, *Annals of the New York Stage*, 1931, VI, 218 (by permission of Columbia University Press), completes this cast as follows:

"Hunter Savage....................Mr. Lester Kitty....................Miss Tayleure
Hannibal....................Mr. Durant"

[66] Joseph N. Ireland, *Records of the New York Stage, from 1750 to 1860*, 2 v., 1867, II, 611. See also, Odell, *op. cit.*, VI, 213 ff.

tact and brought order out of "a mixture of material" which a less delicate and experienced touch might have utterly failed to elicit.

I tried hard to find a cheery-plucky-little note, in pencil, which he wrote to my Father after he was wounded—but in vain—or I w^{d} have sent it to you—

Always truly yours
Lester Wallack

The grammar of this
note is questionable
but—never mind—(I dont mean O'B's note but *mine.*)[67]

The most complete source of information about O'Brien's first play is the review of it in *The New York Herald.* As it contains in addition friendly comment on the adroitness of O'Brien's technique, it is quoted in full:

For the holidays Wallack has brought out two new pieces entitled "My Christmas Dinner," and "Mysterious Rappings," which will be presented for the second time tomorrow evening. "My Christmas Dinner" was written by Fitz James O'Brien, Esq. We congratulate Mr. Wallack on having hit the public taste so dexterously. The story, like that of all farces is easily told. Mr. Hunter Savage, a fast man about town, has received no invitation to dinner on Christmas-day. Naturally indignant, he boldly forces his way into the drawing-room of a house whence a grateful fragrance of sirloin and other good things issues forth. The host, Mr. Iceberg, who is dignity personified, makes vain endeavors to get rid of his unexpected guest. Savage "is not to be pulverized;" he talks and tells stories and makes love to the maiden aunt, whom he finally leads off to the dinner table. While he is still chuckling over the success of his expedient, he meets in the daughter of his host an old flame whom he had seen in the Crystal Palace in London, and renews his protestations of love, gains over the aunt to his cause by an adroit *ruse,* extorts a consent from Iceberg, who is more than half seas over, and the curtain falls on a happy couple. A sprightly dialogue and a profusion of excellent bon-mots give an attraction to this *bluette* which was well appreciated by the audience on Saturday night. We heard but one endless roar of laughter from the first to the last scene. Mr. O'Brien has obviously turned to good profit his acquaintance with the witty vaudevilles of Scribe and the other modern French dramatic writers: without borrowing either an idea or a situation from any, he has caught their peculiar liveliness, and has given us—a rare thing—a very clever and sparkling, though original, piece. We trust that the public will soon be familiar with his name as a successful dramatic author.[68]

[67] A. L. S. in Romm collection.
[68] *N. Y. Herald,* Dec. 27, 1852.

Two years later, with *A Gentleman from Ireland*, O'Brien did become a successful dramatic author, but he never had a sufficient number of plays produced to make his name familiar to the theatregoing public. He was, however, always interested in the theatre, had many managers, actors, and actresses for his friends, wrote and adapted a number of plays, frequently used the life of the theater as background for his stories and sketches, became travelling press agent for a tour of the tragic actress, Matilda Heron, and held the position of dramatic critic on *The Saturday Press*.

At the end of the theatrical season for 1852–1853 the *New York Times* printed the following notice: "During the past season MR. WALLACK has produced eighteen leading pieces; seventeen of them old, one new, and none original (if we except a farce produced on Christmas Eve)."[69] O'Brien must have written this himself, for no one but the author would single out as an exception such a minor production.

My Christmas Dinner was, however, of sufficient drawing power to be repeated on December 28, 29, and 30, and again on January 4.[70] Thus, in a sense, Fitz-James O'Brien ended his first American year in a blaze of glory; and through the years that followed, the blazes occurred with frequency and brilliance. But they were fitful—lacked steadiness and warmth—and so, though O'Brien had quickly found a market for his writing, an outlet for his jerky, exuberant genius, he lacked the steadiness of application which might easily have made him a real power in American journalism. As Stoddard puts it, "No American writer ever had such chances of success as Fitz-James O'Brien at this time, and but one American writer ever threw such chances away so recklessly."[71]

[69] *N. Y. Times*, June 14, 1853.

[70] See advertisements in *N. Y. Herald* for respective dates.

[71] *N. Y. Tribune*, Mar. 6, 1881. The reference is obviously to Poe.

Chapter III

The Start with Harper's

(1853)

The year 1853 marks the beginning of an association which was to prove the most permanent and most important of all those which, during his checkered career, Fitz-James O'Brien formed with various publishers. With the appearance of "The Two Skulls" in the February number of *Harper's New Monthly Magazine* he began a series of writings for the Harper Brothers which continued, with what was for O'Brien a surprising regularity, until the time of his death nine years later.

For the *Monthly* he wrote thirty-two poems, thirty-one short stories, and five articles of a miscellaneous character; while for the *Weekly*, besides "The Man about Town" column, appearing in thirty-two issues, he contributed seven poems and one short story.[1]

It is not unlikely that this association was formed through Henry J. Raymond, who was the first managing editor of the *Monthly*, and who, after having made trial of O'Brien's abilities on the *Times* and having found him useful, introduced him to the publishers of the magazine, which was just then beginning to include some original contributions in the midst of its European reprints. Before long O'Brien was a well-known figure in the Harper offices on Franklin Square; he became acquainted especially with Fletcher Harper, who of the four brothers devoted himself most particularly to the periodicals (the *Monthly*, the *Weekly*, and later the *Bazaar*); he grew to be an intimate friend of the young Joseph W. Harper, Jr.; and he was a fellow soldier of John Fletcher Harper (son of Wesley), when, with the New York Seventh Regiment, they marched away to the Civil War.

Besides these, O'Brien became intimately acquainted with Alfred H. Guernsey, commonly spoken of as Dr. Guernsey, who shortly succeeded Raymond as managing editor of the *Magazine*, when the latter became absorbed in the *Times;* and with Charles H. Nordhoff, later editor of *The*

[1] See Bibliography.

New York Herald, who was for four years in the editorial department of Harper's.[2] To Nordhoff O'Brien addressed a letter which supplies a concrete incident from his nine years' association with the Harpers and which, though belonging to the end rather than to the beginning of this period, suggests the sort of hand-to-mouth existence which was O'Brien's with fair consistency.

Dear Nordhoff

I will try to let you have a poem on the subject you suggest. Will these terms be found suitable?

Half the price of the poem on acceptance. The other half to be passed to my credit.

I am not in a position at present to write on any other terms.

Ever yours

O'Brien[3]

This letter is almost the only documentary evidence in support of like testimony given by many of his acquaintances. Mrs. Fields, recording in her diary in 1865 an account related to her by Aldrich, writes, "He wrote for Harpers, and one publisher and another, writing little and overdrawing funds on a large scale."[4] The letter to Nordhoff indicates one way in which such advances were obtained, while the continuation of Mrs. Fields's story describes a more unique method. "One day he tried to borrow money of Harpers, and being refused he went into the bindery department, borrowed a board, printed on it, 'I am starving,' bored holes through the ends, put in a string, hung it round his neck, allowed his fawn-colored gloves to depend over each end, and stood in the doorway where the firm should see him when they went to dinner. A great laugh and more money were the result of this escapade." This practical-joke sort of highway robbery could hardly have been effective more than once; so it is probably of the same occasion that William Sidney Hillyer tells years later in *The New York Times*. The story has in the years between November 9, 1865, and July 2, 1898, grown considerably, and in spite of the loss of the fawn-colored gloves, it has on the whole become more colorful.

[2] For these and other details about the Harper organization see J. Henry Harper, *The House of Harper*, N. Y. and London, 1912.

[3] This letter is available through the kindness of Capt. F. L. Pleadwell (M. C.), U. S. Navy (Ret.), in whose collection it now is. The poem referred to, "Our Christmas Tree," was printed in *Harper's* for March, 1860.

[4] Howe, *op. cit.*, p. 227.

At another time, when he was not strictly sober, O'Brien found himself out of funds. He wandered into a publisher's office and asked for $25. This was refused him. Angrily seizing a placard, O'Brien reversed it and made in big letters on the blank side:

ONE OF HARPER'S AUTHORS.

I AM STARVING.

Tying a string to the card, O'Brien placed it around his neck and paraded up and down the street, to the great amusement of a large crowd. He was of course requested to desist, but nothing stopped his mad course until a $5 bill was presented to him as a compromise, whereupon he divested himself of his unique sign and went on his devious way rejoicing.

The earliest contribution in the *Monthly* attributed to O'Brien is "The Two Skulls," which appears in the February issue, and this is the only title for 1853 assigned to him in the Harper's *Index* list.[5] The obituary notice in *Harper's Weekly* in 1862 does not mention "The Two Skulls," but its author (perhaps Joseph W. Harper, Jr., though most likely Dr. Guernsey) says instead that the earliest of O'Brien's contributions which he "can now identify appeared in November, 1853. From that time until the month before his death, with a few short intermissions, almost every number contained something from his pen."[6]

Although *Harper's* custom of printing most of its articles anonymously makes assurance of a complete bibliography impossible, the practice, nevertheless, was a decided convenience both to O'Brien and to the Harper Brothers; for the young author was not infrequently represented in the *Monthly* by two, and on one or two occasions by three, contributions in the same number. O'Brien in this way made more money than would have been possible under the present system of signed articles, and the Harper Brothers were able to concentrate their interests and keep in close touch with a smaller number of contributors.

In the issue for November, 1853, only "A Dead Secret" exemplifies any

[5] See *An Index to Harper's New Monthly Magazine, Volumes I to L: From June, 1850, to May, 1875*, 1875. The list had been published previously, in *The Round Table*, VII, 365 for June 6, 1868, in a communication to "Notes and Queries" signed by "L. H. B." This correspondent, who lived in West Springfield, Massachusetts, thanks "the editors of *Harper* and *Putnam* for their kindness in assisting in the compilation of the above list," and says that the prose list in *Harper's Magazine* is almost complete, but that the list of poems is complete only after volume XIX.

[6] *H. W.*, VI, 267.

one of the various styles in which O'Brien was accustomed to write, and it alone deals with the sort of material which later became a source of his strength. The first of O'Brien's mystery stories, this early example does not exhibit the finish of "What Was It?," nor the power of "The Diamond Lens," nor does it so definitely localize the setting as does "Tommatoo," "The Pot of Tulips," or "The Wondersmith"; but it does, following the example of Poe, revel in the weird and gruesome, create a mystery which it does not solve, place its hero in an abnormal situation or an abnormal state of mind, and let him tell his story in the first person. "A Dead Secret"—one of those half-punning titles of which O'Brien is fond—refers to the secret of a dead man, a character in the story, with whose suicide the answer to the secret is lost. It also seems to apply to another dead man, a man who has been recently hanged, the man who is telling the story. This man, or man's spirit, or whatever one may call the yarn-spinning remains of a hanged man, describes the implacable pursuit and fiendish persecution to which he was subjected because his identity was mistaken for that of the man who had committed suicide. Although the story is too long and too melodramatic, the struggles of the hero to free himself from the relentless and ever-tightening coils of an inexplicable dilemma create suspense and sustain it to the end.

"The Two Skulls" is a very much less interesting production and serves as a far from promising introduction to the series of many distinctive pieces which it inaugurates. It tells of how skulls are measured by pouring shot into them, and then launches into a disquisition on the greatness of man, considering chiefly why a great man is disappointing to meet personally.

Besides the start with Harper's, the year 1853 marks O'Brien's association with a new publishing enterprise—the establishment of *Putnam's Monthly Magazine of American Literature, Science, and Art*. With the first number, January, 1853, O'Brien became a contributor, and a number of his writings in both prose and poetry appeared in its pages. Thus the newcomer to the American shores found his earliest opportunities in the younger American magazines, rather than with the older *Knickerbocker* and *Graham's*. The "Introductory" notice in the first number of *Putnam's*, casting aspersions on *Harper's*, says:

It is because we are confident that neither Greece nor Guinea can offer the American reader a richer variety of instruction and amusement in every kind, than the country whose pulses throb with his, and whose every interest is his own, that this Magazine presents itself to-day.

It continues, appealing to the sense of patriotism, to say that it will print pure American stuff, combining "the essential freshness of feeling and true poetic sense of the American," and will heap upon its "pages the results of the acutest observations, and the most trenchant thought," all from native pens.

In line with this policy, the first two articles by O'Brien, under the general heading "Our Young Authors," are, in January, a critical comment on Donald Grant Mitchell and his work, and in February, a review of *Mardi* and discussion of Melville. The style is lively and entertaining; and the comment is outspoken in both its commendation and its blame and, withal, is pertinent as far as it goes—which is only so far as to keep it suitable for a popular magazine. The statements as to the style of the authors and their other characteristic qualities are discerning and stimulating. Mitchell he praises for his naturalness, his sweet breath, and his pleasant smile, and for the delicate, dreamy grace of the "Reveries," charming but unreal. The author does not falsify life; but he softens it: in this lie his charm and his weakness. His writing is

very sweet, pathetic and tender, but there is a want of manly force about it that impresses us with more melancholy than any of the sad details. The author knocks at our hearts with a muffled hand. His grief glimmers like a twilight, soft, hazy, and indistinct. Some of the fine feelings of a heart in sorrow, are disclosed with quiet precision. But we look upon it rather as a curious operation, than the exposition of a terrible interior. . . . His exquisite appreciation of the gentler human sorrows, his tender consideration of all earthly grief, would gain a new soundness and lustre if backed with some solider ground. . . . His books are pure to the very core. They are limpid, pellucid streams of thought, flowing in mid-air, with never a bed beneath them. No dark rocks lie at the bottom, no secret channels in the rifted stones whose very mystery invites examination. All is clear, true and transparent, but we find ourselves sighing for some dark unfathomable pool into which we might gaze and wonder, hour upon hour.[7]

In the comparisons the critic makes, evidence is given of a fairly wide reading in English literature. Laurence Sterne he knows—as would be natural for an Irishman—and Mitchell he credits with a knowledge of

[7] *Putnam's Monthly Magazine*, I, 77 (Jan., 1853).

A Sentimental Journey sufficient to plagiarize from it. Certain elements of Bulwer and Carlyle are also imitated by Mitchell, he says, while "there can be little doubt . . . of his having been inspired by the author of the Sketch Book."[8] O'Brien then contrasts Mitchell with Hawthorne, discussing the scene in *The Reveries of a Bachelor* in which Mitchell describes a husband's feelings on the death of his wife:

> Had Hawthorne been painting such a scene, how differently would he have handled it. Analytic as he is when treating of human sentiments, here he would at once have thrown aside the scalpel, and grasped the subject with nervous, quivering hand, and, Milo-like, rent it asunder. We would have had no gently-sorrowing husband, creeping about the house, with slippered grief! no girlish sentiment over gilt-edged saucers of mignonette, no feeble reflections about empty chairs.
>
> The husband would have sat massively, like Marius, amid the shattered ruins of his love. The sky would have been black above his head; the wind would have shrieked among the fallen pillars, terrible dissonances of sorrow. There would have been no light in the picture, no trustfulness in the Great End, such as Mr. Mitchell paints. All would have been huge, black, mountainous despair, before which we could not help trembling, and which we could not forget.[9]

This is a fairly typical example of O'Brien's style, with its semi-inversions, its periods, and its air of learning. In the last particular he is indebted to the example of Poe, to whom he owes much for his whole critical attitude. Poe had by his *Literati* (1846) criticisms stirred up a hornet's nest and gained wide attention, and he was widely imitated by the young bloods of the period, to whom the conservatism of the older generation seemed a stultifying force. "Our Young Authors" criticisms, like all O'Brien's writing except his poetry, show a manly attitude, such as that which he urges upon Mitchell in the exhortation which closes the essay,—"Let him go to it with a stalwart pen."[10]

In evaluating Herman Melville, O'Brien says that his initial popularity was the result of his fine narrative facility, which was a great relief "after the maudlin journeys in Greece—travels in the Holy Land, full of Biblical raptures, and yacht-tours in the Mediterranean, where monotonous sea-dinners and vulgar shore-pleasures were faithfully chronicled, with such like

[8] *Ibid.*, I, 75.
[9] *Ibid.*, I, 77.
[10] *Ibid.*, I, 78.

trash that had been inundating the literary market for years previous."[11] *Typee* (1846) was also a welcome variation from the sea novels of Marryatt [*sic*], Chamier, and Cooper, says O'Brien, with their repetition of shipwrecks and fires at sea, and all the details of a sailor's life. But he accuses Melville of deliberate plagiarizing of old Sir Thomas Browne's gorgeous and metaphorical manner, and then follows the accusation with a striking example of his own imitative genius, cleverly and closely approximating Melville's style in his analytical description of it. The sentences rush along with the Melville swirl and dash, and succeed in giving the very atmosphere of some of the storm passages in *Moby Dick*.

Typee is a far cry from Broadway; and yet, from the greatness of the contrasts, O'Brien, in a synopsis of the kind of life lived on the island of Typee, manages to give a satirical picture of certain phases of life on the island of Manhattan. The items in the Manhattan state of society against which O'Brien sets up the idealities of Typee are largely those which pinched him personally. The first sentence comes from the heart; for him, in Manhattan, it was constantly otherwise:

> In Typee there were no debts, consequently no duns. The charming inhabitants dispensed with all clothing, and tailors were unknown. No detestable bills to mar one's new year's pleasures with items of "seven fancy vests, $85; three coats, $120; gloves, ties, &c., &c., &c., &c., &c., $200." Tom had no hotel bill to pay. A piece of Tappa, or a quid of tobacco was current coin, and if the girls of the valley got up a ball, there was no subscription list, no lady patronesses, and no enmities gathering out of rejected applications for tickets.[12]

The satire then becomes less personal, being directed, in the Thackeray fashion, against the foibles of pretentious vulgarity. This satirical note, for which in America Mrs. Mowatt had set the vogue with the successful performance of her play *Fashion*, in 1845, recurs frequently in O'Brien, in both verse and prose.

> It does not appear either that there were any "sets," or *cliques* in Typee. Mr. Melville does not mention that they had their Fifth Avenue, or their Bleecker Rubicon. Society was not divided into petty circles, each revolving round some insignificant centre, and fancying themselves the central sun of the universe of

[11] *Ibid.*, I, 156 (Feb., 1853).
[12] *Ibid.*, I, 180.

fashion. Typee ladies did not receive their visitors in drawing-rooms resplendent with gilt vulgarity, and if they had ever been so fortunate as to travel, we doubt if they would have talked one down with the Grand Duke of Fiddeldedeestein "whom they met at Baden-Baden." . . . How Tom could ever have left thee [Fayaway], surpasseth human understanding. Left thee, graceful, artless child of the forest and the stream, to dwell among civilized women—dancing machines; flirting machines, built of whalebone and painted red.[13]

High praise is accorded to Melville's power of words. *White Jacket* is compared with the best in Smollett; *Redburn*, with the worst in Dickens. The final admonition to our young author is: "Let him diet himself for a year or two on Addison, and avoid Sir Thomas Browne, and there is little doubt but that he will make a notch on the American Pine."[14]

With references to Hawthorne, Irving, Poe, Cooper, and other American writers, the Irishman of only a year's residence in New York fulfilled the desires of *Putnam's* patriotic publishers and succeeded in creating the impression of an American point of view. His adaptability in this and other ways was sufficiently striking to cause the editorial writer for the *Leader*, in 1862, to write as follows:

It is some ten years since he came here, an unknown and unheralded stranger, and, in the hurry-scurry of our rapid ways, he soon made himself a recognized position in our literature and affairs, and became so much an American that his foreign birth and education would never be recognized in his writings. The amalgam of his genius moulded itself at once to the temper of the people among whom he had come to dwell. There was nothing more remarkable than this in his singular career.[15]

The May number of *Putnam's* contains a neatly written story, "Elegant Tom Dillar," which, despite the lack of any external evidence, I should like to claim as O'Brien's. The first-person author relates as he learns of them episodes in the career of the most completely accomplished, most perfectly mannered, and most sought-after young man in New York's social circles. Society's standards of judgment are condemned both by satirical implication and by direct attack, as they are in the earlier "Ballad of Sir Brown" and

[13] *Ibid.*, I, 160–161.
[14] *Ibid.*, I, 164. For reference to it see Lewis Mumford, *Herman Melville*, 1929, pp. 198–199 and 226.
[15] *The New York Leader*, Apr. 12, 1862.

in many later sketches, stories, and poems. Elegant Tom loses his fortune through the machinations of the great auctioneer, old Ormolu (a character name used by O'Brien in other stories), and because of an accomplished but useless education (a subject frequently and pointedly attacked by O'Brien) is reduced to starvation and beggary (a condition upon which O'Brien in many stories dwells with circumstantial detail). Tom works his way back into the social world by finding lucrative but secret employment as the most popular singer and dancer in an Ethiopian opera troupe or minstrel show (which takes the reader to O'Brien's oft-repeated scenes of backstage theatrical life); but when his honest means of livelihood are discovered, society again frowns upon him and his beloved jilts him (upon which O'Brien bitterly moralizes in a way habitual with him upon the falsely superficial standards of America's moneyed class).

Besides the new associations with *Harper's* and *Putnam's*, O'Brien was continuing his connection with the *Times*, writing for it scattered articles of purely ephemeral interest, and occasionally contributing a poem. "The Prophecy of Christmas," bewailing in its four stanzas the passing of the Christmas season, was printed on January 15. The first essay for the year, a description of and comment on "Literary Parties" and their flatness, filled over a column and a half on March 9; discussion of burial customs, "The Way to Get Buried," occupied more than two columns on March 19; "Sixpence too Little" commented on human shortcomings on April 16; and "A Sick Bachelor" drew largely upon what seem to have been O'Brien's own difficulties when ill in a cheap lodginghouse on May 13. "Gebhold," a balladlike poem, telling the story of a prodigal son, a father in unrelenting mood, and a final reconciliation, appeared on June 8. This was followed by four numbers of "Écume de Mer,"[16] a series of rambling essays describing various phases of O'Brien's life while on a vacation at Tulipton, on the north shore of Long Island.

Typically the city man away for a vacation, he deals lightly with the inconveniences resulting from his changed environment and with the mishaps brought about by his own ignorance. Discursively, both as to general aspect and as to minute details, he describes the natural phenomena of his shore surroundings; and once again, as he had done with Typee in relation to Broadway, he compares himself, the well-dressed bachelor, with the naked frog, decidedly to the latter's advantage. The last of these articles,

[16] *N. Y. Times*, June 15, 1853, June 24, July 13, and July 19.

written from his retreat on July 5, describes a typical Fourth of July celebration on the coast; and then, as part two, F. J. O'B., as he calls himself, writes about "A Storm." As printed, it looks like prose, but the strongly marked rhythm and the rhyme soon make the reader conscious that it is verse, however jerky and irregular the meters may be. The poem vividly describes the quiet preparation for the storm, the fury of its breaking, and the clearing up in the beautiful sunset. The thought of the last sentence, strikingly like that of the last stanza of "A Child's Prayer" in *Household Words*, runs:

Mounting, mounting to the zenith on a chain of liquid music, floating up o'er clouds and sunbeams where no earthly foot hath trod, did my soul ascend in singing, linked to that wild Robin's music, till they both sank down in silence at the blazing throne of God.[17]

With a poem printed as such, O'Brien completed the list of his signed contributions to the *Times*. It is a poorly written bit of melancholy reflection over the death of a loved one, entitled "The May Wind and the Poet."[18]

Another piece of sentimentalism written by O'Brien was "Beginning the World," a song, with music by Thomas Baker. This was published by Horace Waters as one of a series of so-called *Bleak House Ballads*, a general title designed to capitalize on the popularity of Dickens's novel, which during 1852 and 1853 was running through *Harper's*. The tone of O'Brien's verses is revealed by the quotation from *Bleak House* which appears on the cover sheet: "And with a parting sob he began the world. Not this world—oh not this! The world that sets this right." In collaboration with the same publisher and the same composer the name of Fitz James O'Brien Esq. appeared in large letters as the author of the words of another ballad, entitled "Once a Year." Like "Beginning the World," the sentimentalism of this song can scarcely be surpassed. Its neatly turned rhymes suggest with utmost bathos that you cherish your children and your wife and treasure the bliss they afford in this sad world until you find eternal rest in heaven.[19]

[17] *Ibid.*, July 19.

[18] *Ibid.*, July 29, 1853.

[19] "Beginning the World" consists of 24 lines printed with the music as a seven-page song sheet. A copy is in the Harvard Library, Mus. 403.3; No. 5, in volume entitled *Vocal Music*. "Once a Year" consists of four stanzas on a five-page song sheet. A copy is in the Berg collection, New York Public Library.

In the early spring O'Brien seems to have renewed his connection with *The Lantern*, for it is almost impossible not to regard as his "Pauline. As Seen by Diogenes," a rhymed theatrical review, and "The Lost City Broom,"[20] a close parody of Poe's "The Lost Ulalume." The former, though it reviews the play being acted at Wallack's Theatre by Lester and by Laura Keene, gives the author a chance to express the opinion that audiences generally are inclined to relish a good deal of filth mixed in with their theatrical fare. "The Lost City Broom," like many of the earlier *Lantern* verses a poem of social protest, reveals the same sort of interest in the technique of Poe's poetic method as had "Oinea" of the preceding December. In this case, however, instead of commenting on it, O'Brien imitates it in every detail—meter, alliteration, assonance, repetend, rhyme-scheme, and even diction—but uses it for a satirical attack on the filthy condition of the city's streets. He fastens the blame on a drunken alderman with whom he moves through the suffocating dust blown up by the wind to "the grave of the lost city broom!" Yet even in this parody-diatribe Fitz-James cannot resist a reference to his own impecuniosity, especially as it relates to his trouble with tailors. Speaking of former dustless days he says,

These were days when my tailor was truest,
And heard all the vows that I talked—
All the vows that I recklessly talked;
And still when my prospects were bluest,
To give me long 'tic,' he ne'er balked—
Though my prospects were bankrupt and bluest,
That tailor at 'tic' never balked.

The only other writing of O'Brien's to be located for 1853 appeared in the September issue of the *United States Magazine and Democratic Review*. " 'Sir Brasil's Falcon' By Fitz-James O'Brien" is the superscription which introduces a lengthy poem in blank verse, telling the story of a knight, who, when hot and thirsty at the end of a hunt, painfully filled his drinking horn at an almost dried-up stream. As he raised it to his lips, his falcon with its wing dashed the horn from his hand and spilled the drink. When this occurred for a third time, the knight angrily killed the falcon, and found out too late that the faithful bird had saved his life by preventing his drink-

[20] *The Lantern*, III, 156–158 (Mar. 19, 1853), and III, 204 (Apr. 7, 1853). The identification of the latter was suggested by Charles I. Glicksberg.

ing the poisonous slaver from the jaws of a dragon. The poem contains much ornate description, the interest of the author being largely in style. It is reminiscent of the romantic school as seen in Spenser, or Keats, or in the descriptive parts of the poetical romances of Sir Walter Scott. The method for a time interests, but the ornamentations are not in themselves of sufficient beauty to hold the attention through a too slowly moving story. As Stoddard said, "Ability to write blank verse is absent from 'Sir Brasil's Falcon,' which does not rise above the flowery level of Willis's 'Scriptural Sketches.' "[21] Willis, however, was one of the most popular writers of his day, and that O'Brien himself considered he had done a creditable piece of work is evident from the fact that he had separate copies of this poem struck off for distribution among his friends. Thus "Sir Brasil's Falcon" becomes, with the possible exception of the song "Beginning the World," the first separate publication of any of O'Brien's writings.[22] William Winter was so far from being of Stoddard's opinion that he placed the poem as the first selection in his 1881 volume, and proposed to Osgood, the publisher, that the book itself should be called "Sir Brasil's Falcon, And Other Poems, And Stories."[23]

Besides making valuable literary connections O'Brien was, during the year, increasing the circle of his acquaintances, and from 1853 dates one of his closest friendships. Brougham, Bellew, and the Wallacks were already his friends, and now he added to the list Thomas Bailey Aldrich. Aldrich had come to the city in 1852, at the age of sixteen, to become a clerk in the counting room of his uncle's commission house. Mr. Charles Frost was a successful merchant, whose place of business was at 146 Pearl Street. His attitude toward the things which interested his nephew is made clear by his reply, "Why don't you send the damned fool one every day?" to the announcement by Aldrich "that Dr. Guernsey of 'Harper's' had just accepted a poem and paid him fifteen dollars for it."[24]

[21] *N. Y. Tribune*, Mar. 6, 1881.

[22] The copy in the Harvard Library is a pamphlet of ten pages with a gray paper cover, inscribed in the author's hand to "C. L. Ward with the author's Compliments." Printed on the outside of the cover is "Sir Brasil's Falcon, A Poem. By Fitz-James O'Brien. Published in September No. of the United States Review. 1853."

[23] Winter to Osgood, Nov. 10, 1880, pasted in copy of Winter, 1881, in Yale Library. Winter to Ticknor, Nov. 13, 1880, is to same effect; also in Yale Library copy.

[24] See Ferris Greenslet, *The Life of Thomas Bailey Aldrich*, Boston and New York, 1908, p. 20.

Though Aldrich continued at the countinghouse until 1855, he was writing poetry—"a lyric or two every day before going down town,"[25] he said—and forming acquaintances in a set more appreciative of his poetic aspirations than was his uncle. O'Brien was one of the earliest of these, and they became fast friends. Aldrich lived with his uncle at 105 Clinton Place, now 33 West 8th Street, occupying a little back hall bedroom on the third floor, and it was here that he entertained his friends and discussed his plans for literary fame. Bayard Taylor, Richard Henry Stoddard, and his wife, Elizabeth Barstow, also became intimate friends, as well as Henry Clapp, Jr., Ada Clare, FitzHugh Ludlow, and George Arnold. Later on Edmund Clarence Stedman, William Winter, Edwin Booth, Launt Thompson, and A. D. Shattuck were added to the circle.

The anecdotal accounts of the friendship between Aldrich and O'Brien, though in most cases trivial, nevertheless make vivid their personalities and convey a sense of the aliveness and the erratic qualities of O'Brien. Ferris Greenslet, Aldrich's biographer, speaks of it as a warm, peppery friendship, and he illustrates his point by numerous delightfully related details. Aldrich's letter to Winter, of October 20, 1880, tells a story which Greenslet says he was fond of relating: "I half smile as I recall how hurt I was on an occasion when O'Brien borrowed $35.00 of me, to pay a pressing bill, and, instead of paying the bill, gave a little dinner at Delmonico's to which he did *not* invite *me!* Arnold and Clapp were there, and perhaps you. *I gave that dinner!*"[26]

That O'Brien found Aldrich a convenient person to borrow money from is borne out by two other stories. O'Brien once challenged Aldrich to a duel, but "the matter was amicably arranged," says Greenslet, "by Aldrich's pointing out to the Irishman that according to the 'punctilio of the duello' it was incorrect to challenge a person while one owed him money."[27] This story, as usual, grew with retelling, and Mrs. Fields gives it in this way:

He borrowed once sixty-five dollars for which A. became responsible, and when it was not paid he sent a letter to O'B. saying he must pay it. In return O'Brien sent him a challenge for a duel, which A. accepted, in the meantime discovering that an honorable fight could not be between a debtor and a creditor. However,

[25] *Ibid.*, p. 21.
[26] Winter, *Old Friends*, p. 101.
[27] Greenslet, *op. cit.*, p. 40.

when the time appointed arrived, O'Brien had absconded. We could not repress a smile at the idea of A.'s *fighting*, for he is a painfully small gentleman.[28]

The second story is told by William Sidney Hillyer as follows:

Aldrich . . . was then a small salaried clerk in George W. Carleton's book store on Broadway. O'Brien was in the habit of dropping in to see Aldrich, and one day came in rather more than "half seas over." Aldrich decided to take him across the street to a hotel and put him to bed. Cautiously and carefully he led O'Brien, but before he had got half way across a friend stopped him and asked: "Why do you want to bother with the fellow. Let him go." "I will not," replied Aldrich. "He borrowed a dollar from me a few days ago and I can't afford to let anything happen to him."[29]

That O'Brien also made use of Aldrich to save the room rent which he was so frequently unable to pay is a circumstance alluded to more than once. Mrs. Fields says, "He came and lived six weeks upon Aldrich in his uncle's house one summer when the family were away."[30] This is perhaps the same period of which Greenslet tells:

Once, when Aldrich was living *en garçon* at 105 Clinton Place in the absence of the Frost family, O'Brien said to him, "Let's live for a week after the Venetian manner." "What's that?" said Aldrich. "Why, sleep all day and live all night," was the reply. They tried it for a time, exploring the streets all night and going to bed at seven A. M., but it seems soon to have palled on them.[31]

Two other new friends made by Fitz-James at this time were so impressed by his individual peculiarities and by the force of his personality that each portrayed him as one of the chief characters in a novel. These were Bayard Taylor and William North. North had come to America in 1852, probably some months after the arrival of O'Brien, and, like O'Brien, almost immediately upon his arrival became a contributor to the American magazines. *Harper's*, *The Knickerbocker*, *Graham's*, and *The Whig Review* all printed stories of his, and Burton's theatre successfully brought out a farce called

[28] Howe, *op. cit.*, pp. 228–229.
[29] William Sidney Hillyer, "Facts in O'Brien's Brilliant Career." *N. Y. Times*, July 2, 1898 (Saturday Review of Books and Art), p. 445.
[30] Howe, *op. cit.*, p. 227.
[31] Greenslet, *op. cit.*, 40–41.

The Automaton Man.[32] He became a comrade of O'Brien, and his most intimate friends were also friends of O'Brien and fellow members of the same club—Frank Bellew, the artist, and Charles B. Seymour, who wrote for Raymond on the *Times*. Then North and O'Brien quarreled and became enemies; and North in his novel held O'Brien up to contempt and ridicule by the satirical thrusts in his portrait of the character Fitzgammon O'Bouncer.[33] The novel was first known as *The Slave of the Lamp* and was published posthumously in 1855; for North in dire poverty and unhappy about a love affair had committed suicide by drinking prussic acid on November 14, 1854. As the portrait of O'Brien contained in North's novel, prejudiced and unfair though it manifestly is, is the only one dating from so early a period and is one of the few descriptions of him written while he was still alive, it is here rather fully quoted.

He was well educated, had edited, even to the death, a magazine in London, wrote in every style but his own (not having any in particular), and was what, even in the best European society, would be considered an accomplished man. His verses were very sweet, if not very strong—like French tea. His lively writings were pleasant, if hastily written, and, therefore, diluted—good negus, if not rare wine. His farce was not damned, if not actually successful. When he wrote, his mind seemed to take its tone from the last book he had read, or the last person he had talked to. Without intending it, he was a wonderful imitator—certainly never a servile plagiarist. In short, he was a man of universal talent and adaptive genius; a brilliant versatility, precociously perfect, in his way, for he was scarcely six and twenty years of age.

In appearance he was handsome, had a fine brow, and a decided nose, which Napoleon would have appreciated. He was carefully dressed, and had palpably trimmed his moustaches and whiskers with laborious exactness. In profile, his head was remarkable for the exaggeration of the organs of self-esteem and love of approval, which, with the flatness of his veneration, gave his cranium a strange angularity. His figure was somewhat tall, and his frame powerful, active, and symmetrical. His complexion was florid, his hair dark, his eyes blue, and of a peculiar softness, though by no means conveying the idea of a peculiar gentle

[32] For above facts see William North, *The Slave of the Lamp*, New York, 1855; Preface, pp. vii–ix. The book is comparatively rare. The copies in the Library of Congress and the New York Public Library are the only ones which the writer has been able to locate. It was republished under the title *The Man of the World* in 1877. For other details about North see Winter, *Old Friends*, pp. 313–317.

[33] See Winter, 1881, p. xxxviii, n.

nature. On the contrary, his general expression was that of a man whose duty to himself would be performed at all hazards, whatever became of the rest of the world.[34]

* * *

O'Bouncer trusted to habit and the inspiration of the moment, both in conversation and in writing. He had the cunning of the man of the world, but little of the soul of the artist in his nature. Indeed art was the one thing which he never could comprehend. A professional critic, he wrote brilliantly but falsely. His imagination dominated his judgment, and worst crime of all, he was superficial—worse yet, *consciously* superficial. That is, he knew and disguised his ignorance of a given topic with consummate dexterity. This his widely spread information enabled him to do with great tact and success. Perhaps few writers for the press possessed the facility and the power of this accomplished personage. Perhaps to say that in his way he was a man of genius would scarcely be an exaggeration.[35]

That O'Brien was consciously superficial is only partly true, for many of his more delicate poems were written with sincere feeling and scrupulous care. But he was guilty of a quality—snobbishness—which especially irritated North and which is referred to almost every time O'Bouncer is introduced.

Mr. Fitzgammon O'Bouncer always spoke to waiters with a lofty and dignified severity. Mr. F. O'Bouncer was intensely aristocratic in his feelings. Like all Irishmen, he came of a great but impoverished family, was heir to an estate of unascertained rental, was a lineal descendant of the ancient Irish kings, and would rather have been damned eternally than admitted that he had had a drop of plebeian blood in his veins, since Adam, or Lord Monboddo's monkeys, whichever legend may be preferred. . . .

Morally, he was good-natured and impulsive, yet politic and selfish. He was extravagant and brave—spurred on by vanity, he could be generous and heroic. The great vice of his character was his inordinate self-esteem, which had taken the diseased form of ambition for superior social position. Even as it was, the young Irish adventurer fondly affected the airs of a scion of nobility—an exiled prince—I know not what *rôle de fantasie*, to the great amusement of his friends. He was not content that those to whom fortune had given inferior education, and antecedents to himself, should practically stand before him in the social scale; he also wished them to feel, and in a manner indirectly acknowledge, this intangible advantage which he believed in as a divine right, and yet half doubted

[34] North, *op. cit.*, pp. 67–68.
[35] *Ibid.*, pp. 71–72.

himself, because he felt that it was not admitted by others. . . . Fitzgammon was ever taken in by the absurd tinsel of New York fashionable society, that ridiculous agglomeration of vulgarity, ignorance, vanity and imitation.[36]

Most of the points made in the last paragraph were certainly true about O'Brien during his first two years in America when North knew him, even though he later became one of the sharpest critics of society's false standards. Indeed Thackeray's description of the Irish snob in London strikingly fits O'Brien's general career in this country.[37] As North puts it:

Poor O'Bouncer! he secretly despised his country. He was an Anglicised Celt. To call him Englishman, was the surest way to flatter him. He lacked the patriotic monomania which often supplies the place of so many other advantages. He was an Irishman because he could not help it. How gladly would he have forgotten it, could the world have forgotten it also. But the O'Bouncer name was legion in the land. There was no evading the destinies; so O'Bouncer contented himself with cutting his own compatriots. To do him justice, O'Bouncer was too much of a man to be an Irishman in America, or mingle in the petty intrigues of American-Irish politics.

* * *

It was really a great pity that he was not a man of large fortune, and Viscount Fitzgammon. He would have enjoyed a title and fortune so intensely.[38]

All this detail emphasizes the fact that Fitz-James O'Brien, in spite of his attractive qualities, managed pretty consistently to indulge in some ridiculous absurdity or other and so to appear to his contemporaries in an unfavorable light.

The publication of *The Slave of the Lamp* did not end the association of the names of O'Brien and North; for upon the appearance of "The Diamond Lens" in January, 1858, some one claimed that it had been stolen from a manuscript of North's. Naturally O'Brien denied this, and the statements for both sides were printed in the *Evening Post.* In spite of the bad blood stirred up, Fitz-James had by March sufficiently recovered from his irritation to write, "Poor North, the Republican philosopher, who hoped so much when he sought this country, and who came to so melancholy an end after he had tried it."[39] Once more, on April 21, 1866, *The Round Table,* in a

[36] *Ibid.*, pp. 66–69.
[37] See W. M. Thackeray, *The Book of Snobs,* Chap. XVII.
[38] North, *op. cit.*, pp. 87–88.
[39] "A Paper of All Sorts" in *Harper's,* XVI, 513 (Mar., 1858).

review of Richard Grant White's *Poetry of the Civil War*, made the statement that

. . . some person or persons pretended ["The Diamond Lens"] was written by the late Mr. William North, who could no more have written it than he could have written "Paradise Lost," "The Newcomes," or Buckle's "History of Civilization." Whatever similarity may have existed between the minds of these two young writers, however much they may have sympathized, together, or apart, with a certain class of subjects, of which Poe was always a master, their methods were utterly dissimilar, and their talents of a different order, Mr. O'Brien writing like a scholar and a man of the world, Mr. North as it pleased the gods at the moment, frequently like a Choctaw.

It was ten years after North wrote *The Slave of the Lamp* and two years after O'Brien's death that Bayard Taylor drew upon his recollections of Fitz-James for the character of Brandagee in his novel *John Godfrey's Fortunes* (1864).[40] Of this book Albert H. Smyth, one of Taylor's biographers, writing of Taylor's early literary and journalistic career, says, it "is a reminiscence of certain moods of that life and of literary and social experience in New York."[41] John Godfrey, the hero, dines at the home of Mr. Clarendon, the publisher, and there makes the acquaintance of Mr. Brandagee.

He was the author of several dashing musical articles, which had been published in the *Wonder*, during the opera season, and had created a temporary sensation. Since then he had assailed Mr. Bellows, the great tragedian, in several sketches characterized rather by wit and impertinence than profound dramatic criticism: but everybody read and enjoyed them none the less. . . . He had now adopted journalism, it was reported, as an easy mode of making his tastes and his talents support him in such splendor as was still possible.

Upon his arrival at the Clarendons', "he made his salutations with a jolly self-possession—a noisy flashy glitter of sentences." At the dinner table he focused all the attention so that Godfrey had ample opportunity to study his person.

The man's face interested me profoundly. It was not handsome; it could hardly be called intellectual, it was very irregular; I could almost say that it was disagreeable, and yet, it was so mobile, it ran so rapidly through striking contrasts

[40] Bayard Taylor, *John Godfrey's Fortunes; Related by Himself. A Story of American Life*, 1889 (First edition, 1864).

[41] Albert H. Smyth, *Bayard Taylor*, Boston and New York, 1896, p. 164.

of expression, and was so informed with a restless dazzling life, that I could not turn my eyes away from it.[42]

After this first encounter Godfrey meets Brandagee fairly often. He is taken by him to the Friday evening receptions of the sentimental poetess, Adeliza Choate, otherwise Mrs. Yorkton, where Brandagee plays up brilliantly to the pretentious literary pose and insincere adulation of the occasion by composing and reciting extempore verses apostrophizing his talented hostess. Brandagee was frequently seen also at salons where an atmosphere of true culture and refinement held sway—those of Miss Anna C. Lynch, or Mrs. Botta, as she had become early in the fifties upon her marriage to the Italian physicist. As Taylor says:

I sometimes met him in those delightful rooms which no author or artist who lived in New York at that time can have forgotten, and was not surprised to see that, even in his subdued character, he still inspired a covetable interest.[43]

Mrs. M. E. W. Sherwood also remembered with enthusiasm the "most agreeable circle" that formed about her friend, Mrs. Botta:

At her literary reunions I have met not only many of these most agreeable literary men and women of our own country, but the historians, authors, and artists of England, France, and Italy. Such a grand phalanx as would often gather in a single evening!—Christine Nilsson, Salvini, Ristori, Anthony Trollope, Sala, Thackeray, and George P. Marsh; Mr. W. W. Story, home from Rome, and General di Cesnola, fresh from Cyprus. This was a salon indeed! Everything that was fresh and new. Paul du Chaillu, from Africa and the land of the gorilla, and Charles Kingsley, with his gifted daughter Rose. From time to time a fresh arrival—N. P. Willis, General Morris, or Lewis Gaylord Clark—while in one corner would sit the authoress of *Queechy* and the poetesses Alice and Phoebe Cary, and Bryant, Bancroft, Everett, and Emerson![44]

But even in the gatherings of such celebrities Mrs. Sherwood could not forget Fitz-James; he is one of the three men she met at the Botta salons to whom she devotes at least a paragraph,—the other two being John Bancroft, the historian, and Charles Sumner, the orator. She says:

Another genius whom I met at Mrs. Botta's was Fitz-James O'Brien, the young Irish poet, author of *A Diamond Lens*, which, next to the stories of Bret Harte

[42] Taylor, *op. cit.*, pp. 260–261.
[43] *Ibid.*, pp. 321–322.
[44] M. E. W. Sherwood, *An Epistle to Posterity*, p. 123.

(which came ten years later), was the most surprising short story that ever startled the reading American public. Fitz-James O'Brien followed up his successes by delightful poems, and his *Monody on the Death of Kane* was and is worthily remembered. He was a fascinating conversationalist, a rather handsome, dashing, well-dressed young Irish gentleman, very much courted in society for a brief hour. He went to the war, fought bravely, and surrendered his young life gracefully and well after the second battle of Bull Run.[45]

O'Brien could not, however, stand the rarefied atmosphere of such literary evenings too often or too continuously. He needed to relax in more masculine company where he could be his exuberant self. Consequently, with Bellew and others he formed a sort of club, the account of which Taylor (alias John Godfrey) puts into the mouth of O'Brien (alias Brandagee). Brandagee urges Godfrey:

"Come on, you'll find all my coadjutors at the Ichneumon."

"Where is the Ichneumon," I asked, "and what is it?"

"Not know it! You *are* a green Bohemian. Close at hand, in Crosby Street. The name is my suggestion, and I'm rather proud of it. When the landlord—Miles, who used to be bar-tender at the 'Court of Appeals'—took his new place, he was puzzled to get a title, as all the classic epithets, Shades, Pewter Mugs, Banks, Houses of Commons, Nightingales, Badgers, and Dolphins, were appropriated by others. I offered to give him a stunning name, in consideration of occasional free drinks. I first hit on the *Ornithorhynchus paradoxus*, which was capital; but Miles was fool enough to think that nobody could ever pronounce or remember it. Then I gave him the Ichneumon, with which he was satisfied,—he, as well as all Crosby Street, calls it 'Ike Newman.' I've persuaded him to give us a backroom, and keep a bed up-stairs for any fellow who is boozy or belated. We shall make a classic place of it, and if the *Oracle* once fairly open its mouth the crocodiles must look out for their eggs!"[46]

Further on in his novel Taylor suggests that the members of this group later deserted Miles on Crosby Street for not being what they considered sufficiently generous and flexible in the extension of credit and became patrons of and debtors to a new proprietor in Spring Street. The new club, its name, and its signboard are described by William Winter as follows:

There was a notable group of writers and artists in New York, of earlier date than the Pfaff Bohemian coterie, comprising, among its many members (as I heard,

[45] *Ibid.*, pp. 126–127.

[46] Taylor, *op. cit.*, pp. 323–324.

for I was not associated with it), Francis Henry Temple Bellew, Charles Gayler, William North, Sol Eytinge, Charles G. Rosenberg, Charles B. Seymour, and Fitz-James O'Brien, all of whom are dead. That society, unlike the Pfaff coterie, was, after a fortuitous fashion, organized, and it had a name,—the remarkable name of the Ornithorhyncus Club. In New Guinea there is a four-footed animal, having a bill like that of a duck, known to the inhabitants of that country as the Mulligong, but, scientifically, designated the *Ornithorhyncus paradoxus*, or Duck-Billed Platypus. The singular aspect of that quadruped had attracted the amused attention of Bellew, an excellent artist; and when, as happened, a German widow, poor, and wishful to retrieve her once opulent fortune, opened a restaurant, in Spring Street, and wanted a name for it, he suggested that of the eccentric Australasian beast, and merrily persuaded her to adopt it; and he painted a sign for her, which was hung in front of the house, representing the Ornithorhyncus in the act of smoking a pipe, while grasping a glass of foaming beer. At that facetious sign the writers and artists constituting the Ornithorhyncus Club habitually met, for the pastime of talking, singing, joking, drinking beer, and smoking churchwarden pipes. Many of their songs were composed among themselves,—one written by O'Brien and sung to an air from the ever popular "Fra Diavolo," having been an especial favorite.[47]

The song just referred to was entitled "The Ornithorhyncus,"[48] and it was recalled with reminiscent delight by the veteran artist, A. D. Shattuck, when I visited him at his home in Granby, Connecticut, in the summer of 1927:

> "Demnition! I can't remember the name—"

Then he hesitated and stopped, unable to recall the next line; but soon continued with the third, and finished the quatrain as follows:—

> "Just then it clung to the tip of my tongue—
> I fear it will remain unsung."

Taylor sums up the atmosphere of the club, or "the Cave of Trophonius" as O'Brien called it, in the following paragraph:

Though there was rather a repellant [*sic*] absence of sentiment, there was, at least, nothing of the mock article. Nobody attempted to play a part, knowing the absurdity of wearing a mask behind the curtain, and suspecting how soon it would be torn off, if attempted. Thus the conversation, if occasionally coarse, if un-

[47] Winter, *Old Friends*, pp. 308–310.
[48] On the list made by William Winter for a second volume of O'Brien's writings.

necessarily profane, if scoffing and depreciative of much that I knew to be good and noble, was always lively, racy, and entertaining. I surmised that my associates were not the best of men; but then, on the other hand, they were not bores.[49]

It was in this circle that Brandagee (O'Brien) and his associates made elaborate plans for the publication of a paper to be known as the *Oracle*; and the policy enthusiastically sketched for it by Brandagee was later exemplified, as nearly as possible, in the witty, smart, and caustic *Saturday Press* of 1858 and '59, of which O'Brien became dramatic critic. Even this last position, on a paper partly of his own creation, he did not keep very long; for to a person of his irresponsible and mercurial disposition a job imaginatively in the future, on which one might speculate, was ever so much more satisfactory than a job actively present, on which one must work. This attitude Taylor embodies in a concrete example:

He now came to the *Wonder* office but seldom. He could never be relied upon to have his articles ready at the appointed time, and there had been some quarrel between him and Mr. Clarendon, in consequence of which he transferred his services to the *Avenger*. I had become such a zealous disciple of the former paper that I looked upon this transfer as almost involving a sacrifice of principle. Mr. Clarendon, however, seemed to care little about it, for he did not scruple still to send to Brandagee for an article on some special subject.[50]

With changes of allegiance such as this, one imagines O'Brien, as the year 1853 draws to a close, writing now for one publisher, now for another; or one sees him appearing in the best society, or enjoying evenings in a smoky clubroom with his bachelor friends.

[49] Taylor, *op. cit.*, p. 326.
[50] *Ibid.*, p. 322.

CHAPTER IV

VERSE CONTESTS AND A SUCCESSFUL PLAY

(1854)

Bayard Taylor's novel *John Godfrey's Fortunes*, although it vividly characterizes O'Brien and tells much about the habits of his life in New York's literary circles, fails even to hint at the most pleasantly personal relations of the two men. Their real intimacy grew out of their mutual friendship for Richard Henry Stoddard and his talented wife Elizabeth Barstow Stoddard, at whose rooms on Third Street, near Washington Square, Taylor and O'Brien spent many evenings together during the years 1854 and 1855. For Taylor had returned from the first of his long foreign journeys on December 20, 1853; and when he was not out of the city lecturing as a famous traveler, he sought as often as he could the company of his intimate friends. He, Stoddard, and O'Brien, joined occasionally by Aldrich, fell naturally into talk about literary subjects; and as young poets themselves they discussed most frequently the poetry of their American and British contemporaries, analyzing the qualities of style which gave distinction and individuality to each. This led to imitation; and a habit of verse-writing contests originated, which kept not only themselves but their common friends much amused.[1]

Taylor describes one of these contests in a letter (of September 15, 1854) to his Philadelphia friend, the poet and dramatist George H. Boker. After referring to O'Brien as "a very clever young Irishman and a *littérateur*" he writes:

Dick, O'Brien, and I were talking the other evening about German ballads, and it was suggested, on the spur of the moment, that we should try our hands on something in the German vein. We chose "The Helmet" as a subject, and had but fifteen minutes to conceive and carry out our ideas.

[1] For these and other details about Taylor's life, see Russell H. Conwell, *The Life, Travels, and Literary Career of Bayard Taylor*, Boston, 1879, esp. pp. 244–249; and *Life and Letters of Bayard Taylor*, ed. Marie Hansen-Taylor and Horace E. Scudder, 2 v., Boston & New York, 1885, esp. I, 282–287.

The eight lines produced by Fitz-James O'Brien are as follows:

"A warrior hung his plumed helm
On the rugged bough of an aged elm;
'Where is the knight so bold,' he cried,
'That dares my haughty crest deride?'

The wind came by with a sullen howl,
And dashed the helm on the pathway foul,
And shook in scorn each sturdy limb,—
For where is the knight could fight with him?"[2]

Dick Stoddard's poem, comprising twelve lines, told of a young warrior who needed no protecting helmet because his mother had kissed his golden tresses "with the holy lips of prayer." "Taylor came in last," wrote Stoddard, "though not far behind. He could not write upon the helmet, he explained; he had tried it on his head, and there was nothing in it!"[3] But the poem with which Taylor finished last was of twenty-four lines, twice as long as Stoddard's, and told the story of a penniless knight who, to win the old man's daughter, donned his helmet and set out to make his fortune. Unsuccessful, he sent back his helmet filled with his own blood, at sight of which the maiden died.

Through the autumn of 1854 and the winter of 1855 the enjoyment and good-natured rivalry of such verse-making contests continued, and Stoddard's rooms "were to the trio for the night what the Salutation and Cat was to Lamb and Coleridge."[4] In November when he was away lecturing, Taylor wrote of how he longed to be back and, because of a bad cold, concluded the letter as follows:

Give my kide rebebradces to O'Bried, whed you see hib, ad believe be, ever,
Your sidcere Fred.[5]

Stoddard's account of the meetings gives a number of particulars not mentioned by Taylor:

Great was our merriment; for if we did not always sink the ship, we kept it for our own amusement solely. Fitz James O'Brien—whose acquaintance we had

[2] *N. Y. Tribune*, Mar. 6, 1881. Later O'Brien polished his verses, changed the title, and as "The Challenge" they were published in *Putnam's*, V, 504 (May, 1855).

[3] *Ibid.* Stoddard's poem "The Helmet" was printed in *Putnam's*, VI, 395 (Oct., 1855).

[4] *Ibid.*

[5] Hansen-Taylor and Scudder, *op. cit.*, I, 295.

made while Taylor was abroad—was a frequent guest, and an eager partaker of our merriment, which somehow resolved itself into the writing of burlesque poems.

We sat around a table, and whenever the whim seized us, which was often enough, we each wrote down themes on little pieces of paper, and putting them into a hat or a box we drew out one at random, and then scribbled away for dear life. We put no restriction upon ourselves; we could be grave, or gay, or idiotic even; but we must be rapid, for half the fun was in noting who first sang out "Finished!" It was a neck-and-neck race between Bayard Taylor and Fitz James O'Brien, who divided the honors pretty equally, and whose verses, I am compelled to admit, were generally better than my own. Bayard Taylor was very dexterous in seizing the salient points of the poets we girded at, and was as happy as a child when his burlesques were successful. He reminded me, I told him once, of Katerfelto,

"with his hair on end
At his own wonders."

He blushed, laughed, and admitted that his cleverness pleased him, and he was glad that it pleased us, also.

"It is good sport," he remarked; "but not poetry,—that is a very different and very serious matter." I mention these trifling intellectual duels, because they were afterwards a continual source of amusement among our common friends, and because the practice he thus acquired stood Bayard Taylor in good stead when he was preparing The Echo Club, which grew out of these early wit combats of ours.[6]

The *Diversions of the Echo Club*, which ran in *The Atlantic Monthly* from January to July, 1872, is therefore the second book by Taylor in which he made literary capital of his early friendship with O'Brien. The four characters who compose the membership of the Echo Club, who write poems under contest rules similar to those already described, and who afterwards explain and analyze what they have written, were modeled, says Taylor, not on individuals but were designed to represent classes of literary attitudes. He admits, however, that O'Brien was of the type represented by the Gannet. " 'The Gannet'—a name suggested by a poem written by a member of the class, long ago—represents brilliancy without literary principle, the love of technical effect, regardless of the intellectual conception of

[6] R. H. Stoddard, *Recollections, Personal and Literary*, New York, 1903, pp. 248–249. This account appeared originally in "Reminiscences of Bayard Taylor" in *The Atlantic Monthly*, XLIII, 242–252 (February, 1879), and it is only here (p. 248) that the last sentence is complete.

a work. This is a class which is always large, and always more or less successful—for a time."[7]

The main interest of the Echo Club papers lies, of course, not in the characters or their comments but in the burlesque poems written in imitation of the poets who were then prominent in the literary world. One of these, "The Ballad of Hiram Hover," amusingly imitating the style of Whittier, was written by the Gannet;[8] but the poem which caused O'Brien to be called the Gannet is not included in the group of Echo Club verses. Instead, "The Three Gannets" was printed in *Putnam's* for November, 1854. Neither the idea nor the working to a climax through a series of threes is particularly original; but the parallelism is well handled, and the treatment of the three elements, each in one short stanza, gives the poem an effect of dramatic concentration not often found in O'Brien. Stoddard names it as one of three poems which, alone of those in Winter's collection, show power and "are fair examples of lyrical talent."[9] "Willy and I" and "Sea" are the two others thus named, "Sea"[10] being also a contest poem. Haste is apparent in its lack of smoothness; though in the second of its four stanzas the rise and fall of the verse suggests the varying fluctuation of the sea:

> To and fro! To and fro!
> Chanting ever, and chanting slow,
> Thy harp is swept with liquid hands,
> And thy music is breathing of distant lands!

One of O'Brien's acquaintances, Walt Whitman, in the irregularities and unmetered rhythms of "Out of the Cradle Endlessly Rocking" (1859), is infinitely more poetic than this; while a comparison with the sea poetry of Tennyson or Longfellow, Swinburne or Kipling, gives further confirmation as to the second-rateness of Fitz-James O'Brien in the poetic scale. He is not a poet of melodious verse, which by the very sound creates beauty; nor is he a poet of deep thought or high poetic imagination. His verse, at its best, contains interesting or striking figures and fancies; or it is lightly

[7] Bayard Taylor, *The Echo Club, And Other Literary Diversions*, Boston, 1876, pp. viii–ix. In *The Atlantic* the title was *Diversions of the Echo Club*.

[8] See *ibid.*, pp. 61–63. F. L. Pattee reprints it in *The Feminine Fifties*, pp. 295–296, where he definitely assigns it to O'Brien.

[9] *N. Y. Tribune*, Mar. 6, 1881.

[10] *Putnam's*, IV, 666 (Dec., 1854).

playful, with the quaint term or the apt word; or it is satirical, directed against the shams of Society; or, as in "The Three Gannets," it contains the sort of surprise which comes from dramatic condensation. Lacking the highest qualities of poetry, his verses of the "tender passion" often degenerate into sentimentality and bathos, and his attempts at dramatic incident in ballad form turn to melodrama, which is frequently so forced as to be ludicrous. Unfortunately his Irish humor was too often in abeyance and was too frequently offset by his Irish sentiment and credulity.

A month after printing "Sea" *Putnam's* published two more of O'Brien's poems—"Winter" and "Willy and I."[11] The latter, which drew forth the commendation of Stoddard, is a balladlike poem of five stanzas suggesting a deeply tragic story, though the actual statement is concentrated and bare. "Winter," which like "Sea" and "The Three Gannets" was written at one of the evening contest meetings, creates an impression of the bleak desolation of the winter season.[12]

As a fourth poem written at his rooms Stoddard lists "An Old Story." This, it will be recalled, first appeared in *The Lantern* on April 17, 1852, over a year and a half before Taylor returned to America. Stoddard's memory may have been at fault, or even without Taylor it is possible that by April, 1852, O'Brien knew Stoddard well enough to be writing poetry in his rooms; but a third possibility, which accepts Stoddard's statement, must be suggested. If, on a certain evening in 1854 or 1855, the subject that the three friends drew to write upon should have turned out to be the sad fate of a prostitute or something nearly akin, it would not have been at all out of accord with the theatrical bias in O'Brien's character and with his desire to hold the center of the stage for him speedily to have reproduced an earlier poem written for and printed in a dead and forgotten comic sheet. Indeed, he might even have given this subject as his contribution to the hat that evening, with the idea that if it were drawn he would be sure to finish first, an easy winner. Color is lent to such a supposition by the existence of a poem by Stoddard on the same subject in much the same tone,[13] and by the likelihood that O'Brien, having established a reputation for rapid composition and improvisation, must more than once have been tempted to prepare for such feats beforehand.

[11] *Ibid.*, V, 11 and 40, respectively (Jan., 1855).

[12] This comment holds good about the poem even as it appears in *Putnam's*. The version used by Winter, 1881, pp. 89–90, is markedly improved.

[13] "On the Town," *The New York Saturday Press*, Mar. 19, 1859.

The only other poem that can be assigned to the year 1854 is "The Garden Walk," printed in *Putnam's* for June. That this periodical should have accepted it, with its uncouth rhythms and awkward word arrangement, is an indication of the low quality of verse being submitted to the magazines of the period. A sentimental love poem in nine stanzas, it begins:

I sauntered down the garden walk,
  Where she beneath the trees was sitting,
  The faint May shadows round her flitting,
As some leaf moved upon its stalk.

The author who could have written this was sadly lacking in poetic ear, while even an amateur of poetic melody is disturbed by the dissonance of the last line.

The five poems just discussed are the only ones to be definitely identified as O'Brien's for the year 1854; his prose writings for the same period number only seven; and none of this meagre production appeared before May. When it is remembered that all except two of O'Brien's writings for the preceding year were printed before the first of August, thus making a gap of nine and a half months in his literary productivity, the questions naturally arise as to what Fitz-James was doing during this interval, and as to how he was making his living. It is perfectly possible, of course, that he was composing with the same facile fecundity that marks his course both before and after this period and that it is merely the investigator's lack of ability to pierce the pall of anonymity which makes an apparent silence where none really exists. For instance, the musical and dramatic criticism in *The New York Times* may be O'Brien's, and he is easily capable of having written at least one of the short stories or sketches in each number of *Harper's Monthly Magazine*.[14] If such things are his, it is a strange coincidence that

[14] The more one works with Fitz-James O'Brien and comes across his numerous passing references to Paris—for they are seldom more than that—the more the conviction grows upon him that O'Brien must have spent considerable time in Paris, as was pointed out in the first chapter; and this suggests the probability that, with his habit of using familiarly local places as the settings for his stories, he would at times have laid his scenes in Paris. Two such stories, which moreover deal with the backstage life of the theatre (another subject of which O'Brien is fond) and its actors and actresses, appeared in *Harper's* during these months of O'Brien's apparent inactivity; and I herewith submit their names as part of the O'Brien canon—"Celeste Bertin," *Harper's*, VII, 499–504 (Sept., 1853) and "A Peep Behind the Scenes," *ibid.*, VIII, 509–510 (Mar., 1854). "Celeste Bertin" has as its narrator a poor young physician (another O'Brien touch) who haunts the Théâtre Porte St. Martin and becomes infatuated, as does all of Paris,

his friends and acquaintances, through whose help so many items are identified throughout the rest of his career, should reveal none for this particular period. It is also possible that he had for the time being found other means of support, perhaps a woman who could at once satisfy his passionate desires and his love of ease. At any rate the hiatus in his work, be it real or only apparent, at present exists.

"Belladonna," the first authenticated short story for the year, appeared in the June *Harper's*. Oddly mixing many styles and moods, it is in spots delicately sentimental; in spots, slyly, lightly gay; and in many places, charming with the lovely smooth rhythms of a Poe's "Eleanora" (1842). As a whole, however, it is far from deserving praise—the moods are too many, the touches not sure.

For the opening O'Brien used a method which grew to be more or less characteristic of him. He gives an initial setting definitely localized, realistic, and acceptable to the reader. From this he leads to places and incidents less acceptable and less familiar, carrying the reader with him by the confidence he has already established. In his best stories this is done with great skill; in "Belladonna" only an artificial and conventional example of it is seen. A guest visits his friend in his home, made happy by a lovely and loving wife. The host relates to his guest how he met and won her, and by so doing carries the reader from his familiar home to the scene of his penniless wanderings in France. This he follows with the story of his romantic courtship. Another point of O'Brien's technique, later many times repeated but first made use of here, is to have a proud but poor man as the hero. Although this is a conventional subject of the time, the details of poverty and the makeshifts to conceal it are often so circumstantially vivid that the reader, who knows of the author's easygoing shiftlessness and impecuniosity, is constantly tempted to give such details an autobiographical interpretation.

F. L. Pattee in *The Development of the American Short Story* makes the comment that "Belladonna" reads like a travesty "of the feminine romance

---

with a great new actress there. He attends her when she becomes ill and orders rest; but to hold the love of her prince against a rival of noble blood she insists on performing and dies upon the stage. "A Peep Behind the Scenes" is much shorter but has the same atmosphere. The narrator, wandering in Père la Chaise cemetery, meets a French actor, who leads him to the grave of his beloved and there tells him the story of their love and her death and of the necessity of his going on with his comic parts to convulse the audiences of Paris.

so fashionable during the period";[15] and his suggestion receives striking support from references to the Fannie Fern school made by O'Brien over a year and a half later in the story "Sister Anne."[16] The heroine, Anne Plymott, begins her literary career by writing verses over the name Filbert; later she writes a "series of sketches entitled 'Lichens,' under the signature of 'Matilda Moss'." Finally, she is advised to "write some pretty country sketches. You can call them 'Dried Leaves,' or some other vegetable title, and they will be sure to succeed."[17] "Belladonna" and "Sister Anne" bear many points of resemblance to Fannie Fern and Fanny Forrester, especially in their oversweet sentiment and in the ridiculously forced and petty melodrama necessary to assure soft romantic endings; and, after the words of the author himself which have just been quoted, one would be justified in assuming that these stories are indeed satirical of their own style and method were it not that the same offenses of overdrawn sentiment and melodrama are repeated with perfect seriousness in other stories which are unrelieved by the humor that makes this one suspected. "Tommatoo," "My Wife's Tempter," "Dora Dee," "Mary Burnie of the Mill," and "Baby Bloom" prove that where the question of melodrama is concerned, O'Brien sins as woefully and with as sincerely solemn a face as the worst offenders either of the 1850's or of the present decade. Besides, O'Brien was writing to make a living; and, as tenderly sentimental stories were certain of a market, he turned them out frequently, relying on his strongly marked imitative faculty to equal the most tearful of the women scribblers.

Largely sentimental also is O'Brien's next sketch, "The Fiddler."[18] It is so obviously didactic that the autobiographical interest of the introductory paragraphs, depicting a young writer much cut up by an unfavorable review of one of his poems, is soon destroyed.

One other story for this year is based upon the difficulties encountered by a poor author in trying to make ends meet. North, in *The Slave of the Lamp*, says that someone was mean enough to put O'Bouncer and his pecuniary difficulties into a story in P———'s magazine, and to call it "Hard Up."[19] That North is in this case, as well as throughout the novel, patently malicious about O'Brien receives double confirmation from the

[15] Fred Lewis Pattee, *The Development of the American Short Story, An Historical Survey*, New York & London, 1923, p. 157.

[16] *Harper's*, XII, 91–96 (Dec., 1855).

[17] *Ibid.*, XII, 95.

[18] *Ibid.*, IX, 536–539 (Sept., 1854).

[19] See North, *op. cit.*, p. 435.

facts that "Hard Up" was named by *Putnam's* as one of O'Brien's contributions[20] and that Fitz-James included it in his own list of twenty stories picked for publication.[21] The author of "Hard Up,"[22] bragging about his wealth, says he would like to tell a story about a poor acquaintance of his, Belisarius Mynus. Slips, intentionally made, occur just often enough, however, to keep the reader aware that the author is telling his own story. He had come from Ireland, had written for the editors of *Putnam's Monthly* and *Harper's*, and had contributed to the *Occident Magazine* a story called "The Animated Skeleton." Another story of his, "The Phantom Telescope," still in manuscript, shows a greater originality and power than anything of Poe's or Hawthorne's. He was, nevertheless, forced to live in an attic in the midst of the squalor of Elizabeth Street, over the shop of the cheap theatrical costumer, Sollerman Isaacs. When Isaacs pressed him for rent, Mynus replied that he was writing a play for Mr. Tiddles, manager of the Mulberry Theatre, who was to give him five hundred dollars for it when finished. Upon this Isaacs agreed to wait, provided Mynus would help carry costumes to the theatre.

> Poor Mynus . . . felt the humiliation keenly. He was full of pride, though without much of either self-respect or moral courage. He would borrow money of a woman, or live upon a friend without the slightest compunction, yet would revolt against the smallest social slight with all the indignation of an incorruptible gentleman.[23]

The play was at last produced, but being unsuccessful, brought Mynus only one hundred dollars. With this he paid Isaacs and for three weeks lived like a gentleman, but now once more is hard up.

In treatment this story is uneven and jerky, and even the realistic details of debt and theatrical life are sentimentalized. Its style and technique are far inferior to those of O'Brien's last story for the year, "Mrs. Macsimum's Bill."[24] This is the first of a series of stories which deal, in what is usually a neatly concentrated form, with phases of life in fashionable New York society; and four more of them—" My Son, Sir," "The Beauty," "A Drawing-Room Drama," and "The Duel"—appeared in *Harper's* during the next year. The plot of "Mrs. Macsimum's Bill" is a comparatively obvious one,

[20] See L. H. B. in *The Round Table*, VIII, 159 (Sept. 5, 1868).
[21] See p. 230 and note 57.
[22] *Putnam's*, IV, 50–63 (July, 1854).
[23] *Ibid.*, IV, 53.
[24] *Ibid.*, IV, 660–665 (Dec., 1854).

dealing with the extravagance of the society woman, to meet whose expenditures the husband is forced to give out promissory notes and to contract unwise debts. Of course, there is the lover willing to destroy the note against the husband if the wife will pay the price he most desires. The triteness of the devices used to secure the happy ending—the husband overhears the lover's proposals and almost at the same moment receives news which retrieves his credit—would seem unconditionally to damn the story; but the artificial mould in which the whole thing is cast, together with the neatness with which each minor artificiality fits into and helps build up the total effect, is, in its kind, thoroughly admirable. It has the close-knit quality of a Scribe farce, and is French in the fine finish it applies to an inconsequential trifle.

In addition to the stories and poems, *Putnam's* printed three articles of criticism. A review of Charles Halpine's volume, *Lyrics by the Letter H*,[25] gave O'Brien a chance to express his ideas as to what poetry should be, and, in measuring Halpine's verse by this standard, to deride his shortcomings gayly and cleverly, but cruelly. He is right, but not kind. Having pointed out Halpine's servile imitations of Poe, Tom Moore, Charles Mackay, and Samuel Lover, O'Brien says that "there are certain mental and physical elements necessary to the formation of a poet," and implies that these Halpine entirely lacks. "Some imagination is usually required. Strength and boldness are not objectionable. A knowledge of either external or internal life, or both united, is of some advantage, while dramatic fire, and an enthusiasm for the beautiful, add considerably to the excellence of the poetic writer."[26]

He criticizes Halpine's "wit," and to show how easily things like his are done O'Brien produces the following:

THE ANGEL OF THE ASSEMBLY

I met her at the Chinese Rooms,
She wore a wreath of roses,
She walked in beauty like the night,
Her breath was like sweet posies.

I led her through the festal Hall,
Her glance was soft and tender;
She whispered gently in my ear,
"SAY! MOSE—AIN'T THIS A BENDER?"

[25] *Putnam's*, IV, 213–217 (Aug., 1854), entitled "The Last Poet Out."
[26] *Ibid.*, IV, 214.

and then comments, "Our watch is lying on the table, and we find on consulting that faithful chronometer that the composition of the foregoing charming poem occupied us exactly one minute, and three seconds."[27] Like Poe dealing with Joseph Rodman Drake, O'Brien holds the details of Halpine's imagery up to ridicule. He, in the habit of the time, longs for "a great American poet, who shall speak grandly to us, and whose nature shall be veined with the aspects, customs, and instincts of his country."[28] These requirements Halpine does not meet; indeed, concludes O'Brien, "H" is not a poet at all.

Two months later O'Brien is appealing for "a grand original American Drama! Don't let it be historical. . . . Let us have a good comedy of American life; not vulgarly flippant, or nationally slangular, but delicately anatomizing the various shades of our very peculiar and somewhat anomalous society." Two difficulties that will stand in the way of this are that to be successful, like "that trashy drama of Bulwer's, 'The Lady of Lyons,' " the author will have to make his appeal largely to feminine sentiment, and that he must write a play to suit the company who will act it. "Study your actors before you write. Fix upon a certain company, and do not trouble yourself so much about suiting the capabilities of the individual performers, as giving them parts that *they* will like."[29] These suggestions appeared in the second of two rambling, diversified, formless articles entitled "The Editor at Large."[30] In these papers episodes about the life of the town told in an easy conversational way alternate with anecdotes and gossipy details about authors to give the reader a feeling that he is being admitted behind the scenes of the New York literary world. The Bard of the Orient, Bayard Taylor, is introduced, as is the author's immaculate society friend, Dimes, "the adored of Fifth Avenue and Grammercy [*sic*] Park,"[31] who later figures so largely in "The Man about Town" papers; and Belisarius Mynus is quoted—an additional proof that O'Brien, and not an enemy of his, was the author of "Hard Up." One of the best sellers of the day, the *Manuel de Savoir Vivre* by M. Alfred de Meilheurat, meets with the editorial disapprobation on the ground that it tries to mold everybody to one form. In objecting to such a desideratum O'Brien cites examples of great men who were unprepossessing, and claims that debt also

[27] *Ibid.*, IV, 215.
[28] *Ibid.*, IV, 216.
[29] *Ibid.*, IV, 439 (Oct., 1854).
[30] *Ibid.*, IV, 331–337 (Sept., 1854), and IV, 434–442 (Oct.).
[31] *Ibid.*, IV, 434.

should not be despised, for like lack of polish it has been the friend at times of many great men,—Byron, Coleridge, Shakespeare, Leigh Hunt, Thackeray, and Dickens. As Belisarius Mynus says, "Debt, sir, is the umbilical cord of Genius, that binds it to its mother earth."[32]

Though to mother earth O'Brien was bound with a rather unenviable consistency and continuity, still in December, 1854, he might have been hopefully trying his wings and not unreasonably indulging in the flights of fancy to which his aristocratic inclinations were always urging him. His two-act play, *A Gentleman from Ireland*, put on at Wallack's Theatre on the night of Monday, December 11,[33] was a decided hit; and his adaptation of a French play, *The Sisters*, acted for the first time on December 27,[34] was also successful. Together they held the boards for what was then considered a great run, and the part of Gerald Fitzmaurice in *A Gentleman from Ireland* continued to be one of the most popular of John Brougham's characterizations throughout his career.[35] The play ran continuously from December 11 to 21, and then, after a lapse of three nights, was continued, only to make way for the opening of *The Sisters* on the twenty-seventh. On the twenty-ninth and thirtieth, Mr. O'Brien the playwright had the unusual and certainly pleasant experience of having both his plays performed on the same bill,[36] and even as late as January 13, 1855, *The New York Picayune* feels called upon to remark somewhat facetiously upon this circumstance:

"The Sisters" seem to be a decidedly popular pair of young ladies. They have made their appearance before large and gratified audiences at this house ever since they made their *debut*. Of course we cannot keep on criticizing them continually, for criticism must end somewhere—say where compliment begins, but even compliment is exhaustible. Moreover, the Rhadamanthus of the Amusements of the Public should not be complimentary, and therefore—But enough. We have

[32] *Ibid.*, IV, 435.

[33] See *N. Y. Herald* and *N. Y. Times*, Dec. 12, 1854; also FitzJames O'Brien, *A Gentleman from Ireland*, No. CLVI, The Minor Drama, Samuel French [1858], "Cast of the Characters," p. 2; J. N. Ireland, *op. cit.*, II, 635; T. Allston Brown, *op. cit.*, I, 484; and G. C. K. Odell, *op. cit.*, VI, 361.

[34] See *N. Y. Herald* and *N. Y. Times*, Dec. 28, 1854; also Ireland, Brown, and Odell as in n. 33, above.

[35] For information about Brougham and a characterization of his acting see *Life, Stories, and Poems of John Brougham*, ed. W. Winter, Boston, 1881, and W. L. Keese, *William E. Burton, Actor, Author, and Manager*, New York & London, 1885, esp. pp. 55–56.

[36] See advertisements in *N. Y. Times* of respective dates.

succeeded in drawing the attention of our readers to the "Sisters," a play well worthy of being seen. We must not omit to state that the "Sisters" are subjected to an annoyance peculiar to their situation at this theatre—which is, that they are nightly followed by "A Gentleman from Ireland!" But the public having expressed no objections to this, we suppose that we must pass it without censure, until it does.

By January 20 "The Sisters" were still making their appearance nightly, but the Irish Gentleman was following them only occasionally.[37]

Detailed accounts of *A Gentleman from Ireland* appeared in the columns of both *The New York Daily Times* and *The New York Herald* on the morning of December 12. After saying "The story is simple, and develops itself rapidly," and giving a synopsis, the *Times* account continues:

There is much dramatic ability displayed in the elaboration of this plot, and the situations are thoroughly humorous and effective. The tag to the second act is perhaps a trifle too long, but it does not hang fire. In other respects—literary and dramatic—there is nothing to be improved.

The character of *Gerald Fitz-Maurice* is a decided addition to Mr. BROUGHAM'S repertoire. There have been but few delineators of the Irish Gentleman on the stage. Mr. BROUGHAM achieved an unequivocal success in that difficult *rôle.* He was easy and subdued throughout, contributing in no small degree to the benefit of the piece.

... There was a great deal of applause on the fall of the curtain. Mr. O'BRIAN [*sic*] was loudly called for, and made a plunge at the orchestra from a private box; immediately afterwards retiring into private life. This was not considered sufficient by the audience, who insisted on having two more bows from the author—and got them.

The *Herald,* though on the whole favorable, has the following strictures to make:

The plot of the piece is barely sufficient to keep up the interest for the first act.

The dialogue is sometimes smart, but the name of Fitzgerald's castle, "Ballymo-kee," is too often iterated; it ceases to be funny after the twentieth repetition. The dash of sentiment in the character of the Irish gentleman is very weak, and it is difficult to ascertain whether he is a genteel swindler, or a very fine young fellow in difficulties as he represents himself. The weight of the piece rests on

[37] *The New York Picayune,* Jan. 20, 1855; also on Apr. 21 and Nov. 24 *A Gentleman from Ireland* is noted as among the old pieces revived. The writer has been able to locate only broken files of *The New York Picayune,* the files in none of the great libraries being complete.

the shoulders of Mr. Brougham, and its success must be, in a great measure, attributed to his excellent acting.[38]

Then, having spoken of Mr. Brougham's curtain call and Mr. O'Brien's bow, the *Herald* closes with the same request for an original American play that O'Brien had been making in "The Editor at Large": "Mr. O'Brien has shown talent for dramatic writing, and we hope that he will give us an American comedy on an American subject." Such a play never materialized, but *A Gentleman from Ireland* continued perennially to win favor with the audiences before whom Brougham elected to act it.

That the *Herald* criticism was not unfair was shown in an amusing way when the play was revived at Wallack's in November, 1858. At this time Fitz-James O'Brien was dramatic critic for *The Saturday Press*, his column appearing in its pages each week. He naturally attended the revival of his own play and as critic wrote the following review:

My Own Comedy of "A Gentleman from Ireland."

I was startled in the early part of this week by observing on the bills of this theater [Wallack's], in conjunction with Mr. Hoppin's piece, an old comedy of my own—"A Gentleman from Ireland"—announced for representation. I went in the evening to see it, and was as much amused as the audience. Only that they laughed at the piece, while I laughed at myself. I found the Gentleman from Ireland a wonderfully crude production. I had not seen it played for a couple of years, and I think viewed it from as impartial a point of view as any dramatic critic in the city. In the first place, I discovered that it is not a comedy, although announced to be such. It is simply a sort of farce in two acts. The dialogue is sometimes smart, but never witty, while occasionally it rises into the realm of fustian. The ending of the first act is weak and nonsensical. There is no characterization in it from beginning to end, and everybody talks like everybody else. It inculcates no lesson, illustrates no principle, and evidently owes its success to a certain vitality which a young man's writings generally possess—literary animal spirits, so to speak—and a slight vein of sentiment. The equivoque of the piece is well sustained, and the situations tolerably laughable. It is what I would call, for another, a very young piece, but as it has always drawn good houses, and been now played for over fifty times in various parts of the Union, I suppose I ought not to find too much fault with it.

FitzJames O'Brien.[39]

[38] *N. Y. Herald*, Dec. 12, 1854. Gerald Fitzmaurice is the correct name of the character, and Ballypookeen that of the castle.

[39] *The Saturday Press*, Nov. 13, 1858.

By 1856 O'Brien had become sufficiently identified with the play to give point to a cartoon in which he is seen holding in both hands a copy of "Gentleman from Ireland."[40] The play was entered for publication in 1858, and is still on the active list of Samuel French, Publisher, as No. CLVI of "The Minor Drama." The title page of this edition gives O'Brien as "Author of 'The Sisters,' 'Duke Humphrey's Dinner,' 'The Cup and the Lip,' 'My Christmas Dinner,' &c.," and it is this edition which became the basis for the promptbooks used by John Brougham in later performances.[41]

Brougham always considered Gerald Fitzmaurice as one of his best parts; he therefore revived it frequently, not only during O'Brien's lifetime but throughout his long career, and when he took a benefit himself or was called upon to perform in benefits for others, it was generally in this part that he chose to appear.[42] Following its popularization by Brougham, *A Gentleman from Ireland* was performed successfully in various parts of the country—at the Varieties Theatre in New Orleans, for instance, and at the old National Theatre in Washington, D. C., as late as 1893.[43]

As one reads the play today he is entirely willing to believe that the skillful acting of the leading rôle was largely responsible for its unqualified success, for the intrigue and mistaken identity that furnish the plot are quite usual, and the characters are conventional types. Clover is the irate father; Hugh, the jealous lover; Charles, the scapegrace son; and Agnes and Lucy, both charming girls indistinguishable from each other. On the other hand, the dialogue is bright, the puns clever, and there is a sufficient variety of mood and scene, the sentimental alternating with the amusing. Professor Arthur Hobson Quinn, in his *A History of the American Drama*, speaking of Irish plays by Brougham, Boucicault, and others, says:

> The usual caricature of an Irish gentleman is given more semblance to truth in *The Gentleman from Ireland*, by the talented Irish-American FitzJames O'Brien. . . .
>
> Comparatively few of these plays, therefore, were written by native Americans, though men like Brougham and O'Brien became identified to a certain degree with our stage or our literature. They were simply following a British stage

[40] *N. Y. Picayune*, Sept. 20, 1856; see Illustration, p. 114.

[41] A copy in the Boston Public Library was used as promptbook at the Boston Theatre in 1860, at the Academy of Music, Cleveland, Ohio, Dec. 6, 1869, and at the Brooklyn Theatre, Dec. 12, 1871.

[42] For revivals see Bibliography. See also J. N. Ireland, *op. cit.*, T. Allston Brown, *op. cit.*, and G. C. K. Odell, *op. cit.*

[43] W. R. Floyd to William Winter, Oct. 16, 1880 (A. L. S. in Romm collection), and conversation with Frank Winter, May 5, 1925.

tradition in choosing the bizarre features of Irish life, the gentleman in trouble for debt, the servant, or the emigrant, and they rarely placed him on Irish soil. So far as any great interpretation of Irish character is concerned, they are valueless.[44]

This comedy of the Irishman in England was followed not by a play of America as the *Herald* had hoped, but by one skilfully adapted from the French. Unlike *A Gentleman from Ireland* this play did not get into print, and as a result practically the only sources of information are the reviews in the *Times* and the *Herald* and the comment from the *Picayune* quoted above. According to the *Times*, it was "a cleverly constructed and ably written drama, in two acts, called 'The Sisters,' " adapted for Wallack's Theatre by Mr. F. J. O'Brien. It was carefully placed on the stage; the costumes and scenery were all good. "It was eminently successful, and was announced for repetition every evening this week amid loud applause."[45] *The New York Herald* for the same date says:

"The Sisters"—a new adaptation of a French vaudeville entitled "Ange ou Diable"—was produced at this house last evening. The plot turns upon the extraordinary family likeness between two sisters—a stage property at least as old as Plautus; but the manner in which it is wrought up, and the accessories in the shape of characters, dialogue, etc., are original and good. . . . The dialogue is sprightly and amusing. Many of the situations are so happily contrived as to seem original, and the interest is well sustained throughout. Lester, who played an accessory part—Ernest Bridoux—and Blake as the crusty old uncle, labored effectively for the success of the piece. The gentleman who adapted it to our stage—Mr. Fitzjames O'Brien—evinced equal dramatic skill and literary taste in his portion of the work. The piece was perfectly successful; and when Mr. O'Brien was called to the front of a side box, a hearty burst of applause testified to the satisfaction of the audience.

Ireland recorded the play under another title, *Like and Unlike, or the Sisters*;[46] but it seems usually to have been referred to by what he gives as the subtitle. The sisters, though like in appearance, are most unlike in character; and the parts of Baroness de Rosier and Thérèse, both played

[44] A. H. Quinn, *A History of the American Drama from the Beginning to the Civil War*, 1923, pp. 376–377.
[45] *N. Y. Times*, Dec. 28, 1854.
[46] Ireland, *op. cit.*, II, 635.

by the same actress, Miss Rosa Bennett, gave her a chance to show her versatility of characterization. The play was temporarily successful, running "without intermission up to and including January 13th"; but it was not the subject for such repeated revival and renewed popularity as was *A Gentleman from Ireland*.[47]

[47] Both Ireland, *op. cit.*, II, 635, and Odell, *op. cit.*, VI, 362, give the casts. This seems not to be the same as the play called *Like and Unlike* played for the benefit of Laura Keene on May 4, 1857; though it may be another adaptation of the same. The names of the characters are different, and Miss Keene played four parts. See Brown, *op. cit.*, II, 125, and Odell, *op. cit.*, VI, 544.

CHAPTER V

BOHEMIA

(1855)

When the Bohemians established themselves in New York in the 1850's, they acknowledged the suzerainty of a King in the person of Henry Clapp, Jr.; their Queen was Ada Clare; their kingdom the streets of the city, the publishing houses, and the offices of the journals of all sorts; and their court the cellar at Pfaff's. Some sort of foreign trade they carried on with the magazines of Boston and Philadelphia. But their organization never went far enough to include the selection of a Prince. Fitz-James O'Brien might very well have held the title, however, if one may credit the testimony of his contemporaries, both friends and enemies. He belonged to the kingdom even before it received its name or had established its permanent court; in fact, as has been seen, he became a citizen of Bohemia immediately upon his arrival in America, and he may have sworn allegiance while he was still in London.

As editor of *The Lantern* John Brougham was, in 1852, the leader of the Bohemians; and as a regular contributor to this comic magazine O'Brien must have attended Brougham's weekly dinners at Windust's. From this time until he left in 1861 to go to the Civil War, Fitz-James O'Brien played the rôle of prince of Bohemia. He lived Bohemia's typical life of contrasting triumphs and vicissitudes; he shared in all its enterprises, largely journalistic; he championed its cause against its enemies—and all this with a dash, vigor, enthusiasm, and force of personal magnetism which impressed themselves upon the imaginations of his comrades.

These comrades were a group, mostly of young men, who as artists, sculptors, poets, actors, playwrights, novelists, storytellers, journalists, and critics were trying to make a living in New York—a city which was chiefly interested in creating for itself material business advantages, in acquiring wealth, and in spending it ostentatiously—a city not much interested in art. Yet in spite of this, or perhaps better, because of it, New York of the mid-century had its Bohemia, just as the great city of the early twentieth century had its Greenwich Village; or as London had its Grub Street and Paris its Latin Quarter. The term *Bohemia* is today applied with a latitude of connotation far beyond what it suggested when, in the early 1850's, it became popularized as a new word, and in the later fifties took on local significance from its adoption by the Pfaff group. It is only fair, therefore, to take the definition from the man and the book which first gave vogue to the word and its idea—Henri Murger and his *Scènes de la Vie de Bohème.*

This novel, or rather, this series of more or less closely connected episodes in the lives of a group of Parisian artists, sentimentalizing and idealizing as it does the distresses and miseries of a hand-to-mouth existence, attained a wide popularity. It first appeared in parts, running through *Le Corsaire* from 1847 to 1849, and was published in book form in Paris in the latter year. In his preface to the novel, Murger takes pains to define and describe Bohemia (*La Bohème*). "The Bohemians," he says, "which are treated of in this book are not a race born today; they have existed always and everywhere, and can show illustrious origins"; and he traces them from Greek antiquity, through the Middle Ages and the Renaissance, to the seventeenth and eighteenth centuries, and so arrives at this pointed statement: "Today as formerly, everyone who enters into the arts, without other means of existence than the art itself, will have to pass along the paths of Bohemia." He adds that Bohemia exists and is possible only in Paris. These words are later taken up by the enemies of the New York Bohemians and used with violent force against them. And yet, if Henri Murger had been bent on describing the New York Bohemia of a decade later instead of that of his own Paris, he could not have given a more accurate picture of it; nor could he more truly have hit off certain salient traits in the nature of Fitz-James O'Brien, had the model been before him, than he does in his description of the characteristics of the typical Bohemian. It seems worth while therefore to quote at length from the final paragraphs of Murger's preface, especially as the New Yorkers declared their imitation of his book and were fully conscious of their indebtedness to Murger.

After discussing the unknown Bohemian with his lack of ability and the amateur Bohemian, who ultimately returns to the conventional fold, Murger arrives among the true Bohemians.

This [the true] Bohemia is like the others beset with dangers; two gulfs border it on either side,—want and uncertainty. But between these two gulfs there is at least a road leading to a goal, which the Bohemians may behold with their eyes until they can lay their hands upon it.

This is official Bohemia;—so called, because those who compose it have publicly declared their existence, have made known their presence in life, on something more than a registrar's page; finally, to employ an expression of their language, because their names are posted, because they are known in the literary and artistic market, and because their product, which bears their mark, has currency there, though at moderate prices it is true.

. . . Nothing stops these hardy adventurers, whose very vices are strengthened by virtues. Wit is always kept awake by their ambition, which charges before them and urges them to the assault of the future; without giving up to the struggles with necessity, their invention, which always marches with a lighted fuse, blows up the obstacle almost before it troubles them. . . . At need they know how to practice abstinence with all the virtue of an anchorite; but should a little fortune fall into their hands, you will see them suddenly riding the most ruinous hobbies. . . .

Bohemians know everything, and go everywhere, according as they have polished or worn out shoes. They are found one day, comfortably seated before the fireplace in a drawing-room, and the next day lounging in the public dance-halls. They cannot take ten steps on the boulevard without meeting a friend, nor thirty anywhere, without meeting a creditor. . . . Such is, in brief, this life of Bohemia, in ill-repute among the puritans of society, condemned by the puritans of art, insulted by all the fearful and jealous mediocrities, who cannot find outcries and lies and calumnies enough to drown out the voices and names of those who attain to the threshold of fame by adding boldness to their talents.[1]

Fitz-James O'Brien, though he was a dweller in Bohemia, which became a vital part of his life as he became a vital part of it, seldom writes about it. Of course, frequently in his stories and sketches he reflects his life there, from time to time exhibiting the seamy side of the theatrical profession, usually with a touch of humor, and many times giving glimpses of various sorts into the poorer New York lodging- and boardinghouses. Once, in "The Man about Town,"[2] he goes into a tirade against the indignities and discomforts of boardinghouses, an anathematizing description which is so sincere that its basis must have been a long and irritating experience at many such tables. Only once, however, does O'Brien directly name the Bohemian and let him give an account of himself, and even then the de-

[1] Henry Murger, *The Latin Quarter* ("Scènes de la Vie de Bohème"), Translated by Ellen Marriage and John Selwyn, with an Introduction by Arthur Symons, 1901. "Preface."

[2] *H. W.*, I, 179 (Mar. 21, 1857).

scription is half-contemptuous and satirical. This was written before the Bohemians had decided to call themselves such; but even had it been afterwards, it would not have been foreign to the method frequently adopted by O'Brien of depicting in semiludicrous light the hardships and makeshifts of his difficult existence. In "The Bohemian,"[3] a short story, the introduction of the main character is given by means of a dialogue in which a struggling young lawyer questions his odd visitor and receives the replies of the latter:

"A resident of this city?"

"No. I am by birth an Englishman, but I never reside anywhere."

"Oh! You are a commercial agent, then, perhaps?"

"I am a Bohemian."

"A what?"

"A Bohemian," he repeated, coolly removing the papers with which I had concealed my magazine story, and glancing over the commencement; "you see, my habits are easy."

"I see it perfectly, Sir," I answered, indignantly.

"When I say that I am a Bohemian, I do not wish you to understand that I am a Zingaro. I don't steal chickens, tell fortunes, or live in a camp. I am a social Bohemian, and fly at higher game. . . . Have you read Henri Murger's *Scènes de la Vie de Bohème?*"

"Yes."

"Well, then, you can comprehend my life. I am clever, learned, witty, and tolerably good looking. I can write brilliant magazine articles"—here his eye rested contemptuously on my historical tale—"I can paint pictures, and, what is more, sell the pictures I paint. I can compose songs, make comedies, and captivate women."

"On my word, Sir, you have a choice of professions," I said, sarcastically; for the scorn with which the Bohemian had eyed my story humiliated me.

"That's it," he answered; "I don't want a profession. I could make plenty of money if I chose to work, but I don't choose to work. I will never work. I have a contempt for labor."

"Probably you despise money equally," I replied, with a sneer.

"No, I don't. To acquire money without trouble is the great object of my life."[4]

Let it be granted that this picture of a Bohemian and his aims is satirical; nevertheless, it is clear that O'Brien appreciated the point of Murger's

[3] *Harper's*, XI, 233–242 (July, 1855).

[4] *Ibid.*, p. 235.

description, and gives to the Bohemian of the story in concrete details the traits with which Murger had endowed the Bohemians in general terms. Moreover, O'Brien, whether or not he as early as 1855 recognized himself as a denizen of Bohemia, is here, at all events, writing out traits of his own character; for with the utmost self-assurance (the quality most demanded by Murger) he was conscious of his brilliantly successful versatility, and he scorned work except when it was necessary. His own writings are testimony to his versatility, while *The New York Times* bears witness to his ability to make money, had he chosen to do so. It says: "As a literary man, Lieut. O'Brien was completely successful. He never made a failure, and in consequence was much sought after by publishers. It was his whim, however, to be fickle, and hence the writings that would have gladly been taken by one, were scattered among many."[5] The same paper some years later states that "it came easier for him to earn his living by the pen than in any other way; his facility was a fatal gift."[6] But recklessness and fickleness, or instability, were essential traits of O'Brien's character as they were, according to Murger, a usual accompaniment of the Bohemian life.

Murger, however, and his *Scènes de la Vie de Bohème* could not say the final word about Bohemia: first, because it was written about phases of Paris life of which the New York life was an ocean-separated imitation, and next, because the New Yorkers in their vivacious exuberance continued by their actions to add new meanings to the word by which they chose to designate themselves. In addition to this, many of the phases of Bohemian life which were accepted as matters of course by the French mind were to the average American mind, with its background of Puritan moral and religious training, causes of violent denunciation and grave concern; so, to the conservative American, Bohemianism came to signify unrestrained license and immorality.

Part of this reputation, incurred by the Bohemians of the 1850's, was, of course, deserved; but part of it depended on the failure of the critics to understand what the members of the group were truly striving for. Is Bohemia a name which should be applied to the ideal of the artistic type of mind? Or is Bohemia the life which results when a group of artists, hemmed in on all sides by the limitations of their corporeal humanity, strive toward their ideal through the midst of a material world? Perhaps there is a bit of

[5] *N. Y. Times*, Apr. 10, 1862.
[6] *Ibid.*, Mar. 12, 1881.

truth in both these ideas; and if so, the struggle involved in the latter will often, as with other mortals, result in failure. But the failures of the artist are generally more irritating than are those of others, because, Icaruslike, by aiming at the heavens and striving to soar, he exposes himself to the melting rays of the sun of absolute criticism and so falls doubly low, to be drowned in the sea of oblivion. Or, on the other hand, by his much striving, the artist's inability to fly becomes apparent to a wide audience, and his continued attempts only render him contemptible or ludicrous. In terms of the concrete earthly Bohemia in which he exists, the artist or poet desiring to live a life of the imagination unhampered by the conventions and limitations of ordinarily constituted society manages as best he can to get along outside of this society. He ceases to concern himself chiefly with the procuring of material necessities. Let such things vanish or take care of themselves. He gives himself up to the enjoyment of the moment, to most fully experiencing pleasures as they pass. Congenial friends he can enjoy; the discussion of topics of mutual interest delight him. For the time being nothing else exists.

But Bohemia is a land of violent contrasts. After such indulgings of the imagination, such realizations of his ideal life (frequent and delightful though they may be), the poet looking about him finds that his body is still surrounded by a world of material things—that it is in the midst of the growing, spreading city of New York, in which bodies become hungry, and food costs money; in which the air is cold, and clothes can be had only for gold; in which all the senses grow weary, and lodging has to be paid for. And he is likely to find, too, that he has offended the society which controls the supply of the things which now he needs. His freedom from care is called recklessness and extravagance, his delight license, his pleasure immorality. "Ten or twelve years ago there came into favor here the twin abominations, Free Love and Bohemianism—the feculent product of Parisian low life," says a writer of 1864,[7] and he continues to speak of "the Bacchanalian Mutual Admiration Society which has dragged down to its degraded level a score of promising young men, has drunk and smoked not a few of them into premature graves, and is still flourishing in its infernal work." The members of this Society, leading their hand-to-mouth existence, are described as

shiftless, lazy, moneyless, glorying in a condition of poverty that knows not at breakfast where dinner is to come from, borrowing and begging from dollars to

[7] *The Round Table*, I, 43 (Jan. 2, 1864), "Dramatic Critics in New York."

pennies from any one weak enough to trust them, running away from boarding houses at midnight, dodging indignant washerwomen at street corners, getting trusted at every bar-room that would stand it, shinning around the free lunches of porterhouses, often presenting outward evidence of pinching want.

That such disapproval of Bohemia was not one merely of journalistic jealousy and unconsidered spitefulness is indicated by Emerson's reference to Bohemians as "persons open to the suspicion of irregular and immoral living."[8]

In striking contrast to the Emersonian attitude is that of Walt Whitman (on such a subject as Bohemia one would expect a contrast in these two men), who, in addition to his liking for the stage drivers and his friendly regard for the young surgeons of the hospitals, had sufficient sympathy for the Bohemians to have been, during the fifties and up to 1862, a frequent visitor at their general gathering place, Pfaff's. Years later he said:

I can recall it all now, and, through a vista of cigar and pipe smoke and dim gaslight, see the scores of kindly faces peering at me, some in love, some in question, but all friendly enough; for, while "Bohemia" might differ as to a man's work or its results, she usually, once he was in, accepted the man, idiosyncrasies and all. "Bohemia" comes but once in one's life. Let's treasure even its memory.[9]

The last two sentences contain the suggestion of one of the Bohemian attitudes which has been much criticized. Its sentiment has been branded as false, and as such has been attacked and decried. Arthur Symons, however, makes what seems to be a necessary, even if a rather fine, distinction; that is, that the Bohemian sentiment is itself true, but that the expression of it is not quite sincere.[10] In other words, the sentiment is a real one in that it is the sentiment that youth actually does have of itself, "at the flowering moment of existence," and can be regarded as false only by those who confuse the feeling, which is real, with the unreal vision about which it feels—the romantic regarding of life as a vast arena of magnificent accomplishment. That the object is unreal is seen by the fact that with most intelligent people it passes with the passing of youth; but while youth remains the sentiment exists; it is, for the youth, true. Nevertheless, the

[8] Ralph Waldo Emerson, *Letters and Social Aims*, new and rev. ed., 1884, p. 299.

[9] Thomas Donaldson, *Walt Whitman the Man*, New York, 1896, p. 206.

[10] Henry Murger, *op. cit.*, "Introduction" by Arthur Symons.

Bohemian usually gives a real handle to his critics, for in seeking to embody his sentiment he tries to make an art of his life, and so becomes unnatural and guilty of exaggeration. This is, as Arthur Symons puts it, equivalent to saying that "no one is quite sincere in Bohemia, because sincerity is a respectable virtue, tedious in the long run, and the transposition of things part of the charm of existence there."[11]

Probably the best known of all the criticisms of Bohemia and the circle at Pfaff's is that written by William Dean Howells. This man, fresh from Boston, gives ample evidence of the eternal irreconcilability between Bohemia and respectability. He writes in 1900, forty years after his introduction to Bohemia one August morning in the office of *The Saturday Press:*

It would not be easy to say just why the Bohemian group represented New York literature to my imagination, for I certainly associated other names with its best work, but perhaps it was because I had written for the *Saturday Press* myself, and had my pride in it, and perhaps it was because that paper really embodied the new literary life of the city. It was clever, and full of the wit that tries its teeth upon everything. It attacked all literary shams but its own, and it made itself felt and feared. The young writers throughout the country were ambitious to be seen in it, and they gave their best to it; they gave literally, for the *Saturday Press* never paid in anything but hopes of paying, vaguer even than promises. It is not too much to say that it was very nearly as well for one to be accepted by the *Press* as to be accepted by the *Atlantic*, and for the time there was no other literary comparison. To be in it was to be in the company of Fitz James O'Brien, Fitzhugh Ludlow, Mr. Aldrich, Mr. Stedman, and whoever else was liveliest in prose or loveliest in verse at that day in New York. It was a power, and although it is true that, as Henry Giles said of it, "Man cannot live by snapping-turtle alone," the *Press* was very good snapping-turtle. Or, it seemed so then; I should be almost afraid to test it now, for I do not like snapping-turtle so much as I once did, and I have grown nicer in my taste, and want my snapping-turtle of the very best. What is certain is that I went to the office of the *Saturday Press* in New York with much the same sort of feeling I had in going to the office of the *Atlantic Monthly* in Boston, but I came away with a very different feeling. I had found there a bitterness against Boston as great as the bitterness against respectability, and as Boston was then rapidly becoming my second country, I could not join in the scorn thought of her and said of her by the Bohemians. I fancied a

[11] *Ibid.* For the pose and affectation see Bayard Taylor, *John Godfrey's Fortunes*, 1889, pp. 269–283; for the sentiment and pose see Thomas Bailey Aldrich, "At the Café," in *Vanity Fair*, I, 12 (Dec. 31, 1859).

conspiracy among them to shock the literary pilgrim, and to minify the precious emotions he had experienced in visiting other shrines; but I found no harm in that, for I knew just how much to be shocked, and I thought I knew better how to value certain things of the soul than they. Yet when their chief asked me how I got on with Hawthorne, and I began to say that he was very shy and I was rather shy, and the king of Bohemia took his pipe out to break in upon me with "Oh, a couple of shysters!" and the rest laughed, I was abashed all they could have wished, and was not restored to myself till one of them said that the thought of Boston made him as ugly as sin; then I began to hope again that men who took themselves so seriously as that need not be taken very seriously by me.

In fact I had heard things almost as desperately cynical in other newspaper offices before that, and I could not see what was so distinctively Bohemian in these *anime prave*, these souls so baleful by their own showing.[12]

Howells, a little later in discussing Richard Henry Stoddard and his wife, gives as his chief reason for liking them that "they were frankly not of that Bohemia which I disliked so much, and thought it of no promise or validity."[13]

What seems to be the fairest estimate of the Bohemian group of writers, to whom the critics, whether hostile or friendly, unite in allowing an extraordinary amount of energy and vitality, is made by Charles T. Congdon, an editorial writer for the *New York Tribune:*

Some quarter of a century ago, we imported from France, among other things which we could well do without, what is called Bohemianism. A Bohemian in those days was one who was clever in writing smart jokes and pretty poems and lively tales and brisk essays and other newspaper commodities which perish in the reading. If he did not have permanent employment, and generally there was nothing permanent about him, he hawked his wares from office to office, and sold them at tragically small prices, subsequently investing the amount, it was ill-naturedly declared, in a great deal of beer and a very little bread. . . . There was a desperate effort to establish the Bohemian guild in New York, but the climate, I suppose was unfavorable. It figured mostly in weekly newspapers which are dead, long ago, while the performers have followed their works. I do not mean to say, however, that there were not many excellent fellows and men of rare genius enrolled under the Bohemian banner; young gentlemen were there, who soon found that such a way of life was not wise; poets were there, who have since

[12] William Dean Howells, *Literary Friends and Acquaintances, A Personal Retrospect of American Authorship*, New York and London, 1911, pp. 70–71.

[13] *Ibid.*, p. 87.

won deserved and honorable fame, and who now preside with dignity at the family tea-table, and give good advice, with the morning muffin, to their well-grown boys and girls. Such a harum-scarum life, such listening to the chimes at midnight, and utter disregard of the conventionalities and respectabilities and responsibilities, generally tests a man pretty sharply. If he really has brains, he usually gets away from it before it gets away with him. . . .

Brilliancy is all well enough; those talents are not to be despised which attract friends and give a light and evanescent pleasure; the delights of the senses are tempting so long as they last: but when one's head has grown gray, and one's natural ardor has abated; when a bitter suspicion begins to dawn upon the mind that the way of life has been foolish; when the opportunities of work have become fewer, and the ability to do it well much smaller, a man of genius may envy those duller spirits who have not despised a homely prudence, and to whom the humdrum performance of duty, however humble, has brought a little competence and a freedom from daily apprehension.[14]

Such sermonizing the Bohemians would have regarded as ill-advised, utterly bourgeois, and contemptible; and even Congdon cannot help weakening the force of his admonitions almost immediately after by saying, "Yet those were pleasant nights in the old cellar, after all, when the last novel was discussed, the last new play anatomized; and the fun sometimes, but not often, became fast and furious."[15] The participators in the life of Bohemia almost invariably write like this, with a touch of the sentimental—the sentiment being, perhaps, in the sharing, in the abandoning oneself to the common attitude.

When Fitz-James O'Brien described characters of the Bohemian temperament, however, the sentimental phase was not the one he emphasized. On the contrary, he pointed out the weaknesses of the type, and made frequent use of the traits of his own personality to fill out the picture. In the short story "Seeing the World"[16] the hero, a successful poetic *improvvisatore*, closely resembles his literary creator. "Without having all the gifts, he had all the faults of a poet—the innate passion for independence, the incorrigible aversion to manual labor, the habit of awaiting inspiration, the radical want of punctuality. Add to this, the irritability which always accompanies poetic natures, an instinctive tendency to luxury, and an aris-

[14] Charles Tabor Congdon, *Reminiscences of a Journalist*, Boston, 1880, pp. 336–337 and 340–341.

[15] *Ibid.*, p. 341.

[16] *Harper's*, XV, 542–546 (Sept., 1857).

tocratic craving for distinction. He could neither translate nor work by the page or column."[17]

The character of Twitter in "A Screw Loose"[18] is presented with an accumulation of even more intimate and personal details.

> Twitter was a young literary gentleman who was continually occupying the handsomest apartments he could find, which he invariably vacated after a month of luxury. He was of a sanguine temperament, and I will do him the justice to say, that he always intended at the time of taking his rooms to pay for them. But so many extraordinary and unforeseen circumstances intervened between the day of his introduction and pay-day, that when that period arrived he regularly found himself in a state of unprecedented pecuniary depletion. The most unexpected calls would be made on his purse, such as being absolutely obliged to invite six friends to dinner at Delmonico's, with Burgundy and canvas-backs, or some infamous tailor, whom he had dealt with for over two months would suddenly present his bill, and insist on being paid, on threats of publishing Twitter's account in the newspapers. But the most unusual and at the same time unaccountable accident which his circumstances were in the habit of suffering, was a mysterious evaporation of considerable sums of money.
>
> "The oddest thing in life, Sir," Twitter would say to his friend. "I drew a hundred dollars from the Harpers on Tuesday, and to-day, Thursday, I positively cannot tell what has become of it" . . . and Twitter, oblivious of the supper at the Ornithorhyncus, and the twenty dollars he lent Jacobs to go and play faro with, and the coat and boots that he bought, and the expensive engravings that he ordered at Goupil's, moans after his vanished pile, and leaves his sumptuous apartments in disgrace. . . .
>
> It was a part of Twitter's principle of life never to confess himself poor. It produced a bad impression on people, he said. He had studied with great perseverance the art of assuming what might be called "the thousand-dollar-in-your-pocket look," and with immense success.[19]

Nevertheless, to obtain the funds necessary to keep up such an appearance O'Brien had to write, and, naturally, he wrote the sort of stuff for which the publishers would pay. He kept in close touch with the market, and during 1855 turned out a sufficient variety of product to satisfy the needs of Harper Brothers, who printed it in the *Monthly*.

Ten stories are included in the list: four of which use New York society

[17] *Ibid.*, p. 543.
[18] *Ibid.*, XV, 629–634 (Oct., 1857).
[19] *Ibid.*, pp. 630 and 633.

life as a background—"My Son, Sir," "The Beauty," "A Drawing-Room Drama," and "The Duel"; four of which are sentimentally melodramatic—"Baby Bloom," "Duke Humphrey's Dinner," "Milly Dove," and "Sister Anne" (the titles indicate the sentimentality); and two of which deal with the occult. These are "The Bohemian," from which has been quoted Fitz-James O'Brien's definition of the type, and "The Pot of Tulips."

"My Son, Sir" and "The Beauty"[20] are companion stories, as are "A Drawing-Room Drama" and "The Duel." Although O'Brien had frequently written social satire both in prose and verse earlier than this, such satirical thrusts had been mocking and gay, directed for the most part against the foibles of social usage. This type of writing is perennial, and in the eighteen-fifties it was practiced with animated skill not only by O'Brien but by George William Curtis, Edmund Clarence Stedman, and other clever young men of the New York group. In "My Son, Sir" and "The Beauty," however, he develops his satire not in a spirit of playful thrusting but with a cutting edge which seeks to accomplish the reform of dangerous customs sanctioned by the artificial conventions of the wealthy class. Such satirical attacks at false standards, at superficial codes of conduct, at the brutal selfishness of moneyed interests, and at effeminacy in the wrong places continued for the rest of O'Brien's life to be part of his product in both prose and verse. These first two stories, though sharply condemnatory in idea, are comparatively mild in method of presentation; for they are told by Mr. Troy, an old bachelor, who wishes to warn parents as to what will be the sad fate of their children if brought up in the midst of luxurious indulgence and educated in the most fashionable schools. In both cases the father fails in business and the child comes to a tragic end. The son of the first story becomes a drunkard and a gambler and is finally stabbed in a drunken brawl on the East Side. The daughter of the second story, having received the proper finishing at Madame Cancan's, has learned to do nothing useful. So when her father's swindling schemes fail, she becomes a beggar and a brandy sot and dies of delirium tremens. Both stories are interesting in their Thackeraylike pictures of the hollow mockery behind Fifth Avenue society, and in their tragic climaxes; but both are spoiled by the obvious moralizing of Mr. Troy in the final paragraphs.

The second pair of stories deal with duelling. "A Drawing-Room

[20] *Ibid.*, X, 246–251 (Jan., 1855) and XI, 193–196 (July, 1855).

Drama"[21] is brief and pointed, and though the material is that of melodrama, it is handled with such conciseness as not to force the note. Montaigne, jealous of the attentions of a reigning beauty to another man, challenges and kills him, only to learn that the slain man was, in secret, her husband. "The Duel,"[22] which vividly describes an evening gathering at the Chrysanthemum Club in Broadway, builds up its interest step by step to the tragic outcome. Two companions are rivals in love. Drinking leads to tactlessness, tactlessness to insult, insult to giving the lie; the lie is followed by the blow, and the blow by the duel. Pistols unloaded by friends proving ineffective, they resort to swords. One friend kills the other and escapes to Europe. Up to this point the story commands the reader's attention; but when a paragraph is added telling how the victor dies of a broken heart for having killed his friend, the moral is overemphasized and the unity destroyed. Because it stops without moralizing, "A Drawing-Room Drama" shows the better technique. F. L. Pattee says that it is the one bit of O'Brien's art "that its reader does not finish with the last sentence, since it leaves him after the last sentence with a terrible and a strange surmise concerning the woman who has not been charged with guilt."[23]

As a contrast to these stories dealing with the rich and dissipated society of a great city, the three sentimental stories deal with poor but worthy lovers of nature. Of these "Milly Dove"[24] has the most delicate finish of style. In reading it one becomes conscious of other literary voices of the time—it is a Dickenslike idyll in its sentimental tenderness worked out by melodrama; it has the soft, finished cadences of one of Hawthorne's *Mosses from an Old Manse* (1846); it suggests Thackeray in its frequent intrusions of the somewhat genial author; and it contains details of flowers, of music, of panorama mechanisms, of philosophy—all to give an impression of much learning, in the manner of Poe. It is, as Joseph J. Reilly points out, a "sentimental tale of the 'Duchess' variety in which King Cophetua, in the person of the great Alexander Winthrop, falls in love with the beggar maid in the person of Milly Dove."[25] Of course, this pointing out such a wide

[21] *Ibid.*, XI, 397–398 (Aug., 1855).
[22] *Ibid.*, XI, 649–653 (Oct., 1855).
[23] F. L. Pattee, *op. cit.*, p. 158.
[24] *Harper's*, XI, 535–543 (Sept., 1855).
[25] Joseph J. Reilly, "A Keltic Poe," in *The Catholic World*, CX, 751–762 (Mar., 1920), p. 754.

variety of borrowings from sources so dissimilar is in reality calling attention to a type of constructive ability which was O'Brien's.

"Baby Bloom," which came earlier in the year, and "Duke Humphrey's Dinner" and "Sister Anne,"[26] which followed, frequently depart from a strict adherence to the sentimental mood. "Duke Humphrey's Dinner," in fact, contains just as much humor as it does sentiment and pathos; and in a contemporary notice is called, strangely enough, "a racy narrative of fashionable life."[27] It seeks to arouse the reader's sympathy and pity for the young husband and wife, hungry and cold in their garret tenement, who have been used to better things; it would make the reader laugh at their jokes and at the airs they give themselves over the imaginary banquet they consume, while at the same time it would have him become teary at the bravery with which each beguiles his starving senses for the sake of keeping up courage in the other; it asks him to share Richard's glee when he procures two dollars with which to buy himself and wife bread and sausages; and it would have him tearfully rejoice when the long-lost friend unexpectedly appears to repay old debts and supply the young couple with a real dinner. The human sympathy demanded is merely superficial, and, though possible, the coincidence which brings about the denouement is melodramatically forced. The reviewer for *The Critic*, however, considers "Duke Humphrey's Dinner" "the one simple, natural, possible story" in Winter's collection, preferring it to "Mother of Pearl," "The Golden Ingot," and "The Diamond Lens." "This is full of a brightness and pathos which show, if not the burning of genius, at least the warmth of human feeling."[28] Before the year was out Fitz-James had turned this into a one-act play, and after many delays it was produced at Wallack's in the following February.

Both the other stories, "Baby Bloom" and "Sister Anne," have been suspected of being travesties "of the feminine romance so fashionable during the period."[29] In the case of "Sister Anne" this has already been shown to be almost certainly true; but that "Baby Bloom" is travesty seems most unlikely. Sentimental melodrama was fashionable, and Fitz-James O'Brien was a facile complier with fashion. A rural Harlem village is the scene where lives Baby Bloom with her German parents—her father the taciturn

[26] *Harper's*, X, 503–508 (Mar., 1855); XI, 352–357 (Aug.); and XII, 91–96 (Dec.).
[27] *The Home Journal*, Aug. 4, 1855.
[28] *The Critic*, III, 208 (May 2, 1885).
[29] Pattee, *op. cit.*, p. 157.

harness maker, who spends much time over his pipe and his beer, and her fat mother, who busies herself raising chickens (a touch of the sly humor of Irving here). Baby's chief occupation is to be pastorally beautiful, picking flowers, until the carpenter's apprentice has an opportunity to see and fall in love with her. Baby then has an adventure with a maniac ornithologist, who drives her to seek refuge in the woods and pursues her in the most uncanny and terrifying way; and, when she is just about to succumb panic-stricken to his maniacal persecutions, she is rescued by the timely arrival of her loving apprentice.

The part played by the insane ornithologist, the suspense created by the abnormal pursuit, and the terror of uncertainty with which it is followed connect "Baby Bloom" with the occultism of "The Bohemian" and with the supernaturalism of "The Pot of Tulips." Not one of the three characters of "The Bohemian" is normal—the hero who tells the story is money-mad, the heroine is psychically hypersensitive, "a *clairvoyante* of the first water,"[30] while the extraordinary Bohemian is a mesmerist and mind reader. In addition to these elements of the uncanny, the story has the adventure interest of the search for buried treasure, and unusualness of atmosphere is suggested by direct references to Poe's "The Gold Bug." These things make the story interesting; but it is almost spoiled by a too early and too patent suggestion of the catastrophe and by such an obvious pointing of the moral at the end as "Below stairs, in the valise, lay the treasure I had gained. Here, in her grave-clothes, lay the treasure I had lost!"[31] In its ethical undercurrent "it is under obvious obligations to Hawthorne's *The Birthmark*;"[32] as it is in the girl's initial hesitation, in her later acquiescence in risking her life at the instance of the man she loves, and in her sudden death as a punishment for his selfishness.

That O'Brien was familiar with both the prose and verse of Edgar Allan Poe, at least as early as his first year in America, was demonstrated by his imitation of Poe's poetic technique in "Oinea" and by his reference in the discussion thereof to "The Pit and the Pendulum." Though at first O'Brien seems to have been influenced by the weirdness and highly colored romance in the sensational Irish novels of Joseph Sheridan Lefanu, from the time

[30] *Harper's*, XI, 237.
[31] *Ibid.*, p. 242.
[32] J. J. Reilly, *op. cit., loc. cit.*, p. 754.

he wrote "The Bohemian" and "The Pot of Tulips" the methods and moods of Poe became more and more unmistakable in his work.

"The Pot of Tulips"[33] is among the best half dozen of O'Brien's stories. It is a ghost story, smoothly written and convincingly told. It assumes the pose of having been written solely for the purpose of scientific or psychic elucidation; and, by contrast, the terrifying effects are all the more potent. The settings are definitely localized and are entirely acceptable, although a Dutch villa on the Hudson could hardly fail to suggest Sleepy Hollow and Rip Van Winkle. The first element of the unusual is the fanatical jealousy of Mr. Van Koeren, the grandfather. This is followed by the tragic story of his son Alain, by the description of the queerly carved mantelpiece, by the arrangements for the night, and by the appearance of the ghost. The ghost is accompanied by a cold wind, a luminous cloud, and an odor of corpses, and carries in its hands a pot of tulips. The tulips are, of course, the clue to the family mystery, and the working out of the clue forms the last part of the story. The author sticks to his point with extraordinary singleness of purpose, introducing almost nothing to distract the reader's attention. Harry Escott, the narrator, is thoroughly plausible in his mediocrity, and at the end of the story he adds a postscript to the effect that any person "who wishes to investigate this subject, will find an opportunity by addressing a note to Mr. Harry Escott, care of the publishers of this Magazine."[34] That the tale and its postscript were convincing is borne out by the following statement from *Harper's Weekly:* "Scores of letters, and not a few personal applications, were received, asking for means of communicating with Mr. Escott. I remember one young man, who called so often, and was so firmly convinced that in this narrative lay the germs of some great revelation, that I was compelled to tell him that the whole was a pure effort of the imagination. Unfortunately he would not believe me."[35]

Besides the ten stories for *Harper's*, all of which have some intrinsic merit, O'Brien also wrote during 1855 four poems, two reviews, and an essay. All the poems were especially written "For the Evening Post" and appeared over the signature Fitz-James O'Brien within ten days in October.[36] Per-

[33] *Harper's*, XI, 807–814 (Nov., 1855).

[34] *Ibid.*, p. 814. It is misquoted in *H. W.*, VI, 267, and is omitted entirely from Winter, 1881—see p. 354.

[35] *H. W.*, VI, 267.

[36] *The Evening Post*, Oct. 10, 1855; Oct. 19; Oct. 20; and Oct. 22, respectively. Location supplied through the kindness of Charles I. Glicksberg.

haps, because his name was attached, he took more care than usual; at any rate, they are smoothly written, and each successfully evokes a single emotion. "The Song of the Bacchante" is a frank glorification of the joys of life—drinking, loving, and living with Peace—in companionship with the god Bacchus. "The Heath" is described as a sullen moorland which the author dares not approach, because in it lies buried the victim he had murdered. The very next day in "Sing, Linnet, Sing" O'Brien returns to one of his favorite themes, a singing bird; and two days later writes a love poem "To ———," which, however conventional in its devoted dedication to the beloved, achieves its effect through smoothly written quatrains.

Of the two reviews the one for the *Times* attracted considerable attention and is, perhaps, his most thorough piece of critical writing. It is entitled "Alfred Tennyson,"[37] and is a careful analysis and a fair and discerning appraisal of *Maud and Other Poems*, which had but recently appeared. In summing up he finds that, as a whole, *Maud* "lacks coherency and lacks truth," but that "there are some magnificent bits of poetic scorn scattered through the pages" and that "the songs are gems of lyrical composition."

For *Harper's* also O'Brien wrote a review, together with a nondescript article called "Bird Gossip."[38] The latter is one of the four articles referred to in Chapter I as supplying a bit of the Irish background about which he wrote so little. A wandering, gossipy essay written in the easiest of manners, it relates amusing and interesting anecdotes connected with birds of unusual species and refers to various items of bird literature. It appeared in the same number of *Harper's* as did "The Pot of Tulips," O'Brien's best story for the year, and it seems rather obviously to have been written to order as a space filler. A much clearer instance of the fact that O'Brien as a literary Bohemian was frequently reduced to doing hack work and to turning out work on definite commission is furnished by a four-page article which immediately precedes "Milly Dove" in the September issue. Entitled "Your Health!", it is a review of *Letters to the People on Health and Happiness* by Catherine E. Beecher, a book which Harper and Brothers had recently published. The book preaches the attainment of happiness through health and shows how perennial is the interest supplied in our own

[37] *N. Y. Times*, Nov. 13, 1855.
[38] *Harper's*, XI, 820–825 (Nov., 1855).

day by the physical-culture type of magazine. O'Brien's review begins with four paragraphs of florid expatiation upon the beauties of the human body, and is written throughout in an ornate style. It is elaborate in its reform purpose, and especially inveighs against the pale, thin youths on Broadway and the distortion of the female form by tight lacing. It is highly commendatory of the subject matter of the book, yet avoids seeming like a direct advertisement of it. The Harper Brothers could hardly fail to be gratified by such a skilful execution of their order, and Fitz-James would by service well rendered make a little less precarious his foothold on the slippery shores of Bohemia.

Chapter VI

Sentimentalism versus the Macabre

(1856)

It might have been supposed that with his apprentice work done in all the forms for which he was to become known Fitz-James O'Brien would in the year which was to follow (1856) go on and produce some of his best work. Such, however, was not the case. He did not immediately follow up his early successes, and not for two years did he write anything of real importance or show any advance in his art. And yet by the end of 1855 he had written social satire, satirical invective in both prose and verse, literary criticism, plays, and short stories of both the supernatural and sentimental varieties. "The Beauty" contains in its small way satire on the habits and practices of the society of Fifth and Madison Avenues, and is thus closely allied with such verse satires on vicious phases of contemporary life as "The Tenement House," "The Sewing Bird," "The Prize Fight," and especially "The Finishing School" which did not come until 1858. The prose "The Man about Town" papers of 1857 also give vent in their discursive essay style to bits of satirical thrusting. "The Diamond Lens," O'Brien's extravagant masterpiece, did not appear until four years later, and yet in "The Pot of Tulips" he had given evidence of his ability to handle with excellent conviction the tale of supernatural mystery. *Maud* is as carefully thought out a review as any of the criticisms he did for *The Saturday Press* in 1858; *A Gentleman from Ireland* is his best play; and "Milly Dove" is as delicate a handling of the sentimental as he ever accomplished.

The only story in the sentimental genre which at all rivals "Milly Dove" is "Baby Bertie's Christmas." This story, though appearing in the January, 1856, *Harper's*, was written and printed in 1855, and was noticed on December 29 of that year as "a touching tale."[1] A "pathetic and very

[1] *The Home Journal*, Dec. 29, 1855.

pretty love-story," William Winter calls it;[2] and in its kind—a sentimental love story, delicately written, exquisitely finished, consisting entirely of sentiment and religion and love—it is almost perfect. There is nothing to break the sentimental mood, established with the estrangement of the two lovers, built up through the story of the poor but cheerful little invalid, and concluded with the reconciliation of the lovers on Christmas Day at the bedside of the dying child. To be sure the plot now seems conventional and obvious, the mood too frankly tearful, and the religious teaching too complacently Victorian; but in its kind it is almost as good as the Christmas stories of Dickens, which it imitates, and for once O'Brien happily avoids his usual melodramatic denouement depending upon the long arm of coincidence.

The consistency of taste observed by this story lends some color to the claim of John O. Beaty that the author of "Baby Bertie's Christmas" was John Esten Cooke, not Fitz-James O'Brien. Nevertheless, the evidence for O'Brien's authorship is as sound as that for Cooke; and, as it is named in Winter's manuscript list of things collected for the second volume of O'Brien, and as Dr. Guernsey, for a long time editor of *Harper's Monthly* and friend of O'Brien, includes it as one of sixty-six O'Brien items in the Harper's *Index*, it is at least permissible to include it in a general consideration of O'Brien's writings.[3] With this exception his sentimental productions for the year did not appear until the late summer.

"Duke Humphrey's Dinner," however, the sentimental story of the preceding year which contained the largest admixture of humor, had been recognized for its dramatic possibilities soon after its publication in August,

[2] MS list in Charles Romm collection.

[3] In addition to the two O'Brien claims given above the evidence is as follows:—

The Round Table, VII, 365 (June 6, 1868), in its "Notes and Queries" column prints a letter from "L. H. B." dated "West Springfield, Mass., May 23, 1868," in which he gives a list of seventy O'Brien titles, for assistance in the compilation of which he thanks the editors of *Harper* and *Putnam*. *The Round Table* received and printed a reply to L. H. B. from "R. Y." stating that he knew definitely that John Esten Cooke was the author of "Baby Bertie's Christmas." For this correction L. H. B., (VIII, 159, Sept. 5, 1868) thanks R. Y., but adds "The mistake was not mine, however, as I derived my information from Dr. Guernsey." *An Index to Harper's New Monthly Magazine*, (Volumes I. to L.: From June, 1850, to May, 1875. New York: 1875) includes under O'Brien's name sixty-six titles, the second of which is "Baby Bertie's Christmas." Under Cooke's name it lists twenty-three titles, of which this is not one. In John O. Beaty, *John Esten Cooke, Virginian*, 1922, p. 58, it is listed as one of nine prose articles for 1856:—" 'Baby Bertie's Christmas' is . . . very closely akin to 'Peony' and *Ellie*." Also see "Bibliography," *ibid.*, p. 167.

had been turned into a play, and was in rehearsal at Wallack's theatre by the fifteenth of December.[4] The production, however, was postponed so many times that when it actually was presented on February 4, 1856,[5] it was made the butt of facetious remarks by a number of reviewers. The *Times* review after rather copious bantering contains the following paragraph:

"Duke Humphrey's Dinner" is properly called a sketch, and as such is entitled to much praise. It is carefully written, with a little sentiment, a little pathos, and a little fun in it; perhaps a trifle too much of the first named commodity. A piece of this character requires peculiar acting, and it is scarcely probable that any artists can realize all that the text suggests. MR. LESTER as *Richard Birdoon* was in many respects excellent, but he missed some of the points, and especially so in the introduction, where suicide is hinted more in seriousness than in fun. In the sham dinner, however, he was admirable. MRS. HOEY'S *rôle* is a rather embarrassing one, but she is capable of making it eminently attractive if she will eschew all melodramatic effects.[6]

This sympathetic criticism contains remarks that indicate an intimate knowledge of the play, of its delicate shifting of moods, and of the subtlety of acting requisite to bring out all its best points. No better statement could have been made by the author himself had he seen his parts lose some of their effectiveness through the inadequacy of the actors, or had he been subjected to what he felt were undiscerning remarks of the critics. Indeed, it is probable that Fitz-James O'Brien wrote the review himself: the attitudes and stylistic peculiarities contained in other parts of the notice are typical of him, and two years later he wrote a similarly facetious review of his *A Gentleman from Ireland* for *The Saturday Press.*

But O'Brien—or at least the *Times* reviewer whose partisanship is under suspicion—was not the only person to praise *Duke Humphrey's Dinner.* The *Herald*, *The New York Picayune*, and *Frank Leslie's Illustrated Newspaper* all contain fairly elaborate reviews of the sketch. The *Herald* says, "The piece was well acted, and has the merit of being original in its treatment";[7] the *Picayune* calls it "a beautiful combination of the pathetic and

[4] Notice in *N. Y. Picayune*, Dec. 22, 1855. (For week ending Dec. 15).

[5] See announcement in *N. Y. Times*, Feb. 4, 1856; advertisement in *N. Y. Herald*, s. d.; J. N. Ireland, *op. cit.*, II, 646; T. Allston Brown, *op. cit.*, I, 487, where it is called *Dick Humphrey's Dinner;* Lester Wallack, *Memories of Fifty Years*, p. 217, where Richard Burdon [*sic*] is listed as one of his parts; and G. C. D. Odell, *op. cit.*, VI, 444.

[6] *N. Y. Times*, Feb. 5, 1856.

[7] *N. Y. Herald*, Feb. 5, 1856.

humorous" and adds that it "deserved the cordial reception which it met";[8] while *Leslie's* refers to it as "a pleasing dramatic sketch" which "was perfectly successful."[9] In spite of such favorable comment the piece was not so successful as its author must have hoped, and was withdrawn before the week was out.[10]

Nevertheless, O'Brien continued to write for the theatre, as the following notice from *The Home Journal* indicates:

A NEW PLAY AT WALLACK'S

—"The Cup and the Lip" is the suggestive title of a three act play, about to be brought out at Wallack's. It is written by Fitz James O'Brien, the author of several capital pieces. "The Cup and the Lip" is a defence of "good society," attempting to show that our "first families" are not entirely composed of ignorant grocers and successful dressmakers. That will be refreshing.[11]

If the author of *Duke Humphrey's Dinner* was disturbed and irritated by postponements which put off the production of a one-act sketch from December to February, he must have been much more upset by delays which held up his first three-act play until its production was abandoned entirely.

O'Brien's fame as a playwright survives on the strength of a single play, *A Gentleman from Ireland;* and the preeminence and continued popularity of this play were recognized in the same year that saw the comparative failure of *Duke Humphrey's Dinner*. The cover page of the *Picayune* for September 20 consists of a cartoon by Frank Bellew, entitled "Effect of the Dramatic Copyright Law." It shows a "Rush of dramatists to the office of the clerk of the District Court of the United States for the Southern District of New York." Each playwright has in his hands his most popular play, except John Brougham and Dion Boucicault, whose plays are so many that they bring them in baskets. Benjamin A. Baker's hand conceals most of the title of his play, but Cornelius Mathews bears quite plainly his "Witchcraft." Charles Gayler is presenting "Taking the Chances," while the offering of E. G. P. Wilkins, with his sharp features and spindle-shanks, cannot be seen. O'Brien advances in the center foreground, grasping in

[8] *N. Y. Picayune*, Feb. 16, 1856.

[9] *Frank Leslie's Illustrated Newspaper*, Feb. 16, 1856.

[10] The play was repeated on Feb. 5, 6, and 7. See notices in *N. Y. Herald* for these dates.

[11] *The Home Journal*, Dec. 27, 1856.

both hands a copy of "Gentleman from Ireland," and is pictured with the prominent nose, heavy mustaches, and small chin that his friends have described. Of course, the cartoonist who so prominently pictured Fitz-

EFFECT OF THE DRAMATIC COPYRIGHT LAW

Rush of Dramatists to the Office of the Clerk of the District Court of the United States for the Southern District of New York

James as one of the seven outstanding playwrights of America was showing but natural prejudice in favor of his closest friend.

Less than a month after *Duke Humphrey's Dinner* was presented at

Wallack's, O'Brien gave further evidence of his extraordinary versatility of style in a story which, neither sentimental nor macabre, is almost perfect in its delicate, whimsical atmosphere of Oriental magic. It is called "The Dragon Fang Possessed by the Conjuror Piou-Lu"[12] and, set in China, is delightful in its humorous imitation of the flowery epithets of ornate Chinese style, while the magical occurrences are accepted entirely without question and are treated with perfect naïveté. It is unfortunate that O'Brien never repeated the method used here and that "The Dragon Fang," therefore, remains unique in the list of his writings; for the story is exquisite in finish, a gem of its type, and, as Henry Seidel Canby says, shows the influence of Lamb or De Quincey.[13]

After this O'Brien's interest turned once more to a comic magazine, and his hand is found in the pages of *Yankee Doodle; or Young America* from March until June.[14] Its editor was O'Brien's friend, Charles Gayler, the playwright, and it had as its artists his intimate associates, Hoppin and Charles Rosenberg, the former of whom illustrated almost as many of his poems as did Frank Bellew and with the latter of whom he later collaborated on a play. External evidence for the titles of O'Brien's contributions to *Young America* is entirely lacking; but many sporadic squibs and some of the verse may easily have been his. Among the former are "Bachelor's Buttons. By Benedick" and "Fashionable Lexicon," which consist of series of punning definitions exactly in the manner of the earliest items he sent to Philp's *The Family Friend;*[15] while even more certainly his are two articles written in florid style describing the seasonal changes upon the approach of spring, the details given as if they were notes on the latest fashions. "The Spring Fashions" and "Beauties of the Vernal Season"[16] are almost identical in style and subject matter with two letters O'Brien wrote to friends when in the spring of 1862 he was sick and wounded and under the influence of strong opiates. Under such circumstances it is not uncommon for the mind to revert to past performances, and these early *jeux d'esprit* seem to have

[12] *Harper's*, XII, 519–526 (Mar., 1856).

[13] See H. S. Canby, *The Short Story in English*, N. Y., 1909, p. 282.

[14] For details about *Young America* see F. L. Mott, *A History of American Magazines, 1850–1865*, pp. 182–183.

[15] *Young America*, I, 95 (Mar. 1, 1856), and I, 144 (Mar. 22). "The Counterfeit Joke Detector," which analyzes puns, is much in the same vein—see *ibid.*, I, 58 (Feb. 2).

[16] *Ibid.*, I, 154 (Mar. 29, 1856), and I, 161 (Apr. 5).

furnished the basis for his later gaiety. Quite like Fitz-James also are two numbers of "The Green Curtain,"[17] in each of which a prominent actor, presumably criticizing himself and his art, so overpraises himself that his foibles and shortcomings are satirically emphasized.

Conjecture ceases with the internal evidence which positively identifies O'Brien as the author of a series of sixteen "Brown Studies" appearing in the magazine each week from March 1 to June 14.[18] In the second number the orchestra breaks "into the Ornithorhyncus waltz,"[19] and the whole group satirizes once more (as he had done in *The Lantern*) the sycophantic sexton of Grace Church and the social circle of Fifth and Madison Avenues. Each number, besides holding up to ridicule some particular viciousness or inanity of social life, tells part of a story centering around the social exquisite Bleecker Lounge, his rival Tom Brevier, the society belle Rose de Chine, the writer Petronius Whither, and the celebrated female astrologer Madame Ponnibell. It is this continued story that keeps one reading through the sharp attacks on expensive balls, on the wrecking of youth and health by all-night dancing, on the desire for foreign travel and the aping of European manners, on social slights and polite society's methods of avenging them.[20] These are only a few of the shams and abuses hit at; some, like duelling and Madame Cancan's fashionable boarding school, O'Brien had already inveighed against, some he would return to in later work with greater force and sharper points. For these weekly tirades are a little heavy-footed, a little lacking in the easy sparkle and clever turn of phrase with which Fitz-James often handled such subjects. They give the impression of having been a chore.

As a relief from this kind of writing Fitz-James early in May wrote two poems for *The Evening Post* which give evidence that he still regarded poetry with the same high seriousness manifested so early in his verses for *The Cork Magazine* and more recently in those for the *Post* of the preceding October. "An Episode,"[21] nicely rounded and rhythmically smooth, remi-

[17] *Ibid.*, I, 42 (Jan. 26, 1856) about W. E. Burton; and I, 149 (Mar. 29) about William Rufus Blake.

[18] See Bibliography.

[19] *Young America*, I, 111 (Mar. 8, 1856).

[20] See respectively *Young America*, I, 111 (Mar. 8, 1856); 123 (Mar. 15); 135 (Mar. 22); 172 (Apr. 12); 243 (May 24).

[21] *The Evening Post*, May 1, 1856. Autograph MS signed in New York Public Library; 2 sheets—9 stanzas on 1st sheet, 5 on 2nd.

niscently reflects upon a summer wooing aboard ship, of which nothing now remains but "a faded flower between the leaves" and "one in my heart that will not fade"; while "The Lake"[22] builds up through elaborately ornate descriptive details a picture of an ideal bit of natural scenery:

For the soul of a poet is sheltered here,
Wrapped in the joy of a perfect sphere;
And all the beauty he loved and prized,
Is here ineffably realized.

So Shelley, outlawed by dogmatists
From the orthodox Heaven that for them exists,
In this fairy realm has built his throne,
And made a Paradise of his own.

In the July number of *Putnam's Magazine* appeared a story which, though it has been attributed to O'Brien, may not be his; the weight of evidence, which at best is slight, could be made to throw the balance in favor of O'Brien or of Lucretia P. Hale. "The Spider's Eye"[23] is based on the text that there is more romance and excitement in everyday life than in three volumes of the wildest incident an author can invent. An odd preachment this for a writer whose chief power lies in concocting weird stories, were it not for the fact that the means through which the hero learns the conversations admitting him to the private affairs of ordinary mortals is in itself eery and extraordinary. By an unusual set of circumstances he finds himself in the sound-center of a well-filled theatre, enabled to read "the unspoken thoughts of those around him." Such application of the pseudoscientific to the increase of interest in fiction had been made with great artistry by Poe; but the inspiration for this particular story, as Dorothy Scarborough points out, was "The Owl's Ear" by Erckmann-Chatrian.

[22] *Ibid.*, May 6, 1856. Both these poems are signed "Fitz-James O'Brien." Their location was kindly supplied by Charles I. Glicksberg.

[23] *Putnam's Magazine*, VIII, 11–18 (July, 1856). Dorothy Scarborough in *The Supernatural in Modern English Fiction*, N. Y. and London, 1917, pp. 62 and 274, notes, lists this story as having been written by Lucretia P. Hale. It appears, however, in *Stories by American Authors*, New York, 1884, III, pp. 5–29, under the name Fitz James O'Brien, both on the title-page and on p. 5 under the title. On the other hand this same volume is listed in *The American Catalogue, 1876–1884*, 1885, with, "No. 3. *The Spider's Eye*, by L. P. Hale"; and when it was republished in 1898 the name Lucretia P. Hale appears in both places. In the copy in the library at the University of Pennsylvania Hale's name is crossed out in both places and O'Brien's written in, and in the card catalogue there the story is under O'Brien's name.

The author here "applies the laws of acoustics to mentality and spirituality, making astounding discoveries."[24]

By this time it was summer; so in order to escape the heat of the city Fitz-James visited at the home of his poet friend George Arnold, in Strawberry Hills, New Jersey. He went there frequently and found vacation retreats in other nearby places, with the result that New Jersey supplies the setting for two of his stories printed in the fall. If the converse were true, the setting for a third story would indicate that O'Brien had spent part of the summer in northern New York. Whether or not such was the case, he returned to his journalistic job after a considerable vacation, and his poems and stories appeared in the magazines throughout the fall.

Two of the stories, "How Nellie Lee Was Pawned" and "Mary Burnie of the Mill,"[25] are sentimental ones. The first of these is told in the first person, and begins with numerous circumstantial details about the prosaic life of the author. This method of introduction O'Brien had used before—in the preceding year in "The Bohemian," "The Duel," and "The Pot of Tulips"—and with it he was to achieve some of his best effects—in "The Diamond Lens," "Mother of Pearl," "The Lost Room," "The Golden Ingot," "My Wife's Tempter," and "What Was It?" In this way the reader is beguiled by a series of minor details and by the commonplaceness of the author and the setting to an unconscious acceptance of the later uncanny, bizarre, or supernatural incidents which form the nucleus of the story. A century and a half earlier the method had been perfected by Daniel Defoe, notably in *The Apparition of Mrs. Veal* (1705), but with the reintroduction of the supernatural into fiction with *The Castle of Otranto* (1764) and *The Mysteries of Udolpho* (1794) the practice had been to assume tacitly and immediately the reader's belief in the miraculous and the superhuman. This assumption continued to affect the writing of the romantic period of the early nineteenth century, as seen in the poetry of Coleridge and the horrors of "Monk" Lewis (1795) and Charles Robert Maturin (1820), until it reached a culmination of artistic handling in *The Masque of the Red Death* (1842), *The Tell-Tale Heart* (1843), and others of the grotesque tales of Poe. Fitz-James O'Brien, trying his hand at the story of weird and

[24] Dorothy Scarborough, *The Supernatural in Modern English Fiction*, p. 274, courtesy of G. P. Putnam's Sons.

[25] *Harper's*, XIII, 500–504 (Sept., 1856) and XIII, 782–784 (Nov., 1856).

grotesque atmosphere at a time when the impulse of the romantic movement was on the wane, could not improve on Poe; and so, while imitating many of Poe's technical devices, he rediscovered and added what may be regarded as the modern touch of the commonplace setting. Thus he forms an important connecting link between the tale of terror and the methods of modern realism.

In the two stories at present under discussion, however, this method is made to subserve the purpose of sentimentalism rather than that of the macabre. For "How Nellie Lee Was Pawned" it is almost as necessary an introduction as it is for the weirdness of "The Lost Room" (1858); for the circumstance of the girl who was pawned by her artist father in order that he might raise money to buy canvas is as difficult of acceptance as is the tale of the man who, in his own house, one night extraordinarily finds his way into a mysterious room which he can never discover again. "Nellie Lee," therefore, begins with details of the author's many dealings with the pawnbrokers of Chicory Street. As he is on his way to the shop of Lazarus Levi to see what he can raise on a chessboard, he tells incidents of his former life in London and in Paris and of having at one time written an article for *Blackwood's Magazine*.[26] This time the author calls himself not Harry Escott but M. Papillote; and M. Papillote, neatly finished though his story is, is revealed as not nearly so skilled a raconteur as Escott, who was responsible for the uncanny relation of the mysteries of "The Pot of Tulips" and is used again as the narrator of "What Was It?"

"Mary Burnie of the Mill" also bears but little scrutiny in comparison with other O'Brien stories, though if compared with those of most of his contemporaries it stands high. Contrary to his usual practice in the sentimental type, O'Brien ended this story tragically; but, in accord with his practice, he definitely localized the idyllic setting and placed the mill on the Passaic River, New Jersey, thirty miles below its source. Here, at the overheard suggestion of Nellie Bryce, Mary Burnie, her rival, drowns herself in the milldam, so that she will not be a drag upon the man she loves. The moral at the end is as offensive as usual—Nellie (like the heroine of "The Beauty," a product of Madame Cancan's finishing school) is revealed as essentially a murderess, and when her hero is butchered in one of the Central American wars, she comes to a realization of the justice of heaven.

[26] See *Ibid.*, XIII, 501–502.

Not only in prose, but also in verse—though here even less adequately—O'Brien was, in compliance with a constant demand of the magazine readers of the eighteen-fifties, working out the sentimental vein. In "When We Husked the Corn"[27] the husband on his silver jubilee recalls the days of his wooing. It was corn-husking time, and the climax comes as follows:

> Away you fled, and I pursued,
> Till all too faint you were to warn;
> And—know you not how well I wooed
> A husking of the corn?

"How It Happened"[28] is also a reminiscence of early love (probably they all hark back to "John Anderson, My Jo" and the older songs that suggested it, and will remain perennially popular, as the songs "When You and I Were Young, Maggie" and "Silver Threads among the Gold" would seem to indicate). It is neither good nor bad, simply typical, and ends on the same key as the above:

> And now the white snow, come again,
> Once more peeps through our window-pane,
> And Ben and I sit side by side,
> Nor has the flame we burned with died.

Such obvious, flat conclusions to such pallidly sentimental verses make one thankful that O'Brien indulged in so few tender poems; and it is a relief to turn to even such a trifle as "The Crystal Bell,"[29] a story in which magic and oddity supply the keynote for a short dream. The author finds himself in possession of a bell which tinkles when anyone tells him an untruth. With it he tests the girl he loves; the bell tinkles. He denounces her; she smashes the bell; he wakes up; and the story ends, "I never told Annie Gray that I had ever doubted her even in a dream, until we had been a month married."

Young Tom Bailey Aldrich, O'Brien's early and always intimate friend, had in 1855 won his first popular success with the "Ballad of Babie Bell," with the result that during the summer of 1856 he found himself, at the age

[27] *Ibid.*, XIII, 382–383 (Aug., 1856).
[28] *Ibid.*, XIV, 56 (Dec., 1856).
[29] *Ibid.*, XIV, 88–91 (Dec., 1856).

of twenty, practically in control of Willis's paper *The Home Journal*.[30] In need of a little more material to fill his columns, Aldrich turned to O'Brien; and the latter, thus put in line for an additional paid contribution or two, replied as follows:

Waverley House, Madison, N. J.,[31]
Sept. (something or other), Tuesday.

Dear Sir: I send you a poem. If I finish another before I go to bed to-night, I will enclose it also. If you do not find it, conclude that it is not finished. The one I send is a ballad, horrible and indigestible.

Make such corrections as you think fit, preserving carefully, at the same time, the language, spelling, punctuation, and arrangement of the verses. Anything else you find "out of kilter" you can alter.

Seriously, if you can improve, do it fearlessly. It is the Augur who speaks to Tarquin. "Cut boldly"; an *auger* who trusts that he does not *bore*.

Paradox as it may seem, "the Fall" has already arisen. I saw her veil fluttering on the hills the other day, and some of the earliest and most servile of the trees have already put on her livery. Come out and be presented...

Yours sincerely,
Fitz-James de Courcy O'Brien.[32]

The poem referred to is indeed "a ballad, horrible and indigestible," which appeared in *The Home Journal* under the title "What Befell."[33] That the second poem was finished that night before the letter was posted is also likely, for in its very next issue *The Home Journal* printed a second weird ballad, "By the Alders."[34] These are two of the three macabre pieces that O'Brien wrote during the year 1856, all three, seemingly, having been written about the same time and probably from the same place, his New Jersey retreat. "A Terrible Night," a story published in the October *Harper's*, is the third treatment of the gruesome and supernatural.

The nine stanzas of "What Befell" tell of a ghost or demon that snatched

[30] For details of his rise in the journalistic world see Greenslet, *op. cit.*, pp. 28 ff.

[31] In "The Crystal Bell" the scene is the Hominy House, Hopskotch, N. J. See *Harper's*, XIV, 88.

[32] Quoted from Winter, *Old Friends*, p. 103. The signature has been referred to on p. 9 and n. 21.

[33] *The Home Journal*, Oct. 18, 1856. Winter, 1881, pp. 73–74, prints "What Befell" under the title "The Demon of the Gibbet."

[34] *Ibid.*, Oct. 25, 1856.

an eloping bride from the seat behind her lover as he spurred his horse "hard by the terrible gallows-tree." It is technically correct, but it fails to convey the horrible impression that was intended. "By the Alders" is weirdly and uncannily suggestive of evil impulses and of crime. A woman led her lover (who tells the story) to the riverside where she flung her babe into the water. For a moment he hid his head in agony, but when he looked up to cry, "Still loved, a pardon!" she was not there.

> But I saw a dint in the weedy bed,
> And I felt a ghost in the troubled air!

If the reader can safely get over the third line,

> She gripped my arm, she clutched my hair,

without ridicule, the gruesome atmosphere of the poem will establish itself.

The pity of it is that O'Brien's verse so often contains lines of just this sort; his sense of humor when he was writing poetry often failed him. His prose is always more successful, and "A Terrible Night" is no exception. It is a ghastly tale of lonesomeness and fear in the woods of northern New York, done with tremendous effect. The tension of suspense is most powerfully worked up and culminates in the horror of a most startling and awful surprise ending—an ending worthy of Frank R. Stockton, O. Henry, or any other of our most skillful technicians of the short story. In its dream horror it is the best of O'Brien's tales up to the time of its appearance in October; but it was followed in November by such a weak piece of sentimentalism as "Mary Burnie of the Mill," and in December by such an inconsequential treatment of dreams as "The Crystal Bell." That O'Brien resorted so constantly to the flippantly satirical or the flabbily sentimental when he could be so vivid in the macabre was due to the unreliability of his taste and to his lack of self-discipline and unsteadiness of application, even in the field where he excelled. Also, as he was a free lance in the journalistic field, and as a certain volume of production with selling qualities was necessary to keep him alive, he turned out what came easiest to him and what would have the readiest and widest market. In the decade of the eighteen-fifties this was romantic sentimentalism; so for a time O'Brien joined the ranks of Donald Grant Mitchell and Thomas Bailey Aldrich (the best of the sentimentalists) and turned out "sob stuff," until, with the publication of "The

Diamond Lens" (1858) and "What Was It?" (1859), his unique gift in the macabre was recognized.[35]

[35] O'Brien's achievement for 1856 as just discussed seems a slight one; and it will be recalled that the statement was made that from November, 1853, "until the month before his death, with a few intermissions, almost every number of *Harper's Monthly* contained something from his pen." As there are a number of months in the 1856 volumes of *Harper's* for which no O'Brien pieces have been identified, it becomes a great temptation to hazard conjectures; and after careful consideration of the style and subject matter the following surmises are offered. The fertile Fitz-James may very possibly have contributed the stories "Milicent" in June, and "Twice in Love" in August. Three poems which were originally included in this list of possibles, "When We Husked the Corn," "What Santa Claus Brought Me" and "My Valentine," have been since, through other sources, definitely assigned to O'Brien.

CHAPTER VII

PFAFF'S, AND "THE MAN ABOUT TOWN"

(1857)

As far as the records show, it is in his life as a social being rather than in the results of his literary production that interest in Fitz-James O'Brien centers during the year 1857. The popularity of Pfaff's and its congenial circle was by this time well-established, a smaller group of intimate friends had organized a club called "The Bees," and O'Brien and three of his friends were initiated into a college fraternity. His most prominent writings for the year, columns he contributed regularly to *Harper's Weekly* upon its founding early in January, are papers interesting as journalism rather than as literature. They appeared under the heading "The Man about Town" and as a series reflect more plainly than anything else he wrote the dynamic quality of the man and his vivid personality, and they thoroughly reveal him in his New York setting with a wide variety of interests and a tremendous gusto for participation in them.

The favorite rendezvous of the Bohemians was "Pfaff's." This restaurant and saloon of Charles Pfaff, who came from Germany to America in 1855, and who shortly afterwards set up his establishment in the cellar of 645 Broadway, a few doors above Bleecker Street on the west side, was for them a meeting place where bright friends gathered, full of a zest for life and of enthusiasm for the latest literary venture. Conviviality was a part of the atmosphere, and a few of the habitués, Fitz-James among them, drank too much and too frequently. Henry Clapp discovered the place one day in 1856, when, in company with O'Brien, he lounged into it and "was so delighted with the beer served him that he straightway sounded its praises among his comrades."[1] Pfaff's thereupon became the favorite resort of the Bohemians, and a table around which thirty could sit was reserved for their use. Nearly all of them were writers for *The Saturday Press* or for *Vanity Fair*, which were established a year or two later, and the group held pretty well together until the failure of these journals and the advent of the Civil War. Walt Whitman, Thomas Bailey Aldrich, and William Dean Howells

[1] Rufus Rockwell Wilson, *New York, Old and New*, 3d ed., Phila. and London, 1909, II, 141.

have, among others, recorded their impressions of Pfaff's, and their accounts of the evenings spent there vary widely as to mood and as to detail presented. Whitman had once planned to make use of Pfaff's as the subject of a poem to be called "The Two Vaults":

The vault at Pfaff's where the drinkers and laughers meet to eat and drink and carouse,
While on the walk immediately overhead, pass the myriad feet of Broadway
As the dead in their graves, are underfoot hidden
And the living pass over them, recking not of them,

Laugh on Laughters!
Drink on Drinkers!
Bandy the jest! Toss the theme from one to another![2]

He also described the place and its proprietor in an interview published in *The Brooklyn Daily Eagle* in 1886:

I used to go to Pfaff's nearly every night. It used to be a pleasant place to go in the evening after taking a bath and finishing the work of the day. When it began to grow dark Pfaff would politely invite everybody who happened to be sitting in the cave he had under the sidewalk to some other part of the restaurant. There was a long table extending the length of this cave; and as soon as the Bohemians put in an appearance Henry Clapp would take a seat at the head of this table. I think there was as good talk around that table as took place anywhere in the world. Clapp was a very witty man. FitzJames O'Brien was very bright. Ned Wilkins, who used to be the dramatic critic of the Herald, was another bright man. There were between twenty-five and thirty journalists, authors, artists and actors who made up the company that took possession of the cave under the sidewalk.[3]

These are kindly glimpses, and they are corroborated by a report of Thomas Donaldson from his conversations with Whitman. The words are Whitman's:

At the old Pfaff's the food was well cooked, German method, and cheap; the ale (beer was but coming in then) good, and other liquid refreshments healthy. There

[2] Emory Holloway, *The Uncollected Poetry and Prose of Walt Whitman*, Garden City, N. Y. and Toronto, 1921, II, 92, reprinted by permission from Doubleday, Doran and Company, Inc.

[3] *The Brooklyn Daily Eagle*, July 11, 1886. (Parts of it are quoted by Oscar Lovell Triggs in *Selections from the Prose and Poetry of Walt Whitman*, Boston, 1898, pp. xxvi–xxvii; and by Leon Bazalgette, *Walt Whitman The Man and His Work*, tr. by Ellen FitzGerald, 1920, p. 76).

was no formality—"Bohemia" sat around in groups. It is difficult at this distance to recall all who dwelt in "Bohemia." . . . It took hard work and merit to have full membership. The top lights recognized themselves, and made a bit of an inside clique or cabal. I can recall John Swinton, Stoddard, R. H. Wilkins, Fitzjames O'Brien, Henry Clapp, Oakley Hall, Stanley, Mullin, Wood, John Brougham, and Arnold among the leaders. Ada Clare and Daisy Sheppard were among the women of "Bohemia." I was very friendly with Ada Clare. She was brilliant, bright, and handsome. She went on the stage, I think, and then melted out of sight. Pfaff's "Bohemia" was never reported, and more the sorrow. What wit, humor, repartee, word wars, and sometimes bad blood! The "Count Joannes"—George Jones, the actor—used to come there; and an able man he was, barring the "Count." Many actors afterward stars, but then in the great stock companies of the New York theatres, were frequent visitors.[4]

Thomas Bailey Aldrich in the mocking sentimentalism of his verses reflects one mood of the place, the touch of exaggeration giving a delightful turn to the last three lines:

At the Café

We were all very merry at Pfaff's. Did you think
While I laughed with the rest, just a trifle too gay,
That ma mignonne was false, that I buried my friend,
That my castles in Spain had been plundered that day—
Did you think?

. . .

You will kill me with laughter, some day, you dear owl!
I was happy that night, though the girl was a cheat:
Could I grieve for a flirt, when the man that I loved
Was so sweetly at rest from his head to his feet—
Did you think?

T.B.A.[5]

Howells, in a very different mood, writing of his arrival in New York, says:

That very night I went to the beer-cellar, once very far up Broadway, where I was given to know that the Bohemian nights were smoked and quaffed away. . . . I felt that as a contributor and at least a brevet Bohemian I ought not to go home without visiting the famous place, and witnessing if I could not share the revels

[4] Thomas Donaldson, *op. cit.*, p. 206.

[5] *Vanity Fair*, I, 12 (Dec. 31, 1859).

of my comrades. As I neither drank beer nor smoked, my part in the carousal was limited to a German pancake, which I found they had very good at Pfaff's, and to listening to the whirling words of my commensals, at the long board spread for the Bohemians in a cavernous space under the pavement. There were writers for the *Saturday Press* and for *Vanity Fair* (a hopefully comic paper of that day), and some of the artists who drew for the illustrated periodicals. Nothing of their talk remains with me, but the impression remains that it was not so good talk as I had heard in Boston. At one moment of the orgy, which went but slowly for an orgy, we were joined by some belated Bohemians whom the others made a great clamor over; I was given to understand they were just recovered from a fearful debauch; their locks were still damp from the wet towels used to restore them, and their eyes were very frenzied. I was presented to these types, who neither said nor did anything worthy of their awful appearance, but dropped into seats at the table, and ate of the supper with an appetite that seemed poor. I stayed hoping vainly for worse things till eleven o'clock, and then I rose and took my leave of a literary condition that had distinctly disappointed me.[6]

William Winter, who in 1860 was himself fresh from Boston, in commenting on these statements of Howells, suggests that the "orgy" was the result of "the fine fancy and fertile invention that have made Mr. Howells everywhere illustrious," and adds that "the 'types' whom he met at Pfaff's Cave, and by whom he was 'distinctly disappointed,' were quite as 'distinctly disappointed' by him. They thought him a prig."[7]

Howells is mild, however, compared with an article of 1864 on the "Dramatic Critics in New York" containing the following tirade:

The leading male professors [of irregular living] fell upon Bohemianism, pipes, lager-beer, and literature, as so many means for assuaging their sorrows. . . . Out of this mass of moral and physical corruption has come for years the greater portion of "Dramatic Criticism" in New York. What it has been the public well know. Its low, egotistic, unfair, malicious character; its blind partialities and undying hates; its brazen ignorance and insulting familiarity, have given it wide notoriety, and brought upon it equally wise contempt. Its writers—the actual inner priesthood of the Cyprian Temple—have generally been "smart young men," as the phrase goes, who . . . have been flattered by the *clique* that literature was their forte: the bait was taken, and the neophyte rapidly rushed through a course of lager-beer flattery, oysters, and theatres (at his expense), until he was duly hatched as a professor of arts in the society. Now and then one has contrived,

[6] W. D. Howells, *op. cit.*, pp. 71–73.
[7] Winter, *Old Friends*, pp. 91–92.

by strong will, to resist the Siren, and has escaped, as Lot did from Sodom, just in time to save health and reputation; but to the greater number the first descent of the steps in Broadway near Bleecker Street had proved that Dante's inscription over the door of hell ought to be set up there.[8]

Abandonment of hope was not the mood, however, with which most of the young men descended the steps to Pfaff's cellar, nor did it seem like hell to them; and the statements of two of the participants give touches of especial intimacy to the group that gathered almost nightly about the large table there. One is a diary note by Edmund Clarence Stedman which, written at the time, gives a sense of life to what in many of the later accounts do not get beyond the point of being mere names. "Supper at Pfaff's cellar, Broadway, 1860; Present: Clapp, Jr., Arnold, O'Brien, Wood, Wilkins, Ada Clare, Jenny Danforth, House, Winter, Whitman, Artemus Ward (Browne), Aldrich, Stedman."[9] There they are, a definite table full, fourteen of them, on one particular evening, and for a moment they are no longer a mere generalization.

The other item is even more vivid and represents a unique experience. It was my fortune to meet in Granby, Connecticut, on August 20, 1927, A. D. Shattuck, the artist, one of the charter members of the National Academy of Design, known especially for his canvases of cattle and sheep. This ninety-five-year-old gentleman, still in full possession of his faculties, was both pleased and proud to recall the days of his youthful ambitions, when as a young man he was studying art in New York City before the Civil War. His closest friend was also the intimate friend and companion of Fitz-James—Thomas Bailey Aldrich. These three—the two New Hampshire boys and the Irishman, "A.D.", "Fitz", and "Tom"—were often together, and though the meetings were sometimes in Shattuck's studio, sometimes in Aldrich's rooms, the usual get-together was at Pfaff's for

[8] *The Round Table*, I, 43–44 (Jan. 2, 1864). *The Round Table* printed its first number Saturday, Dec. 19, 1863.

[9] Laura Stedman and George M. Gould, *op. cit.*, I, 207. Besides this list of Stedman's those of Howells (see p. 99), and Whitman have already been given. In addition to these an article, "Charles Pfaff of 'Bohemia' Fame Dead," in *N. Y. Tribune*, Apr. 25, 1890, lists Olive Logan, Frank Bellew, and Augustin Daly; and "Death of Charles I. Pfaff," *N. Y. Times*, Apr. 26, 1890, adds John Winthrop, Georges Clemenceau, Nat Childs, William E. Marshall, Max Strakosch, Charles G. Halpine (Miles O'Reilly), and Thomas Dunn English. Besides these William Winter, *Old Friends*, pp. 64–66, includes Charles Dawson Shanly, N. G. Shepherd, Charles D. Gardette, Launt Thompson, George Boughton, and Sol Eytinge, Jr.

supper. Launt Thompson, the sculptor, was at that time an intimate also, though later most sadly he drank himself to death. Mrs. Shattuck, active at ninety, shared her husband's recollections of Aldrich, who was best man at their wedding, and of Thompson, who was a groomsman. "Gay, one of the gayest of the lot, O'Brien was, and he could write so easily. One December he turned out a sketch for the *Times*—almost without effort it was—and received a hundred dollars for it, a nice sum to have coming in about Christmas time." Mr. Shattuck went oftenest to Pfaff's during the life of *The Saturday Press* (started October 23, 1858), because Clapp, the editor, found that the most convenient place for a daily meeting with his assistant, Aldrich.

Whitman, though he frequently came to Pfaff's, was older than Shattuck, Thompson, Aldrich, and O'Brien and did not belong to their club. Besides he was different and did conspicuous, uncouth things. His beard and his open shirt made him noticeable; his friendly hobnobbing with the stage drivers showed a vulgarity of taste inexplicable to the younger men of the Bohemian group; and his habit of riding up and down Broadway on the tops of the omnibuses beside the driver was—well, one simply would never think of such a thing.[10]

This conversation with the old gentleman, who in his striving young manhood, nearly seventy years before, ate his suppers in Pfaff's dingy basement at the same table with Fitz-James has given the freshness of present reality to the whole Pfaff group.

Pfaff "was a model host, and personally looked after the comfort of each of his guests. He had a cook in his service who could prepare the large German pancake, or 'pfanne-kuchen,' and beefsteak to perfection, and hundreds of people used to visit his place to taste these edibles, drink his famous 'best' Rhine wine, and get a look at the lions of Bohemia."[11] The earliest of these was Henry Clapp, their brilliant and erratic King;[12] a later one was Georges Clemenceau, afterwards premier of France, who, in New York for a couple of years beginning in 1866, was vainly trying to make a living as a

[10] The statements in the two paragraphs just ended are almost entirely indirect quotations from the words of Mr. Shattuck written down two hours after my visit with him. A. D. Shattuck died on July 30 1928.

[11] Obituary notice in *N. Y. Times*, Apr. 26, 1890. Pfaff died Apr. 23, 1890, in his seventy-second year.

[12] For details about Clapp see Charles T. Congdon, *op. cit.*, 336–347.

physician;[13] but the most conspicuous during O'Brien's time was Walt Whitman, who, with *Leaves of Grass* but fresh from the press, came there with his slouch hat, gray suit, soft shirt open at the neck, and long, flowing hair.[14] Ada Clare, whom Whitman referred to as "brilliant . . . and handsome," was an actress, noted for her mass of beautiful yellow hair and for the deftness of her wit in the repartee which, with cut and thrust, flew about the table at Pfaff's.[15] Rather persistent rumor has it that Fitz-James was in love with this "Queen of Bohemia" and that she was for a time his mistress. With Jenny Danforth, too, another witty and beautiful woman belonging to the Pfaff circle,[16] O'Brien was on the most intimate terms, an intimacy clearly suggested in a letter to the "Baron," the title by which his friends often chaffingly called him in reference to the aristocratic airs he gave himself and to his being reputedly regarded as Baron Inchiquin.

Saturday A.M.

Mon Cher Baron

Adieu! I leave to-day! but to return Tuesday P.M. I go to classic Syracuse. I take the "Judge" because—Well its—confounded stupid en route *alone*. N'importe. Remember me while I am away. Come when I return. I will not say I shall pray for you nightly but I shall certés think of you much.

I am in earnest about the matter we have spoken of. I think of you ce soir at your Club dinner. Drink me silently.

Be good. And let the festive cup alone.

Ever faithfully
Yours
Jenny[17]

Relationships of the kind indicated by this letter gave rise to the severe criticisms directed against the Bohemian group, but although Jenny's admo-

[13] For Clemenceau's life in America (1865–1870) see *The Encyclopedia Americana*, 1925, VII, 83; and James L. Ford, *Forty-Odd Years in the Literary Shop*, 1921, pp. 61–62.

[14] See R. R. Wilson, *op. cit.*, II, 141. Critics agree as to the general effect of Whitman's appearance, though they differ somewhat as to the details of his costume; e. g., see Bliss Perry, *Walt Whitman*, Boston and N. Y., 1906, p. 131; Winter, *Old Friends*, p. 64; and Emory Holloway, *Whitman. An Interpretation in Narrative*, 1926, p. 137.

[15] For details see R. R. Wilson, *op. cit.*, II, 143; and T. Allston Brown, *op. cit.*, I, 484, or *The Round Table*, III, 308 (May 19, 1866). The latter contains a review of her novel, *Only a Woman's Heart*.

[16] See R. R. Wilson, *op. cit.*, II, 143.

[17] That this letter, now in the Charles J. Romm collection, was written some years later than 1857 is proved by the fact that the paper contains an "1860" watermark. It was probably written in 1861.

nition to Fitz-James to "let the festive cup alone" bears witness to her acquaintance with one of his chief failings—as indeed it was a failing of a number of the Pfaff circle—still the Bohemian ideal as such was far from despicable, as its adherents in *The Saturday Press* point out. It exalts, they say, "the freedom, the honesty, the sincerity, the good-fellowship, the devotion, the reverence for truth, the scorn and contempt for hypocrisy, which characterizes the genuine Bohemian."[18]

The Club dinner that Jenny Danforth mentions may have been one given either by the Bees or by the Theta Delta Chi's. "The Bees" was the name given to a group of associates more intimately friendly than the varied company who met at Pfaff's. The club, formed in 1856, had rooms on the south side of East Houston Street, a few doors from Broadway, and its membership was composed of actors, dramatists, and journalists. John Brougham, the playwright and actor who had made and kept alive the popularity of *A Gentleman from Ireland*, was the president, and other members besides Fitz-James were Ned Wilkins, the dramatist and critic, and Mark Smith, the comedian.[19] "The Bees" took as their motto "Honey Soit" and, as O'Brien says, they were a gay, lively, witty crowd, and because of their clever ridicule of plays came to be feared by the theatrical managers.[20]

As for O'Brien's membership in an American college fraternity, that also came about through the instrumentality of John Brougham. At the old Astor House this actor had met and become a fast friend of Charles Stetson, who was a member of Theta Delta Chi. In the summer of 1856 this fraternity formed a graduate chapter or charge, known as the Lambda Graduate Association; and, although this charge was discontinued in the summer of 1857, it was in existence just long enough for John Brougham and his friends, Fitz-James O'Brien, Ned Wilkins, and Mark Smith, together with six others, to be initiated in January, 1857, by a group of graduates who had themselves become members of the fraternity during their undergraduate days. O'Brien and Brougham were admitted as having been students of Trinity College, Dublin; Wilkins, as from Columbia; and Mark Smith, as from Dartmouth.[21] This makes it evident that O'Brien persisted in his story of

[18] *The New York Saturday Press*, June 16, 1860. "New York" was added to the title, beginning Dec. 4, 1858.

[19] See *The Shield. A Magazine Published Quarterly in the Interests of Theta: Delta: Chi*, XIV, 325 (Sept., 1898); quoted from *The Shield*, II, 9.

[20] See *H. W.*, I, 67 (Jan. 31, 1857).

[21] See *The Shield*, *loc. cit.*, and XIV, 418 (Dec., 1898).

having been educated at Trinity College, the claim being in itself an excellent gesture and likely to help his pose as a gentleman.

On April 29, delegates from nine chapters met in convention in New York, and at the literary exercises held in Hope Chapel, on Broadway, in the evening "John Brougham as poet delivered his famous 'Age of Gold'."[22] "It was characteristically humorous, and kept the audience in a continual roar of laughter."[23] As "The Man about Town" had referred to his club, the Bees, so he uses this convention as an excuse to give publicity to ΘΔΧ, puffing it as "one of the largest and most influential of the collegiate societies in America."[24]

With the rooms of Theta Delta Chi in a small house on Fourth Street, at the corner of Broadway, with Pfaff's at 645 Broadway, a few doors above Bleecker Street, and with the Bees just off Broadway on East Houston Street, the convivial Fitz-James had a number of convenient places for social contacts, which supplied him at the same time with material for "The Man about Town" papers, such as the latest gossip of the journalistic and theatrical worlds or the most recent choice morsel of society scandal.

Harpers had on January 3, 1857, published the first number of their new periodical, *Harper's Weekly. A Journal of Civilization.* Theodore Sedgwick was appointed editor, and he engaged O'Brien as one of his collaborators.[25] O'Brien's duty was to prepare each week a paper of from one and a half to three columns long to be called "The Man about Town." Circumstances thus contrived to furnish him with an almost ideal combination of work and play. The first paper appeared in the issue of January 31, and set the key for the brilliant and successful ones to follow; and for as long as they continued they remained a popular feature of the *Weekly*. But the weekly requirement was for O'Brien's erratic disposition and restless temperament too severe a test, and he wrote his last number on September 26. The habit and practise of regular production seems, nevertheless, to have been good for him, for it was but shortly after "The Man about Town" ceased his gay badinage that Fitz-James did some of his best writing and achieved his masterpiece.

[22] *Ibid.*, XIV, 325 (Sept., 1898). A copy of the poem, a fifteen-page pamphlet, is in the Harvard Library. Brougham was Convention Poet in 1873 also.

[23] *N. Y. Times*, Apr. 30, 1857.

[24] *H. W.*, I, 291 (May 9, 1857).

[25] See Frederic Hudson, *op. cit.*, p. 707.

During the months from January to September,[26] however, O'Brien expended his vitality in the clever, malicious, satiric, or vituperative exuberance of his column and exhausted his creative forces in collecting the material and preparing the copy for it. His few original poems and stories for the period, therefore, reach with one or two exceptions almost the low-water mark of worthless composition.

"The Man about Town" papers make Fitz-James O'Brien America's first columnist in the modern sense, instituting as they did the column of personal and pertinent comment, which, with the decline in influence of the heavy, serious editorial, becomes one of the prominent features of contemporary American journalism.[27]

Some of O'Brien's papers are more personal than are those of the columnists of today, or at least the personalities with which they deal are more narrowly local; and the comments resemble more nearly the society notes in Sunday editions of the modern yellow journals. It was because of the gossipy material with its spicy flavoring of scandal that the series attracted attention and comment. Even after the lapse of nearly ninety years, with the people and episodes unknown, the sketches retain their vitality, and the portraits and stories seem real.

As usual O'Brien does not spare himself but, under cover of clever bantering, reveals numerous details of his appearance and his pecuniary difficulties, though the exaggeration is always sufficient to prevent one from implicitly trusting the details. As these can be checked, however, from other sources, and as the general impression given is substantially accurate, O'Brien's sketch of himself as "The Man about Town" deserves to be quoted almost in its entirety. It is entitled "Walk Up, Ladies!" and tells of a lottery and peep show which he is getting up. For this, "The Grand Penny Peep-Show Gift Bachelor Association," he asks subscriptions, especially as he is the bachelor to be drawn for in the lottery six years later.

My qualifications may be thus set forth. I am turned of twenty-seven years, of medium height, while in my figure, symmetry and strength are harmoniously mingled. My nose and forehead form the Phidian line. My hands and feet are small and aristocratically shaped, and my eyes by turns melt with the soft emotions of the heart, or flash with the nobler passions of the hero. My hair is

[26] See Bibliography.

[27] The sharp, brief editorial paragraphs of George D. Prentice (*Louisville Journal*, 1830–1859) do not at all anticipate the easy, anecdotal sketches of O'Brien's column.

chestnut, and flows in long ringlets over my neck, somewhat like the hair of the Apollo Belvidere, only that I employ a much better *coiffeur*. Words fail me in endeavoring to describe my whiskers and mustache. I have been informed by the most excellent female judges that even in their dreams they never imagined any thing more lovely. My accomplishments are varied. I play on the banjo, and my Redowa is the eighth wonder of the world. I have been in Paris, and can talk about baronesses whom I met in the *Chaussée D'Antin*. I go to the opera, know all the singers by sight, so that I can point them out to my friends in bar-rooms, and have a slight acquaintance with a few ballet-dancers—a most important item for a young man, as it gives him a social standi g among his male companions. I can play an excellent game of billiards, can drink an unlimited number of cocktails, and, in short, I think that there are few men about town that can take me down on any thing.

With regard to my fortune, I may as well say at once that I advertise myself as having nothing in particular in my own right. In other words, I haven't a cent. But hang it! what's money after all? If any good-looking girl with a decent fortune draws me, she won't lose by it, that's all I've got to say. I'll bring her into society. I'll teach her how to dress; and, if she has tin enough, why, I'll run over to France or Germany, buy a title, and, come back a count or baron, so that ever after her relations can talk of their dear Countess de Quelquechose.

Now that I have been so candid about the matter, I trust that the readers of *Harper's Weekly*, who so far have done me the honor to express themselves pleased with me in print, will each one subscribe without delay to the Grand Penny Peep-show Gift Bachelor Association.

P.S.—If any gentleman draws me, and is not satisfied, I will be most happy to meet him with any weapons he may choose. Can I say more?[28]

"The Man about Town" had already introduced himself in the first number, but without giving any details. He was content there simply to say that he was in partnership with his friend Dimes, Dimes supplying the dress and the position and he, the author, furnishing the brains.[29] Within three weeks he admits the success of the column in the following doggerel:

There is a gent I've noted down, Sirs,
Who calls himself the Man About Town, Sirs;
He's thought to be a clever scribe, Sirs,

[28] *H. W.*, I, 163 (Mar. 14, 1857). On p. 195 (Mar. 28), he also speaks about his "heavy mustache."

[29] See *H. W.*, I, 66 (Jan. 31, 1857). Dimes had earlier been made use of as a character in "The Editor at Large," *Putnam's*, September and October, 1854.

So I hope he'll ask me to himbibe, Sirs;
And though he looks so meek and quiet,
His articles they make a riot.[30]

Besides references to his person O'Brien gives, in continuation of his earlier practice, many a reflection of his financial embarrassments, particularly as they necessitate his living in cheap boardinghouses. On February 14, he says that "Dimes, the other morning, rushed into my little room in the Hotel de Liâson—it is so small and cheap that Dimes is the only person I ever allow to visit me there." On March 21, under the title "My Hotel" he gives descriptive details of this uninviting boardinghouse. "It is cellular from top to bottom; and in its queer, ill-proportioned chambers, is hived a swarm of discolored Cubans, third-rate French clerks, mingled with frowzy, stupefied, married couples, who generally exist in a state of chronic lethargy, from which they occasionally awake to give the boarders the benefit of a matrimonial quarrel." The Cubans are noisy; the service is dirty; the food is monotonous—yet they all fight for it. The mistress of the boardinghouse "is an anomalous being—neither woman nor man, but a monster, who, like the Dragon of Wantley, cold-bloodedly feeds on the vitals of the population."

Because of the many disagreeable features of the Hotel de Liâson, "The Man about Town" dined out when he could. As Dimes remarked,

Man was a dining animal only when he had credit at a restaurant.

"Pecuniary questions," I replied, severely, "are out of place in a scientific discussion."

"My dear fellow," the good-natured Dimes hastened to say, "I meant nothing personal, I assure you. I think it is the most delightful thing in the world to owe for your dinner."[31]

In the spring of 1857 it was predicted that a comet would strike and destroy the world, and, in anticipation of such a finality, "The Man about Town" lived riotously. "For the last fortnight I have exhausted every pleasure. Dinners, suppers, horses, clothes, jewelry, cards. What boots I ordered! What entrancing coats! what seraphic waistcoats! My convivial parties have been the talk of the town." But when the comet fails to arrive, and the world still whirls on in its old way, he laments, "I am

[30] *Ibid.*, I, 115 (Feb. 21, 1857).
[31] *Ibid.*, 147 (March 7).

besieged. My bell is going all day, and creditors are ten deep round my door." Tailors' boys bring bills, restaurants dun him, tradespeople spring at him on Broadway, sheriffs' summonses deluge him. "I am growing thin and pale. . . . If the wealthy and respectable firm of publishers with whom I am connected do not immediately advance me twenty thousand dollars on account of literary matter to be hereafter furnished, I see no resource left me but to take Prussic acid, or go back with General Walker to Nicaragua."[32]

The following week the results of the above confession are made public. Although the "wealthy and liberal firm" of Harper's refused to advance him the twenty thousand dollars, Dimes "immediately furnished me with that paltry sum. To those correspondents who so liberally offered to supply my small wants, I however now offer the thanks of a free Man about Town."[33] In less than two months, however, he is once again in difficulties, as "My Money Article" of August 29, a punning parody on the market reports, shows.

> During the past week money has been rather tight with me. The *Illinois* brought in $1,658,072 in gold, but I have not got any of it yet. Specie payments have been small, but I have found a difficulty in obtaining money of any species. . . . The decrease in loans was inconsiderable; Mr. Simpson having advanced this week on my watch within a few shillings of the sum he gave me last time. . . . I conclude here, because I want to borrow five dollars of Smith, and want to catch him before he goes out for the evening.

Other features of the column are the running comments on local happenings and the satirical or vituperative handling of society scandal or social abuses. Gambling dens come in for severe attack more than once, and other evil conditions are periodically inveighed against. At these times the column, which otherwise seems carelessly flippant, takes on an air of righteous reform purpose, and the author's crusading spirit expresses itself in no uncertain terms. On May 23 "The Man about Town" shows the Comet how it can help with the cleansing process needed in the city by burning up certain splendid barrooms on Broadway, all of Wall Street and its Exchange, the City Hall with its graft, especially "street-contractors that don't do their work," and "Mayors that make a job of politics." Horace Greeley and *The Tribune* also deserve annihilation, and the Central Park Commission, and "the gentleman who has been promising the public a catalogue of

[32] *Ibid.*, 403 (June 27).
[33] *Ibid.*, I, 419 (July 4).

books in the Astor Library ever since that institution opened." The faro table in Quatremain's rooms led to the ruin of a young man of brilliant promise who later became a thug.[34] "The Board of Green Cloth," surrounded by faces strained, silent, decorous, leads to evil courses, murder, and general ruin—the girls go on the street, and the boys take up thieving at the Five Points.[35] To such a gambling club, over which is thrown an air of respectability, Dimes has been elected. "Come, Mr. Mayor Wood, here is work for you to do! Exterminate this pestilential haunt ere it infects the town. Burn its furniture. Quarantine its inhabitants. Level its walls to the ground. You know not how many wives and children will bless you for the deed; how many young men you will save from misery and crime."[36] This is the sort of moral tirade in which "The Man about Town" frequently indulges. The cheap dance hall, the filth of the slaughterhouses, the leering in omnibuses and on steps of hotels, and the idle dissipation of hotel life generally are other abuses upon which he vents his virtuous wrath.[37] Especial animus, repeated in a number of issues, is poured out upon the proprietor of a hotel which he calls the Bunkum House.[38]

On the other hand, it is with evident gossipy relish that he retails the juicy bits of scandal in which his society folk figure. The names for most of his characters he had used in stories and sketches previously, such as Mrs. Honiton, Mrs. Ormolu, Miss Halibut, and Croton Poole; and the best incidents about them are told as anecdotes, or short stories in miniature, related with pointed, malicious gaiety. Such are "Love among the Roses," "Schiller's 'Glove' Revised," "The Fatal Sneeze," and "A Tale of the Great Saratoga Trunk."[39]

Other miniature stories done in different moods give variety and interest to the column. "A Day Dream"[40] possesses the same weird power as do O'Brien's longer stories. The author dreams of killing his friend Dimes, and describes the murder and the effects on the assassin with intense, morbid vividness. The dead man appears to him like a Moslem at prayer; then like a fiend bearing consciousness of guilt; and the dreamer is rescued only

[34] See *ibid.*, I, 99 (Feb. 14).
[35] See *ibid.*, I, 259 (Apr. 25).
[36] *Ibid.*, I, 179 (Mar. 21).
[37] See respectively *ibid.*, I, 387 (June 20); 196 (Mar. 28); 227 (Apr. 11); and 563 (Sept. 5).
[38] See *ibid.*, I, 242 (Apr. 18); 291 (May 9); 339 (May 30).
[39] Respectively in *ibid.*, I, 99 (Feb. 14); 274 (May 2); 387 (June 20); and 611 (Sept. 26).
[40] *Ibid.*, I, 114 (Feb. 21).

with his awakening. The sentimental tale is represented by "A Story for April,"[41] in which a poor little girl selling violets is recognized by a wealthy couple as their granddaughter, the child of their long-lost son. The same mood is treated tragically in the story of Sahara. At this quiet seaside everything is drowsy; only the landlord's boy is full of life. Next morning he is drowned by the undertow, and his father mourns in quiet anguish.[42]

The filthy squalor of out-of-the-way slum districts of New York is graphically and indignantly described;[43] in fact, a tour of the slums was definitely planned to supply material for an article for the *Weekly*. As this article was to be illustrated, "The Man about Town" was accompanied on his tramp by Triangle, his artist friend (Frank H. Bellew). "Triangle and

TYPES OF BEARDS

myself belong to a mutual admiration society," writes O'Brien. "Triangle has agreed to caricature me into notoriety. . . . I am at present writing a history of the world, in the first chapter of which I allude to Triangle no less than five times."[44] He also praises the work of Triangle in caricature and compares it with the wonderful sketches of John Leech and Gavarni. For this publicity Bellew reciprocates the very next week and illustrates O'Brien's article describing the various fashions in beards by picturing O'Brien's own head as one of the ten examples.[45]

[41] *Ibid.*, I, 227 (Apr. 11).
[42] See *ibid.*, I, 451 (July 18, 1857).
[43] See *ibid.*, I, 114–115 (Feb. 21); 195–196 (Mar. 28).
[44] *Ibid.*, 195 (Mar. 28). See also I, 355 (June 6).
[45] *Ibid.*, I, 212 (Apr. 4). O'Brien's is the head in the lower left-hand corner.

Other friends are personally mentioned in the column from time to time. Bayard Taylor, his gifted friend, is referred to, and his delightful books of travels;[46] Frank S. Cozzens and his "Sparrowgrass" papers come in for notice;[47] and Walt Whitman is written of in the following complimentary words: "I for my part, love the passing panorama of countenances as much as did ever Walt Whitman, who has sung the hymn of the human face divinely."[48]

O'Brien manages to get in a word of attention and commendation about his young artist friend, A. D. Shattuck, in one of the two articles he devotes to the annual exhibit of the Academy of Design:

> But *revenons à nos moutons*—I don't mean the artists, nor their pictures, though, now that I think of it, there *are* sheep in the calm, delightful picture of The Lowland Pasture, by Mr. Shattuck. I think the foreground is excellently painted. The trees are too thick, as if the artist had put on too many leaves. I can not conceive the wind blowing through such clotted vegetation. Still the picture is delightful, and Mr. Shattuck has begun at the right end by painting through studies upward.[49]

The week previous he had regretted having to stop before being able to say what he wanted to say about "Shattuck's verdant Studies from Nature."[50] His critical attacks on some of the other artists are fierce and satirical, though he awards praise to S. W. Rowse, Leutze, Lambdin, Kensett, and especially Church for his landscape of the Andes of Ecuador.

Although O'Brien wrote no new plays in 1857, his interest in the theatre continued unabated. It centered about this time in the acting of Matilda Heron, with whom he became infatuated. He praises her in the *Weekly;*[51] he traveled as her press agent in the fall of 1859; and in 1860 he motivated the climax of his story "Mother of Pearl" from her performances of *Camille* and *Medea*. Since her withdrawal from the Bowery Theatre as leading lady, in January, 1853, Miss Heron had not appeared in New York until she played *Camille* on January 22, 1857. Her appearance was a tremendous success, and *Camille* ran for forty-five nights, followed by frequent revivals. "Fry in *The Tribune* uttered a multitude of adjectives in her honor. Sey-

[46] See *ibid.*, I, 83 (Feb. 7); 307 (May 16); and 387 (June 20).
[47] See *ibid.*, I, 83 (Feb. 7); 515 (Aug. 15); and 547 (Aug. 29).
[48] *Ibid.*, I, 212 (Apr. 4).
[49] *Ibid.*, I, 355 (June 6).
[50] *Ibid.*, I, 339 (May 30).
[51] See *ibid.*, I, 323 (May 23); and 595 (Sept. 19).

mour, in *The Times*, pronounced her greater than Rachel, and Wilkins, in *The Herald*, put in all the French of his dramatic wardrobe."[52] By May 23, "The Man about Town" is wondering whether the comet paid the patient man with the long brass telescope, on the pavement opposite the New York Hospital, "as well as Miss Heron must have paid her enterprising New York manager."

The method of her "naturalistic" acting is described by O'Brien in "Mother of Pearl."[53] Not indulging in the conventional elocution, in the swimming entrances and graceful exits, in the hysterics and eye-rolling which were the usual stock in trade of the emotional actress, Miss Heron made a sensation by being different. Her first entrance was

> wonderfully unconventional. The woman dared to come in upon that painted scene as if it really was the home apartment it was represented to be! She did not slide in with her face to the audience and wait for the mockery that is called "a reception." She walked in easily, naturally, unwitting of any outside eyes. The petulant manner in which she took off her shawl; the commonplace conversational tone in which she spoke to her servant, were revelations. . . . Here was a daring reality. . . . We felt ourselves in the presence of an inspired woman! . . .
>
> Miss Heron's figure was commanding, and there was a certain powerful light in her eyes that startled and thrilled; but there was none of the beauty of the "favorite actress." The conquest that she achieved was purely intellectual and magnetic.[54]

The next season Matilda Heron opened at Wallack's in another play from the French, called *La Fiammina*. While O'Brien greatly praises the actress, he expresses his disapproval of the play:

> Miss Heron is made for better things than playing singers under a cloud and women of pleasure with the consumption. There can be found a noble and pathetic character in woman, without her running away from her husband or ruining a young man. I am not in the least what is called "old fogy." I am not distinguished for a Cromwellian sternness of morality, but I think, nevertheless, that "Camille" and "Fiammina" both belong to a bad school of play.[55]

[52] T. Allston Brown, *op. cit.*, I, 491.
[53] *Harper's*, XX, 392–399 (Feb., 1860).
[54] *Ibid.*, XX, 395–396.
[55] *H. W.*, I, 595 (Sept. 19, 1857).

When in 1859, however, Miss Heron acted in *Geraldine,* a play about which he could wax enthusiastic, O'Brien became for a time her press agent, and as such accompanied her to Boston for her engagement there.

Another stage celebrity to whom "The Man about Town" pays his compliments is Agnes Robertson, whose singing of Scotch and Irish ballads he much admires. He tells the story of a fairy child brought up and taught to sing by a family of blackbirds, until she far outsang her teachers. You can hear her birdlike singing now, if you will only go to the concerts at the Academy of Music. The boost is neatly humorous, and the compliment graceful.[56]

The last of "The Man about Town" papers appeared on September 26; but signs of disaffection, indicative of the breakup which was to follow, are noticed in the column two weeks earlier, when the writer tells of being interrupted in his efforts to keep cool on a sweltering day by the arrival of the printer's devil. The boy tries to help him out and incite him to work, by suggesting subjects for the *Harper's Weekly* article which is due. Finding his suggestions received without enthusiasm, the boy departs with the remark that the seventy thousand subscribers are perhaps "not waiting for your article, Sir." This piques the author to such an extent that, inspired by the fact that his feet are in an ice bath, he determines to write on baths.[57]

This is the longest record of steady employment in the entire career of Fitz-James, with the possible exception of his editorship of *The Parlour Magazine* at the Crystal Palace in 1851; and the prominence gained by "The Man about Town" must have been of mutual benefit to the author and to the newly launched "Journal of Civilization." The reason for his quitting was probably nothing other than his temperamental instability and his dislike of regular habits. The regular income, however, must have been

[56] See *ibid.*, I, 531 (Aug. 22).

[57] See *ibid.*, I, 579 (Sept. 12, 1857). A similar column, "Bohemian Walks and Talks," began in *Harper's Weekly* on Nov. 7, 1857, and continued until Apr. 3, 1858. This had neither the spice nor the verve of O'Brien's column; and in spite of the fact that L. H. B. cites nineteen numbers of "The Bohemian Papers" in his list of O'Brien's writings (*The Round Table,* VII, 365—June 6, 1868) he apparently confused them with "The Man about Town" papers, which he does not include. The following statement in the almost contemporary *New York Picayune* for Mar. 26, 1859, would seem to settle the question: "Wilkins, theatrical critic of the *Herald* used to *Bohemianize* in *Harper's* until his articles, being an amusing feature, died a natural death." This is Ned Wilkins. F. H. Bellew in a letter to Winter (Oct. 7, 1880) says that O'Brien "continued his series of the Man about Town in the Picayune."

welcome, even though it gave him too much money to spend on his favorite form of dissipation; and only two weeks after his last article appeared he is found as one of the chief figures in a barroom brawl. *The New-York Daily Tribune*, which reports the whole affair under date of October 10, 1857, refers to him as "formerly of *The Daily Times*, and now known as the 'Man about Town'." The article, headed "A Rumpus among Distinguished Journalists,"[58] gives the story from the sides of both antagonists. Though neither version is particularly commendable, O'Brien's seems the more accurate.

On Thursday night, October 8, he met in a Broadway saloon George Wilkes, the chief writer for *Porter's Spirit of the Times*. Wilkes had in some articles been casting animadversions upon the character of actors and he is said that night to have asserted that all "actors are blackguards." O'Brien, some of whose best friends were actors, naturally resented this, saying that he had a number of personal friends in the theatrical profession who were eminent and every inch gentlemen, and assured Wilkes that "if old James Wallack were twenty years younger he would thrash him for his insolence." Wilkes left.

The next night, Friday, they met again at Niblo's Saloon, without exchanging any word. Later, however, when O'Brien entered the saloon at 609 Broadway, he found Wilkes there with "a number of fighting men, among whom were the notorious California ruffians Billy Mulligan and Charley Walsh, with a number of hackmen." O'Brien was alone and obviously in a trap. Wilkes came over and said that O'Brien had insulted him the other night and proceeded to punch O'Brien's head. When O'Brien sought to retaliate, he was seized and held by Mulligan while Wilkes struck him twice more in the face. O'Brien was then permitted to leave. But outside he was again assaulted by the friends of Wilkes, members of his "gang," who knocked him down and so punched and mauled him that he showed many cuts as the result of the fray.

Though O'Brien's career is dotted with episodes of this sort, it may well be that the success of his column, with its unchallenged attacks on slums, on slaughterhouses, on the filth of New York streets, and on vice, hypocrisy, and oppression of all sorts, had made him more cocksure, more truculent than ever. Certainly the column had attracted so much attention that Frank Bellew, feeling it would be an asset to *The New York Picayune*, per-

[58] This item was supplied through the kindness of Charles I. Glicksberg.

suaded his friend Fitz-James to continue it in that comic weekly. Under the old title, then, the Man about Town once more addressed his public from the pages of the *Picayune* on November 21; and in characteristic fashion he spends the first three paragraphs speaking facetiously about himself and his transfer of allegiance from *Harper's Weekly* to the "standard which the sleepless Doesticks guards." After that he returns fearlessly to the attack of local abuses: he scathingly berates the insolent and unscrupulous practices of certain lawyers in the courtroom, and he satirically ridicules the misguided efforts of the society lady who wants to help the starving poor. But the next two numbers—all that appeared—show a decided falling off in wit and power. On November 28 he writes about Thanksgiving and turkeys, and on December 5 gives too much space to personal animadversions of a former editor who now writes puffs for advertisers. His friend Dimes and the Bunkum House figure as before; but the old verve is so lacking that the reader is glad that O'Brien did not further continue the column.

Of his other writing for the year 1857 the only bit which was not done for the Harper firm represents a return to the articles he wrote for *Putnam's* upon its inception in January, 1853. *Putnam's* printed this one too—it is again a book review—and once more the subject is Melville—this time about the "Confidence Man" instead of the earlier *Mardi.* But the whole treatment is similar: he praises the originality of such American authors as Jonathan Edwards, Benjamin Franklin, Bryant, Cooper, Irving, Hawthorne, Emerson, Poe, Longfellow, Lowell, and Mrs. Stowe; then he reviews the style and subject matter of Melville's books from *Typee* through "Israel Potter"; so he reaches his discussion of the metaphysical but brilliant "Confidence Man"; and finally ends with the warning that Melville should "give up metaphysics and take to nature and the study of mankind."[59] All this is done in such a vivacious style and with such discriminating comments that the reader wishes O'Brien had more often applied his critical faculties to his own work before sending it to the publishers. The title is "Our Authors and Authorship. Melville and Curtis,"[60] and the last two pages discuss as rather an anticlimax George William Curtis's unfortunate imitation of Thackeray, Thackeray's somewhat superficial cynicism, and the shallowness of the too popular *Potiphar Papers.*

[59] *Putnam's,* IX, 391 (Apr., 1857).
[60] *Ibid.,* IX, 384–393.

In addition to "The Man about Town" column O'Brien contributed to the Harper publications during the year nine poems and five stories. "Dora Dee,"[61] the first of the stories, is a melodramatic incident in three parts. Dora Dee, found in an ash barrel and adopted by a sexton, becomes the beautiful rival of the woman with whom she has a position as companion. Dora, driven out into the snow and the bitter cold, gets lost near Washington Square and succumbs near some stables on Fifth Avenue. Her lover follows her tracks through the snow, finds her, carries her home, and marries her the next morning. Totally forced and unreal, yet interesting as to plot, it is a horrible example of what was the popular literature of that day—or for that matter of the present. William Winter complacently says it is "well enough;"[62] but would that it were intentionally satirical.

This is matched in badness, and in a rhyming title—"Helen Lee"[63]—by the worst poem of the year. It is so servilely imitative of Longfellow—of *Hiawatha* (1855) and *Evangeline* (1847)—that it becomes unbearable.

> Oh, the pleasant, pleasant autumn!
> How it seemed like spring-time to them!
> How the flowers budded, blossomed
> In their hearts afresh each day!
> Oh, the walks they had together
> From the singing schools and parties,
> In the white and frosty moonlight,
> In the starlight cold and gray!

So it goes on—with the description of the cornhusking and the country scenes like Whittier, and the use of similes pure Longfellow. If atmosphere is for a moment created, it is ruined almost immediately after by false, flat notes.

> When she sought her little chamber,
> Long she could not sleep for thinking
> Of his looks, his voice, his language,
> For the youth had turned her head.

The next to the last stanza leaves the bride smiling at her teasing husband Richard. Then, to end, Farmer Lee weeps and attitudinizes:

> "For I have not lost a daughter,
> But a worthy son have found!"

[61] *Harper's*, XIV, 369–371 (Feb., 1857).
[62] Winter, MS note.
[63] *Harper's*, XV, 809–810 (Nov., 1857).

Up to this final moment there had been no idea that he had lost or would lose her. Why bring it up now?

With "Dora Dee" and "Helen Lee" the writing of Fitz-James O'Brien reaches its lowest point, which, it may be noted, coincides almost exactly with the halfway mark in his career of authorship in America. After this there is nothing so poorly done; everything shows a little improvement; and some of the things show marked power and become intrinsically valuable.

Of the other eight poems of the year all preceded "Helen Lee" except one. This one, "Bacchus,"[64] in which the all-powerful god of drink extols the use of alcohol, is a parody of Emerson's recently printed "Brahma."[65] The other seven are a miscellaneous assortment: "What Santa Claus Brought Me"[66] tells a sentimental love story; sentimental too is "The Little Maid I Lost Long Ago,"[67] an elegy written smoothly and delicately, and containing a touch of mysticism; "My Valentine,"[68] has the clever turns of the half-sentimental, half-humorous *vers de société;* while similar in type is "By the Passaic,"[69] a trivial, graceful, attractive *jeu d'esprit*, written in slyly elaborate verse.

The poem which on its appearance received the largest amount of contemporary comment is a memorial to Elisha Kent Kane. This arctic explorer died on February 16, 1857 "at Havana, Cuba, whither he had gone in the hope of regaining a health shattered by his sufferings in the north."[70] On March 14 "Kane," a poem in his memory, appeared in *Harper's Weekly*. This ode *The New York Times* calls "a piece of poetry full of dignity and beauty, and which strikes the highest note of all that O'Brien produced."[71] Parts of it are unquestionably done with stately power, notably the third stanza and the vivid descriptions of the arctic trials in the sixth. The

[64] *H. W.*, I, 735 (Nov. 14, 1857). It was immediately reprinted in *The Evening Post*, Nov. 11, 1857. By Jan. 8, 1858, the *Post* had printed eight other parodies of "Brahma."

[65] *The Atlantic Monthly*, I, 48 (Nov., 1857).

[66] *Harper's*, XIV, 196 (Jan., 1857). Reprinted over the author's name (but without acknowledgment) in *The New York Saturday Press*, Dec. 25, 1858.

[67] *H. W.*, I, 125 (Feb. 21, 1857). It is signed by "Origen Od," the mystic, who in 1852 wrote some of the "Fragments from an Unpublished Magazine."

[68] *Harper's*, XIV, 505–506 (Mar., 1857).

[69] *Ibid.*, XIV, 767 (May, 1857). Brander Matthews calls it "On the Passaic" and includes it in *American Familiar Verse*, 1904, pp. 173–174; and F. L. Pattee, with the same title, includes it in *Century Readings for a Course in American Literature*, Third Edition, 1926, p. 651.

[70] Burton Egbert Stevenson, *Poems of American History*, Boston and New York, 1908, p. 379.

[71] *N. Y. Times*, Mar. 12, 1881. It then quotes three stanzas of the poem. "Kane" had appeared complete in William Cullen Bryant, *The Family Library of Poetry and Song*, 1870, pp. 933–934, and in two other collections before Winter's 1881 volume. See Bibliography.

simile of the fourth stanza, however, likening Kane to an iceberg melting away in a southern sea, is too farfetched in its conceit to sustain the mood. The whole poem is sufficiently rhetorical to gain greatly when its periods are subjected to oral delivery. As the *Harper's Weekly* account not only analyzes the poem and tells the story of its genesis, but also makes clear the relationship between publisher and author, it is quoted in full:

When the tidings of the death of the Arctic hero reached us O'Brien was asked to write a poem on Kane for the next number of this paper. He set to work at once, but for a time, it appeared, vainly. The thought was there, but it would not shape itself into form. All at once the whole flashed before him in a series of pictures. He saw where—

"Aloft upon an old basaltic crag,
Which, scalped by keen winds that defend the Pole,
Gazes with dead face on the seas that roll
Around the secret of the mystic zone,
A mighty nation's star-bespangled flag
Flutters alone.
And underneath, upon the lifeless front
Of that drear cliff a simple name is traced:
Fit type of him who, famishing and gaunt,
But, with a rocky purpose in his soul,
Breasted the gathering snows,
Clung to the drifting floes,
By Want beleaguered and by Winter chased,
Seeking the brother lost amid that frozen waste."

Then came visions of the burst of welcome which greeted Kane from the whole land—from the deep woods of Maine to "Texas wild and grim;" and of the brave young heart seeking to recover in a sunny clime the vital heat of which it had been robbed by the Arctic winds; and of the solemn end; when,

"Ere the thunders of applause were done,
His bright eyes closed forever on the sun!
Too late, too late the splendid prize he won
In the Olympic race of Science and of Art."

Then came the two magnificent strophes in which are condensed into two-score lines that long tale of peril and self-sacrifice, with the noble choral close:

"No grander episode doth chivalry hold,
In all its annals back to Charlemagne,
Than that long vigil of unceasing pain,
Faithfully kept through hunger and through cold,
By the good Christian knight Elisha Kane."

The poem sprung up as a series of pictures, which were to be disposed in proper order. We went over the proofs as he had arranged them, and agreed that the order was faulty, and should be changed in the types; and so it was done. Early next morning he came to me. "We were wrong," he said; "the poem was right as I had it." I had meanwhile come to the same conclusion, and it was altered back precisely as it stood at first. I have more than once heard the same order suggested in which the poem was placed at the first change. But I am sure that any one who enters fully into its spirit will agree with me that, as it originally stood and now stands, it is perfect in thought, structure, and arrangement.[72]

"A Summer Idyl"[73] tells a love story with a certain frank sensuousness of expression very different from what was the habit of the New England group of poets. With the age-old combination of a mild night, the moon, a stream, and a girl, O'Brien makes an attractive setting, beginning

It was a moonlit summer night;
The heavens were drenched with silver rain;
And frowning rose Katahdin's height,
Above the murmuring woods of Maine.

Then follow the suggestions of the passionate situation so foreign to the Longfellow method of treatment; yet with what a delight of relief the subscribers to *Harper's* must have read in the details of the poem, reflections of their own—the eternal—love-making:

Her stooping face, no longer wan,
Flushed in the harvest-time of love,

and

I drew her down upon my breast.

[72] *H. W.*, VI, 267 (Apr. 26, 1862).
[73] *Harper's*, XV, 219–220 (July, 1857).

Already some of the readers were no doubt too much shocked to continue; but the rest finished it with:

> And in the vague electric spark,
> Felt only when cheek touches cheek,
> I knew through all the shadows dark
> The promise that she did not speak.

Then, fortunately, O'Brien knew enough to stop, with only a repeated variation on the first stanza.

On the Fourth of July *Harper's Weekly* printed a patriotic poem which has since become well known under another title, through its inclusion in many school readers. It appeared originally under the caption,

HOW THE BELL RANG.

July 4th, 1776.

But since as early as 1883 it has always been entitled "Independence Bell—July 4th, 1776,"[74] and it has from its first appearance continued to be printed anonymously. Fitz-James O'Brien, however, is the author, as is made clear from a notebook of William Winter in which he includes "How the Bell Rang" as one of twenty-four poems which he had collected as "Material for Second Vol. of O'Brien's Works." The copy which he had in hand for the purpose was clipped from *The New York Saturday Press* for July 7, 1860, where it had been reprinted with its original title. Here the poem is preceded by a prose paragraph explaining the background of the incident related by the poem.[75] In almost all succeeding reprints this introduction is used. The story of the boy who waits to notify his grandfather when the Continental Congress shall have signed the Declaration of Independence, and of the old bellman who rings forth the glorious news is so familiar as to need no retelling. Suspense is well sustained, and the subject is handled with such a vivid sense of the dramatic as to give a patriotic thrill. The

[74] See Bibliography.

[75] This copy and Winter's MS list are in the Charles Romm collection. The list is written in a small leather-covered notebook, with the following inscription in Winter's hand on the cover: "O'Brien—List of things for Volume 2." The line quoted above appears inside the book. In A. L. S., William Winter to B. H. Ticknor, October 26, 1880 (pasted in Yale copy of Winter, 1881), occurs the following: "I know of TEN excellent things, verse and prose, by O'Brien that I haven't yet been able to capture. Vol. II (should we make it), will be very strong, and 'no slouch'."

exhortation of the last stanza had especial point during the time of the Civil War, and has since made the application of the poem general:

> The old bell now is silent,
> And hushed its iron tongue,
> But the spirit it awakened
> Still lives forever young.
> And while we breathe the sunlight,
> On the Fourth of this July,
> Let us not forget the Bellman,
> Who, 'twixt the earth and sky,
> Rang out our Independence,
> Which, please God, shall never die![76]

Finally, as part of O'Brien's verse accomplishment for the year it is necessary to notice "A Storm in Summer," a descriptive sketch from "The Man about Town." This shows O'Brien at his trick of reproducing old material when in need of copy for a new purpose, for this seemingly prose essay for July 4, 1857, is the identical poem that he had written in the same prose way on July 5, 1853.[77]

Of the short stories, "Uncle and Nephew"[78] appeared a month after "Dora Dee." It is an interesting story, dealing with cases of monomania in the two chief characters, an uncle and his nephew. The abnormal states of mind are treated in Dr. Auvray's sanatorium, the setting being given with much circumstantial detail as to time, place, and character. First the nephew is insane and ties up his uncle; then the conscience-stricken uncle becomes insane, and the nephew is cured. The style is clever—"manifestly French," says Pattee[79]—and the effect of short, seemingly irrelevant sentences is telling. The ways of insanity and the cures for it are, in the Poe way, written up with a great show of authority and learning.

Poesque, also, is the fantastic story of "Seeing the World."[80] Cipriano

[76] *H. W.*, I, 418 (July 4, 1857). The above is quoted exactly as it appears in *Harper's Weekly*. Later reprints, besides the many changes in words and punctuation, omit two stanzas of the poem as it originally appeared, and substitute eight new lines (equivalent to a complete stanza) in the third from the last stanza. It is these new lines that contain the boy's well-known, thrilling shout, "Ring! Grandpa! Ring!" which can, consequently, not be attributed to O'Brien.

[77] See *N. Y. Times*, July 19, 1853. The verse and diction have been polished in places for the reappearance in *Harper's Weekly*.

[78] *Harper's*, XIV, 518–526 (Mar., 1857).

[79] F. L. Pattee, *op. cit.*, p. 157.

[80] *Harper's*, XV, 542–546 (Sept., 1857).

has thought and the creative faculty, but cannot express himself. A physician from India offers him facility in verse-making, with the proviso that, if he accepts, the gift shall remain irrevocable, and that it shall be accompanied by a power within him to know and to comprehend everything. Cipriano agrees to the conditions and from that time sees only the material, scientific bases of things. He sees in his loved Charlotte only an anatomical specimen; he sees instead of a picture only canvas and paint; instead of water he sees molecules, germs, and gases. At the same time he finds that by his astounding performances in feats of poetic improvising, he can make money and live in luxury. His mind revolts, nevertheless, at his terrible gift, and his reason totters.

The next story, "A Screw Loose,"[81] in style, background, and names used is closer to the manner of "The Man about Town" than to the startling extravagances of "Uncle and Nephew" and "Seeing the World." Its descriptions of Twitter, with their autobiographical implications, have already been quoted at some length, and the story, though depending on coincidence, is tolerably well told—"after the Dickens Christmas-story manner," as Pattee says.[82] It is not so neat and compact, however, as the stories of two years earlier—"My Son, Sir," "The Beauty," "A Drawing-Room Drama," and "The Duel"; and it is therefore with a feeling of progressive accomplishment that one returns to the weirdness of atmosphere which is uppermost in the last story of the year.

The interest in "My Wife's Tempter"[83] depends on the fear of the unknown, the curiosity about the unsolved, which was growing to be typical of O'Brien. In this story it is secured by the use of the Mormons, whose proselyting activities, because of general ignorance as to their methods and their religion, inspired great fear in the popular mind. A Mormon ruins the happiness of a man's home, secretly converts the man's wife, and tempts her to run away with him. The story is too long, but the weird atmosphere is a worthy precursor to that of "The Diamond Lens," which followed close on its heels as the first of O'Brien's output for 1858.

[81] *Ibid.*, XV, 629–634 (Oct., 1857).
[82] F. L. Pattee, *op. cit.*, p. 157.
[83] *H. W.*, I, 795–796 (Dec. 12, 1857).

Chapter VIII

The Heights of Bohemia

"The Diamond Lens," "The Finishing School," "The Saturday Press"

(1858)

With the year 1858 Fitz-James O'Brien won recognition and acclaim through his story "The Diamond Lens" and his poem "The Finishing School." "The Diamond Lens," with the possible exception of "What Was It?," remains his best short story, and "The Finishing School" the best of his social satire in verse. As O'Brien's best critical writing, contained in the dramatic reviews of *The Saturday Press*, also belongs to 1858, it is apparent that this year marks the height of his achievement. The success of his masterpiece, a tale of an abnormal mind under unnatural conditions, stimulated him to emulate its success in other supernatural tales, and during the year he wrote "From Hand to Mouth," "The Golden Ingot," and "The Lost Room;" while he repeated "The Finishing School" method in "The Prize-Fight," satirically flaying the organized exploitation of "the manly art."

The year started auspiciously, for "The Diamond Lens" appeared in the January number of the recently established *Atlantic Monthly*.[1] This story has been generally recognized as the best example of Fitz-James O'Brien's literary output, and is the only one of his stories which is at all widely known. At the time of its appearance it created, according to various reports, something of a literary sensation,[2] and, since, it has been more often reprinted and referred to than any other O'Brien writing.[3] In fact, from the time of its publication Fitz-James O'Brien was generally advertised and referred to as "author of 'The Diamond Lens.' "[4]

[1] *The Atlantic Monthly*, I, 354–367 (January, 1858). The first number of *The Atlantic* had appeared in November, 1857.

[2] E. g., see Winter, 1881, p. xix; M. E. W. Sherwood, *op. cit.*, p. 126; M. A. DeW. Howe, *op. cit.*, p. 227.

[3] See Bibliography and *The Round Table*, III, 245 (Apr. 21, 1866).

[4] See *N. Y. Picayune*, Mar. 27, 1858; and Sherwood and Howe, as in n. 2, above.

The story shows very plainly the use that O'Brien made of the Poe technique—what he learned from Poe and made use of, what he added, and in what points he was incapable of following Poe's example.

The plot of "The Diamond Lens" immediately takes advantage of the interest in scientific discovery and scientific speculation which characterized the mid-nineteenth century, and in its pseudoscientific way suggests the possibility and the far-reaching results of the finding of a perfect lens. It invents as its principal, almost its sole, character a man to whom such a search becomes a monomania, which stifles all other ideas and purposes in life and which blunts his moral sense. Under such stimulus he commits a cold-blooded, carefully carried-out murder. Through this crime he secures and creates the perfect lens, with the result that by its means he is able to see in a drop of water, moving there and having her being, the ideal of feminine beauty, the perfection of women. He calls her Animula and falls in love with her; but with ironic retribution, though he can watch her free, beautiful life as she moves within the water drop, he cannot communicate with her. Animula must remain for him a wholly unattainable ideal, and when, in spite of all that he can do, the drop of water begins to evaporate, he is forced to witness her gradual fading away. So brooding upon his frustration and consumed with longing for her, he becomes mad.

This is almost pure Poe. Un-Poelike, however, is the way in which O'Brien creates his mood of queerness, of unreality. Poe, by his use of suggestive, colorful, atmospheric words, in the first paragraph, in the first sentence even, secures the feeling of brooding horror, of impending doom. O'Brien, on the other hand, starts with a paragraph or two of details that set before the reader what, though perhaps not entirely usual, are nevertheless elements belonging to a perfectly acceptable and almost normal situation. The germs of the ensuing abnormalities are, of course, present, but it is only after beguiling the reader into a confident acceptance of his initial premise that O'Brien makes his transitions into the realm of the weird and supernatural. In "The Diamond Lens," which is told in six parts, the entire first part is devoted to this purpose of inspiring faith in the storyteller and belief in the subject of his narrative. It deals with the curiosity and natural enthusiasm of a boy for a pet hobby, admits his egotism, selfishness, and colossal ignorance, and tells of his desire to get away from unsympathetic parents at home and of his accomplishing this by being sent to study medicine in New York. It should perhaps be stated that part of the apparatus for securing the "suspension of disbelief" is to have the hero tell his own story, to have the narration made in the first person—another particular in which O'Brien is imitating Poe. For that matter, nothing of the method just described is original with O'Brien; Defoe had shown the possibilities long before. But to O'Brien must be given the credit for showing how the Defoe elements could be successfully combined with the type of grotesque tale that Poe so highly developed.

Section two continues the story of Linley's settlement in a New York lodginghouse and of his development as a microscopist. All this is continued in a matter-of-fact way, but a few details, and more hints, are introduced which suggest that all is not quite normal. Finally, in the third section, in which is described a spiritualistic séance, the borders of the acceptable and natural are broken through; but any reader who has continued thus far will not balk at the supernatural spirit-rappings for which he has been well but subtly prepared by constant suggestions of the abnormal. Then follows the murder, and at last in section five the revelation of the radiant being, the infinitesimally tiny Animula. By this time there is absolutely no question of either acceptance or repudiation on the part of the reader. He is following the story for what it will give him, his curiosity is caught, he shares the emotions of the hero, and is as curious as is the latter in the discoveries to be revealed by the wonderful diamond. The sixth section gives the scientifically probable, tragic results of the discovery, returns to everyday life in telling of the hero's present situation, and ends with "They say now that I am mad; but they are mistaken."

The foregoing analysis has already indicated wherein lies what is perhaps the chief limitation which has prevented O'Brien from rivaling the power of suggestive horror and the artistic perfection of Poe. He lacks Poe's concentration; his stories are always just a trifle too long. Whereas Poe makes every word, every sentence, count in building up and producing a single unified effect, O'Brien by his very attempt to carry over from the acceptable to the impossible has to work in at least two moods. This makes for discursiveness, and though the variety of effect obtained may in itself be good and interesting, it never possesses quite the compelling intensity of the best of Poe's horror stories.

With all these reservations in favor of Poe, it is nevertheless certain that "The Diamond Lens" remains what its contemporaries thought it, an excellently executed and absorbingly interesting short story.

The similarities and the differences between Poe and O'Brien are carefully pointed out by Joseph J. Reilly in an article, "A Keltic Poe," written for *The Catholic World* in 1920. After suggesting that Poe would have relentlessly "cut away the visit to Madame Volpes [*sic*], the medium, and pruned down the incident of Simon to a single paragraph," Reilly lists the many touches in which Poe would have recognized "a skillful student of his own methods"—the preliminary self-revelation, the marshalling of the names of great scientists, the discussion of references to scientific discoveries, the confession that the narrator "supposes he is mad," the cold-blooded determination to compass a murder, the choice diction and poetic fervor of the description of Animula. In further detail he compares the murder of Simon with the murder in "The Cask of Amontillado;" and finally he distinguishes between the emotional and imaginative qualities of the two men.

Both men were opinionated, but Poe was vastly more the egotist. Both had the dramatic instinct to a marked degree; O'Brien employed his in writing for the theatre, Poe his in arranging his world as a stage upon which he himself played the leading rôle. . . . O'Brien was sociable; he liked life and delighted to feel the hum and thrill of it about him. Poe, with his peculiar attitude of mind, spent lonely years, . . . self-centered and self-pitying. . . . With Poe melancholy was a habit of mind; . . . O'Brien's melancholy was a phase of his Keltic temperament which, in the ardor of today, plays joyously among the stars, only to find itself on the chill morrow plunged in the slough of despond.[5]

Even before "The Diamond Lens" was printed, O'Brien seems to have been conscious that he had written something a good deal better than usual. This is interestingly shown in two letters addressed to the editors of *The Atlantic Monthly*. The story was written in the fall of 1857, probably soon after he gave up "The Man about Town" column; for by the date of the first letter, November 28, "The Diamond Lens" had been written and accepted.

Harper's
Franklin Sq^{re}.
Nov. 28th

Dear Sirs

I am much pleased that my story has met your approval, and shall be glad at some future time to present you with other articles.

[5] *The Catholic World*, CX, 760, 761, and 762 (Mar., 1920).

I have not calculated the number of pages which the Diamond Lens will make and will thank you to have the computation made and remit to me the amount according to whatever scale of prices you see fit to include it in.

It will be in a great measure a labor of love to write for a Magazine of so high a tone as the Atlantic. I have long felt the want of a channel in which to place articles on which I might bestow labor and thought. Here in New York we are far too apt to neglect the higher aims.

Will you permit me to express the great pleasure I have experienced in reading "Skipper Ireson's Ride" in your last number. It abounds in lyrical fire, pathos and strength.

Yours truly,
FitzJames O'Brien.

Messrs. Phillips Sampson and Co.[6]

The second letter followed a few days later and reveals his desire that the style be as finished as possible.

Harper's
Franklin Sq^re^
Dec. 1st

Gentlemen

If not too inconvenient I will feel particularly obliged by your letting me have a proof of my story, which I will return to you corrected with all possible speed. I remember some inelegancies which I would like to alter. I forgot to mention this in my last note to you.

Yours very truly,
FitzJames O'Brien.

Messrs Phillips Sampson & Co.[7]

"The Diamond Lens" attracted so much attention—William Winter says it "electrified magazine literature"[8]—that a claim of original authorship was made for O'Brien's old rival William North. This report was given publicity in William Cullen Bryant's newspaper *The Evening Post* on January 14. Under the heading "Who Wrote 'The Diamond Lens'?" the *Post* printed the following paragraph from a correspondent who signed himself "Guy":

'Who wrote that brilliant and original story in the last *Atlantic*, called The Diamond Lens?' Miss Sophronia asked; and while Bob answered 'Hawthorne, of

[6] A. L. S., in Yale Library, pasted in copy of Winter, 1881.
[7] A. L. S., in Yale Library, pasted in copy of *The Atlantic Monthly* for January, 1858.
[8] Winter, 1881, p. xix.

course,' James said it was a posthumous work of Poe; but, a gentleman in spectacles, a stranger to me, although evidently from Boston, asserted positively that it was written by a young man of New York, named O'Brien. Thereupon, a reporter to one of the unrivalled dailies asserted no less vehemently that he had read it in the manuscript, years ago, of the late William J. North, an accomplished young English writer, who met with so sad a fate in this city not long ago.

To this "The Author of 'The Diamond Lens' " wrote an indignant reply denying that North had had anything to do with the idea on which he had been working for several years but on which he had been held up because of technical difficulties.

In the composition of "The Diamond Lens" I derived considerable aid from Doctor J. D. Whelply of this city, himself an accomplished writer and practical microscopist. To him I am indebted for some valuable suggestions connected with the scientific mechanism of the plot, and he was a witness of the gradual development of the story under my hands.[9]

The letter ends with a reference to "the uncertain reporter of a certain daily newspaper" who has unauthorizedly attributed the story to various men of letters.

Despite O'Brien's statement reports continued to circulate and to increase in the viciousness of their attacks on O'Brien's plagiarizing. Fitz-James investigated and on February 20 over his full name wrote to the *Post* his account of the slander. He traces the original assertion to a reporter or editor of the New York *Daily Times*, who, however, upon direct inquiry wrote "*a point-blank denial.*" "J. J.," a lady journalist, had also been spreading the story, and in a particularly malicious form full of circumstantial detail had written it to the New Orleans *Delta*, an account which O'Brien transcribes in full. He then threatens action if the scandalous falsehoods continue and concludes with a reiteration of his own authorship, saying that "in its conception and composition I have been indebted to no one." To allay the bad blood his paper had stirred up, Bryant three days later printed a nice little biographical note about Fitz-James, adding that "volumes of his poems and tales are soon to be published."[10] The final word on this subject, definitely supporting O'Brien's claim, was written by Dr. Guernsey of Harper's who knew the stories of both men. He first

[9] *The Evening Post*, Jan. 20, 1858.
[10] *Ibid.*, Feb. 23.

regrets the appearance of "The Diamond Lens" in *The Atlantic* rather than in *Harper's*, saying, "It was owing to a misapprehension that" it, "after having been accepted, was withdrawn and published elsewhere." And then he continues:

Some circumstances gave special notoriety to "The Diamond Lens." The story is founded on the old idea that time and space are mere accidents; that, for instance, a drop of water is a world in itself. . . . The late William North had written a story called "Microcosmus," based upon the same general idea. He had spoken of it to many, though I know of no person excepting myself who has read it; for it was offered to the Magazine. Shortly afterward he committed suicide, and the story, so far as I know, was not found among his papers. Some one charged O'Brien with stealing the "Diamond Lens" from North, slightly altering it, and passing it off for his own. The charge was wholly unfounded. I am confident that he never saw North's story, and I think he never heard of it until after the "Diamond Lens" was published. At all events the two were wholly unlike in every point except the suggesting idea, which has been in writing for two thousand years.[11]

In addition to its many other interests "The Diamond Lens" claims the distinction of being the first writing of O'Brien's to be published in book form with his name attached. During his life his work, with the exception of the three Irish poems, "Loch Ine," "The Boatmen of Kerry," and "Irish Castles," was printed, for the most part anonymously, entirely in magazines and newspapers. After his death "The Diamond Lens" was one of the fourteen stories printed in *Atlantic Tales* in 1866, with the table of contents, announcing: "THE DIAMOND LENS Fitz James O'Brien. pp. 21–49."[12]

Nothing of O'Brien's is identified for two months after the appearance of "The Diamond Lens," and one imagines him, elated by the success of his story, resting on his laurels until the dinner invitations ceased and more money was necessary. Before March he has again renewed his connection with the Harper Brothers and has written for the *Monthly* a nondescript sort of article called "A Paper of All Sorts,"[13] in which he points out the differences in Bohemianism as practiced in Paris, London, and New York,

[11] *H. W.*, VI, 267 (Apr. 26, 1862). Testimony to the same effect is given in *The Round Table*, III, 245 (Apr. 21, 1866); by George Arnold in Winter, 1881, p. li; by Winter's note, *ibid.*, pp. li–lii; and by Winter, *Old Friends*, pp. 67–68, which says, "It was prompted by a remark made to him by Dr. A. L. Carroll . . . relative to the marvellous things contained in a drop of water."

[12] *Atlantic Tales, A Collection of Stories from the Atlantic Monthly*, Boston, 1866.

[13] *Harper's*, XVI, 507–515 (Mar., 1858).

describes the poverty-stricken makeshifts of a typical Bohemian, and draws a splendid analytical contrast between the humor of Thackeray and Dickens.

This was followed by a story which began to run serially in *The New York Picayune.* The first number, appearing in the issue for March 27, contained three chapters, and the ensuing chapters ran through six succeeding issues, to the conclusion on May 15. "From Hand to Mouth"[14] is the title of this extraordinary story written, as the *Picayune* is careful to announce, "By the Author of 'The Diamond Lens.' " The notoriety acquired by the earlier story was thus quickly recognized as having advertising value; and even a poem in the same issue was headed "*An Old Story* By the Author of 'The Diamond Lens'." It will be remembered that the *Picayune* was Bellew's weekly, and that "An Old Story" had appeared six years before in *The Lantern,* the comic paper on which Bellew and O'Brien had worked together. Within six weeks three more of O'Brien's early *Lantern* poems were similarly used by Bellew.[15]

The May 1 installment of "From Hand to Mouth" is very short, running only a little over a column and ending with the formula "to be concluded in our next." But the next issue fails to fulfill this promise. Instead, under the usual title-caption, is the following: "We regret to state that owing to the sudden illness of the author of 'From Hand to Mouth,' the conclusion of that tale is unavoidably postponed until next week's number of the Picayune."[16] The following week the story is concluded, not by O'Brien, but by Frank H. Bellew, who writes, "O'Brien failed and I finished it."[17] Thus, as with "The Man about Town," for the second time within a year O'Brien failed to fulfill his contract.

"From Hand to Mouth" begins with a definite setting, "The evening of the 8th of March, in the present year,"[18] and describes a heavy snowstorm and the opera—the first performance of Meyerbeer's *The Huguenots*—which he, the author, attended that night. From this setting the author, telling his story in the first person, makes a very skillful transition to the super-fantastic setting of the Hotel de Coup d'oeil. Here, surrounded by thousands of disembodied eyes, ears, hands, and mouths, which though stationary

[14] *N. Y. Picayune,* X, 2–3 (Mar. 27, 1858); 10 (Apr. 3); 18 (Apr. 10); 26–27 (Apr. 17); 34 (Apr. 24); 42 (May 1); 50 (May 8); 58 (May 15).

[15] See *ibid.,* X, 6 (Mar. 27), "The Ballad of Sir Brown"; X, 9 (Apr. 3), "To April"; and X, 50 (May 8), "The Demon Tie."

[16] *Ibid.,* p. 50 (May 8).

[17] F. H. Bellew to Winter, Oct. 7, 1880.

[18] *N. Y. Picayune,* X, 2 (Mar. 27).

function like normal organs, a most unheard-of set of complications takes place. Unlike Animula of "The Diamond Lens," the impossibilities of this story never become convincing, but instead the whole is suffused with an atmosphere of fantastic queerness, which invites not sympathy or belief but which stimulates the curiosity and wonder of the reader as to what even passably plausible conclusion the author can invent for such outlandish premises. In Chapter XII[19] the hero describes himself and, as usual, O'Brien uses this opportunity to describe his own features. Consequently, when "From Hand to Mouth" was printed in book form in 1868, S. Eytinge, Jr., who illustrated it, drew as a full-page frontispiece a portrait of O'Brien seated at a table taking breakfast. The fantastic, talking, green bird, which plays such a large part in the story, is there, too, and one each of the disembodied eyes and ears is on the door.[20]

Once again, with the May number of the *Monthly*, O'Brien is seen in the Harper fold, lured there perhaps by promise of display space for his next contribution; for on no other basis does "Amazon," a trite poem about a scornful Amazonian maiden and her rejected lover, deserve the prominence given it. The Harpers realized the value of keeping on good terms with, and even flattering a bit, this old contributor who had suddenly gained prominence and whose two latest stories had been sold to magazines other than theirs.

During the summer Fitz-James had had an unfortunate experience. He was hotheaded and reckless, and among his friends the allusions to his challenges to a duel or a fight are numerous. On June 14 at the New York Hotel, however, he picked on the wrong man and had his nose broken by the blow of a pugilistic barkeeper. This encounter decidedly marred his appearance, as is humorously related by the surgeon who immediately thereafter attended him. "He looked . . . like Cruikshank's picture of 'the man wot wun the fight.' Never have I seen the human nose more completely comminuted than in my patient's case. Even his tailor wouldn't have recognized him. I remember that nose particularly, on account of his urgent solicitude that I should make it slightly aquiline, but avoid the Israelitish extreme. *Romans* rather than *Hebrews* furnished his text."[21]

[19] *Ibid.*, X, 26 (Apr. 17, 1858).

[20] *Good Stories*, Part IV, Boston, 1868, pp. 3–49. Title page and illustration may be seen in copy in the American Society Library. They are missing from the copy in the Library of Congress.

[21] Winter, *Old Friends*, pp. 98–99.

George Arnold speaks of O'Brien's muscularity and says that he was "a gymnast of some ability, and a firm disciple of the church of St. Biceps,"[22] and Stephen Fiske reports that he "had not only the figure but the training of an athlete" and that "his skill was considered wonderful. He was an

FROM HAND TO MOUTH

admirable swordsman," and Fiske had seen "several instances of his skill with the pistol."[23] Similar testimony is given in the *Leader* editorial: "He was of athletic build, of extremely courteous and winning manners; prompt

[22] Winter, 1881, p. xlvii.
[23] *Ibid.*, 1881, p. liv.

to resent a fancied affront, and quick to forget and forgive when the first flush of angry feeling was spent."[24]

Before the disfiguring blow to his nose O'Brien is described by William Winter as follows: "He had a fair and glowing complexion, and waving brown hair; his eyes were gray-blue, large, brilliant, and expressive; his smile was honest and sweet, and his countenance frank and winning; he was of the middle stature, an athlete in person, and he moved with negligent grace. His voice was rich in quality, loud and clear, and he had a bluff and breezy manner of speech, tending at times to a joyous turbulence."[25]

Another reference to the summer of 1858 is made by Mrs. M. E. W. Sherwood. She writes:

> We were all in the Summer of 1858 looking at Donati's comet—that superb visitor in our twilight skies which O'Brien declared looked like a mighty quill pen, and indeed it did, although the feathery part of it was more like a beautiful ostrich plume, which a lady might wear in her hair to a Court ball. He therefore claimed it as the sign manual of a newspaper correspondent and wrote a brilliant address to it as the pen which some demigod had seized from his hand and had placed in the heavens with Berenice's hair.[26]

In August *The Knickerbocker Magazine* printed both a poem and a story by O'Brien. The poem, "The Boatman of Whitehall," is an obvious melodramatic ballad telling of Ben's success in love through the defeat of his rival in a rowing match. The story is much better. Powerfully melodramatic, "The Golden Ingot" tells of a girl sacrificing herself in order to save the life of her father, who believes he is an alchemist. The doctor, who tells the story, does it with earnestness, sympathy, and conviction. And when, finally, he and the daughter, Marian, undeceive the father in regard to the secret he thinks he has discovered and the ability he thinks he possesses to transmute baser stuff into gold, the father dies from the shock. Once more, certain elements of the O'Brien-Poe formula are present—the monomania, the local setting (Seventh Avenue above Twenty-third Street), and the pseudoscience aired with the seeming casualness of great learning. One example of the display of learning, a sentence spoken by the old alchemist, is "That which Nicholas Flamel did in 1382, that which George

[24] *The New York Leader*, Apr. 12, 1862. Editorial notice.

[25] Winter, 1881, p. xxi. See also George Arnold's description, *ibid.*, p. xlvii.

[26] *N. Y. Times*, July 2, 1898,—*Saturday Review of Books and Art*, p. 444. This address of O'Brien's I have been unable to locate.

Ripley did at Rhodes in 1460, that which Alexander Sethon and Michael Scudivogius did in the seventeenth century, I did in 1856."[27]

An especially interesting point of technique is the way in which O'Brien makes triple use of one of his favorite devices. As has been said, the doctor is the chief narrator, but when he makes his professional visit to the old man, that character at some length tells his own story to the doctor, and later the daughter in justifying herself indulges in another personal narrative. The story is, then, a sort of elaborate monologue containing within itself two other fairly developed monologues. It sticks much more closely to the point than do most of O'Brien's stories—there are practically no digressions—and its only flaw seems to be a slight stiltedness of expression in the conversation between the doctor and Marian.

The chief interest of "The Golden Ingot" is not in ingenuity of device as it is in "From Hand to Mouth," nor in power of the imagination as in "The Diamond Lens," nor in morbidity of conception as in "What Was It?" or "The Lost Room," but lies rather in the sympathy evoked by the great suffering which can result from following a delusive obsession.

The following number of *The Knickerbocker* contains another story of O'Brien's, which in this case makes use of the Hawthorne method in that, though a supernatural cause for the catastrophe is definitely suggested, there is also a plausible solution through natural means contained in the circumstances of the story. "Jubal, the Ringer"[28] is a legend of the type common to German romanticism, and a medieval effect is produced by the description of the pageantry and the supernatural visitation of the bats. As Jubal sits "high in the brown belfry of the old Church of St. Fantasmos" awaiting the dawn, he can reflect on how he, now old, and the old church, and the old cock weather vane crowning the steeple are all neglected by the people below. Even the woman he loved will on the morrow wed another. So Jubal summons a horde of bats, who dig out the mortar and hide themselves in the stones of the belfry. The wedding procession, gay and beautiful, arrives. As it reaches the altar Jubal begins to ring harsh discords on his bells. They sound with a terrible clamor and cry with a wild, discordant jangling. The bats fly away; the bells crash outrageously; and the turret rocks and falls, smashing through the ceiling and killing Jubal and all beneath. The pageant of the world below as seen from the belfry recalls

[27] *The Knickerbocker, or New-York Monthly Magazine,* LII, 180 (Aug., 1858).

[28] *Ibid.*, LII, 230–234 (Sept., 1858). Aldrich in a letter to Winter in 1880 confused its title with that of Poe's story and speaks of it as "The Devil in the Belfry."

Hawthorne's "Sights from a Steeple" (1831), and the description of the wildly clanging bells cannot but have been influenced by Poe's poem (1849).

In the same month, September, *Harper's Monthly* printed two of O'Brien's most interesting productions. Scattered among a number of his stories and articles O'Brien, in speaking of New York society and the education of its young ladies, had referred slightingly or satirically to Madame Cancan's fashionable boarding school.[29] Not satisfied with such passing references, however, he wrote a long and elaborate poem devoted especially to Madame Cancan and called it "The Finishing School." This poem, given full-page spread and illustrated with twelve large line drawings by A. Hoppin, was made the feature article of the issue.

It is divided into three parts, the first two of which tell most of the story, while the third part describes the horrible degradation to which such an education as that dispensed by Madame Cancan must lead, and from this draws a very long and elaborate moral. The poem is written easily in swinging anapestic tetrameters, varied frequently by internal rhyme. The rhyme is often a forced double or triple one written as a *jeu d'esprit,* and occasional puns add to the poem's informal, bantering mood. Yet, when the moral is being driven home, the feeling changes to one of great seriousness and earnest indignation.

In part one Miss Mary Degai, the heiress, is introduced as ready to make her debut from Madame Cancan's school. This gives opportunity for sarcastic digs at finishing schools and their training:

> No Puritan modesty marred their *tournure*—
> Being modest is nearly as bad as being poor—
>
> No flirting of course was permitted. Oh dear!
> If Madame Cancan such a word were to hear
> She would look a whole beltful of dagger-blades at you,
> And faint in the style of some favorite statue.
>
> *Au reste*, Madame's *pension* was quite the fashion:
> None better knew how to put shawl or pin sash on
> Than did her young ladies; 'twas good as a play
> To watch the well-bred and impertinent way
> They could enter a room in. Their gait in the street
> Was five-barred—one might say—'twas so high and complete.[30]

[29] See "The Beauty," *Harper's*, XI, 196; "Mary Burnie of the Mill," *ibid.*, XIII, 783; "Dora Dee," *ibid.*, XIV, 369; "The Man about Town," *H. W.*, I, 259 and 355; and "Brown Studies. No. VII," *Young America*, I, 172.

[30] *Harper's*, XVII, 434–435 (Sept., 1858).

The Ball, part two, is made the opportunity for many a fling at the idle dissipation and artificial life of the New York winter season. Miss Degai flirts violently with the bogus Count Cherami, and "while poor Madison Mowbray—a rising young lawyer"[31]—is looking for her to claim the next dance, she elopes with the count.

A sad denouement follows; for in a den of vice, starving and shivering in a filthy attic, the disillusioned wife is beaten and abused by her drunken husband. In seven years he has squandered her fortune, and now neither will nor can work.

> No help from herself—thanks to Madame Cancan,
> She had not a notion of getting along.[32]

After this, begins the moral application, which, though lengthy, is kept interesting and alive. It begins:

> Oh! young ladies who sigh over novels in yellow,
> And think Eugene Sue an exceeding smart fellow,
> There are more aims in life than a crinoline skirt,
> And a maid may be charming and yet not a flirt;
> And merit is better than title, my dears;
> In this country we've no occupation for peers.
>
> . . .
>
> Be this axiom forever with you paramount,
> Don't you ever advance all your cash on a Count.[33]

At last comes the divine retribution: Madame Cancan is "called up before the great Teacher of all" to account for the many pure young souls which had been sent to her for guidance.

> Were they harbored or wrecked?
> You didn't take trouble to think, I expect.
>
> . . .
>
> Ah! Madame Cancan, our great Master above,
> Who instructs us in charity, virtue, and love,
> When he finds you deficient in all of your lessons,
> A deliberate dunce both in substance and essence,
> Will send you, I fear, to a Finishing School,

[31] *Ibid.*, p. 442.
[32] *Ibid.*, p. 444.
[33] *Ibid.*, p. 445.

Which differs from yours though, in being less cool,
And kept on the corporal punishment rule.[34]

From these extracts the appeal of the poem to a large majority of the *Harper's* readers is easily seen. Its exaltation of the moral virtues, its implication of a sensible homemaking education for girls, and its appeal to American patriotic pride, all had their effect. In addition, it tells the old but ever interesting story of how pride will have its fall, and it berates the idle rich. For the social satire, as well as for the supernatural story, O'Brien had found an excellent recipe.

But he by no means gave up the writing of supernatural stories, for in this very number of *Harper's* he tells the story of a room much loved by its occupant, which, after a frightful, uncanny experience suffered by him, disappears from the house in which it was located. Far less concentrated than "The Golden Ingot," "The Lost Room"[35] works through a discursive introduction of the familiar-essay type into an atmosphere which wins acceptance for the gruesome supernaturalism of the climax. The story, though not so divided, consists of three parts. In part one the storyteller sits in the oppressive heat of the gathering twilight and makes an inventory of the various objects in his room, dwelling upon the personal associations with which each object is surrounded. In one instance he mentions an ancestor on his maternal side, "Sir Florence O'Driscoll by name,"[36] and gives the history of his piracies, of his affair with Queen Elizabeth, and of his being dispossessed. Like the description of his own appearance in "From Hand to Mouth," like the details of his pecuniary embarrassments in "The Man about Town," this is only another example of the use O'Brien makes of his personal background for literary material; and the difficulty for the investigator is to know how to separate such authentic details from the highly imaginative ones with which they are frequently intermixed. Part two emphasizes the growing sultriness of the night, describes the peculiar, lonely atmosphere of the house with its endless corridors and its gibbering ghoullike servant, and tells of the author's extraordinary encounter in the blackness of the cypress-shrouded garden. The story reaches its culmination in the third part, with the author's rapid return to his room, to find it completely transformed—brilliantly illuminated, set with Renaissance fur-

[34] *Ibid.*, pp. 446–447.
[35] *Ibid.*, XVII, 494–500 (Sept., 1858).
[36] *Ibid.*, p. 495.

nishings, and occupied by people of a corresponding era. Yet in all the objects, transformed as they are, he recognizes the basis of his familiar possessions. Refusing to eat of the horrible banquet of these sensual ghouls, he is ousted from the apartment, which during the moment of his ejection returns to its original form. Then the door closes; he turns; a blank wall faces him; and he never finds a trace of his room or possessions again.

The descriptive passages of "The Lost Room," with their touches of wit, of sentiment, of weirdness, and of awful suggestion, are especially well done; and the part dealing with the familiar so transformed as to be only eerily suggestive of itself, inextricably entangled in the manner of a bad dream, is vivid and convincing. The cause of this gruesome experience is never positively stated, but the suggestion made is clear enough and is even more uncanny than the happening itself.

In October O'Brien became an associate editor of, and the dramatic critic for, *The Saturday Press*, in which venture he was associated with Clapp, the editor, with Aldrich, and in general with the Pfaff group of Bohemians. To some of the excellent criticisms which he wrote for this paper O'Brien must have given considerable attention; yet before the year was out he had printed elsewhere three more poems and one short story.

The most striking of these poems, "The Prize-Fight," was published in the December number of *Harper's Monthly* and was immediately copied in *The Saturday Press*.[37] Like "The Finishing School," "The Prize-Fight" is a poem of satirical purpose. It is "an indignant protest against the brutalities of the Ring and its backers and abettors."[38] Since his June encounter with the barkeeping pugilist O'Brien had probably become especially sensitive to men disfiguring and ruining each other with blows of the bare fist, and he could write feelingly on the subject. In strong, pounding verse, which strikingly recalls the rhythms of John Masefield's "The Everlasting Mercy" of half a century later (1911), this "spirited satirical poem" treats of "the great fight between those combative gentlemen, Mr. John C. Heenan and the late Mr. Thomas Sayers."[39] The effect of the beating thuds is in the verse, and the varied repetition of the refrain hammers itself into one's consciousness.

Some pages earlier in the same issue appeared a gay little poem, telling

[37] *The Saturday Press*, Nov. 20, 1858.
[38] *H. W.*, VI, 267 (Apr. 26, 1862).
[39] *The Round Table*, III, 245 (Apr. 21, 1866).

a simple love story in a lightly humorous way—"Love at a Lattice."[40] Its running diary form is neatly handled and, as William Winter says, it is "pretty."[41]

The third poem and the last story for the year give voice to the kind of sentimentality which was the stock in trade of the female writers of the period. To a man who is alone and "Homeless"[42] only Death is true. What an appeal to the charitable feelings which lie close to the surface near Christmas time! Even more pointed is the story "Three of a Trade; or, Red Little Kriss Kringle,"[43] which implicitly hopes that purse strings will open to help others situated like the two little orphan boys who, huddled in the cold and snow with the organ-grinder's monkey, become drowsy and freeze to death. And this under date of Christmas Day!

This is all for 1858 except *The Saturday Press* criticism; for "The Red Petticoat" never materialised, in spite of the prominent advertising given it, three times repeated, in *Frank Leslie's Illustrated Newspaper:*

> Frank Leslie has the pleasure to announce that the leading Original Story commenced in the First Number has been written especially for
>
> THE STARS AND STRIPES
>
> by
>
> FITZJAMES O'BRIEN, ESQ,
>
> (Author of "The Diamond Lens," &c., &c.) entitled,
>
> THE RED PETTICOAT:
>
> A Tale of the Great Panic;
>
> which, in thrilling and startling interest—human, real life interest—has rarely been equalled and never excelled. As a work of literary merit, it is worthy the scholarly reputation and the brilliant imagination of the distinguished author.[44]

The Saturday Press[45] began its brilliant but precarious career on October 23, 1858, under the editorial guidance of the erratic "King of Bohemia,"

[40] *Harper's*, XVIII, 58–60 (Dec., 1858).
[41] MS note.
[42] *The Knickerbocker*, LII, 587 (Dec., 1858).
[43] *The New York Saturday Press*, Dec. 25, 1858.
[44] *Frank Leslie's Illustrated Newspaper*, Dec. 11, 1858; Dec. 18, and Dec. 25.
[45] *The Saturday Press* appeared with this title, Oct. 23 to Nov. 27, 1858. With the issue of December 4 it changed its title to *The New York Saturday Press*. Beginning with Jan. 1, 1859, it used a hyphen in the word *New-York*.

Henry Clapp, Jr. It was witty, clever, and fearless, cynically attacking literary shams, opposing especially respectability and Boston, and protesting continually—sometimes apparently without any very distinct idea of what it protested against. Needless to say it kept the literary pot stirred up, and must have shocked any of the staid respectabilities of the mid-century who had the temerity to read it. Even William Dean Howells, whose general disapproval of Pfaff's and the Bohemians has been quoted at length, was, it will be remembered, especially interested in *The Saturday Press* and in the young men who wrote for it. He was not so commendatory, however, about the irregular hours kept by its editors.[46] Further testimony to the paper's unbusinesslike methods is supplied by James C. Derby:

> There were about twenty young literary people connected with the *Saturday Press*. There was no cash book or other account books kept, thus avoiding the expense of a book-keeper. Whatever money was received went into the hands of whichever proprietor happened to be in the office at the time. Mr. Aldrich once told me that Mr. Clapp could not sleep in the morning, while he, being young and in excellent health, slept until about nine o'clock. Through this habit he got little or nothing of the money which came in for advertisements, as Mr. Clapp, being the first on hand, confiscated the receipts.[47]

Additional information as to Clapp's superb disregard of honest business methods is given by Edmund Clarence Stedman: "The paper was usually hard up, and Mr. Clapp took in several business partners, one after the other. When he got what he called 'fresh blood' he used to divide it up among the boys."[48]

Under such conditions the wonder is not that the paper was discontinued in December, 1860, but that it ran so long. At its initiation Thomas Bailey Aldrich was the assistant editor and Fitz-James O'Brien dramatic reviewer. Others closely associated with the enterprise were George Arnold and Edward G. P. Wilkins, and a little later Charles F. Browne ("Artemus Ward") and William Winter. O'Brien, on no such plane of economic independence as to be able to give his time and effort gratuitously, severed his connection with *The Saturday Press* in January, 1859, his last article appearing on January 29. Aldrich, who remained a few months longer, wrote of this

[46] See W. D. Howells, *op. cit.*, p. 68.
[47] J. C. Derby, *Fifty Years among Authors, Books and Publishers*, New York, 1884, p. 232.
[48] Laura Stedman and G. M. Gould, *op. cit.*, I, 208.

association that "in the years 1858–'59 O'Brien and I were very intimate; we never let a day pass without meeting."[49]

The work done by O'Brien as theatrical critic for *The Saturday Press* was contained in a column headed "Dramatic Feuilleton." In the first number, which praises Joseph Jefferson's performance in Tom Taylor's *Our American Cousin*, but which berates the play, this column is signed "Dodo."[50] In the next issue the column concludes with the following notice:

PERSONAL. My first article was signed "Dodo," as all persons who read the first number of *The Saturday Press* are aware. It has been suggested to me since that the Dodo, being a bird which was remarkably deficient in feathers, its name was inappropriate for a *nom de plume*. I accordingly subscribe myself,

Fitz James O'Brien[51]

Over this signature, then, for the next three months followed a series of critical articles. Once or twice he mentions theatregoing experiences of his years in London: he recalls a play seen at the Royal Olympic Theatre in February, 1851, and he has heard Herr Formes sing at the Covent Garden Opera House.[52] One number is devoted to a commendation of the acting and theatrical productions of the French; in another number he inveighs against the not uncommon occurrence of actors appearing on the stage when drunk, and refers to the popular *The Lady of Lyons* as "that melancholy piece of fustian;" in a third, he deprecates the constant cry among the critics for "a national drama" and shows how attempts at comedies of American life and Revolutionary melodramas will only result in poor plays; and in a fourth he advises about the proper use of the voice—read a part with intellect and the proper "elocution" will follow.[53]

In three cases he writes interesting criticism of plays,—twice about Shakespeare's and once about his own. The review of *A Gentleman from Ireland* was written almost four years after it was originally produced, and shows with how detached a manner he could write, upon seeing the revival at Wallack's of the brain child of which he had once been proud and enthusiastic. Even if the criticism was done as a magnificent and clever pose, the semblance of

[49] Winter, *Old Friends*, p. 101.
[50] *The Saturday Press*, Oct. 23, 1858.
[51] *Ibid.*, Oct. 30.
[52] See *ibid.*, Oct. 30, and Nov. 13, respectively.
[53] See *ibid.*, Nov. 20, Nov. 27, Dec. 25, and Dec. 18, respectively.

cold-blooded detachment is there.[54] Of the Shakespearean articles the first contains enthusiastic but discriminating praise of Wallack's revival of *The Merchant of Venice*.[55] The second is a much more pretentious article. It was written after O'Brien had been to see Barry Sullivan's production of *Hamlet;* but rather than a criticism of that performance, it is a discussion of what O'Brien would consider an ideal portrayal of the character of Hamlet. The proper interpretation of the play and the appropriate method of acting, especially in the soliloquies, are dwelt on with some particularity.[56] He had "elaborately considered Hamlet from a Bohemian point of view," as he said in the column the following week.[57]

On this latter date (January 8, 1859) the column is very short, the writer complaining that there is no news. For the next two weeks there is no dramatic column at all; and finally, on January 29, appears the last one. It rather bitterly complains of the niggardly unfairness of the money returns that authors receive for their plays, and expresses the writer's opinion of pirating managers.

Thus with dramatic criticism, poetic satires, and supernatural stories Fitz-James O'Brien rounded out a year of successful and varied activity and made for himself a name in the fields of journalism and literature.

[54] See *ibid.*, Nov. 13. Quoted on p. 88, above.

[55] See *ibid.*, Dec. 18, 1858.

[56] See *ibid.*, Jan. 1, 1859.

[57] *Ibid.*, Jan. 8.

Chapter IX

Supernatural Stories and a Trip to Boston

(1859)

The outstanding production of the year 1859 was "What Was It? A Mystery,"[1] the startling success of which almost if not quite duplicated the sensation made by "The Diamond Lens." With the exception of the latter this story far excels any other of O'Brien's stories. It tells of an encounter with a monster which can be felt and heard, but not seen. It is weird and uncanny, and suggestive of terror beyond anything else O'Brien wrote. The mystery of the inexplicable, the fear of the unseen, permeate the atmosphere. The reader is held fearfully wondering what is to be the next dreadful revelation. If imitation is a sign of admiration, "What Was It?" has been most flatteringly admired; for Guy de Maupassant a few years later in "La Horla" (1886) repeated with powerful effectiveness the terror and horror of the invisible ghost. Still later Ambrose Bierce in "The Damned Thing" (1898) and H. G. Wells in "The Invisible Man" (1897) took advantage of the same device.

In contrast with "The Lost Room" this story is direct and to the point, containing no digressions. Even the introduction is shorter than usual, and most of it necessary and purposeful giving the story local place and time and relating circumstantial details about the first-person author. Such a technical device had by this time become a distinctive mark of O'Brien's short-story writing; and the signature of "Harry Escott" at the end definitely connects "What Was It?" with the earlier "A Pot of Tulips," the narrator of ghostly mystery seeming in both cases to vouch for the truth of the tale by affixing his name.

Amid the chorus of contemporary praise for "What Was It?" only one dissenting note was heard, and although voiced by the *Boston Courier* it was again the New York *Evening Post* which copied the attack to give it wide publicity. Originality in character and treatment are denied to a story

[1] *Harper's*, XVIII, 504–509 (Mar., 1859).

for which, as it says, the scene of "The Dweller of the Threshold" in Bulwer's *Zanoni* supplied the model.[2] Nevertheless, Brander Matthews reprinted the tale in his specimens of *The Short Story*; and, in spite of his making a number of cuts in the text, his estimate of it is high and his criticism well considered: "The originality of the invention is most evident, and there is a realism in the story-form which is more than mere similitude. The matter-of-fact telling of the tale recalls De Foe, while the theme itself suggests Poe. But Poe would never have condescended to the prosaic plaster cast at the end."[3] To this last statement C. Alphonso Smith replies, "But why not? The taking of the plaster cast emphasises the characteristics that were known of the terrible creature." "As it stands it is the best short story in Poe's manner, and of it the last half century may be proud."[4]

Following the lead of Brander Matthews, many editors have since 1907 reprinted "What Was It?," and a number of critics besides Dr. Smith have considered its place in the development of the short story.[5] Especially interesting analyses and critical evaluations of the story are given by J. Berg Esenwein, Henry Albert Phillips, Carolyn Wells, and Dorothy Scarborough.[6] With Esenwein's reference to it as a solved ghost story I disagree, however; for though the plaster cast which is taken pretends to solve the mystery, it actually does not do so, the invisibility still remaining unexplained. As Phillips says, the fact that the mystery is unexplained is one of the story's distinctive points. In addition to Maupassant's "The Horla," Carolyn Wells speaks of "What Was It?" in connection with Kipling's "They" (1904), Henry James's "The Turn of the Screw" (1898), and F.

[2] See *Evening Post*, Mar. 4, 1859.

[3] Brander Matthews, ed. *The Short Story, Specimens Illustrating Its Development*, New York-Cincinnati-Chicago, 1907, p. 246.

[4] Translated from Dr. C. Alphonso Smith, *Die Amerikanische Literature.* Vorlesungen, gehalten an der Königlichen Friedrich-Wilhelms-Universität zu Berlin, Berlin, 1912, pp. 354 and 353.

[5] For citations and list of reprints see Bibliography, esp. p. 263.

[6] See J. B. Esenwein, *Studying the Short-Story*, The Writer's Library, Springfield, Mass., 1912, pp. 71–72; H. A. Phillips, *The Plot of the Short Story, An exhaustive study, both synthetical and analytical, with copious examples, making the work A Practical Treatise*, (The Authors' Handbook Series), Larchmont, N. Y., 1912, p. 69; Carolyn Wells, *The Technique of the Mystery Story*, The Writer's Library, Springfield, Mass., 1913, pp. 31–32; and Dorothy Scarborough, *The Supernatural in Modern English Fiction*, 1917, pp. 61 and 96, and *Famous Modern Ghost Stories*, 1921, pp. xiv, and 253–273.

Marion Crawford's "The Upper Berth" (1894); and Dorothy Scarborough analyzes the elements of its haunting effectiveness.

One other story of interesting supernatural invention, though without the undefined horror of "What Was It?," also marks the year 1859. "The Wondersmith,"[7] the second and last of O'Brien's stories to be contributed to *The Atlantic Monthly*, deals with evil people, who through evil impulses produce instruments of evil and who, being caught in their own toils, perish by the means they had produced. The gypsy wondersmith, maker of wicked mannikins; the fortuneteller, with her black bottle full of the evil souls which animate them; the French artisan in artificial eyes, with the huge glass eye placed outside the door to warn against interruption of their evil rites; and Oaksmith, the English gypsy, make a rare quartet of criminals. Through their uncanny skill at their respective crafts they become the wielders of supernatural agencies. Yet their machinations are frustrated, not through outside aid as the introduction of Solon, the humpback, and Furbelow, the monkey, would seem to predict; but through their own evil, in its premature triumph, overreaching itself. Worse than futile are their schemes as they perish in the tortures of the frightful poison and, together with the mannikins, are burnt out of existence in the flaming house.

The powerful impression of this plot is somewhat diluted by the introduction of Zonéla, the stolen child of the wondersmith, whose love episode with Solon, though it adds a sentimental touch to the story, affects the conduct of its development not at all. One other weakness in the plot is the elaboration of detail with which Kerplonne's great glass eye is introduced. Its supernatural properties make one expect that at some crucial moment it will by its weird warning aid evil and thwart good; but it does absolutely nothing.

In spite of these strictures, which point out minor irritations rather than major defects, "The Wondersmith" remains a marvelously interesting story. The main episode of the diabolical, murderous toys, of the pigmy slaughter in the birdshop, and of the toys' final attack on their vengeful creators is told with real skill and imaginative intensity. As the hero in "What Was It?," abnormal from the use of opium, lives in a perfectly believable boardinghouse on Twenty-sixth Street between Seventh and Eighth Avenues, so the chief character in "The Wondersmith," abnormal from his fierce hatred

[7] *The Atlantic Monthly*, IV, 463–482 (Oct., 1859).

of humanity, especially of Christians and children, inhabits a shop in a vividly described slum district of New York, on a street the authenticity of whose details is unquestionable. The sordidness of the squalid street is so accurately described that when the supernatural is introduced it seems perfectly plausible.

In addition to its inherent interest, "The Wondersmith" sounds many echoes of other work. As Fred Lewis Pattee says, the first part is "redolent of Dickens, but the rest of it reads like a translation of a Hoffman tale of 'The Sand Man' variety or 'Nutcracker and the King of the Mice'."[8] Almost identical is the statement by Joseph J. Reilly that O'Brien "imitated Poe in studying Hoffman, to whom his obligations in *The Wondersmith* are unmistakable."[9] The organ-grinder's monkey he had used recently in "Three of a Trade," and earlier in the old *Lantern* poem, "The Street Monkey," while the use of the artificial eye had been suggested to him by Henry Clapp, who told of once being with Albert Brisbane when the latter fell asleep with his eye wide open.[10] The meaningless but dauntless repetitions of the Mino-birds also connect with a Henry Clapp anecdote, though in this case O'Brien's story was the earlier. In "The Wondersmith" one Mino-bird asks, "What'll you take?" "Brandy and water," constantly replies the other.[11]

Some years afterward when Artemus Ward was "beginning to be known as a lecturer, he was in at Pfaff's and received a telegram or letter from California, 'What will you take for forty nights?'

" 'Brandy and soda, answer them,' sang out Clapp. Browne [Artemus Ward] did, and established a reputation on the Pacific coast."[12]

With the publication of "The Wondersmith" Fitz-James O'Brien had completed the writing of his best stories. During the two and a half years of life remaining to him he did not again equal the performance of "The Diamond Lens," "What Was It?" and "The Wondersmith." It is, therefore, chiefly upon these that his claim to a place in the development of the short story in America must rest. The critics contemporary with O'Brien, however, seem generally to have regarded his poetry as superior to his stories, and Henry A. Beers, in 1878, when he attempted for the first time

[8] F. L. Pattee, *op. cit.*, p. 157.

[9] J. J. Reilly, *op. cit.*, *loc. cit.*, p. 753.

[10] See Winter, *Old Friends*, p. 69.

[11] *The Atlantic Monthly*, IV, 474–475.

[12] Stedman and Gould, *op. cit.*, I, 208.

to assign O'Brien a place in American literary history, represented him by selections in both verse and prose, reprinting "Kane" and the last two sections of "The Diamond Lens."[13]

Since the Beers anthology, and especially since Winter's collection of 1881, although unmentioned in the shorter histories of American literature, the work of Fitz-James O'Brien has in the longer surveys been granted at least a sentence or a paragraph, and in the more recent studies of the development of the short story in America it has received considerable attention. Just how thoroughly the addition of a Defoelike verisimilitude to the Poelike tale of terror marks a new technical departure is minutely analyzed by Henry Seidel Canby in *The Short Story in English.* Published in 1909, two years after the reprint of "What Was It?" by Brander Matthews, Canby's book is the first to give O'Brien's work anything like adequate consideration. This passage is, therefore, quoted at some length:

O'Brien, it is true, succeeded only when he worked up his local color and his contemporary portraits under the stress of a sensationally grim plot, which fused all into one definite impression. But at least, in some measure, he was applying the impressionistic story, hitherto used consciously only in pursuit of the terror of the soul, to reasonably familiar life. Of *The Diamond Lens* and *The Wondersmith* Mr. Winter says, "They electrified magazine literature, and they set up a model of excellence which, in this department, has made it better than it ever had been, in this country, before those tales were printed." Now Poe's technique had certainly been more original and more perfect, and Hawthorne's stories more fully charged with matter and with meaning. Surely, electrification could only have come from the example of a new story-telling used in tales which, for all their extravagance, had more of the common clay of life than was to be found in earlier examples of the impressionistic short story.

O'Brien's imagination might have carried him far, and did place him unquestionably among the ranks of remarkable narrators. The idea of *The Diamond Lens* is at least unique; the invisible man-monster of *What Was It?* is one of those conceptions which insure a story; but the plot of *The Wondersmith* is still more indicative of power. . . . The imagination which conceived and moved this tale without absurdity did much, even in this very unequal narrative. There is nothing else quite like *The Wondersmith* in American literature. Hood might have done it, had he known how to tell a good short story; Hawthorne might have hit upon the fancy, and made the tale far more serious, more gloomy, more sen-

[13] See H. A. Beers, ed., *A Century of American Literature, 1776–1876*, 1878, Leisure Hour Series,—No. 100, pp. 372–385. This contains also a short biographical sketch of O'Brien.

tentious, but scarcely so pleasing; neither could have blended so much life, imagination, extravagance in one reasonably coherent whole, and contrived to leave a very definite impression of the heart of the story. O'Brien, with all his journalistic carelessness, accomplished just that because, in his amateur fashion, he really understood Poe's technique for the short story.[14]

Four years later in *A Study of the Short Story*, Canby reiterates much of the above, and then regretfully notes that of all the fertile storytellers of the mid-nineteenth century, only Edward Everett Hale and O'Brien have been worthy of remembrance. The three milestones of the fifties and sixties, he points out, are O'Brien, "a man of those times only, whose brilliant career was nipped in its beginning by death in our Civil War, . . . Edward Everett Hale, whose just finished work attained to what may prove its most lasting triumph in the early sixties;" and "Bret Harte, the first writer to gain recognition in England for our short story."[15] Margaret Ashmun, Edward J. O'Brien, and F. L. Pattee also consider O'Brien's work as marking a distinct step in the development of the short story.[16]

O'Brien wrote only the two stories during 1859, and but little else in prose. In March appeared "A Nest of Nightingales,"[17] an article of the essay-story type like "A Paper of All Sorts" or like some of the sketches in "The Man about Town." It was to have been included in the 1881 volume, *The Poems and Stories of Fitz-James O'Brien*; but a letter of October 26, 1880, from Winter to Ticknor the publisher in Boston, discussing the contents and arrangement of the volume, contains the following sentence: "I particularly wish, under any circumstances, to OMIT '*A NEST OF NIGHTINGALES*'—as I think it is a *translation* from the French". If this is so, it is not at all unlikely that Charles Nordhoff or some one else at Harpers, being in need of a space filler, called upon O'Brien, who supplied the gap with a foreign translation in accord with what had been the Harper policy at the time of the *Monthly's* establishment. There is no other prose, except that a notice in the *Evening Post* states that O'Brien is responsible for a review in the May *Atlantic*.[18] The one which exhibits his lightness of tone and which in subject matter is similar to his earlier "Your

[14] H. S. Canby, *The Short Story in English*, 1909, pp. 284–285.

[15] *Ibid.*, p. 281.

[16] See Margaret Ashmun, ed., *Modern Short Stories*, 1914, pp. xxvi and 197–199; E. J. O'Brien, *The Advance of the American Short Story*, 1923, pp. 88–91; and F. L. Pattee, *The Development of the American Short Story, An Historical Survey*, 1923, pp. 155–159.

[17] *Harper's*, XVIII, 520–522 (Mar., 1859).

[18] *New York Evening Post*, Apr. 29, 1859.

Health!" reviews Dr. Donné's book on the importance of the proper nursing for infants—a treatise on eugenics really—and on the microscopic analysis of milk. (Shades of "The Diamond Lens"!)

Besides the writing of "What Was It?" and "The Wondersmith," the year 1859 is marked for O'Brien by an actively renewed interest in things theatrical. Through his startling supernatural stories he had gained prominence and notoriety, and he had got himself often referred to and frequently laughed at. Though on January 29 he had written his last "Dramatic Feuilleton" for *The Saturday Press*, nevertheless, on February 5 his old friend Bellew writes about him in the *Picayune*, referring to his recent activities as a dramatic critic in such a way as to suggest that O'Brien must have turned almost immediately from *The Saturday Press* to some other organ. Over the signature "Triangle" Bellew gives the following estimate of *The Veteran*, the new play in which Lester Wallack had scored a decided hit:

> Oh, ye gods, that such a thing should be put upon the stage—be called a DRAMA! and, above all, find critics to approve it. *Herald! Times!! Tribune!!!* and last, not least, the great, inflexible Judge, Fitz James O'Brien, all soaping, soaping, soaping! Oh, gentlemen, gentlemen, this is too bad! Mr. Lester may be, he is, without doubt, a very fine fellow, popular, and all the rest of it, but is it consistent for you judges of the supremest of supreme courts to—but no matter, the "Veteran" will be a great success.

In this account Bellew seems to have been impressed by his friend's cocksureness and growing arrogance; and a cartoon of Bellew's, which only a month later appeared on the cover page of the *Picayune*, shows that such loftiness on the part of O'Brien and his assumption of even lordly airs had procured for him among his associates the nickname of "Baron." It will be recalled that William North had been unpleasantly impressed by his arrogance, that the letter from Jenny Danforth was addressed to him as "Mon cher Baron," and that Aldrich said he used to call O'Brien Baron Linchpin when they were merry. Bellew's full-length caricature pictures O'Brien walking by a shopwindow carrying in his hand a rolled manuscript, and wearing upon his head an enormous baronial coronet. His long nose, small chin, side whiskers, and large flowing mustache are prominently emphasized.[19] On July 2 O'Brien is again referred to as "the Baron," this

[19] *N. Y. Picayune*, Mar. 12, 1859.

time by Winter, his successor on *The Saturday Press*, who, writing as "Personne," comments at some length on the naming of one of O'Brien's plays:

The Slip, Sir, the Slip! I remember that some time ago the Baron was a good deal exercised in his mind about a title for a magnificent play which he was blocking out. There was much profound cogitation on the subject. The Baron inclined towards "There's Many a Slip 'Twixt the Cup and the Lip." Others

MR. FITZ JAMES O'BRIEN, AS WE MAY EXPECT TO SEE HIM SHORTLY PROMENADING BROADWAY

suggested that it was too long and proposed "The Cup and the Lip;" or "There's Many a Slip." I suggested "The Slip," and was duly snubbed for it.

Well, now Gayler, whom the Baron ranks among the finest minds of the age, has written a play for the Florences with the Baron's title, and as some of the papers say, somebody else's plot, but that is probably an accidental resemblance in certain situations.[20]

[20] *The Saturday Press*, July 2, 1859. O'Brien's play was called *The Cup and the Lip*. Gayler's farce had its first performance on June 27 under the title *The Railroad Contractor; or, There's Many a Slip Between the Cup and Lip*. (See Odell, *op. cit.*, VII, 125). For a third play with the same title translated from the French by Maria Grace Walcot see T. Allston Brown, *op. cit.*, I, 452, and Odell, *op. cit.*, VII, 390. (First acted Oct. 7, 1861).

On August 27 Matilda Heron, the actress whom O'Brien so greatly admired, began her season at Wallack's Theatre in a performance of Mrs. Sidney F. Bateman's new play *Geraldine*. Of this play O'Brien wrote a somewhat lengthy and complete account. After praising Mrs. Bateman's choice of a far distant historic period as the setting for her tragedy and the play as a piece of "wonderful emotional power," he shows what was expected of a tragedy in the ante-bellum days, and what to be successful was the effect it should exert on the audience:

> Act after act the torrent of the play is swollen with tributary streams of dramatic event, until, at length, in its passion and its strength, it inundates the public heart, and fertilizes it into a wholesome harvest of tears.[21]

In this emotional tragedy, then, O'Brien's admired emotional actress had a great opportunity to show the full range of her powers. And it was to advertise her that, after a run of "twenty-one consecutive nights to Crowded, Intelligent and Fashionable Audiences,"[22] O'Brien went to Boston as literary assistant to her "energetic, resolute, intrepid, tumultuous theatrical manager H. L. Bateman."[23] On Monday, September 19, "the Great Tragic Actress MATILDA HERON!" made "her first appearance in Boston In Two Years,"[24] and performed the title role in *Geraldine, or Love's Victory*, so movingly and effectively that the play ran at the Howard Athenaeum for three and a half weeks. Such a run was a decided success, and throughout its course it is punctuated by extravagant display advertisements, by enthusiastic comments, and by little items of personal interest, supplied to the daily press by Bateman's ingeniously fertile and alert press agent. On September 29, the *Boston Courier* announces that "the beauty of the new play, *Geraldine*, aided by the exquisite performance of Miss Heron, continues to fill the Howard Athenaeum every night." On October 3 part of a display advertisement in the same paper flatters literary Boston with the following words: "Night after night the walls of the theatre have enclosed persons who are celebrated in the worlds of SCIENCE, LITERATURE, ART AND FASHION. Thus stamping A Great Work And A Great Actress with the seal of Intellectual Approbation!" Bateman and O'Brien made a gala night of October 5, with the Putnam Phalanx from Connecticut

[21] Quoted from *Wilkes' Spirit of the Times*, May 24, 1862.

[22] *The Atlas and Daily Bee*, Boston, Sept. 19, 1859.

[23] Winter, *Old Friends*, p. 100.

[24] *The Atlas and Daily Bee*, Boston. Advertisement repeated on Sept. 20.

in attendance; and on the eighth, O'Brien carefully reported that on the previous evening a lady in the audience swooned from the power of Miss Heron's acting. Finally on Wednesday, the twelfth, Miss Heron gave her last performance of *Geraldine* at an author's night.[25] Upon this occasion *The Atlas and Daily Bee* contains a lengthy article in "The Man about Town" vein, referring to "the elegant and well-dressed Dimes," wittily, yet greatly, praising Miss Heron's acting, and ending with the following plea for the rights and recognition of the playwright:

It is but right that the author of a piece should obtain the same public recognition that an actor does. The author's triumphs are few—confined to the first night of production—while the actor's triumphs are nightly. . . . Audiences are frequently in the habit of forgetting . . . the poor solitary brain that constructed the panoramic display of Life which warns, soothes, and instructs. . . . In many cases the author has a better right to be known than the artist—because the author produces a piece, which, perfect in composition, fails through interpretation.

This is in line both with the comment of O'Brien's made in *The Saturday Press* and with his earlier criticism of the acting of his *Duke Humphrey's Dinner*.[26]

Of the social side of O'Brien's life during these four weeks in Boston (for Miss Heron completed the last week by acting in *Medea* and *Camille*),[27] there are some interesting traces. It was at this time that he met William Winter, who shortly after left Boston for New York; and in the latter city they renewed the acquaintance which ripened into a close and lasting friendship. At the time of their first meetings, Winter says, "His countenance bore a slight trace of rough usage; his hair, closely cropped, had begun to be a little thin; but his expressive gray-blue eyes were clear and brilliant; his laughter was bluff and breezy; his voice was strong and musical; his manner was gay; and he was a cheerful companion,—making the most of To-day, and caring not at all for To-morrow."[28] Of their early acquaintance in Boston, Winter wrote:

I remember that he considerably astonished some of the quiet literary circles of that staid and decorous region by his utter and unaffected irreverence for various

[25] See *Boston Courier*, Oct. 6, 8, and 12, respectively.
[26] See pp. 170; and 112.
[27] See *Boston Courier*, Oct. 13, 14, and 15.
[28] Winter, *Old Friends*, p. 100.

camphorated figure-heads which were then an incubus upon American letters. It was there and then that I first met him, and first observed that stalwart mind and that formidable frankness of temperament for which he was remarkable. . . . In his face and carriage there was the strong and splendid freedom of the wild woods; yet at times there came into his eyes a weary look of unrest, and a quite indescribable light of dangerous, half-slumbering wrath—as of a soul that was a hunted vagabond standing sentinel over its own desolation. I was attracted toward him by a profound sympathy, and we became comrades and friends, and so remained to the end.[29]

Boston boasted a kitchen that held much the same place in the lives and affections of its actor folk that Pfaff's did in New York. It was that of Miss Fisher at No. 2 Bulfinch Place, and here Fitz-James found congenial company. William Warren, the comedian, the favorite of Boston theatre-goers, presided here much as Henry Clapp, Jr., presided at Pfaff's. Joseph Jefferson, who, as well as Warren, lived for a time at Miss Fisher's, has described it most attractively in his autobiography:

There was a grand old kitchen here where, in company with many passing stars, we supped together after the play. Warren always sat at the head of the table, and was usually concealed behind a huge pile of lobsters, and as he served them liberally the scarlet edifice would slowly sink as if it were going through the stage in pantomime, revealing as it descended the fine face of the feast. For many seasons after this when I came to act in Boston, our suppers in the old kitchen were among the agreeable features of the engagement.[30]

That O'Brien was an intimate at Miss Fisher's is made clear by letters written to him by his young friend, Frank Wood. One of March 16, 1862, was sent to "Fitz" while he was away at war, and is full of personal, theatrical, and literary gossip. It devotes a paragraph to Boston:

Did you get the letter I wrote you from the Parker House, Boston? I passed a month at the "Hub." Stupid place. Morals of a village without its quiet. The lechery of the ape combined with the hypocrisy of the crocodile. While there I suborned the press for the Bateman as you used to do for the Heron.[31] I did

[29] Winter, 1881, p. xx.

[30] *The Autobiography of Joseph Jefferson*, N. Y., 1889, p. 407.

[31] Miss Bateman during this season revived *Geraldine*, the play for which O'Brien went to Boston to advertise Matilda Heron. She opened with it in New York on May 12—see *Wilkes' Spirit of the Times*, May 24, 1862, and Odell, *op. cit.*, VII, 394.

better than you, though. I am a finer writer.—Lived at Miss Fisher's three weeks of the time. Queer old body. Holds yr memory in sacred reverence. I made a motto for her—"*Simper paratus.*"—Warren was to me the great attraction of Boston. He was the only thing I regretted in leaving it. I consider him the finest comedian in America. Don't you?—We used to have very jolly times at our 11 o'clock suppers in that old kitchen, and when Jim Wallack and his wife came they were jollier still.[32]

Another letter remains from the Boston sojourn, one written by O'Brien himself. This, although addressed only "Dear Sir," was almost certainly sent to James Russell Lowell:

Tremont House
October 10th

Dear Sir

Will you come and hear some very charming singing on next Friday? This somewhat mysterious query resolves itself in this way. There is a small gathering of gentlemen—some of whom are your friends—to be held at the Tremont House on Friday next at six o'clock, the first object of which is dinner, and the second, music. Mr. Squires a very sweet native tenor will sing on this occasion. The host of the evening will be Mr. H. L. Bateman, but he has kindly asked me to invite some of my friends. This will perhaps account for the informality of inviting you to another man's party. Mr. Bateman will be very happy if you will come, and I am sure that you will find the symposium a pleasant one.

Mr. Underwood who has kindly undertaken to deliver this note will give you a more seductive programme than perhaps I can offer.

I am dear Sir

Yours truly
F. J. O'Brien[33]

Although O'Brien did not move in the circles to which Lowell belonged, he could well consider him as his friend through the correspondence they must

[32] Frank Wood to Fitz, March 16, 1862; in the Romm collection.

[33] A. L. S. in New York Public Library, F. J. O'Brien to Dear Sir [James Russell Lowell], Oct. 10, 1859. This letter was the gift of Thomas Ollive Mabbott, who appends the following note: "This letter, which came from Goodspeed's is stated in their 1922 Catalogue to be 'docketed in James Russell Lowell's hand.' As they had many autographs from C. C. Norton's collection, I do not doubt the correctness of this note." The party referred to took place on the night before the closing of the Bateman-Heron engagement; and the singer was Mr. Henry Squires, who made his first appearance in *La Traviata* the next afternoon and who later attained great success in Italy. See *Boston Courier*, Oct. 15, 1859, and *The Boston Herald*, Apr. 28, 1924.

have had when Lowell, as editor, accepted "The Diamond Lens" and "The Wondersmith" for publication in *The Atlantic*. The odd thing about the letter is the signature—it is the only instance I know, with the exception of the war documents, in which O'Brien uses the initials "F. J." instead of the name "Fitz-James."

During his month in Boston, however, the man of baronial airs and amorous proclivities had not been forgotten in New York, as witness this item from *The Saturday Press* of November 12: "The pretty actresses are going off rapidly. Lucille Western is married. (Eheu! M. le Baron) so is Josephine Gougenheim."

In addition to his theatrical experiences and his short stories, the year 1859 is marked by a scattered group of poems. That versemaking did not, however, hold O'Brien's interest at this time is sufficiently clear from the mediocre quality of the performance. The poems are not bad; they are not good; they are merely flat, revealing sufficient technical ability without inspiration or even sincerity behind it. "The Ghosts"[34] is a sonnet; "January"[35] is a rather musical, but entirely conventional, description of winter; "My First of April"—given display space in the April *Harper's*—is a sentimental poem of love and loss, done with the requisite smoothness; "The Meeting by the Hemlocks"[36] repeats the same graveyard theme with even more sentimentality, and imitates many of Poe's technical poetic devices while handling his typical subject, the death of a beautiful woman. Finally "The Enchanted Titan"[37] recalls, both in its reference to "the Cloud Compeller" and in its attempt to handle grotesque rhyme with serious effect, "The Song of the Immortal Gods," written for *The American Whig Review* in 1852 by "Origen Od." These rhymes, "enchanter-instanter," "pulp-gulp," and "hazy-crazy," though almost ridiculous in the first two stanzas, in the last two become effective.

"Wanted—St. Patrick"[38] is a satire of contemporary life done in jerky verse with a weighty seriousness and a lack of humor, not apparent in "The Finishing School." It is more like "The Prize-Fight," but differs from it in that it is an invective against a particular situation rather than against

[34] *The Knickerbocker*, LIII, 40 (Jan., 1859).

[35] *The Saturday Press*, Jan. 8, 1859.

[36] *Harper's*, XIX, 512 (Sept., 1859); identified not by the Harper *Index* but by *Evening Post*, Aug. 25, 1859.

[37] *Ibid.*, XX, 52–53 (Dec., 1859).

[38] *Ibid.*, XVIII, 525 (Mar., 1859).

the general practice behind the specific instance. It is, in fact, a political editorial in verse; and, while it is almost the only poem of such a type definitely assigned to O'Brien, it makes one wonder about the authorship of much verse like it, which began during the next year to appear in *Vanity Fair*. The plea of the poem is for St. Patrick to come today and rid the land of the modern reptiles, Gambling, Theft, and Murder.[39]

"In the autumn of 1859, just preceding the War, our society, 'best' and otherwise, had attained a point of efflorescence at which it began to crystallize," says Edmund Clarence Stedman. "It had begun naturally, to attract the attention of satirists, who weighed it with more reason than in the provincial days of that first fashion writer, Willis; and, inevitably, it attracted the smart young Bohemians who knew it only by report, and by observation of its more obvious functions and episodes."[40] George William Curtis, William Allen Butler, and Stedman himself all wrote social satires which attained considerable notoriety.[41]

This satirical attitude became so general, and the brilliant young authors and artists had so many clever things to say and draw, that once more they were led to launch a new comic weekly, whose fame and success they ardently, if not too confidently, hoped would rival the prestige of the English *Punch*. Accordingly *Vanity Fair*, the first really successful American comic magazine, planned and constructed largely around the table at Pfaff's, slid into the sea of public print on the last day of the year 1859.

[39] A sixth poem for 1859 has been doubtfully attributed to O'Brien by being included in *The Round Table* list of June 6, 1868. After the title, *The Lamentable Complaint of Katharina Maria Poppelle, Spinster*, there is, however, a question mark; and, though in subject it is a satire of fashionable society like "The Finishing School," the fact that the Harper's *Index* attributes it to the authorship of Rose Terry Cooke would seem to settle the point.

[40] Stedman and Gould, *op. cit.*, I, 184.

[41] The most famous of these were: Curtis, "The Potiphar Papers" of 1853; Butler, "Nothing to Wear," printed anonymously in *H. W.*, I, 84 (Feb. 7, 1857); and Stedman, "The Diamond Wedding," printed in *N. Y. Tribune*, Oct. 18, 1859. A full account of the latter—its inception and the aftermath from it—is given in Stedman and Gould, *op. cit.*, I, 183–203.

Chapter X

"A Fallen Star"

(1860)

The year 1860, though strangely destitute of work by O'Brien of much intrinsic literary importance, nevertheless shows a return to production almost as copious as that for 1857. The most interesting of these writings are those which reflect his personality or supply evidence of his friendships or activities. Only one story appeared this year from the hand of the man whose stories had been so effective in their uncanny way; and this one, though morbid and abnormal, avoids the pure supernatural, the material he could handle with such brooding power. Of the poems "The Lost Steamship" is a weird ballad that received much praise from his contemporaries, and "The Sewing Bird" is an indictment, done in the form of fantasy, of the desperate conditions under which women must work in the great city. It too attracted attention. But the poem deserving most consideration is "A Fallen Star," one in which he gracefully and sadly describes himself and much of his own fate; and the course O'Brien traveled, which led from "The Wondersmith" of one October to "A Fallen Star" of the November a year later, was so violently irregular as to make even the devil-may-care Fitz-James realize the dejected condition of himself and his fortunes.

As for the short stories, "Mother of Pearl," the only one for the year, interesting as it is and powerful as are many of its episodes, nevertheless shows a dissipation of the concentrated vigor that was so strong a quality in "The Wondersmith" and the stories that preceded it. Yet nothing better, nothing nearly so good, was in the future to come from O'Brien's pen. Did he try to emulate the fantastic power of his earlier inventions and fail? Or did he realize that he no longer possessed the mental and physical vigor necessary for success in the field where he had won his triumphs and his literary fame? If, conscious of this, he refrained from trying, he was the wiser man. To his poetry, on the other hand, the Civil War with its heightening of all the emotions brought a renewed gleam, and in a poetical as well as a military way the meteoric O'Brien ended in a blaze of glory.

A new market for contributions of the kind O'Brien was able to furnish became available in 1860 with the establishment of *Vanity Fair*. The first number was issued on December 31, 1859, and it ran to be the longest lived of the comics, before it was swallowed up in 1863 by the Civil War. This comic weekly was originated amongst members of the Pfaff group, and its staff and contributors were all friends of O'Brien. George Arnold wrote over a hundred articles for it; Frank Wood, O'Brien's young friend, not yet twenty, was the first editor and ran the magazine for some months with great credit to himself and the paper; "Artemus Ward" was brought in, in the fall of 1860, from his place on the Cleveland *Plaindealer* to join its staff; Frank Bellew was from the start one of its regular cartoonists; and Ada Clare and Thomas Bailey Aldrich appear as contributors in the first number. For this the latter wrote his poem "At the Café" beginning, "We were all very merry at Pfaff's."[1]

In the second number O'Brien himself is represented. The verses of "Song of the Locomotive" have for the first three stanzas something of the rattle and smash of the roughly rolling train, and the refrain is effective:

> Mighty with motion resistless I sweep.
> Bong! bong!
> Smashing along!
> I lighten my road with a bit of a song![2]

The locomotive's joy in its own motion keeps up, until broken into by a bit of sentimentalizing. This is followed by its reflection that it would rather perish while pounding along than rust in a junk yard. It is, nevertheless, a bit unexpected to have the poem end joyfully with a head-on collision.

After the collapse of a cotton factory with an appalling loss of life *Vanity Fair* came out for the next two or three weeks with an assortment of scathingly bitter poems, articles, and cartoons directed against the criminal carelessness of the contractors and owners. The earliest of these was O'Brien's "Pemberton Mills," a rhymed invective against factory owners who do not exercise proper supervision or make needed repairs:

[1] *Vanity Fair*, I, 12 (Dec. 31, 1859).
[2] *Ibid.*, I, 20 (Jan. 7, 1860).

A curse on ye, ye Millionaires
Who sit at home in your easy chairs,
And crack your nuts and sip your wine
While I wail over this son of mine![3]

Two more poems about the same catastrophe were printed in the next two weeks, and either or both of these may easily have been written by O'Brien. "Death, the Builder"[4] points out the suffering resulting to families from the death of their wage earners and makes use of the same sort of contrast as did "Pemberton Mills." "No One to Blame"[5] states satirically in its title the inevitable verdict which follows the investigation of such accidents; and the refrain of the poem is similar to that of "Song of the Locomotive," and "The Prize-Fight." Still another poem on the same subject, "Twenty Per Cent,"[6] is almost certainly O'Brien's. In the form of a dream it decries the building of rotten mills and tenement houses and the poor wages paid to workers so that the owners will be sure of their twenty per cent. The laborers are driven to

Poverty, misery, want and shame,
Miserly thrift and sin,

and the buildings collapse—"a terrible dream!"

That the reforming fit had for the time seized strongly upon Fitz-James is further manifested by a second poem in the issue of February 4. "The Song of the Shirtless" cries out for a thorough cleaning up of the filthiness of the city streets, for which graft among the councilmen is responsible. These details almost duplicate those of "The Lost City Broom," written for *The Lantern* seven years before, and the general tone is also much the same; but the sympathy expressed for the little boy who while starving sweeps the street of its disease- and death-breeding mud reveals a genuine growth in O'Brien's humanitarian spirit.

For February 11 O'Brien wrote the first number of a column entitled "Here and There," which ran irregularly until July 7. Much like "The

[3] *Ibid.*, I, 52 (Jan. 21, 1860).
[4] *Ibid.*, I, 70 (Jan. 28, 1860).
[5] *Ibid.*, I, 85 (Feb. 4, 1860).
[6] *Ibid.*, I, 142 (Feb. 25, 1860). Identification of this poem and of "The Song of the Shirtless" as O'Brien's is confirmed by Charles I. Glicksberg.

Man about Town" it consists of unrelated paragraphs on a variety of subjects, but the columns themselves are not so long nor the treatment so elaborate. In the "Opening Andante" he discusses theatrical fare, Mademoiselle Zoyara the circus bareback rider who is really a man, the tight-moneyed men like old Croesus who oppose the development of Central Park, and "the barbarous state of the streets."[7] In other numbers he refers to his old characters Dimes and Madame Cancan;[8] and from time to time he attacks conditions in the city that cry for reform—Mayor Wood's appointment of a ruffian as street inspector, the lack of quarantine for yellow fever, and the attempts at political pressure and bribery to rescue a thug from a deserved sentence.[9] Most frequently, however, he deals with things theatrical: on March 3 he brilliantly pierces the artificial hypocrisy and pretentiousness of the new chivalric pageant at Niblo's, ridiculing its ignorance and tawdriness; on March 17 he exposes Captain Morton Price of the British army as a fraud and his entertainment as phony; after a reply from Price he still shows on March 31 that if he were a British officer he could not be giving public entertainments; on April 5 in his brightest style he analyzes Dion Boucicault's interesting new play "The Colleen Bawn," explains the Irish terms used, and berates the author for his strident publicity methods; and on May 19 he reviews the circus. For weeks *Vanity Fair* had been full of articles and cartoons about the arrival of the first Japanese Embassy, and O'Brien, after passing mention in two issues, devotes a third to the special visit paid by "the entire *Vanity Fair* office" to the foreign princes. As they stopped at each important bar on their walk up Broadway, O'Titian, the artist, was by the time they arrived in such high spirits that he interrupted the exchange of elaborately ornate official greetings with an invitation in Irish brogue for the princes to come to Ireland. Then bursting into song he became so raucously unruly that he was thrown in jail.[10] This Irishman O'Titian with his propensity for getting drunk had been introduced by *Vanity Fair's* editor, Charles Godfrey Leland, in two earlier numbers as the artist who accompanied "Bister," the critic, when their assignment was to "visit the Academy of Design" and report on the new

[7] *Ibid.*, I, 108 (Feb. 11, 1860). For complete list of "Here and There" see Bibliography.
[8] See *ibid.*, I, 125 (Feb. 18, 1860), and I, 391 (June 16).
[9] See *ibid.*, I, 125 (Feb. 18); I, 324 (May 19); and I, 391 (June 16).
[10] *Ibid.*, II, 22 (July 7, 1860). See also I, 324 (May 19) and I, 391 (June 16).

pictures.[11] O'Brien, being amused by O'Titian, appropriated him and made him play his usual role.

In spite of the lighter mood of the "Here and There" column, O'Brien continued to write poems of social criticism and did his part in a lengthy campaign conducted by *Vanity Fair* against "men in the places where women should be!"[12]—especially male clerks in dry-goods stores. The opening attack was launched in a prose article called "The Sybarites of the Shop" on January 28, and was followed for months by a whole series of supporting verses, squibs, and cartoons; although O'Brien may have supplied many of these, only two items are definitely identified as his, with three others very likely. In the latter category stands "The Sybarites," which tells how women, forced out of their accustomed and proper type of employment, have to become streetwalkers. On such a subject the author cannot "be funny." The other likely ones are "Lines to Zoyara" and "Opening-Day. (After Tennyson)."[13] In both of these the effeminate, dry-goods-selling man is called a counter-jumper and is ridiculed for his superdelicate manners and his handling of cloaks and shawls. The parody on the song from "The Princess," which comprises the second poem, is in accord with O'Brien's best imitative style. Parodies also are the two undoubtedly O'Brien poems on the same subject: "Counter-Jumps. A Poemettina.—After Walt Whitman," illustrated by a cartoon of Walt picking up his hat to reveal under it a diminutive effeminate clerk and composed in a parody of his "I am" style; and "The Counter-Jumper Swell. The Poem of a Very Little Life that was a Great Deal Too Long. An humble imitation of the Author of 'Babie Bell'."[14] Cleverly pointed as are these attacks on the simpering artificiality of the male caterers to women shoppers they do not reach their consummation until the indignant elaboration of "The Sewing Bird" later in the year.

Only one other item in *Vanity Fair* for the year 1860 is definitely identified as O'Brien's—"Meriam's Address to the Great Meteor,"[15] a poem which

[11] See *ibid.*, I, 275–276 (Apr. 28, 1860), and I, 316–317 (May 12).

[12] "The Sewing Bird," *Harper's*, XXI, 442 (Sept., 1860).

[13] *Vanity Fair*, I, 101 (Feb. 11, 1860), and I, 120 (Feb. 18).

[14] *Ibid.*, I, 183 (Mar. 17, 1860), and I, 263 (Apr. 21).

[15] *Ibid.*, II, 65 (Aug. 4, 1860). The MS in O'Brien's handwriting is in the Historical Society of Pennsylvania, with a note added at the end—"The above poem of Fitz J O'Brien was contributed by him to No 32 of Vanity Fair. Charles Godfrey Leland."

conceives the astronomer Meriam contemplating and questioning about the meteor from his Brooklyn roof. Yet Louis H. Stephens, who came to the magazine as business manager and artist "some five months after the date of its first publication," bears witness to the fact that O'Brien wrote a great deal more for this brilliant comic weekly:

It was a custom, in the early days of *Vanity Fair*, in the old editorial rooms at No. 113 Nassau Street, New York, for the writers and artists who were then associated with it to assemble every Friday afternoon, and, over a glass of wine and a cigar, submit and discuss suggestions for subjects for the next issue. On these occasions O'Brien's arrival was always the signal for an outburst of welcome, and our interest immediately centred in the newcomer. His personal magnetism and bright intelligence brought him at once to the front; for, in the friendly encounter of wit and humor, O'Brien—always self-reliant, brilliant, well-tempered, apt at repartee, and piquant with a jovial aggressiveness—imparted new vitality to the little circle, and made lively work for all about him. Amid the laughter, buzz and hum of voices, and the quick interchange of quip and jest,—to which he invariably contributed his full share,—he would take his place at the table, and turn off paragraphs, writing off-hand and rapidly, (how well it is needless for me to say,) upon almost any subject that presented itself.[16]

As one reads through the pages of this still lively magazine, he is tempted to claim for O'Brien many of the witty or censorious satires as the paragraphs mentioned by Stephens. Certain stanzas also he feels sure of as O'Brien's; but lacking positive proof (he has only hints from subject matter and style) he avoids hazarding guesses other than the following: many of the other indignant stabs at the counter-jumper are probably O'Brien's, as are almost certainly "The Sorrows of a Dead-Head," which expresses a love of the theatre but a disgust for the awful aping, fiddling, and shouting which pass for acting; "Set a T— to Catch a T—," which, in the same spirit as the "Here and There" column, scoffs at Dion Boucicault the archplagiarist for howling about others who plagiarize; "Those Little Bills," which treats facetiously the inconvenience of debt, a combination of style and matter reiterated by Fitz-James since his earliest contributions to *The Lantern*; "A Sermon to Organ Grinders," a poem on one of his favorite subjects—humane treatment for the monkey; and "The Song of the Beggar," which accompanies its sympathetic plea for the starving poor with a typi-

[16] Winter, 1881, p. lx; Louis H. Stephens to William Winter, Aug. 3, 1880.

cally O'Brien refrain.[17] As the statement by Stephens gives assurance that for some months at least every number of *Vanity Fair* contains something by O'Brien, the selection of one item from each weekly issue to call his would be a comparatively easy matter, were it not that George Arnold, who was

Waiter.—Have anything more, Sir?
Dramatic Critic.—No—aw, yes—give me another cup of coffee, extra strong. I have to see a new American Comedy to-night, and must keep awake!

also writing copiously for the magazine, was sufficiently versatile to have produced most of them himself.

Besides the many contributions made by Fitz-James, he is the subject of a number of references by his friends: one, in a facetious squib on "Ages of American Authors," mockingly says "Mr. Fitz James O'Brien is 51 (but looks older)"; another written while his new play was holding the stage names him as the last of nineteen prominent actors and playwrights in a list which begins with Shakespeare and Boucicault; while a third, in a

[17] *Vanity Fair*, I, 116 (Feb. 18, 1860); I, 294 (May 5); II, 53 (July 28) two items; and II, 87 (Aug. 18), respectively.

punning article about "Literary and Other Gems," includes "Mother of Pearl," the title of his best short story for the year, and mentions its author as Fitz James O'Inchiquin, the name his friends called him when joking about his aristocratic airs.[18] Also the cartoon of the dejected dramatic critic who needs extra strong coffee in order to keep awake over a new American comedy is a portrait of O'Brien.[19]

Besides Frank Wood, with whom O'Brien had recently become acquainted, two other young men became during this year his fast friends. William Winter, whom he had met in Boston, was one; Edmund Clarence Stedman was the other. Winter had come to New York and had been almost immediately seized upon by Henry Clapp, Jr., to write for *The Saturday Press*. On that paper, with his admirable reviews and criticisms, he made his journalistic reputation. He became its subeditor and writer of its leading articles.[20] Stedman was a contributor to *Vanity Fair*, and made an immediate hit with "The Prince's Ball," which ran in the magazine on October 13 and 20. This elaborate rhymed satire brought him to the attention of Winter, with whom he remained in the closest friendship for nearly fifty years. "Fitz-James O'Brien and Edward H. House were also numbered among those who sought out young Stedman, who while *among* these 'Bohemians,' was, as he used to say in after years, with a something that conveyed a tinge of poetic regret—not exactly *of* them."[21]

Early in the year, before O'Brien had begun his almost hectic activity for *Vanity Fair*, *Harper's* had printed his story "Mother of Pearl."[22] This tale of abnormality and horror seems to be building up to a revelation and acceptance of the supernatural, and when the climax occurs without anything supernatural having taken place the reader feels a bit cheated. The story contains some powerful parts, however, though also some that are less well written. The description of the shark in the southern seas is perhaps the most vivid touch: "The only thing visible in this spot was a black, sharp blade, thin as the blade of a penknife, that appeared slowly and evenly cutting through the still water. No surgical instrument ever glided through human flesh with a more silent, cruel calm." This comes in the first chapter, which tells of a baby rescued from these terrible creatures,

[18] See *ibid.*, I, 172 (Mar. 10, 1860); II, 45 (July 21); and II, 205 (Oct. 20), respectively.
[19] *Ibid.*, I, 46 (Jan. 14, 1860).
[20] See Winter, *Old Friends*, p. 57.
[21] Stedman and Gould, *op. cit.*, I, 207.
[22] *Harper's*, XX, 392–399 (Feb., 1860).

restored to its parents, and named by them Pearl. Chapter two discusses the mother's strange symptoms while under the effect of hasheesh. In chapter three the mother is frustrated in an attempt to kill her husband, the narrator of the story; but in the last chapter she succeeds in murdering her daughter, after which the husband and father, to preserve his reason, resorts to hasheesh himself. Ada Clare in *The Saturday Press* gives as fair a judgment of the story as has appeared:

> The February number of *Harper's Magazine* publishes a story by Fitz James O'Brien, which attracts much notice. The story "Mother of Pearl," opens with an exquisitely beautiful chapter on pearl-fishing, but it seems to me that the crisis of the story is a little uninteresting.
>
> The drug called hasheesh has become too well domesticated to assist in a crisis now. It is on too good terms with the digestion. Let us have some drug more awful and mystic to round off our harrowing climaxes.[23]

In its next number *Harper's Monthly* published a poem pointing out social injustice by means of sharp contrast. Much like the *Vanity Fair* poems which O'Brien was doing at the same time, it was written on a sheet of paper with the letterhead of *Vanity Fair*, 113 Nassau St., New York, and was entitled "Our Christmas Eve."[24] It makes a comparison of the home of Madame Millionaire and its rich and brilliant Christmas tree with the home of the man so "very, very poor" that he cannot supply any Christmas tree for his almost destitute family. Nevertheless, in thorough accord with the conventional sentimentality of the day, the rich woman is not to be envied, for the poor man's "heart at least is true," and his ideals are noble.[25]

An entirely different type of poem is "The Lost Steamship."[26] In conception it is worthy of a place beside O'Brien's uncanny stories, but in workmanship it is frequently crude. It is a ballad reminiscent of "The Rime of the Ancient Mariner" (1798) and "The Wreck of the Hesperus" (1841). William Winter tells most interestingly of an incident connected with it.

[23] *The Saturday Press*, Jan. 21, 1860.

[24] The MS of the poem was furnished through the kindness of Capt. F. L. Pleadwell (M.C.), U. S. Navy (Ret.), of whose collection it is a part; and the transcript was made by Dr. Thomas Ollive Mabbott. This MS was formerly owned by A. H. Joline.

[25] See MS and *Harper's*, XX, 513–514 (Mar., 1860). These ideals are not described in the manuscript but are the subject of ten additional stanzas that belong to the poem as it appears in *Harper's* under changed title, "Our Christmas Tree."

[26] *Ibid.*, XX, 678–679 (Apr., 1860).

He [O'Brien] came into the cave [Pfaff's] late one night, I remember, adorned with a black eye, which had been bestowed upon him by a casual antagonist in Broadway, because of a difference of opinion respecting the right of passage on the side-walk; and, producing from one pocket a vial with a leech in it, which,—concealed in a white handkerchief,—he applied to the region of his damaged optic, he produced from another pocket the manuscript of a poem that he said he had that evening written (his residence, then, was the old Hone House),[27] called "The Lost Steamship"; and he read that poem to our circle in a magnificent manner, with all the passionate vigor, all the weird feeling, and all the tremor of haunted imagination that its tragical theme requires.

A steamship had recently been wrecked, on the Atlantic coast, with much loss of life. The poem is the story of the disaster, and that story is told, to a fisherman on the shore, by a person who seems, at first, to be the only survivor of the wreck. That speaker declares that all on board the ship were drowned,—the last man to go down with her being the Second Mate; then, suddenly, he stands revealed as the ghost of the mariner, the final victim engulfed by the sea. I have heard many readings: I have never heard one in which afflicting reality, hysterical excitement, shuddering dread, and tremulous pathos were so strangely blended as they were in O'Brien's reading of his "Lost Steamship."[28]

The Saturday Press reprinted the ballad almost immediately (March 24), and commented upon it as a "strong, simple, and rugged poem, instinct with the dim mystery and wild terror of the sea." The twentieth-century critic is inclined to agree with the critic of 1860, that "the idea of this poem has the vivid simplicity which only genius attains"; but he is quite sure that he does not agree that "its execution has the power which only genius displays;" for without O'Brien's voice to lend color to the verses some of the "afflicting reality" seems to become overdone sentiment, and some of the poetic phrases turn pedestrian.

During the next three months, however, there is no verse, either good or bad, except for the pieces he was contributing to *Vanity Fair*. Then late in June there appeared in the July *Harper's* another ballad of the sea; but the story of "When I Came Back from Sea" is so trite, and the diction is so obviously that of the conventionally poetic school or, avoiding that, is so unpoetic that the poem fails to create the pathos it intended. Indeed, it barely succeeds in missing the ridiculous, when the returned whaler finds his loved one gone—

[27] The Hone House was in Broadway, at the southeast corner of Great Jones Street.

[28] Winter, *Old Friends*, pp. 97–98.

A tale of shame and a ruined name
When I came back from sea.[29]

Wit and humor, however, were always consciously O'Brien's when he wanted to use them, which he did in collaborating with Charles G. Rosenberg on a play called *The Tycoon, or Young America in Japan.*[30] This burlesque, or extravaganza, took advantage of the sensation caused by the arrival of the first Japanese embassy earlier in the year, and was written for Joseph Jefferson, who on May 16 had opened a summer season at Laura Keene's Theatre. There he produced it on July 2, where it ran until July 21, accompanied by the usual journalistic comment and criticism.

William Winter gives the piece a preliminary boost in *The Saturday Press*;[31] but the reviews are not too enthusiastic. The *Herald* says, "The modern edition is neatly written, but lacks those sharp bits which are absolutely required in pieces of the extravaganza order";[32] while the *Times* makes fun of the play as extravagant and unreal, and praises Jefferson, Mr. Burnett, and Mrs. John Wood for making poor parts interesting.[33] The *Leader* comments, "The songs, the dresses, and the scenery of this piece save it. The music might be a little more popular, but the words of the songs (Mr. O'Brien's I am told) are very good. Mrs. Wood's rowdy chant, that wherein she expresses her admiration of a spree, is eminently characteristic."[34] Of all the accounts the *Tribune's* is the lengthiest and the most favorable. In one paragraph "we believe" that Mr. O'Brien is "responsible for all of the songs and the greater part of the dialogue. When we add that the songs are all excellently written, and that the language is for the most part good, and at times absolutely brilliant, we do but simple justice to Mr. O'Brien."[35]

However divergent the opinions about the play itself, there is perfect unanimity as to the splendor of the costumes and the setting (probably by Rosenberg), and as to the entertaining performances of Mr. Jefferson and Mrs. Wood. The authors did not have the bother of inventing a plot, for

[29] *Harper's*, XXI, 238 (July, 1860).

[30] See J. N. Ireland, *op. cit.*, pp. 698–699.

[31] See *The Saturday Press*, June 30, 1860. Winter when he first succeeded O'Brien as dramatic critic wrote as "Personne," but in May, 1860, changed his pseudonym to "Quelqu'un."

[32] *N. Y. Herald*, July 3, 1860.

[33] See *N. Y. Times*, July 4, 1860.

[34] *N. Y. Leader*, July 7, 1860.

[35] *N. Y. Tribune*, July 3, 1860. It contains an outline of the plot.

The Tycoon was merely a clever adaptation of an earlier burlesque by William Brough, founded upon the *Arabian Nights* story of Prince Camaralzaman and the Princess Badoura.

While *The Tycoon* was still running, the *Leader* compared the comic dramatic dialogue of O'Brien with that of his friend, the comedian and playwright, John Brougham:

Brougham has a great advantage over the other writers hereabouts, in knowing just what will make the people laugh. O'Brien may give them, as he often does, a clear, well-cut diamond-pointed Attic witticism, which they fail to appreciate; and, while he is doing that, Brougham has made four jokes, two good, one indifferent, and one awfully bad. The good ones carry the others along, and give the author a reputation which he may not, in a purely literary point of view, fully deserve. In the matter of song-writing, the same general comparison will apply.[36]

Earlier in the summer Sam Cowell, an English actor who was making a concert tour of America, met Fitz-James—an incident recorded by his wife in her diary on June 9.[37] Months later when he occupied the room next to theirs in the same "hotel" or boardinghouse, they became well acquainted, as Fitz-James was an assiduous, almost daily caller. Mrs. Cowell enjoyed his company. "I like Mr. O'Brien very well indeed," she writes; "and his conversation is quite a relief after that of our usual visitors. *Not* because he is an heir to an Earldom [the rumor still persists], but that he is perfectly well educated and has the manners of a gentleman. His great peculiarities are pride and an affectation of eccentricity, but neither of them appeared tonight, and one feels the pleasantness and friendliness of such a character, more than the good humor of those who 'have smiles for all'." As the night referred to by Mrs. Cowell is that of New Year's Day, 1861, she "congratulated him on his remaining free from 'tightness' after so many calls; he attributed this to his 'eccentricity.' 'Sometimes, I am ashamed to say, that I am very dissipated, but as it is a rule for every male person to get intoxicated on New Year's Day, I determined to keep sober: besides it is a duty to the ladies on whom we call, not to disgrace ourselves before them'."[38]

After this O'Brien called regularly in spite of the disapproval of Sam and

[36] *N. Y. Leader*, July 14, 1860.
[37] M. Willson Disher, ed., *The Cowells in America*, London, 1934, p. 115.
[38] *Ibid.*, p. 234.

the consequent coldness of his lady. Another story she tells reveals the impetuous quality of O'Brien's temper:

Mr. O'Brien was once 'sold' by a newsboy who cried out 'Arrival of the Argo' when that vessel was feared for, and a friend of Mr. O'Brien's in her, so he actually jumped out of an Omnibus, and pursued the child who had a large bundle of the obnoxious paper, which only informed the people that 'The Argo has not yet arrived.' Mr. O'Brien got the papers from the boy and deliberately destroyed them all, saying to the crying urchin that it was a lesson not to excite people's feelings falsely.[39]

But these diary comments of Mrs. Cowell have carried the story of Fitz-James far beyond the mid-summer of 1860. So to return.

In the last week of July there arrived in New York a contingent of the Chicago Zouaves, who attracted much attention by their precise, animated, gymnastic drilling and by their uniforms. *Harper's Weekly* immediately pictured them in a full-page drawing, and on the page opposite printed "a spirited poem" by "Mr. Fitz-James O'Brien."[40] The lines have a certain dash that is not unpleasing:

The Zouaves

To bugle note and beat of drum
They come—the gallant Zouaves come!
With gleams of blue and glints of red;
With airy, light, elastic tread;
With dashing, wild, insouciant air;
With figures sinewy, lithe, and spare;

. . .

They come—the gay Zouaves![41]

A month later *Harper's Monthly* printed a more important poem, "The Sewing Bird,"[42]—the culmination of the counter-jumper verses of the early numbers of *Vanity Fair*. Written under pressure, the author being sadly in need of funds, it was sold at once to Harpers and was made a feature of the September *Monthly*. Unlike the *Vanity Fair* poems "The Sewing

[39] *Ibid.*, p. 239.
[40] "Quelqu'un" in *The Saturday Press*, July 28, 1860.
[41] *H. W.*, IV, 469 (July 28, 1860).
[42] *Harper's*, XXI, 433–442 (Sept., 1860).

Bird" is developed, not by satire, but by a series of descriptions. First, the poor seamstress is seen in her desolate attic; then, led by the silver sewing bird, she passes before a series of pictures—the dapper young clerks demonstrating Cantator's Sewing Machines, the exquisite dummies murmuring over a dry-goods counter, and, by contrast, the manly labor of the California goldminer, of the Maine lumberman, and of the Ohio farmer. The poem is smooth and clear; but somehow it fails to arouse the emotions, as it was evidently intended it should—as it evidently did; for it greatly impressed both Winter and Louis H. Stephens, and *Harper's Weekly* speaks of it as the "best of all" the poems, "worthy of a place beside Hood's 'Song of the Shirt'."[43] Perhaps its problem no longer appeals, perhaps the gospel of work was a more popular subject in the days of Longfellow and Whittier; at any rate, "The Sewing Bird" today seems self-conscious, and deliberately ambitious—well written, but uninspired.

In the same issue (*Harper's* for September) is a much less pretentious jingle. "My Johnny" is a lightly humorous *jeu d'esprit* after the manner of Oliver Wendell Holmes, and quaint rhymes give a touch of fun to the smoothly running verses. "Battledores," not quite so attractive because of the too often repeated *b* rhyme, is another example of O'Brien's ability to handle *vers de société*. It depends on the old idea,

> How happy could I be with either
> Were t'other dear charmer away.[44]

The solution in this case is:

> By loving each, and loving both,
> I know not how to lie,
> So here's to both, however loath,
> Good bye, good bye, good bye!

"*Battledores* by Fitzjames O'Brien" was "written for the Household Journal," and appeared as the initial item in its initial number, Saturday, October 6, 1860.[45]

[43] *H. W.*, VI, 267 (Apr. 26, 1862).

[44] John Gay, *The Beggar's Opera*, 1728, Act II, sc. ii.

[45] That periodicals appeared as they do at present, some time before the nominal date of publication, is indicated by the fact that "Battledores" is printed in *The Saturday Press* of Sept. 22, as quoted from *Household Journal* of October 6.

The verse of "The Man at the Door"[46] is too facilely and carelessly over-anapestic, and the outcome of the situation—a rejected suitor murdering the bride and groom at the cathedral door—is so trite that the poem builds up no suspense. The ballad devices are obvious—the contrast of wedding gaiety and funeral mourning, both typified in the face of the old sexton; the swift revenge of the Gipsy Prince; and the final unadorned statement that

> BERTHA and ALBERT have gone to their rest
> And the Prince of the Gipsies is swinging on high.

Although this poem, with the exception of "A Fallen Star," completes the meagre assortment of O'Brien's writing for the year 1860, especially for the last half of it, a letter addressed to the comedian John E. Owens shows that he still had hopes for the production of a play he had written—probably *The Cup and the Lip*, referred to by William Winter more than a year before:

November 21, 1860.

Is your name Owens? This is a query which I wish to have distinctly answered. I remember, on a recent occasion, meeting a person whose mental attractions were only equalled by the beauty of his physical development. That person answered to the name above mentioned. As I learn that an individual bearing the same cognomen is now managing an insignificant theater in New Orleans, I address this epistle to that place, in the hope of discovering whether the Knight errant Owens and the manager Owens are one and indivisible—which it seems the Union is not. Independent of the personal interest which I feel in ascertaining the welfare and locality of my New York friend, I have a small interest in a comedy of surpassing beauty which he bore away with him from this city, as Jason bore the golden fleece from Colchis. You see this matter is ad-Jasoned to the other. Now, if you are the lovely and fascinating Owens that whilom I knew, I wish you to tell me whether you will take the comedy on the terms named, or any other man? If you take it, please get it copied, and charge me, out of the first instalment, with copying charges as well as with a certain ten dollars, money lent, and forward balance. If not let me have a line, and I will enclose the last mentioned filthy lucre, and forward at same time express expenses for the transmission of the

[46] *The Knickerbocker*, LIV, 71–72 (Jan., 1861). This number appeared in 1860, and from it the poem was reprinted in *The Saturday Press* of Dec. 15, 1860.

MS. here. I have no other copy of the gorgeous production, and do not want to lose the chances of getting it done here. Please reply at once. If your name IS Owens, I may tell you without breach of confidence that all our friends are well. Tom Placide has multiplied into ten acts instead of his usual five. Wilkins has lately been convicted of a deaf-alcation. Cushman, thank God! is going, and Booth is come. Presenting with all due incoherence the assurance of my distinguished consideration, I remain (if your name IS Owens), your sincere friend,

F. J. O'Brien.

Address, Harper Brothers, Franklin Square, New York.[47]

This letter plainly intimates that in 1860, as in 1854, O'Brien was hard up; and by this time his circumstances and his fortune were so Bohemianly irregular that a number of his friends and acquaintances have commented on them. Frank Winter, the actor, oldest son of William Winter, recalls a story told by his father, of O'Brien's coming to Winter's room late one night—about three o'clock in the morning—very drunk. He said, "Will, I have no home." Winter, of course, took him in; and then O'Brien wanted more to drink. Winter had nothing on hand, and gradually O'Brien sobered. He remained with Winter three days.[48] This is probably the time about which Winter himself writes that once O'Brien remained with him in his room in Varick Street for two nights and a day. "I never saw him so deeply depressed as he was then,—and with good reason, for he was destitute, cheerless, and hungry; and whenever that was his case he would not share with a comrade, and even when food was left in his way he would not take it."[49] It was during this stay that he wrote "The Sewing Bird." In the morning he left, sold it to Harper's for one hundred dollars, and at four in the afternoon Winter found him in Delmonico's, at Broadway and Chambers Street, dressed in new clothes, treating his friends, and very gay. "The Lost Steamship," it will be recalled, was produced "under very similar circumstances." "A Fallen Star," too, was written at Winter's room "between midnight and morning, at one sitting, and he left the original draft upon the table, having made a clean copy of it for the press."[50] In direct disagreement with Winter about "The Sewing Bird" is Louis H. Stephens,

[47] Winter, *Old Friends*, pp. 74–75.
[48] Related by Frank Winter at University Club, Denver, May 7, 1925.
[49] Winter, 1881, p. xxii.
[50] *Ibid.*

who recalled that it was "The Sewing Bird" which O'Brien wrote in his presence. When Stephens expressed astonishment at O'Brien's rapidity of composition, the latter said "that when especially interested in a subject for a poem he thought over it and had it so mapped out in his mind that it was well on to completion when he commenced putting it on paper."[51]

George Arnold confirms this statement, but also emphasizes O'Brien's erratic habits: "He often let days and weeks pass without putting a line on paper. Then, when the inspiration came, he wrote steadily and easily on to the end, often without interruption." He lacked moral courage and intellectual restraint, and Arnold continues:

> He loved luxuries but could not acquire them. Left to himself, he became instantly reduced to a half-furnished bedroom in some dingy hotel, a solitary suit of clothing, and—nothing else. He was frequently without a pen, a bottle of ink, a sheet of paper, or money enough to purchase either,—a condition of things not highly favorable to the entertainment of the Muses. . . .
>
> I do not think that Fitz ever incurred a debt in his life without feeling perfectly sure of its immediate payment. But, somehow, when he had the money, he had also so many other uses for it that the debt was crowded over "till next time." Meanwhile he came to be afflicted with a certain curious fear of his creditor, that increased with every day of credit, until meeting him voluntarily was far beyond Fitz's strength of mind; so the debt went forever uncancelled. This . . . was exceedingly unfortunate for O'Brien—and for others.[52]

The above was written in 1865, but an even more closely contemporary account carries the same testimony. Mrs. Cowell writing on Monday, January 28, 1861, says that "O'Brien has run away or indeed, had the doors shut upon him by Mr. Plinta's orders, on the night of the 14th instant. He owed $45, and has got the key of No. 21.—Is in debt everywhere, and is being 'kicked out' of all his haunts. Poor O'Brien."[53]

Thomas E. Davis, who knew him only in these last years, also tells of "his carelessness in worldly matters," while one dunning letter followed him

[51] Louis H. Stephens to William Winter, Aug. 18, 1880.

[52] Winter, 1881, pp. xlix and l.

[53] M. Willson Disher, ed., *op. cit.*, p. 242. On April 16 Mrs. Cowell also mentions O'Brien's having gone away "without remembering to pay," and says that her husband told her things about him "too dreadful to repeat."—p. 295.

even into his military service, much as that did to blot out unpleasant memories:

Washington
June 4, 1861

FitzJames O'Brien, Esq.

Dear Sir

I write to ask that you will give immediate attention to my note which I sent you at Camp Cameron by one of the Officers of the 7th. As I said in my note I was obliged to take up the draft and also had to pay expenses of Protest (a notice of which I sent you). I will be obliged if you will send me the amt. $41.00, by a draft or check on New York by an early mail and I will return the draft and Protest.

Yours respectfully
ORSON H. BESTER

direct care of Franck Taylor.[54]

Another incident that carries an unsavory tang and that relates to "one of the brightest, best-read, and most reckless of the Bohemians of the city" is told by Augustus Maverick. This trick, at least, was played on people who knew him, for the *Times* had printed O'Brien articles many times. He,

> suddenly nipped by evil fortune, secluded himself for a day from the gaze of his fellows, and then appeared in the editorial room with a roll of manuscript. It was a Carrier's Address in verse, intended for the first of January, admirably written, full of local hits, crackling with fun. It was gladly accepted. "Could you let me have forty dollars?" asked the poet. In violation of a rule in force in newspaper offices, which prohibits prepayment for literary contributions, the money was given, and in the evening there was high revel at Pfaff's,—an underground saloon on Broadway much frequented by the Bohemians of the day. The New Year arrived; and the *Times* Carriers' Address was widely distributed and generally read. It was a creditable literary performance,—in fact, far superior to the average character of these annual inflictions. But a stray copy was found by a reader of the *Times* in a western town; and this person, struck by lines in the poem which seemed familiar, made some investigations. It then appeared that the dishonest poet had "adopted" an old Address, changing the order of the verses, adding bits of local color, interjecting a few allusions to the principal events of the year, and then successfully passing it off as an original production.[55]

[54] MS in the Romm collection.

[55] Augustus Maverick, *op. cit.*, p. 251. Also see statement of A. D. Shattuck, p. 129.

Two other practical jokes, as related to Frank Winter by his father, show that gay spirits, late hours, and mad pranks are not the exclusive privilege and recent discovery of college youth, as the modern novels would lead one to suppose. One morning as O'Brien, Winter, and a group of others were on their way home from a night at Pfaff's, they came to cross St. John's Square, a triangle in Greenwich Village, about five o'clock. There was a big stone post in the middle of the "square," and Winter and O'Brien getting on either side of it pretended to push or pull the post into line upon the direction of the others, who were sighting on it and squinting at it from a point down the street. The shouted orders, and the maneuvers of the two at the post pretending to move it this way or that, soon drew a huge crowd of people on their way to early work, who stopped to watch and wonder at the performance. When the unbudgeable stone was satisfactorily in line, the youthful jokers calmly marched away.

Another time O'Brien, Winter, and Aldrich went to the market just off Broadway near Broome Street and, going to every butter stall and cheese stall, tasted samples of the butter and cheese. They smacked their lips, looked at each other, in almost every case disapprovingly shook their heads, and moved on to the next. The market was soon in a stir, the marketmen naturally thinking they were inspectors. The commotion grew over this untimely visit, until finally the trio gave the whole thing away by going up to a butcher's stand, where, taking hold of a string of sausages, they began measuring them off on the length of their arms. Upon this the incensed men they had fooled quickly drove them out.[56]

Readiness to enter into such pranks, or into whatever gaiety the moment offered, was one of the things that endeared O'Brien to his more youthful companions. Wood, Winter, and Aldrich were all his juniors, and they were captivated by his prodigious animal spirits and his zestful enjoyment of the passing hour. Another distinction that procured O'Brien many admirers was his marvelous voice and his extraordinary command of it for reading. The effect of his reading of "The Lost Steamship" has already been quoted, and many similar anecdotes exist.

"I never enjoyed anything more than hearing him read his own writings," wrote Thomas E. Davis;[57] and George Arnold related the following:

His voice, in speaking, was the richest, the sweetest, the most persuasive and expressive, of all the male voices I can now recall. It was a power in itself.

[56] Conversation with Frank Winter, May 7, 1925.

[57] Winter, 1881, p. xxxiii. Thomas E. Davis to William Winter, Oct. 22, 1880.

I shall never forget the impression he made upon a little party, one evening, by the manner in which he read several of Emerson's poems. He threw so much warmth, so much human tenderness and sympathy into them, that we were all astonished. Then, artfully turning the leaves, as if still reading from the book, he recited his own "Bacchus":

"Pink as the rose was his skin so fair,
Round as the rosebud his perfect shape,
And there lay a light in his tawny hair,
Like the sun in the heart of a bursting grape!"

You can fancy how we marvelled to hear such luscious tropes from Emerson, and how we laughed over the deception when O'Brien informed us of it."[58]

Just seven years after O'Brien's first contribution to *Harper's Monthly* the same magazine published his poem "A Fallen Star."[59] According to Dr. Guernsey this poem

contains, I think, the best description of him as he appeared to me in those bright, early years. I remember well when he read the poem to me. He was a magnificent reader—the only person, in fact, to whose reading of his own poems I was always glad to listen. I copy a few verses which seemed then and now to me to describe O'Brien as I had known him five years before:

"A figure sinewy, lithe, and strong—
A laugh infectious in its glee—
A voice as beautiful as song,
When heard along the sea.

"On me, the man of sombre thought,
The radiance of his friendship won,
As round an autumn tree is wrought
The enchantment of the sun.

. . .

"Thus rearing diamond arches up,
Whereon his future life to build,
He quaffed all day the golden cup
That youthful fancy filled.

. . .

[58] Winter, 1881, pp. xlvii–xlviii. The lines quoted are not from O'Brien's poem "Bacchus" in *H. W.*, I, 735 (Nov. 14, 1857), but from his "The Song of the Bacchante" in *The Evening Post*, Oct. 10, 1855, where the word arrangement is slightly different.

[59] *Harper's*, XXI, 834–835 (Nov., 1860).

"Like fruit upon a southern slope,
He ripened on all natural food,
The winds that thrill the skyey cope,
The sunlight's golden blood.

"And in his talk I oft discerned
A timid music vaguely heard;
The fragments of a song scarce learned,
The essays of a bird."

The whole poem is of wonderful power; and I call to mind how burdened with emotion grew the voice of O'Brien as he read the verses which describe the downward career of this friend so highly gifted—from the leading spirit in wild, bacchanalian orgies down to the poor, shivering mendicant asking alms in the public street.[60]

Having lived the first part of the poem—the gifted young poet dedicated to the creation of true beauty in verse—Fitz-James was living now the second part of his own description:

The smile, once honest as the day,
Now waked to words of grossest wit;
The eyes, so simply frank and gay,
With lawless fires were lit.

He was the idol of the board—
He led the careless, wanton throng—
The soul that once to heaven had soared
Now groveled in a song.

He wildly flung his wit away
In small retort, in verbal brawls,
And played with words as jugglers play
With hollow brazen balls.

He wrote much less frequently than before, and when he did write he seems to have aimed not quite so high. He was dissipating his powers; he was living precariously. Yet neither in poem nor story is there a word or attitude not wholly pure. He was still something of an idealist about his work, and besides—he knew the demands and prejudices of both the

[60] *H. W.*, VI, 267 (Apr. 26, 1862).

magazine publishers and their readers. Nevertheless, he dodged his debts, he was truculently defiant, he drank too much and too often, and he alienated numerous friends by his affairs with such women as Ada Clare and Jenny Danforth. He was indeed a star whose original bright magnitude was much diminished, and perhaps in his sensitive Celtic imagination he saw for himself in prospect only the third part of "A Fallen Star"—that of a whining drunken beggar. But if he did, the course of the universe served him well—the Civil War deflected the star in its descending orbit, it took on new light, and ended blazing brightly.

Chapter XI

A Poet with "The Seventh"

(1861)

O'Brien's achievement for 1861, although it has much to do with his part in the Civil War, shows also a marked renewal of poetic activity. It begins early in the year with his contributions to *The Knickerbocker Magazine*, of which his friend Charles Godfrey Leland had just take over the editorship upon the retirement of Lewis Gaylord Clark. "The Man at the Door" of the January number was noted in the last chapter; "Jack's Valentine" in February pictures a dark, rough night at sea with Jack the sailor confiding his messages of love to the stormy elements; and "Treachery" in March briefly tells of an old knight poisoned by his brother. More interesting is the prose tale of the hopeless love of a paralytic youth who has trained a bobolink to be his messenger. The fantastic quality supplied by the bird and the weirdly tragic suicide of the youth evoke in "Bob O' Link"[1] an unexpected power of pathos.

During the same months O'Brien was also writing for *Harper's Monthly* and *Vanity Fair*. "The Skaters"[2] tries to create an effect of horror and suspense and tragedy; but the adjectives are just wrong, the incremental repetition is forced, the names of the characters are pretentious or ludicrously insipid—handsome Madge, the heroine; Rupert Clare, the villain; and the hero, Willy Gray—and the rescue of Madge on the ice from the grip like a vice, ends for the modern reader, not with relief at the rescue of the heroine and horror at the fate of the self-immolated villain, but with the joy of unrestrained hilarity.

The next contribution to *Harper's* is as oversentimental as "The Skaters" is overmelodramatic. "The Ballad of the Shamrock," however, possesses an interest as one of the few bits of writing in which O'Brien makes use of the background of his native land. Also, that it was of a type popular with

[1] *The Knickerbocker Magazine,* LVII, 253–257 (Mar., 1861).

[2] *Harper's,* XXII, 350 (Feb., 1861).

the generation that produced Louisa May Alcott and Donald Grant Mitchell is borne out by the circumstance of its acceptance by *Harper's* and of its being honored by them with the first place in the March issue, illustrated with an art title and three large drawings by Ed. F. Mullen and B. Fostor. Among the hundreds of thousands of Irishmen who emigrated to America during the terrible Irish famine of 1848 and 1849 was Donal, a mother's only son. After ten years he sends for her; but when she lands at the Battery, with her heart full of love and longing, she finds that he is dead. So the shamrock she had brought to give him she plants on his grave, and there by his side she herself hopes soon to lie. The theme of maternal love is a perennially acceptable one; but in this case the reader's sympathy is soon alienated by the awkwardness of the versification.

"The Strawberries. A Summer Picture"[3] is a sentimental little love poem, conventionally adequate, and neither bad nor good. Unlike the poems just discussed, however, it has a certain delicacy and does not overstep the bounds of taste.

"The Legend of Easter Eggs"[4] unfolds an interesting tale of Christ's burial and resurrection and of the singing bird in the nearby tree, which voices at first a universal grief and then a sweet delight. The religious exaltation, the thrill of the great Easter story, is imaginatively conveyed in the smoothly running lines of this beautiful legend.

"The Wreck of the Hesperus" (1841) has much to answer for, and "Minot's Ledge"[5] repeats the trite and obvious subject of the storm at sea and the consequent shipwreck. This and the improbable, forced situation once granted, the ballad is well written. In faultless meters it quickly tells the story of the lighthouse keeper's rescue of his own son.

> Without, the world is wild with rage,
> Unkennelled demons are abroad,
> But with the father and the son,
> Within, there is the peace of God.

Further improvement of handling is seen in the descriptive effects of "The Child That Loved a Grave."[6] This story, of the sad little boy who

[3] *Vanity Fair*, III, 143 (Mar. 23, 1861).

[4] *Harper's*, XXII, 637–638 (Apr., 1861).

[5] *Ibid.*, XXII, 660 (Apr., 1861). This poem and "The Ballad of the Shamrock" are both signed, as are all the *Knickerbocker* pieces.

[6] *Ibid.*, XXII, 682–684 (Apr., 1861).

loves and tends the grave of a child in the old churchyard and who dies when five men come and dig up the bones to bear them back to Europe for burial, is tender with a lovely, soft melancholy. Never once is the mood disturbed or broken, every detail fits perfectly, and the prose rhythms in their smooth loveliness have the effect of poetry. Poe, Hawthorne, and Dickens had all shown how this sort of thing could be done, and the lessons of the Christmas stories and "Eleanora" (1842) were not lost on O'Brien. Only the last clause seems to stretch a point, and to bring the reader from the land of the imagination rather too suddenly back to earth.

With the next poem, "The Wharf Rat,"[7] O'Brien's literary activity ceased for many months in the excitement of war and the exactions of military service. Six days before O'Brien marched down Broadway for his first service in the Civil War, *Vanity Fair* printed three short stanzas which tell of the silent wharves at night, of the singing sailor followed by the wharf rat, and of a missing sailor next day, gone where "the wharf rat alone can tell." It is imaginatively and concisely done, but not smoothly.

The excitement and disturbances which culminated in the firing on Fort Sumter and the outbreak of the Civil War had been gradually accumulating, and Fitz-James O'Brien, sharing in the excitement and desirous of action should it come, enlisted in Company "G" (7th Co.) of the New York Seventh Regiment.[8] This regiment had a well-established tradition of opening its ranks to only the socially eligible, and it was proud of its drill and its uniforms. When active hostilities began, and troops were called by President Lincoln for the defense of the Capital, the Seventh mobilized immediately; and, preceded only by the Massachusetts Sixth, who were attacked while passing through Baltimore, the Seventh moved to Washington. The confused excitement of preparation, the brilliant ovation of their farewell march down Broadway, the turbulence of the country as they moved to Philadelphia, the dangerous uncertainty of conditions in Baltimore, the trip down the Delaware and up the Chesapeake, the landing at Annapolis, and finally the difficult forced march to Washington, are all graphically

[7] *Vanity Fair*, III, 172 (Apr. 13, 1861). MS in O'Brien's handwriting among Leland papers in Historical Society of Pennsylvania.

[8] The records of the Seventh Regiment do not show the date of O'Brien's enlistment. Frank Wood says he joined "in January" (Winter, 1881, p. xl); William Swinton says he entered the service "in the winter of 1861" (*History of the Seventh Regiment*, 1870, in the "Roll of Honor," p. 463); Winter and Louis H. Stephens say, more indefinitely, that he joined when the war broke out (Winter, 1881, pp. xxv and lxi).

described by Fitz-James O'Brien in a letter written from Washington on April 27 and printed in *The New York Times* on Thursday, May 2. This account, written with such vivid fullness of detail and with the accurate knowledge of a participant, has become a recognized part of the records of the early days of the Civil War.[9]

It was on April 19 that the Seventh, in all the feverish bustle of a sudden call to arms, prepared itself for the field, and late in the afternoon marched from the Armory on Third Avenue nearly opposite the Cooper Union, swung into Broadway, and so down the aisles of hysterically cheering thousands to the ferry for Jersey City. As the effect of the war on O'Brien's life and attitudes is important, one may be pardoned for quoting somewhat at length from this contemporary account of the earliest troop movements of the Civil War:

The scene at the armory on Friday was one to be commemorated. For the first time since its formation, the Seventh Regiment left its native City on active service. All day long, from an early hour in the morning, young men in uniforms or civilian's dress, might have been seen hurrying up and down Broadway, with anomalous looking bundles under their arms. . . . Hardware stores were ransacked of revolvers. A feverish excitement throbbed through the City—the beating of that big Northern pulse, so slow, so sure, and so steady.

At 3 o'clock, P. M., we mustered at the Armory, against which there beat a surge of human beings like waves against a rock. Within, all was commotion. Fitting of belts, wild lamentations over uniforms expected but not arrived. Hearty exchanges of comradeships between members of different companies, who felt that they were about to depart on a mission which might end in death. . . . At last the Regiment was formed in companies, and we marched. Was there ever such an ovation? . . . The marble walls of Broadway were never before rent with such cheers as greeted us when we passed. . . . An avenue of brave, honest faces smiled upon us . . . and sent a sunshine into our hearts that lives there still. . . .

The first evening, April 20, on board the *Boston*, passed delightfully. We were all in first-rate spirits, and the calm, sweet evenings that stole on us as we approached the South, diffused a soft and gentle influence over us. The scene on board the ship was exceedingly picturesque. Fellows fumbling in haversacks for rations, or extracting sandwiches from reluctant canteens; guards pacing up and

[9] It is quoted in Frank Moore, *The Civil War in Song and Story*, 1882 (1st ed. 1865), pp. 228–233. Extracts are quoted in Colonel Emmons Clark, *History of the Seventh Regiment of New York, 1806–1889*, 1890, I, 474 ff., and in William Swinton, *History of the Seventh Regiment*, 1870, pp. 37, 42, 96, 106, 153.

down, with drawn bayonets; knapsacks piled in corners, bristling heaps of muskets, with sharp, shining teeth, crowded into every available nook; picturesque groups of men lolling on deck, pipe or cigar in mouth, indulged in the *dolce far niente*, as if they were on the blue shores of Capri rather than on their way to battle; unbuttoned jackets, crossed legs, heads leaning on knapsacks, blue uniforms everywhere, with here and there a glint of officers' red lighting up the foreground—all formed a scene that such painters as the English WARREN would have reveled in. . . .

Notwithstanding that we found very soon that the commissariat was in a bad way, the men were as jolly as sandboys. I never saw a more good-humored set of men in my life. Fellows who would at DELMONICO'S have sent back a *turban de volaille aux truffes* because the truffles were tough, here cheerfully took their places in file between decks, tin plates and tin cups in hand, in order to get an insufficient piece of beef and a vision of coffee. But it was all merrily done. The scant fare was seasoned with hilarity: and I here say to those people in New-York who have sneered at the Seventh Regiment as being dandies and guilty of the unpardonable crimes of cleanliness and kid gloves, that they would cease to scoff and remain to bless, had they beheld the square, honest, genial way in which these military Brummells roughed it. . . .

Some men in the regiment who have fine voices—and their name is legion—had been singing, with all that delicious effect that music at sea produces, several of the finest psalms in our liturgy. . . . While we were singing, the moon swung clear into air, and round her white disc was seen three circles, clear and distinct—*red, white and blue!* The omen was caught by common instinct, and a thousand cheers went up to that Heaven that seemed in its visible signs to manifest its approval of the cause in which we were about to fight. . . .

On the afternoon of the 22d we landed at the Annapolis dock, after having spent hours in trying to relieve the *Maryland*. For the first time in his life your correspondent was put to work to roll flour barrels. He was entrusted with the honorable and onerous duty of transporting stores from the steamer to the dock. Later still he descended to the position of mess-servant, when, in company with gentlemen well known in Broadway for immaculate kids, he had the honor of attending on his company with buckets of cooked meat and crackers. The only difference between him and Co. and the ordinary waiter being, that the former were civil.

After this I had the pleasing duty of performing three hours of guard duty on the dock, with a view to protect the baggage and stores. It was monotonous—being my first guard—but not unpleasant. . . .

All surmises were put an end to by our receiving orders, the evening of the 23d, to assemble in marching order next morning. The dawn saw us up. Knapsacks, with our blankets and overcoats strapped on them, were piled on the green. A brief and insufficient breakfast was taken, our canteens filled with vinegar and water, cartridges distributed to each man, and after mustering and loading, we started on our first march through a hostile country. . . .

We marched the first eight miles under a burning sun, in heavy marching order, in less than three hours; and it is well known that, placing all elementary considerations out of the way, marching on a railroad track is the most harassing. . . .

The tracks had been torn up between Annapolis and the Junction, and here it was that the wonderful qualities of the Massachusetts Eighth Regiment came out. The locomotives had been taken to pieces by the inhabitants, in order to prevent our travel. In steps a Massachusetts volunteer, looks at the piece-meal engine, takes up a flange, and says coolly, "I made this engine, and I can put it together again." Engineers were wanted when the engine was ready. Nineteen stepped out of the ranks. The rails were torn up. Practical railroad-makers out of the Regiment laid them again, and all this, mind you, without care or food. These brave boys, I say, were starving while they were doing all this good work. What their Colonel was doing I can't say. As we marched along the track that they had laid, they greeted us with ranks of smiling but hungry faces. One boy told me, with a laugh on his young lips, that he had not ate anything for thirty hours. There was not, thank God, a haversack in our Regiment that was not emptied into the hands of these ill-treated heroes, nor a flask that was not at their disposal. . . .

After a brief rest of about an hour, we again commenced our march; a march which lasted until the next morning—a march than which in history nothing but those marches in which defeated troops have fled from the enemy can equal. . . . As we went along the railroad we threw out skirmishing parties from the Second and Sixth Companies, to keep the road clear. I know not if I can describe the night's march. I have dim recollections of deep cuts through which we passed, gloomy and treacherous-looking, with the moon shining full on our muskets, while the banks were wrapped in shade, and each moment expecting to see the flash and hear the crack of the rifle of the Southern guerrilla. The tree frogs and lizards made a mournful music as we passed. The soil on which we traveled was soft and heavy. The sleepers lying at intervals across the track made the marching terribly fatiguing. On all sides dark, lonely pine woods stretched away, and high over the hooting of owls or the plaintive petition of the whip-poor-will rose the bass commands of Halt! Forward, march!—and when we came to any ticklish spot the word would run from the head of the column along the line, "Holes," "Bridge, pass it along," &c.

As the night wore on the monotony of the march became oppressive. Owing to our having to explore every inch of the way, we did not make more than a mile or a mile and a half an hour. We ran out of stimulants, and almost out of water. Most of us had not slept for four nights, and as the night advanced our march was almost a stagger. This was not so much fatigue as want of excitement. . . .

The secret of this forced march, as well as our unexpected descent on Annapolis, was the result of Col. LEFFERTS' judgment, which has since been sustained by events. . . . The fact that since then all the Northern troops have passed through the line that we thus opened, is a sufficient comment on the admirable judgment that decided on the movement.

At Washington the Seventh was encamped for five weeks. It had been called into the service of the United States for a term of thirty days; and after arrival in Washington the organization was mustered in on April 26, and again on April 30 and May 14.[10] Throughout this term O'Brien served as a private in the Seventh Company, under the command of John Monroe, Captain.[11] Colonel Emmons Clark in a letter to Winter says that "during that time O'Brien became a universal favourite, as he was a brilliant, dashing fellow and very brave though his fault was intemperance. He wrote several camp songs, which were much sung. He never in any way did anything calculated to hurt the good name of the regiment."[12]

In spite of the commendation of Colonel Clark, a letter from his friend, Tom Davis, shows that O'Brien's record with his company and regiment was not entirely clear. The paragraph quoting the Colonel's sense of the injustice done, however, seems entirely to exonerate O'Brien from any serious charge. The letter was written on February 8, 1862, after O'Brien had a second time left the city on active military service, and the references of its paragraphs contain all that is known of the affair:

I have great pleasure in informing you that I have had an interview with your quondam Col — Lefferts of the 7th Regt. He received me very affably, seemed to know who I was, and said he remembered you. I opened my business at once by giving him a detailed account of your doings last summer and fall, your correspondence with Monroe and your anxiety to have your affairs with your Company regulated according to its by-laws. I concluded by calling his attention to the fact that you had had manifest injustice done to you.

Lefferts was a little stiff about it, *at first*, but I charged him again and again, and at last he met me fairly by owning that he thought the Company had been

[10] See Col. Emmons Clark, *op. cit.*, II, 490.

[11] See *ibid.*, II, 497; and records in the Seventh Regiment Armory.

[12] Col. Emmons Clark to William Winter, n. d. [1880]. Owned by Alfred F. Goldsmith, 42 Lexington Ave.

hasty and unjust. Then I went at Monroe, and after explaining Hoffman's position, family, &c, told Col. Lefferts that I thought Capt. Monroe had deliberately told a falsehood.

The Col. seemed to acquiesce, and I then hinted that the Capt. might have been influenced by some secret dislike or enmity to you. Judge of my surprise when Lefferts honestly told me that he was almost sure that such was the case from remarks that he had heard.

With these points to work on, I set at once about enlisting sympathy &c. I evidently succeeded, for Lefferts told me he would call on Capt. Monroe for the papers, would speak privately to some of the members of yr. company about the case, and would try and obtain a revision of their decision. When we parted he told me to express to you his sense of the injustice, done you, and his appreciation of the rankling you seem to feel, and asked me to call on him in about ten days when he hoped to have a favorable report to make me. As to Monroe, I have greater pleasure in saying that, he is dangerously ill with typhoid fever, than I ever expected to have in reporting the illness of any human being. Thus have I had the interview with Lefferts I was so anxious for, and, if I can do anything more to serve your purpose in this matter, need I say, I am willing to perform it.[13]

Of the songs written by O'Brien, one, "The Seventh," to be sung to the air of "Gilla Machree," is a rollicking lilt in Irish brogue, and was included in the letter to the *Times*. Another poem, not found elsewhere, is given by Colonel Clark in his *History of the Seventh Regiment*. It is called "The Midnight March" and begins:

All along the weary miles
Down through the dark defiles,
Through the woods of pine and larch,
Under midnight's solemn arch,
Came the heavy sounding march
Of the Seventh!

Then follow six similar stanzas, describing what has been given above in prose.

After a few days of guard duty in Washington, the eight hundred men of the Seventh together with other regiments were during most of May stationed at Camp Cameron, a little north of the Capital. Later, with something of a show of force, they were marched across the Potomac to Arlington, and finally, on June 1, they returned to New York, where they

[13] A. L. S., Tom Davis to Fitz, Feb. 8, 1862.

were mustered out on June 3, after almost twice the thirty days for which they had been called into service.[14]

O'Brien, who had had merely a taste of war, now cast about for the best opportunity to see active service. With some of his comrades he became interested in forming a volunteer regiment, with himself included in its list of officers as a captain.

Certain details about the early volunteer recruiting are brought out in the following letter of O'Brien's to an unidentified correspondent:

July 17th 1861
Headquarters, Clinton Rifles
62, William Street
N. Y.

Dr. Sir

My friend Mr. Frank Goodrich mentions to me the fact that you have control of a military company in your neighbourhood. If you and your men have no better engagements in view I can offer your immediate acceptance into the Clinton Rifles. The advantages are these.

We are accepted by government the moment the Army bill passes the Senate. We go into Camp on Staten Island on Thursday 18th. We give the men immediate subsistence and quarters. We will in the course of three weeks have 1000 Enfield Rifles and sword bayonets furnished.

The officers are mainly drawn from the 7th Regt. National Guard. The uniform is that of the French *Chasseurs a pièd*, and will come from France made by the French Government. The whole kit complete, so as to avoid piecemeal distribution to the soldier.

If these facts offer any inducement to you to influence your men I have the honor of placing a First lieutenancy in my Company at your disposal.

We have now 600 men on the rolls and expect to be ready for the field in September.

Pray answer me at your earliest leisure——

I remain your very
obedient sevt
FitzJames O'Brien
Capt. C. L.[15]

By August 3 the scheme was so far advanced that *The New York Leader* refers to it as "A Regiment of Beaux." The well-dressed J. Augustus Page

[14] The reasons for this are fully discussed in Clark, *op. cit.*, II, 21–22, and 31–35.

[15] A. L. S. in the possession of the author.

is the colonel, and Frank Wood is a second lieutenant. The Clinton Rifles as they are called "are now encamped on Staten Island, near New Brighton, and will be off for the seat of war about the first of September."

Within a week, however, trouble developed in the Clinton Rifles, and Colonel Page "felt called upon to dismiss 'three captains and eight lieutenants for insubordination.' "[16] O'Brien was one of the former, and, with his fellow insubordinates, organized a new regiment called "The McClellan Rifles," with headquarters at the corner of Nassau and Beekman Streets. Colonel Eugene Le Gal, formerly of the Fifty-fifth French Regiment, accepted the command of the embryo regiment; and by August 14 three companies of thirty-two men each were ready to be mustered in, and had gone into camp at Fort Hill, Staten Island. On August 16 Company A was mustered into the service by Captain Hayman, and after the mustering, "the company elected Fitzjames O'Brien, Captain, and George Stewart, Lieutenant."[17]

Recruiting for a time continued with fair rapidity, but before long obstacles began to arise. Captain Thomas E. Davis, Jr., who was Paymaster for the regiment, says that after a fair start in the business he found himself "unable to bear the exposure of the camp, and so left the affair" to O'Brien;[18] and Frank Wood, the young lieutenant, reveals the general difficulty of the situation in the following words: "The people's first patriotic spasm had passed, the Union army seemed to have as many men as was necessary, and recruits to the new regiment came in but slowly."[19] The McClellan Rifles had, by September 18, 250 men encamped on Staten Island ready to be mustered into the service of the United States.[20] But the remaining seventy men necessary to fill the minimum regimental requirements were unobtainable. All during these delays "O'Brien was chafing like a caged eagle,"[21] and that he did everything in his power to persuade or even drag men into joining his regiment is humorously depicted in a cartoon by Edward F. Mullen. It appeared in *Vanity Fair* for November 9, and shows the uniformed Captain O'Brien, the flowing mustaches and small chin especially exaggerated, with a huge hand grabbing by the coattail an angry and

[16] *N. Y. Leader*, Aug. 10, 1861.
[17] *N. Y. Herald*, Aug. 18, 1861.
[18] Winter, 1881, p. xxxii.
[19] *Ibid.*, p. xl.
[20] See *N. Y. Herald*, Sept. 18, 1861.
[21] Winter, 1881, p. xl.

resisting recruit. By the third week of September recruiting was so slow that the Hancock Guard was consolidated with the McClellan Rifles;[22] but still the quota was not complete. On October 16 O'Brien was tested by the board of examiners for the New York Depot of Volunteers in the School of the Soldier and Company and was found qualified to serve as a Company Officer.[23] Things dragged on, and O'Brien, eager for action, was fretting at the delays. Finally, giving up all idea of going into action with a complete regiment, he early in December withdrew from the McClellan Rifles and went to Washington to seek a position on some general's staff.[24]

O'Brien Recruiting

From a Caricature by Mullen in "Vanity Fair"

In the meantime his mother, Mrs. DeCourcy O'Grady, had heard of O'Brien's service with the Seventh, and on October 25, 1861, wrote to her son from London. Though full of erroneous ideas as to the type of service to be performed by the Seventh and as to the exaltedness of her son's position in the organization, the letter nevertheless conveys such a vivid impression as to the personality of the mother and contains so many details

[22] See *Evening Post*, Sept. 20, 1861, and *N. Y. Tribune*, Sept. 30, 1861.

[23] Certificate, State of New York, Depot of Volunteers, (Division Armory, co. White and Elm Streets). New York. Oct. 16, 1861. In Romm collection.

[24] See *N. Y. Leader*, Dec. 7; and Winter, 1881, p. xl.

suggestive of the life and of the people from which O'Brien had now been separated for almost ten years that it is given in full:

30 Craven Street, *Strand* London October 25th 1861

My dearest Fitzjames

On the 11th of last August I enclosed a letter for you, to your friends and Publishers "Harper Brothers" and which letter from me also contained another to you from De Courcy. I know that the packet was received by Harpers, as I had a most *kind* and *courteous* reply from them relieving my mind from the terrible anxiety I was in respecting you, and mentioning you in terms the most flattering and cheering and for which I will *ever* feel most truly grateful to them.—In my letter I desired you to address your answer to *Brussels* but as we left that place sooner than I thought I fear your reply may have gone astray or be detained in some of the Continental post offices where we found it most difficult to drag our letters out of their clutches. They detained Messrs Harpers for a fortnight when after many entreaties they forwarded it to me to Paris.—This is what makes me hope you wrote and I think it right to let you know that I never received any answer.

DeCourcy wrote to you to offer you £30 and I hope on receipt of this you will write *at once accepting* the offer for though the sum is small yet it may go a little way towards your outfit in the 7th N. York regiment into which Harpers have announced to me that you have got into.—Dear Fitzjames write at once and dont refuse this little gift and take the offer as it was meant, KINDLY—

Messrs Harper merely mention that you have got into the 7th "a gentlemanlike regiment with their own son" but since then DeCourcy met some American or rather N. York gentlemen in Paris who assured him that it was quite a distinction to get into that regiment for that none but men of *colossal* wealth or most brilliant talent could get a commission in it. They described it as a service like the Horse Guards here, always kept in the city which I promise you was *great happiness* to me to hear.—We will be very anxious to know all about it from you.—What the pay is, and what you rank in the regiment Lieutenant or Captain—You need not answer any of these questions if you don't like. All I want is to hear from you and to have you *write* of all things to DeCourcy and accept his offer this would make me very happy—We left Paris for "Boulogne sur mer" on October the 7th and arrived in London on the 10th after crossing the channel in one hour & 30 minutes—We intended to have stopped in Boulogne for a week but had to fly from the gnats which bit us both nearly to death and I have not yet recovered from the bites. These insects were brought over in an Australian vessel in a cargo of wool and everyone in Boulogne suffered more or less from them.—DeCourcy called on William Henry[25] who with his wife is living there for some time. Mrs. William Henry refused to appear and sent word she was OUT though DeC. saw her coming in. William returned the visit the next day *without* his wife. Never asked me to his house, made no apologies and that is all we saw of him or Mrs. O'Driscoll—He is anxious to know and so am *I* if William Cornelius[26] will suffer in a commercial way by this American war. I hope not—DeCourcy left for Ireland this day week. I remained dreading to encounter the IRISH WINTER I have suffered so dreadfully for the last four years whatever part of that kingdom I was in that I am now going to try how London will agree with me. Even the *fogs* are preferable to the easterly winds and *continual* bad weather in the Sister Isle—Lodgings as well as every thing else are very high in London—I pay 15 per week for two very small rooms *next* the *Slates* but I prefer them infinitely to the grand gloomy rooms under me—I am as poor Nancy used to say "high and dry"—I have the light of heaven and good air *for London*—I am literally sky high "all earth beneath and all Heaven around me" and only for solitude and *your silence* would be both comfortable and happy—If I only had one letter from you I would not envy any one in my cock loft. DeCourcy I can not see for *over 3* months. I don't know *an individual* in London, so I hope you will take pity on me and write to me. I can not *even guess* what I could have done or written to make you so obdurate. If I have unfortunately offended you in any way be assured it was most *unintentional* and if so I *sincerely* ask for your pardon and Mercy! More I could not do to God Almighty! and if he deals as hardly with me at the last day then Heaven have Mercy on me.

I have a good deal of news to tell you if I thought you would care to hear it—DeCourcy paid a visit to Mrs. Cullock Chester Square and had a long chat with her.—Kemp Philp is living at St. James' Terrace Regent's park—I intend to write to him for *your Portrait* which he said he had to give me and only for DeCourcy I would have done so long since—I now regret I did not—

I have subscribed to "Harper's Weekly" for six months through the American agents here, Samson, Low & Co. I intend to remain in London until the end of next summer—in hopes something might bring you over to see the "Great Exhibition." Now that I suppose you are a *paid* officer you could better afford the expenses of the voyage—and whilst *here* you would be under no further expense *as of course* you would stop with your own Mother who would receive you with *open arms* and make you comfortable in *every* way.—Could it [be] possible such happiness is in store for me.—They tell me you could be an officer in the American

[25] William Henry O'Driscoll (b. June 16, 1803), son of William (brother of Michael of Baltimore) and therefore first cousin of Eliza. See J. O'Donovan, *op. cit.*, pp. 398–399.

[26] William Cornelius O'Driscoll, son of Cornelius (fourth brother of Michael), and cousin of Eliza, lived in Charleston, South Carolina, U. S. A.

Army and *live* in this country if you liked. God grant it. Let me know this—would any thing induce you to take a run over here this winter and bless your [*sic*] with a visit in her solitude—How comfortable I could make ——— [word torn away] there are bed rooms of every kind in this house. *Grand* ones if you liked and I could get one for you of any grade.

In *my next* if you answer this I will give you my impressions of my Continental trip with which in most respects I was greatly pleased. We stopped in Brussels, Cologne, Coblentz, then up *the Beautiful Rhine*, worth ALL I saw. Mayence, Wiesbaden, Strasbourgh, Nancy, Chalons, and ending with Paris, and I detest the French where the men are all brutes & the women Demons!—Paris I make no doubt will be a beautiful City if the Emperor goes on demolishing all the narrow filthy *purlieus*—but at present Paris is half in ruins, and sevrel of the Churches, Palaces & sights invisible to sight seekers whilst remodelling and repairing. However we contrived to see a great deal.—I suppose you are tired of this long scrawl and besides I am afraid to add another sheet lest it might be *over weight* so must conclude My ever dearest Fitzjames by assuring you in spite of all coldness neglect or silence of the unalterable affection of your loving Mother.

E OGRADY[27]

After Fitz-James's service with the Seventh "he felt that the opportunity had come for him to redeem the time he had so carelessly used." So says Louis H. Stephens, and adds, "At this time he was much in my society, and I remember with what a sad earnestness he occasionally referred to the past, and how well and hopefully he dwelt upon the possibilities of the future."[28] The other side of his desire is revealed by Mrs. Sherwood:

I saw Fitzjames O'Brien in his uniform before he left for the war, and he gave me a little packet of letters to send to a lady in Ireland if he should be killed. He had all the enthusiasm of an Irishman about being killed. I think he enjoyed the idea. I am afraid, this love of adventure and this heroic intoxication has sent many a man to the war. It is a greater draught than patriotism. It is an amusement, and this arousing a man out of what may be torpor and a habit of ennui is immense. It is more powerful as a factor in the young man's nature than we are apt to imagine. It is what "makes the puppies fight well." "And then," says O'Brien, who laughed at this side of himself, "we feel such a delicious egotism. Why, when I am marching down Broadway I do not know whether I am a part of the universe, or whether the universe is a part of me."

[27] A. L. S. in the Romm collection.
[28] Winter, 1881, p. lxi.

One can hardly imagine how valuable were his letters from the front, written in this gay spirit. He denounced wrongs and abuses with the force of Poultney Bigelow. He was not afraid of anything. He threw a grace and beauty over grim-visaged war, and bore his part with uncommon patience.[29]

One poem of the denunciatory kind was printed in *Vanity Fair* on July 6. "Whom This Cap Fits Let Him Wear It" flays, in uneven verse but no uncertain terms, a certain brigadier for the reckless ignorance and stupid incompetence with which he led his men into a slaughterous ambuscade. He had better be dead

Than to hear blood at the Heaven gate crying,
And walk through the world with a murderer's face.

O'Brien had been writing other things in the many leisure moments that were his after the Seventh had settled down to camp routine in Washington and during the days of slow recruiting that followed. The first of these is a graceful little story, "Captain Alicant,"[30] told with such a light, amusing ease that the rescue in the snowstorm, with its marked coincidence, does not strike one as melodramatic. The mood is more like Irving's than like Poe's; and the story returns for its scene to Hopskotch, New Jersey, on the Passaic River, and revives General Dubbley and the Hominy House of earlier stories.[31]

Another story, "The Bullfinch,"[32] reverts to subject matter he used frequently in earlier sketches—the backstage life of the theatre. Charles Kamm in his shop on Crosby Street takes great pride in making all sorts of costume footwear for the actors and actresses whom he admires, though when he attends a play he notices nothing above the knees of the performers. In spite of the oversentimental conclusion the reader enjoys the story for its humor, especially the characterizations of Umber the scene painter, of Kamm humble yet obstinate teaching his bullfinch to whistle, and of the heroine's vulgarly pretentious mother, and the episode of Kamm in a fit of sudden jealousy pummeling the leading man.

With "Mrs. Jujube at Home,"[33] O'Brien revived the prose social satire,

[29] *N. Y. Times*, July 2, 1898.
[30] *Harper's*, XXIII, 105–108 (June, 1861).
[31] See "Mary Burnie of the Mill" and "The Crystal Bell."
[32] *The Knickerbocker*, LVIII, 29–40 (July, 1861).
[33] *Harper's*, XXIII, 378–381 (Aug., 1861).

a genre in which he had also written some years before. It is, however, lighter in touch than "My Son, Sir" or "The Beauty"; and it remains more consistently on the key of social persiflage than the verse satires like "The Finishing School." In subject matter and in clever presentation of certain aspects of New York society with the veils of outward splendor somewhat cynically pierced, it is, in fact, strongly reminiscent of Thackeray or a French play. The plot is of no particular consequence, but the pictures of Madame Larami's fashionable dressmaking establishment and of the *bal poudre*, together with the revelation of spicy detail through the pointed observations of minor members of this disillusioned set, make the story of Mrs. Jujube's daughter worth reading.

In addition to this story the August *Harper's* gave space to two of O'Brien's poems. "The Countersign" deservedly attracted a good deal more attention than did "The Pot of Gold." The latter is the worst sort of sentimentalism—"Excelsior!" seems to have been its inspiration—and from its meaningless bathos one turns hastily to the preceding page of the magazine to find a poem which, though sentimental also, is timely and true in its picture of war conditions and feelings. The reflections of the sentry on duty—his fears, his adjustments, his memory of fond partings—are not merely conventional, but have the authenticity of experience behind them; and they are broken into by the approach of troops with the countersign. The last stanza—inevitable in wartime, and with Fitz-James at almost any time—expresses the sentry's hope that if he falls he may know the heavenly countersign for entry into the "camp divine." That this poem hit the popular taste is interestingly attested by the following paragraph in the *Leader* for November 30:

Mr. Fitz-James O'Brien's charming poem, "The Countersign," which appeared a few months since in *Harper's Monthly*, is going the rounds of the papers as having been written by one Frank G. Williams, a private in the Federal army, who is said to have sent it a fortnight since, in manuscript, to a Connecticut paper, as his own composition. If this statement be true, Private Williams ought to be drummed out of his regiment forthwith. As a matter of justice to Mr. O'Brien we republish the poem with his name.

The timeliness of "The Countersign" is also seen in the fact that it was one of the poems printed in 1863 in J. Henry Hayward's collection, *Poetical*

Pen-Pictures of the War; and its inclusion in this volume makes it the first of O'Brien's American writings to find its way between the covers of a book.[34]

"The Havelock,"[35] another war poem, tells, without any special inspiration but in an interesting way, the history of the havelock from the time it is grown as cotton on the southern plantation to the time it is worn as a havelock on the head of a Union soldier who is back on that same plantation ready for the coming fight. The last stanzas, telling of the bride who fashioned the havelock from the cotton cloth to protect the head of her beloved husband, are full of the tenderness that war separations bring uppermost.

As the prospects for his early participation in the war waned and as the enlistments came in more slowly, O'Brien turned from the poem with war background, with its comparatively temporary appeal, to his old types of perennially appealing sentiment and satire. "Of Loss"[36] describes the beauties of an Indian summer landscape, where, through the calm and peace of the scene, or amid the merry relaxations of the farmers at their harvest, only the poet is unhappy, mourning the death of his beloved. Whittier's "Telling the Bees" (1858) has this same combination of the farm scene and the loss of a loved one; indeed the loss motive, common to poetry down the ages, took in the mid-nineteenth century this sentimental form not only in the verses of Whittier and O'Brien, but in those of Longfellow, Lowell, Aldrich, and many others as well.

"The Tenement House"[37] brings to a climax the long series of O'Brien's poems about social injustice, such as "The Finishing School," "The Prize-Fight," "Pemberton Mills," and "The Sewing Bird." It flays in scathing satire the selfishness and greed of the rich and their callous indifference to the loss of life for which they are directly responsible; it pictures the sybaritic comfort of their opulent homes; and in contrast it depicts the

[34] J. Henry Hayward, *Poetical Pen-Pictures of the War: Selected from our Union Poets*, 1863. The book was privately printed and is now rare. As the poem appears in it the lines of the last stanza are quite changed, and at the end of the poem, instead of "Camp Cameron, July, 1861," are the words "Found on the Field." This may be the way the "Williams" version had it. It will be recalled that "Loch Ina," "The Boatmen of Kerry" and "Irish Castles," written in Ireland, were printed in Edward Hayes, *The Ballads of Ireland* in 1856. (In *Poetical Pen-Pictures* a poem by Bret Harte also first appears).

[35] *Harper's*, XXIII, 512–513 (Sept., 1861).

[36] *Ibid.*, XXIII, 650 (Oct., 1861).

[37] *Ibid.*, XXIII, 732–734 (Nov., 1861).

utter filth and degradation of the poverty they have caused. The poem opens with carefully polished lines containing vivid touches:

> A nice little dinner at Ormolu's;
> A chosen few, and no ladies there:
> Every man is a millionaire,
> With ample waistcoat and creaking shoes.
> The dinner, of course, is a great success—
> Dinners at Ormolu's always are—
> From the delicate bisque to the caviar,
> And the wild boar's head in its gaudy dress.

Over the wine they talk about money and how to make it, and Ormolu is at ease with the world.

> And somehow he sees, in a dreamy way,
> His tenement houses:—He owns a few,
> And capital profits they bring him too;
> For he knows how to make the tenants pay:—
>
> He sees them squalid and black and tall,
> With rotten rafters and touch-wood stair,
> The scant rooms fetid with stagnant air,
> And the plaster membrane that's called a wall.
>
> . . .
>
> Crazy, filthy, and insecure,
> Hastily builded, and cheap and nasty,
> About as strong as fresh-baked pasty,
> But almost too good for vagrant poor.

Ormolu has had complaints that they are a fire hazard, but they

> Are all insured to their fullest figure—
> Appraised and valued with utmost rigor—

so he gaily continues with his gentlemanly drinking. Then it comes:

> One, two, three, four!
> Ormolu hears the fire-bell toll;
> It is his district—but, bless your soul!
> All is insured, and fires are a bore.

The spectacular fire with its shocking incidents is impressionistically described, until

> down with a roar, in a crimson ruin,
> Ormolu's tenement building tumbles.

And then, not to leave any doubt in the reader's mind as to what he thinks is the criminality involved, O'Brien concludes:

> Crushed and mangled with beam and girder,
> Five corpses lie in those tenement houses;
> And Ormolu with his guests carouses,
> Guilty, by Heaven, of all that murder!

The poem is full of movement and vivid interest; and its bold strokes and sharp, violent contrasts give it such force and such crude power as to establish Fitz-James as a poet to be reckoned with in the field of social protest even had the long line of similar poems that preceded it been almost entirely lacking.

In spite of many shortcomings in his poetic taste and technique due largely to his hasty composition, O'Brien's verses appearing, often with his signature now, in the best magazines were attracting attention; and he had barely returned from his military service with the Seventh, when his services as a poet were flatteringly recognized by his receiving the following letter:

University of Vermont
Burlington, June 3, 1861.

FitzJames O'Brien, Esq.
New York City
Dear Sir:

I am instructed by the Literary Societies of the University to ask you to present a poem before them at their next Annual Celebration. They unitedly hold a celebration on Tuesday Aug. 6th of the present season. It will afford us great pleasure to hear a Poem from yourself if you can be here and deliver one at that time. Will you be so kind as to inform me early whether you can accept the invitation.

With great respect your obedient servant.

P. F. LEAVENS
Secy and etc.[38]

[38] MS in Romm collection.

Such complimentary recognition of his work must have been gratifying; and yet an almost contemporary letter written by himself shows that neither appreciation of his poetic ability by the academic world nor high resolves for military glory could long curb his intemperate habits. A drunken quarrel and a heavy "hang-over" are patently the background for the following:

Albermarle Hotel
June 10th, 1861

Sir

I regret much that a sick headache precluded my receiving to-day even my intimate friends. I am still more sorry that I could not have the pleasure of seeing you, as I learn by your note that you had business of an exigent nature.

I am entirely at a loss to understand your communication. As I am not aware of having had any personal difficulty with you I cannot comprehend your allusions to either giving or taking satisfaction. If those allusions tend to another gentleman of the party, you will excuse my saying that it must be somewhat unnecessary to address me on the subject, inasmuch as the supposed person is not a friend of mine. All affairs between you and such person must be conducted without my aid. If you require a formal report from me of the circumstances of that evening to which you allude, I shall furnish it at your request at 62 Williams Street, where I shall be to-day at 4 o'clock P. M.

I shall be found in the office of Mr. J. A. Page.

I have the honor to
remain your very
obedient servant
FitzJames O'Brien[39]

The difficulty suggested in this letter was no doubt quickly adjusted; but a fracas occurring in September or October in connection with O'Brien's recruiting efforts threatened to become serious. One night about eight o'clock as Captain O'Brien was returning from the boat to the camp at Factoryville, Staten Island, accompanied by Private Frank Opeltt, of Company B, McClellan Rifles, he saw Sergeant Davenport standing talking with two other men. Captain O'Brien asked the Sergeant why he didn't go into camp, and then if he had a pass. Sergeant Davenport answered,

[39] MS in Romm collection. 62 Williams Street was at this time the recruiting office for the Clinton Rifles, in which O'Brien was interested. Later the McClellan Rifles were at the same address. See *N. Y. Leader*, Aug. 24, 1861.

"Our passes are all right." A moment later Captain O'Brien was walking backwards crying out, "Stand back! Stand back!" closely followed by the Sergeant. As they came opposite a blacksmith's shop they halted for a moment, and Davenport called O'Brien a liar and other abusive epithets. O'Brien again commenced retreating followed by Davenport, and then, with his pistol pointed at the Sergeant, O'Brien said, "Stand back or I will shoot you." As they got near a ditch, Davenport still following, O'Brien said, "Stand back, or, so help me God, I will shoot you!" One of the two men who were with Davenport said, "If you shoot Sergt. Davenport you will have to shoot us, too"; to which O'Brien replied, "Well, I will shoot you, too." The Sergeant then laid hands on the Captain, and threw him into the ditch; but, when he raised a hand to strike him, O'Brien fired. The Sergeant cursed, "You damn shit, you didn't hit me anyhow"; and the other two men rushed forward to help him. Still in a clinch O'Brien fired again, and the Sergeant cried, "I'm struck; I die." Then Captain O'Brien got up, advanced to the gate of the camp, and was arrested.[40] One ball took "effect in the leg and the other in the abdomen," and as a result of the first examination the sergeant was not "expected to survive his injuries."[41]

A Court Martial sat on the case and O'Brien was exonerated as firing in self-defense. Nevertheless, considerable bad blood was stirred up by such a serious encounter between members of a volunteer regiment; and the article in the *Evening Post* of November 7 under the title "Fitz-James O'Brien under Arrest" did not help matters any—with its statement that the captain "made an attempt upon the life of the sergeant" because of jealousy, with its slur at his literary connections, and with its repetition of the old slander "that O'Brien had filched North's ideas and given them a new setting."[42] So, until the thing blew over, with the assurance of Sergeant Davenport's complete recovery some weeks later, O'Brien lived in retirement on Staten Island at the home of his friend and fellow officer, Thomas E. Davis.[43]

It was here that he wrote the poem, "A Soldier's Letter," which he read

[40] From a copy in the Romm collection of testimony given by Frank Opeltt, taken before the Court Martial in the case of O'Brien—tried for the shooting of Sergeant Davenport.

[41] *Evening Post*, Nov. 7, 1861; copied from The Stapleton (Staten Island) *Gazette*.

[42] *Ibid.* On Nov. 8 the *Evening Post* grudgingly makes "A Correction" in "Mr. O'Brien's Case" by saying, "He acted, we are told, in self-defence, and has not been arrested."

[43] See Winter, 1881, p. xxxii.

to Davis just after completing it. It was here too that he probably wrote the other stories and poems that were left in manuscript or that for some months continued to appear in the magazines; for after he received his appointment and again went into active service, there could have been but little time for writing. Besides "A Soldier's Letter" and "The Prisoner of War," which are noticed in the next chapter, there remain to be considered five poems, four stories, and four plays.

Of these the only one to be printed during O'Brien's lifetime was "Amy Scudder,"[44] a sentimental ballad, insipid in story and undistinguished in verse. "Down in the Glen at Idlewild,"[45] printed in the following July, is a crude ballad of "The Skaters" type, so crass in its striving for tragic effect as to be almost ludicrous. Of the other three poems all are unfinished and two exist only in manuscript. "Watching the Stag" was published as a fragment in *The Continental Monthly*.[46] Of the manuscripts[47] one without title tells of a gull from whose back drips human blood; the other, much better written, is called "Rose de Mai" and tells of a lover going to the woods for a secret meeting with his "little white Rose." In the fourth stanza (unwritten) Winter says the lover was to have found her dead by the hand of his rival, Sir Hugh. Another idea for a poem which remained unwritten was jotted down by O'Brien, and the manuscript, with a notation by Winter, was recently acquired by the New York Public Library. It was to be called "Nemesis,"—"Poem on the burning of Charleston the spot where the flag was first fired on.

"Flag first raised there on soil South Carolina. First desecrated there also."

Here also must be mentioned "The Cave of Silver,"[48] a balladlike poem in eight stanzas, which tells of a haughty Norwegian maiden who sets for her lover an impossible task but who then grieves when he loses his life attempting its accomplishment.

[44] *H. W.*, VI, 122 (Feb. 22, 1862). A MS. copy of this poem, lacking the last eight stanzas, was sent by William Winter to be printed in *The Sword and the Pen* published during the ten days of the Soldiers' Home Bazaar held in Boston, Dec. 7–17, 1881. Also the MS. was to be sold there.

[45] *Harper's*, XXV, 236 (July, 1862).

[46] *The Continental Monthly devoted to Literature and National Policy*, II, 105 (July, 1862). Under the title is the line, "[An Unfinished Poem, By Fitz-James O'Brien.]"

[47] In the collection of Alfred F. Goldsmith, bookseller, 42 Lexington Avenue, New York City.

[48] Unlocated in original printing. Found in Rev. O. H. Tiffany, ed., *Gems for the Fireside*, Boston, 1882, pp. 362–363. It was included in Winter's list as "The Silver Seeker."

Two of the four stories are also in manuscript. "Violina, the Birth of a Poet" fills five and a half folio pages, containing all of Chapter I and the first paragraph of Chapter II.[49] The scene is laid on upper Lexington Avenue where still exist two dilapidated, old-fashioned houses with gardens, and the story concerns two young men who are rival geniuses on the violin. "On a Rock," the opening paragraphs of which describe O'Brien's familiar state of financial destitution, is also unfinished.[50] "Tommatoo" (in *Harper's Monthly* for August, 1862) could scarcely be rivalled for the bad taste of its mixed melodrama and sentimentalism. It possesses, however, all the elements requisite for popular success—satire, sentimentality, gaiety, horror, hairbreadth escapes, a nick-of-time rescue, beauty in distress, and through it all the reader taken into the confidence of the author, who shares with him his joy in the story and occasionally reveals his own personality. The story in its elaborately detailed handling of a New York slum district recalls the method of "The Wondersmith"—a combination of swamps, slaughterhouses, and scavenger dogs, six years ago at Thirty-second Street between Twelfth and Thirteenth Avenues, supplying the circumstantial setting. "How I Overcame My Gravity,"[51] which did not appear until two years later, is an interesting, convincing, and well-written dream story, and imitates "The Diamond Lens" in having as its hero an inventor and pseudo-scientist, who attempts to make a globe which shall whirl at a speed so great that it will overcome gravity.

Among the other things left in the custody of Davis was the manuscript of a play, *Blood Will Tell.* O'Brien was hopeful of having this produced, and Frank Wood wrote him about it and about the disposition of two other plays shortly after O'Brien had returned to the war:

New York, Jan. 14, 1862.

My dear Fitz:

Being confined to my room by sickness last Thursday and Friday I did not get your notes until Saturday. I immediately applied to Mr. Davis for your MSS. On Monday (yesterday) he sent me "Blood Will Tell." I took it up to E. L. Davenport's hotel, but E. L. D. was not at home. I shall try to see him again to-day. I then went to Wallack. He says he has no use for "The Cup and The Lip" at present; that there is a part in it which he himself, or Blake must

[49] MS in possession of the author.

[50] MS in Romm collection.

[51] *Harper's*, XXVIII, 779–781 (May, 1864).

play; that he (Wallack) cannot do it now and that Blake is too poor a student to be entrusted with it. He will hunt up the play and return it to me in a few days. Has Laura Keene ever seen it? "The Two Ophelias" I will do my best to dispose of.[52]

By February 1, however, when Wood wrote again, he had a discouraging report to make: "The plays have been unfortunate. Wallack says he can do nothing with the New York comedy at present and Davenport says ditto about 'Blood Will Tell.' "

Two other plays are mentioned in connection with O'Brien, but the references to them are not so positive. Louis H. Stephens says, "Looking to more ambitious work, he had selected the story of Samson as a subject for a drama, and, I think, had partly written it."[53] On September 30, 1863, Wallack's Theatre was opened for the season with a new play, *Rosedale, or The Rifle Ball.*[54] This was a great success, being acted 125 times during the season. It is a conventional melodrama of almost the worst type, with lost sons and lost daughters, missing heirs and adopted children hopelessly mixed up, until the final, grand reconciliation scene. Lester Wallack was posted on the playbills as its author; but Charles Gayler, the prolific playwright and something of a rival of O'Brien's, at a dinner given in New York in 1890, stated that Wallack had paid O'Brien $100 to dramatize it from a novel, *Lady Lee's Widowhood*, which had some years previously appeared in *Blackwood's Magazine.*[55] Such a course of action seems unlike Lester Wallack, but there is no other evidence either way.

It must have been during the last months of 1861 also that O'Brien "contemplated publishing, in collected form, those of his writings which he thought worthy of preservation,"[56] and that he wrote out a list of twenty stories headed "The Diamond Lens and other tales By Fitz James O'Brien."[57]

[52] A. L. S. in Romm collection.

[53] Winter, 1881, p. lxi.

[54] See T. Allston Brown, *op. cit.*, II, 252, and Odell, *op. cit.*, VII, 542.

[55] See *ibid*. *Lady Lee's Widowhood* ran as a serial in *Blackwood's Edinburgh Magazine*, LXXIII, 77 to LXXIV, 450 (January to October, 1853). It was written by Captain Edward B. Hamley, R.A., and published by Harper & Brothers in book form as No. 186 in "Library of Select Novels," 1854.

[56] *H. W.*, VI, 267 (Apr. 26, 1862).

[57] This list, in the possession of Mr. Alfred F. Goldsmith, of 42 Lexington Ave., New York City, contains the following stories: "The Diamond Lens," "Duke Humphrey's Dinner," "The Golden Ingot," "The Pot of Tulips," "The Lost Room," "Three of a Trade," "My Wife's

Sixteen of his best stories are in the list, but the inclusion of the inferior "One Event" and "Carrying Weight," as well as such an anomalous piece as "Bird Gossip," would seem to indicate that, for all the welter of production in which he had indulged, O'Brien was hard put to it to find even twenty stories which might justify his claim to a place of literary permanence. When he sent the list to Harpers, he gave it a less matter-of-fact title, truer to his habit of facetious punning: " 'Flotsam and Jetsam'—Things lost by Shipwreck, or thrown overboard to save the Vessel."[58] But such a volume never appeared, and the vessel's voyage was soon to be over.

Tempter," "Jubal the Ringer," "Belladonna," "Hard Up," "Mrs. Macsimum's Bill," "Mother of Pearl," "The Bohemian," "The Dragon Fang possessed by the Conjuror Piou Lou," "The Wondersmith," "Bird Gossip," "Lost," "One Event," "Carrying Weight," and "The King of Nodland and his dwarf." In front of each of the last four titles is a small circle, which might indicate that he preferred not to include them. "Lost" I have not been able to locate. "Amy Scudder," the title of a poem, is written in much lighter at the end, and after "other tales" of the heading, is written in ". . . & poems."

[58] *H. W., loc. cit.*

Chapter XII

War and Death

(1862)

In December, 1861, after O'Brien had returned from Washington, unsuccessful in his attempts to secure a staff appointment,[1] he wrote to General Lander applying for a position on his staff. He had special hopes in this direction because to Tom Aldrich, who had earlier in the year applied to the same general, Lander had after long delay sent an appointment by telegram—a message which through lack of forwarding address remained unopened and unanswered.[2] This place missed by his friend might by chance still be open to Fitz-James. In the meantime his friends were doing all they could by letters of recommendation to help him secure the sort of service he so ardently desired.[3] To one of these letters, General Lander, who was something of a poet himself, replied as follows:

December 31, 1861.

Dear Bierstadt

I received your note but have not seen O'Brien. I have a place as Aide-de-Camp with the rank of Lieutenant of Vols. which would not be worth his while. I was much struck with his Sea Poem, "I Was The First Mate" etc., etc. I think it the best in the country of the class. I have had a hundred applications for staff appointments. I go now to Romney. Should he join me can find the place if he were to come at once. Simon F. Barstow, Washington City, Aidedecamp, can give him particulars of route.

Respy and truly in haste
F. W. Lander
B. G. U. S. A.[4]

[1] See p. 217; and Winter, 1881, p. xl.

[2] See Greenslet, *op. cit.*, p. 54; and Winter, 1881, p. xxvi, n.

[3] See Thomas E. Davis to Hon. A. W. Van Wyck, Dec. 12, 1861; Thos. E. Davis, Jr. to Brig. Genl. Shields, Jan. 8, 1862; and Jos. W. Harper, Jr. to FitzJames O'Brien, Esq., Jan. 13, 1862; and Frank Wood to "My dear Fitz," Jan. 14, 1862, last paragraph—"Wallack sent his letter of introduction to Gen. Marcy, to 84 Nassau St. for you, but as you failed to give Davis's name, the errand was fruitless. W. supposes the letter would be of no use to you, now." (For the first paragraph of this letter see p. 229). All these letters are in Romm collection.

[4] MS in Romm collection.

O'Brien, as yet ignorant of this letter and its contents, probably celebrated its date in characteristic fashion and spent the New Year's Eve at Pfaff's "with a group of hopeful young litterateurs to enliven the present, and the memories of dear Wilkins and Neill to lighten up the past."[5] During the week following O'Brien made renewed appeals to his friends to write letters to military commanders; but on January 8 he received Lander's letter and joyfully jumped at the opportunity for active service which it seemed to offer. That night he dined with Tom Davis, and he promised him that on his return he would settle down with him, and "devote himself to the production of something in literature that might live. He had 'a great work,' he said, prepared in his mind, which he had 'thought out through years of thinking,' and this he would write when his soldiering was over."[6] This may have been "a novel of American Life and Society," of which he had spoken,[7] or it may have been the play *Samson*, which he had mentioned to L. H. Stephens, "when he went 'to the front' " and left with the latter a copy of *The Soul of Strength Wisdom and Patience* by Rev. John Selby Watson.[8] As O'Brien parted from Davis he said, "I can say nothing to you, but you know where my heart is."[9] Besides saying farewell that evening to Davis and Stephens and Frank Wood, he bid good-bye to Dr. Guernsey and took him the poem, "A Soldier's Letter." "The next day he set out for Lander's department, happy and joyful, and after many tribulations and difficulties succeeded in reaching his command."[10]

"A Soldier's Letter" the Harpers printed in the March number of the *Monthly*, which came out about February 20; and they dated the rhymed epistle as of "January 20, 1862." This, by bringing the poem closer to the date on which it would be read, gave it a more immediate interest, and was thoroughly in accord with O'Brien's own practice of assigning definite dates and settings to the products of his imagination in order to increase the interest and belief in their subject matter. Similarly "The Countersign" had been dated as from "Camp Cameron, July, 1861," or a month after O'Brien had returned from there; and "The Prisoner of War"[11] is dated

[5] *N. Y. Leader*, Jan. 4, 1862.
[6] Winter, 1881, p. xxxiii.
[7] *H. W.*, VI, 267.
[8] L. H. Stephens to William Winter, August 18, 1880.
[9] Winter, 1881, p. xxxiv.
[10] *Ibid.*, p. xli.
[11] *Harper's*, XXIV, 348 (Feb., 1862).

"In Camp, December, 1861." Printed in January "The Prisoner of War" immediately became popular, making its appeal through its exaltation of comradeship. Two staunch friends, both in the army, are now separated, and the soldier in the northern camp expresses his longing for the friend held in a southern prison, and tells of his affection, his vicarious suffering, and his determination to share his comrade's fate or get him free. Though its roughness prevents it from being one of O'Brien's best efforts, its feeling rings true, and as the poet says,

> I sing the irregular song of a soul that is bursting with pain!
> There is no metre for sorrow, no rhythm for real despair.

Frank Wood in a letter to his "dear Fitz," written from Boston on February 1, says,

> Yr poem, by the by, "The Prisoner of War" is receiving an intellectual ovation already. Everywhere I hear it spoken of with enthusiasm. Bateman and Ned House—who are not gushing friends of yours by any means—are quite *exalté* on the subject. Coming on here in the train B. requested permission to recite to us the "no rhythm for real despair" verse, and then gave the same in a voice of tragic earnestness. I know that you care more for my opinion than for any one else's and I will therefore state that I consider "The P. of W." immense. Was it intentional, though, or the consequence of haste, that repetition of the figure "as the stream finds its way to the sea." You use it in the second and in the penultimate stanza.

As with "The Prisoner of War," the dominant note of "A Soldier's Letter" is sincerity; and although not a great poem, in its simple straightforwardness it builds up an emotional effect. A soldier describes to his sweetheart his life in camp and tells the comfort it is to him to share his thoughts of her with another young fellow, a tent-mate, who is equally in love. The writing is interrupted by the sound of firing; and ten days later, "January 30," the letter is finished by dictation to the comrade, because

> That was a skirmish that came, as I wrote to you, out on the hill;
> We had sharp fighting a while, and I lost my arm—
> There! don't cry, my darling!—it will not kill,
> And other poor fellows there met greater harm.[12]

[12] *Ibid.*, XXIV, 508 (Mar., 1862).

Upon receipt of Lander's letter O'Brien set out from New York without delay, leaving probably on the morning of January 9; and it is to be presumed that, as the letter directed, he consulted S. F. Barstow in Washington. There he was delayed for some days, and during this time he gave the Willards Hotel, care of Stephen Mirzan, as his mail address.[13] Finally he reached Camp Kelley, General Lander's Divisional Headquarters, on Patterson's Creek, Virginia; and from there, on January 21, he wrote to Davis: "I am in harness, and am staff officer of parade, and am already intrusted with the rather arduous but important duty of posting the pickets all through this devil of a wilderness."[14] That O'Brien had had to sacrifice his captain's rank for the sake of active service under Lander is officially confirmed by "General Order No. 111," issued at Camp Kelley the next day (January 22):

FitzJames O'Brien is hereby appointed an Aide de Camp. to Brig Genl Lander with the rank of Lieutenant, and will be respected and obeyed accordingly.

By command of
Brig Genl Lander,
(signed) S. F. Barstow
A. A. Genl.[15]

O'Brien continued, in the midst of his picket posting, to write to his friends Wood and Davis; and the next time Frank Wood replied (February 1) he addressed his letter to Lander's Brigade at Cumberland, Maryland:

I was very glad to hear—and so were all the boys to whom I read your letter—that you have such a bully posish. When you come back to New York as a Lieutenant-General please let me arrange your ovation for you. I can get you up a gorgeous one for $100.

[13] See envelope in Romm collection, postmarked "New York Jan 14," and addressed:

"Capt. F. J. O'Brien A.D.C.
Care of Stephen Mirzan
Willards Hotel
Washington
D. C."

[14] Winter, 1881, pp. xxvi–xxvii, note. Two little note books still exist, one inscribed "*Details of Guard,* F. J. O'Brien," the other, "Picket Stations. F. J. O'Brien." A scrap of paper in O'Brien's hand giving the Parole as Prescott and the Countersign as Bunker Hill are probably from this same period.

[15] See copy in Romm collection.

Something of O'Brien's life at the front and of his attitude is revealed in a letter written by his artist friend Albert R. Waud. He says of O'Brien:

After he became Aid on Lander's staff a feeling took possession of him that he should not long survive the commission: under its influence he became, at times, strangely softened. His buoyant epicureanism partly deserted him. He showed greater consideration for others and was less convivial than was his wont.

One night I rode with him to the camp of the First Massachusetts Battery, where the evening passed pleasantly, with cigars and punch. Some one sang the song, from "Don Caesar de Bazan," "Then let me like a soldier die."

Next morning he started to join the General (Lander) at Harper's Ferry. As we rode along he kept repeating the words of the song; said he appreciated the sentiment of it the more, as he had a presentiment that he should himself be shot before long.

He would not be rallied out of it, but remarked that he was content, and when we parted said good-bye as cheerfully as need be.[16]

By February 8 General Lander and his command had moved south and reoccupied Romney, West Virginia.[17] The time was one of general advances, and the particularly aggressive Lander, whose decisiveness and dash won him great popularity with his men but brought him into frequent disagreement with higher officers, was certain not to be found lagging behind.[18]

On the night of February 13, with seven regiments of infantry and five hundred cavalry, General Lander pushed on about fourteen miles further to Bloomery Gap. They arrived there after a forced march, which included some bridge building, about five o'clock in the morning. For some hours there was no sign of any opposing force, and then "Col. Anastanzel encountered the enemy at the head of the pass, two miles from Blooming. He was met by a sharp fire, and halted his command."[19] Lander immediately jumped upon his horse and, followed by O'Brien, dashed away toward the

[16] A. R. Waud to W. Winter, Esq., Dec. 7, 1880, in Romm collection. Printed with minor changes in Winter, *Old Friends*, p. 104.

[17] See *The War of the Rebellion: A Compilation of the Official Records of the Union and Confederate Armies*, Washington, 1881. Series I,—Volume V, p. 388.

[18] See *Evening Post*, Feb. 17 and Feb. 19, 1862; *N. Y. Tribune*, Feb. 25, 1862, and Mar. 6, 1881; and *H. W.*, VI, 165–166 (Mar. 15, 1862).

[19] *N. Y. Tribune*, Feb. 20, 1862,—dated "Cumberland, Md., Feb. 15, 1862." Reprinted in Frank Moore, *Rebellion Record*, 1862, IV, 128–129. See also issues of Feb. 17 and Feb. 25. On Feb. 17 and 20, the *Tribune* calls the place "Blooming Gap"; on Feb. 25 this is corrected to "Bloomery Gap," as it is in accounts printed elsewhere.

scene of the firing. An ambuscade opened up on the left, and General Lander stopping "only long enough to tell the men to remember their holy mission," cried, "Follow your General to victory."[20] The cavalry, however, seemed paralyzed before the musketry of the enemy; and when the General, wheeling to the left, charged the enemy, he was accompanied by only three of his staff officers and one private, John Cannon. The officers were Lieutenants H. G. Armstrong, Asst. Adjutant-General; Fitz-James O'Brien, Aide de Camp; and Major Bannister, Paymaster, U. S. A.[21]

A group of Rebel officers were distant about three hundred yards, encouraging their men. Gen. Lander being mounted on his celebrated horse, outran the rest of the party, and cut off the rebel officers, "Surrender, gentlemen," he said, and coolly dismounting, extended his hand to receive the sword of Colonel Baldwin, whom an instant before he had appeared to outside observers to be riding directly over. Five of the Rebel officers surrendered to Gen. Lander, and four more, immediately afterward, to the officers of his staff.[22]

The chief of these, Captain Baird, Assistant Adjutant-General of the Sixteenth Brigade, attached to General Carson's staff, surrendered to O'Brien, who kept his sword and accoutrements as trophies.[23]

"By this time the Rebel infantry, perceiving the small number of their adversaries, commenced a heavy fire from the woods, but the cavalry had recovered from its panic, and now poured up the hill." In the general engagement that followed, lasting nearly an hour, thirteen of the enemy were killed and seventy-five taken prisoner, while the victory cost the Union forces two killed.[24]

Afterwards the General had Private John Cannon made a Lieutenant, and in his report of the affair to General McClellan mentioned that "Lieuts. H. G. Armstrong, A. A. G., and FitzJames O'Brien, Aid-de-Camp, joined me in the charge by which the Rebel officers were captured, and confidence restored, after the cavalry had been checked."[25] Secretary of War Stanton

[20] *Ibid.*, Feb. 20 and Feb. 25.

[21] See "Report of Brig. Gen. Frederick W. Lander," in *The War of the Rebellion*, 1881, Ser. I, Vol. V, pp. 405–406. Report also printed in Moore, *Rebellion Record*, 1862, IV, 127.

[22] *N. Y. Tribune*, Feb. 20.

[23] See "Report of Col. J. Sencendiver," the Confederate commander, in *The War of the Rebellion*, Ser. I, Vol. V, p. 407; Winter, 1881, p. xli; and *H. W.*, VI, 267 (Apr. 26, 1862).

[24] See *N. Y. Tribune*, Feb. 17 and Feb. 20, 1862.

[25] *N. Y. Leader*, Mar. 1, 1862.

sent a dispatch of high commendation to Lander for his exploit, which made possible the opening up of the Baltimore and Ohio Railroad as far as Hancock, Maryland.[26]

Two days later, about four o'clock in the morning of Sunday, February 16, O'Brien was sent out on a scouting expedition with a company of thirty-five cavalrymen. Their objective was to capture a hundred head of cattle belonging to the secessionists. A skirmish resulted. The enemy, consisting of sixty of Jackson's regular cavalry and one hundred and fifty infantry, opened fire on O'Brien's advance point from behind a bluff. The advance fired a few random shots and retreated upon the main body. A cross fire opened on them from the hillside, and O'Brien charged down the road leading his men against the enemy cavalry. The Confederate officer raised his hand and cried, "Halt! who are you?" O'Brien shouted back, "Union soldiers!" and the two officers fired at each other almost simultaneously. This was the signal for a general engagement, in the midst of which the duel between Lieutenant O'Brien and Colonel Ashley continued. At the second shot O'Brien was hit, the ball passing through his breast near the left shoulder and splintering his scapular bone. Nevertheless, they both shot again, and O'Brien's "men aver that he killed Ashley with his last, as that officer fell when he fired."[27] O'Brien's onslaught against such odds had been so audacious that the enemy thought he must have reserves somewhere; and even after he was wounded he "continued to rally his men, until a subordinate officer, seeing him reeling in his saddle from loss of blood, got him to the rear; after which he brought our men off."[28] No one except O'Brien was hurt, while the enemy suffered two killed and four wounded. Weak and in pain, O'Brien now had to ride back twenty-four miles to a base, where he was placed in the hands of a surgeon, who in his ignorance did not consider the wound a dangerous one and gave

[26] See *N. Y. Tribune*, Feb. 18.

[27] Winter, 1881, p. xlii (from *N. Y. Leader*, Apr. 12, 1862). Practically the same story is told in *N. Y. Times*, Apr. 10, 1862, and in *H. W.*, Apr. 26, 1862. Mr. Shattuck, too, recalled with pride the story of O'Brien's duel on horseback with a Southern officer. Winter, in his own copy of the 1881 volume, made some marginal corrections, the most important of which is that the name of the rebel colonel was not Ashley, but Ashby; and that he did not die from O'Brien's shot, but "was killed at Cross Keys, in June 1862, five months later." (See *The Catholic World*, XXXIII, 138—April, 1881.)

[28] Winter, 1881, pp. xlii–xliii.

it insufficient care and treatment. The next day there was forwarded to him the following dispatch:

GENERAL LANDER,—Please say to Lieutenant O'Brien that I am much pleased with his gallantry, and deeply pained to hear of his wound. I trust he will soon be well enough to give the cause the benefit of his services again.

GEORGE B. McCLELLAN.[29]

Lander's official report, printed in the New York papers, caused great anxiety among O'Brien's friends, and Davis immediately wrote:

February 24.

My dear, dear Fitz:

What is the meaning of the paragraph stating that you had been shot? For God's sake, my dear boy, send me some word of yourself. Draw on me for anything you may want, or come home to me, and recruit.

Yours etc.

TOM[30]

Frank Wood got in touch with General Lander; and O'Brien sent word that his shoulder wound, though serious enough to keep him laid up for the moment, was not dangerous.[31] To this letter Wood replied immediately:

V. F. Office
Thursday. March 7/62

My dear Fitz:

We were all much relieved to hear from you and rejoiced to hear that your wound was no worse. I rec'd a letter from Lander (written the day before his death) informing me that you were at Cumberland, Md. in a private house under good medical attendance.

The boys all join me in love to you and are anxious to know if there is anything they can do to lighten up the tedium of your sick bed. I, myself, should go on to see you if I had the money necessary.

. . . Your health was drunk last night heartily at a meeting called for the purpose of organizing a new club "THE IRREGULARS," the principles of which, by the

[29] *Ibid.*, p. xliii.
[30] MS in Romm collection.
[31] See *N. Y. Leader*, Mar. 8, 1862.

way, would suit you to a • Your gallant action is appreciated here, as you will find.

Ever your friend
Frank Wood.

Lieut. F. J. O'Brien,
formerly Aide-de-Camp Lander's Division
Cumberland,
Md.[32]

In the meantime O'Brien was having difficulty about the army pay which was due him, but which was being held up through a technicality, the General having appointed him from civil life instead of waiting for the appointment to come first from Washington.[33] This circumstance Wood refers to in a long letter full of intimate gossip:

132 West 40th St.
Sunday, March 16, 1862.

My dear old Fitz:

Yr. jolly letter of the 10th was yesterday rec'd. It gladdened us all to learn that you were in such good spirits. Having read the letter to the Vanity Fairies I took it to Tom Davis. Mullen went with me. Tom was so elated that he immediately sent out for wassail, and we drank to yr speedy recovery. One of yr. McClellan Rifles lieutenants, a Mr. Doddesley something, (I never can remember names) happened to be in the office at the time. This happy coincidence suggested more wassail. Then Mullen proposed that we should 'wassail' again. Whereupon we 'wassailed.' On this Mr. Vincent came in, and we had some drinks. —On the whole I consider it a fortunate thing that you are unable to write very often. The Bacchic consequences are something awful.

Yr. wound, now that you are out of danger, makes you very interesting. Yr proposition to "curdle maidens' blood" with the story of yr prowess is a good one. You are coming on here to "curdle," aren't you? I don't suppose there are any maidens in Cumberland. Our army has been in that vicinity too long.—There has been a great deal of good feeling to you manifested of late. And by people from whom I had least expected it. Even yr enemies are softened. Bateman desires me to express to you his sympathies and best wishes. Little Bella (whom you have shamefully abandoned, sir!) burst out crying when her father read at the breakfast table that you were shot.—Many tender damsels, who know you

[32] MS in Romm collection.

[33] See copy in Romm collection of letter from S. F. Barstow to Dr. Salter, Feb. 28, 1862.

through me evince the liveliest interest in yr fate. I shall stop talking about you, I think.

It's a shame that you don't get yr pay. You did not make the necessary provisions in time, though, I suppose. You were always troubled with fiscal ophthalmia, you know. But, if I were you, I w'd go down to Washington when I was able and see Stanton about it. He never gives fighting men the go-by. And I feel convinced that he w'd right you. The arm in the sling, and the documents you have got w'd gain the case for you.—Don't you think this a good plan?

I am glad that Shields has retained you on his staff. Make sure of yr papers there! . . .

Katie Bateman plays at the W. G. next month, the 21st. Her 'pa' has taken the theatre. Harry Placide is engaged in the company. We have laughed Bateman off his tragic pedestal at last, and he begins to believe now what you told him two years ago, viz: that his daughter is best fitted for comedy. You should see her play *Indiana* in the "Honeymoon"! *Rien de plus pimpante!*—I saw the gaunt Hoey do it the other night. Ugh!—Mark Smith has been engaged by Wallack in Blake's stead, and has signed a two years' document. I am glad of this, for Mark is a nice fellow to have about.—Matilda Heron's new play "The Belle of the Season" is colossal in its dreariness. I have had two shies at it, but couldn't stand more than $\frac{1}{4}$ hour session either time. Matilda, as the "Belle" looks and dresses like a Biddy out for a holiday.

In compliance with your request I send you to-day a bundle of papers. I shall send you a thousand, more or less, in the course of the week. William has promised to send you the *Albion*.[34] The *Leader* will commend itself to yr Celtic heart on account of the report which it contains of the quarrel between the O'Donoughue and Sir Robt. Peel. I enclose you a slip from the *Budget of Fun*—one of Bellew's articles. You know where he got his facts,—poor fellow! F. B. has full charge of the *Budget* now, takes it on a contract, I presume. Evans, too, is in the Frank Leslie interest. He is writing a story for "The Illustrated" now. I will send you the paper. The story is talked of as a good one. When will you be able again to flash yr lambent pen. You ought to write a poem, or something, about Lander. We all expect it of you. . . .

As soon as you are equal to pen and ink I expect you to send on that letter of introduction to Miss Georgiana Bedell. I have waited in silence long enough. You needn't think I am going to let you come the "wounded hero" business over her. No sir!—Come, fair play!

I shall get you a patent sling, if possible. It will have to come cheap, though. We are all as poor as pis—so much so that it is entirely superfluous to spell the

[34] William Winter was on the staff of *The Albion* as dramatic critic.

word with two s's. I myself am on a rock compared to which Popocatepel is an ant-hill. This is the effect of a fratricidal war which turns brother against brother, father against father, mm,mm,mm.—Please get those $400.[35] and come and stay with me.

My brother Jim was in the hospital the day before the army moved to Manassas. But I don't think he is in the hospital now. We haven't heard from him for more than a week. In his last he said he was sorry to hear of yr wound for you were "a brave fellow." Why don't your letters travel quicker? The last was written on the 10th, posted on the 12th, but did not get to me until the 15th. Write again this week. The others have promised to write, but of course they won't. Get well soon and come back to us.

Your friend,
Frank Wood.[36]

Another letter in intimately bantering tone reached O'Brien from a friend who was also serving in the Union army. Especially noticeable are the series of punning references to titles of O'Brien's work, and the string of jocose references to colorful episodes in O'Brien's personal career:

Bolivar, Va.,
March 20, 1862.

My dear old Fitz—

Can it be that you are wounded? Perhaps there is nothing so surprising after all in it but I have always thought of you as one who would go through everything unharmed. The wars of Bacchus and Venus you have survived—and you know in the former you have played a heavy hand "non militans sine gloria"—encounters with ruffian Pitchers, the interchange of wine glasses with the bellicose steams, prospective and present duels with all the formalities attendant upon the departure of the virtuous to the land of the blessed such as "last wills and testaments" dire catastrophes upon the conjunction of Cambridge Street, Horse R. R. Rails and Chaises, the massacre of Sgts of McClellan rifles, Chelsea beach and a thousand other things have not interfered with the O'Brien—And after all these that you should be reserved for the damnable pistol shot of a more damnable traitor!

Well old Fitz I am very sorry for you and whatever I thought I could do for you I would. We have been waiting here a week—stupid d-d hole, mud without food, tedium without money and when Jack Saunders told me Sunday last of y'r wound etc. I made an effort to come up and see you but I found it impossible. I am alone with my Company and we await a move from here to home.

[35] The army pay due O'Brien.

[36] MS in Romm collection.

What can I get you if we go through Baltimore or Washington for y'r comfort and how and to what address shall I send to you—you must be rather lonely after the lively time with Lander to be reduced to a sick bed which I can hear you cursing over and over again—

However, my boy, Bohemia produces children not easily overcome I expect and you are of them—may that shot not interfere with that "Easy brogue and huge moustache" and you will yet be out I hope to dwell in another Cave of Silver, or make another Wondersmith—This won't be your Finishing School and my old Fitz D'OLens will be thriving whining no meager "*quondam* puellis gratus eram" but magnificent and erotic as of old!

Goodbye and take care of that shoulder—I am writing sitting on a dirty floor with a devil of a noise and confusion about—so excuse

With regard

CHAS. A. WHITTIER[37]

O'Brien at first had hoped to be well of his wound in about twenty days, but by March 8 he was no better. The surgeon, Maccabe, seems to have entirely mistaken the character of his patient's injury, and on March 20 a new surgeon of ability was sent by General McClellan to take the case in hand. He discovered the serious extent of the injury and said that the shoulder blade "rattled like a bag of marbles,"[38] because "the point of the arm at the shoulder had been smashed into a hundred fragments."[39] *The Leader* of March 22 remarks that "LIEUT. FITZ-JAMES O'BRIEN was expected in town this week, but his wounds are not sufficiently healed to warrant his leaving the camp;" and the next week (March 29), *The Leader* quotes extracts from a letter to Wood in which O'Brien describes something of his own plight.

MY DEAR FRANK: ****** I have nothing to write about except myself, a rather one-sided subject. Still I must write or die. I haven't yet told you of my suffering, and didn't intend to; but the fit is on me, and I must harrow you a little. I hope to God you will never have to go through what I have experienced, and what I am liable to. For the first week of my wound, nothing but enormous doses of morphine kept me from going crazy with pain. I had to be kept all day in a lazy, half-slumberous condition, in which I felt like a kind of hot-house plant, dozing and living, and that's all.

[37] MS in Romm collection.

[38] L. H. Stephens to Winter, Aug. 18, 1880.

[39] Winter, 1881, p. xliii. *N. Y. Leader*, Apr. 12, 1862, contains a scathing note about Maccabe, omitted in Winter.

It was at this period I conceived that prejudice against my left arm, which has since ripened into hate. I cannot express the feelings with which I now regard that limb. I long to cast it off, to disinherit it, to cut it off with a (sharp) shilling, and thrust it out upon the world to beg. Its hand at present is fit for no higher occupation than to clutch pennies. While highly morphinized, and in a semi-conscious state, I formed the idea that the aggravating limb did not belong to me, but was a vagabond and malicious arm that had attached itself to me for the purpose of preventing my becoming Commander-in-Chief, which I was to be as soon as I had fought Beauregard in the Colisseum with a trident and a fish net. All my arrangements had been made. Both armies of the Potomac were to assist at the spectacle, when, during my sleep, a Rebel spy took away the arm on which I depended for using the shrimp net, and left me a mutilated member instead. This is the true history of the case, although prejudiced persons might be apt to call it a morphine hallucination.

I left off morphine completely four weeks ago. It was a hard struggle to part with the great consoler, but I gave it up and took to brandy. They gave me a good deal of this in egg-nog and milk-punch to sustain my really wasted frame. Imagine the hundred and sixty-three pound man you knew, down to about a hundred and twenty, and so weak that the falling of a book startles him as if it were the bursting of a shell. I wish Mullen were here to sketch me as I am engineered out of bed to a big chair, with haggard face, spider limbs, and body fairly contracted with the pain of moving. The day after to-morrow I am to have a probe put into the wound and shoved down as far as my elbow, after which they will cut the flesh of the fore-arm open to the bone for six inches in length. So you see I have quite a pleasing prospect before me. . . .

My amusements are not various. I can see from my window a railroad depot and a locomotive; but steam, although a giant, a reformer, and an industrial power of vast etceteras, is not strictly cheerful. To-day is, I think, spring-opening day of the season. The display is very tasteful and elegant. We noticed quite a chaste and novel thing in the way of sunshine which will, no doubt, be extensively patronized. A very neat and delicate article of budding elm, trimmed with early blue-birds, attracted much attention, as did also a little *chef d'oeuvre*, consisting of a pot-pourri of hepaticas, crocuses, and snow-drops. Jesting apart, the day is lovely. The sun shines on the distant hills. The singing of the birds comes through my window with a grateful sound as I lie sad, and silent, and suffering. Oh, liberty of motion, health, and strength! I never knew what treasures you were till now.

A letter of similar tone, written probably the same day to Mrs. Sherwood, seems to be laughing in the face of death; but it may be, instead, the magnificent gesture by which a tortured mind and body seeks relief from itself and from its own affliction. The idea of the spring opening is repeated, but the details are quite different:

This is the day of the Spring opening. You are going to see the new bonnets; I am awaiting the surgeon, who comes to torture me for an hour. I have fever and constant thirst, but I lay on my tongue some of the slippery elm lozenges you sent me. They are an infinite comfort, and here comes dear W. P. with some ice. I see out of my window a very good thing in blue-birds. They crowd a tree which is all delicate greens. Would not that make a pretty Spring bonnet? What is a slippery elm? I never heard of a slippery oak, or a dishonest maple, or a treacherous lime tree. How does an elm continue to be slippery? But I thank the elm tree for this departure from the usual dull tenuosity of a tree, and for its adroitness in bringing refreshment to my fevered tongue. A slippery elm! May it be followed by a rollicking poplar and a luscious pine, an intoxicating hemlock. Do you know of any tree which bears a mint julep? Consider what an apostolic tree that would be that could concentrate into a lozenge the essence of mint julep, such as you used to give us on hot June evenings? Your butler was a past grand master in mixing them.

Great Jupiter! I believe in spooks. Here comes W. P. with a mint julep and two straws! I drink your health. Distant cannonading reaches my ears! And I may meet the enemy and I am his! There is the great enemy of all not far away, so the doctor tells me, but here or there I am yours gratefully,

F. O'B.[40]

After the examination, a thorough one, the new surgeon decided that a resection of the joint was the only resource, and though this is one of the most difficult and dangerous operations in surgery, he advised O'Brien to submit to it. The operation was performed; and on April 1 O'Brien wrote to Davis—his last letter, scribbled in pencil—describing the agony of the operation and his present desperate plight:

Cumberland, Md.

I gave up the ghost, and told him to go ahead. There were about twelve surgeons to witness the operation. All my shoulder bone and a portion of my upper arm have been taken away. I nearly died. My breath ceased, heart ceased to beat, pulse stopped. However, I got through. I am not yet out of danger from the operation, but a worse disease has set in. I have got tetanus, or lock-jaw. There is a chance of my getting out of it,—that's all. In case I

[40] *N. Y. Times*, July 2, 1898.

don't, good-by, old fellow, with all my love. I don't want to make any legal document, but I desire that you and Frank Wood should be my literary executors,—because after I'm dead I may turn out a bigger man than when living. I'd write more if I could, but I'm very weak. Write to me. I may be alive. Also, get Wood to write.[41]

On the same day George A. Thurston, who had been caring for O'Brien in his home during the long weeks of suffering, wrote Davis that O'Brien's condition was regarded as desperate.[42] These letters reached New York on April 4, and the next day Wood and Davis took an early morning train for Cumberland; but on arriving in Baltimore they learned that there would be no train from there for twenty-four hours. They immediately telegraphed to Cumberland, and Thurston replied: "O'Brien is very low. He is glad you are coming."[43]

Of these hours W. P., O'Brien's faithful nurse, a young man of Boston, who left luxury to nurse the wounded in the hospitals wrote:

He showed the patience of a sage and the cheerfulness of an Irishman all the way to painful death. His talk was full of classic, historical, romantic episodes. It was wonderful! He had that varied armory which is needed for debate. I used to listen with delight as he gave back witticism for stupidity from his neighbors. We were always listening for his funny retorts. Then he would become brilliant, fervid, eloquent, pathetic; even as death came on he desired to see the priest, who spent his last hours with him on earth, hearing his confession and commending to God one of the gentlest and most gifted souls whom it has been my good fortune to meet.[44]

On the morning of Sunday, April 6, O'Brien felt a little better than usual, and, being helped up by the attending surgeons, Drs. Folsom and MacMahon, sat for a time on the side of his bed; but while sipping a glass of sherry he turned pale and fell back dead.[45]

So ended the life of Fitz-James O'Brien—the vitality, the manliness, the intense verve and joy of living, together with the flashes of true poetic feeling and the touches of vivid, weird imagination.

Wood and Davis received the news while still waiting for the train at

[41] Winter, 1881, p. xliv. MS. in Romm collection.

[42] See *ibid.*, p. xxxv.

[43] *Ibid.*, p. xliv.

[44] *N. Y. Times*, July 2, 1898,—W. P. to Mrs. M. E. W. Sherwood.

[45] See Winter, 1881, p. xlv.

Baltimore; and the former immediately wrote to L. H. Stephens at the office of *Vanity Fair*, advising him that they would return to New York with the body and asking him to inform O'Brien's friends.[46]

On Monday morning the New York dailies printed the notice of Lieutenant O'Brien's death, and Henry Clapp, remembering that O'Brien had received his appointment in Aldrich's stead, remarked that "Aldrich was shot in O'Brien's shoulder;"[47] while the first words of A. D. Shattuck over half a century later (1927) when asked about O'Brien were "Fitz-James O'Brien!—Ah! he was a brave fellow! and the news of his death was a shock to us all." On Tuesday, April 8, the body arrived in the city and was laid out in state at the Seventh Regiment armory; and from there the following order was issued:

Headquarters, Company Seven, National Guard.—Company Order no. 7. New York, April 8, 1862. The members of the company will assemble at the Armory, in full fatigue dress, with overcoats and white gloves, on Wednesday, 9th inst. at 11½ A. M., for the purpose of paying the last tribute of respect to our late fellow member, Lieutenant Fitz James O'Brien, who died from wounds received while nobly doing his duty in defence of his country. Members of the regiment are invited to join with us. By order of Captain George W. Ely.
Bidwell, Orderly.[48]

The coffin lid bore a plate with the following inscription:

Lieutenant Fitz James O'Brien,
United States Volunteers,
Died April 6, 1862, Aged 33 years.[49]

Upon it rested O'Brien's sword, the sword he had captured from the Rebel officer in the Bloomery Gap charge, "a beautiful wreath of immortelles,

[46] See Frank Wood to L. H. Stephens, Apr. 6, 1862. The statements in Mrs. Fields's diary (Nov. 9, 1865), indicating that Thomas Bailey Aldrich also went to O'Brien at this time, do not agree with what is known of Aldrich's whereabouts: "Being himself (Aldrich) called to take a position on General Lander's staff, he was on his way to Richmond and he had reached Petersburg, when someone told him Fitz-James O'Brien had been shot dead. Then he went to the hospital and saw him lying there dead." Howe, *op. cit.*, p. 227.

[47] Winter, 1881, p. xxvi, n. For the way Aldrich missed Lander's appointment, see Greenslet, *op. cit.*, pp. 54–56.

[48] *N. Y. Herald*, Apr. 9, 1862.

[49] *Ibid.*, Apr. 10, 1862. *H. W.*, VI, 267 (Apr. 26, 1862) also records the inscription with slight differences in form, viz., "Lieut.," "U. S. Volunteers," and "Years."

with a card attached, on which was written, in pencil, 'Farewell! Matilda Heron,' and the regimental flag of the National Guard."[50]

Shortly after noon the services began with Company G, under the command of Captain Geo. W. Ely, in attendance, as well as many of O'Brien's friends and comrades, among them James and Lester Wallack, Frank Bellew, Joseph Harper, Frank Wood, Thomas E. Davis, Thomas Bailey Aldrich, Edward F. Mullen, and William Winter. Then with band and military escort the funeral procession moved to Greenwood Cemetery, Brooklyn, where Company G fired a last salute over the grave. That night while her flowers rested on his tomb, Matilda Heron took her benefit at the Winter Garden, acting the part in which she had so thrilled the ardent Irishman—Camille.[51]

For a time his friends paid him tributes, and then Harpers printed a story and one of the poems that George Arnold says were written during his illness. So often have William Winter's later estimates of his friend been recited that it may not be uninteresting to quote from the eulogy he wrote while the loss of his friend was still a fresh one. It was printed in *The Albion* of April 12 over the signature "Mercutio."

It would be easy to recite his triumphs; to tell the brief and brilliant story of ten years of literary labour; to say that, in the professions of literature and journalism, he was ever active and successful; to recall his poems, his stories, his dramas—weird, imaginative, original, and full of fiery life; to name him a man of real genius, powerful intellect, rich culture, and varied experience; to remember the large scope of thought and observation, the endless variety of character, the sparkling wit, the quick tenderness of feeling that made him, as a companion, so genial and so charming. But all this would avail little to mark their sense of sad bereavement who knew and loved him. With all his frailties of nature and all his faults of life, he was a man to be as deeply loved as now he is deeply mourned. Genuine, fearless, independent, gifted with great powers, true ideals, and vast energy, he aimed to achieve the highest triumph of his art, to interpret the passing age, to beat out the music of human activity,

To shed a something of celestial light
Round the familiar face of every day.

Wood's tribute appeared in the *Leader*, also on April 12, and this number of the paper carried in addition a column-long editorial devoted to "Fitz

[50] *N. Y. Tribune*, Apr. 10, 1862.
[51] See *N. Y. Tribune*, Apr. 10, 1862; *N. Y. Herald*, s. d.; and Winter, 1881, p. xxvii.

James O'Brien." On April 19 *Vanity Fair* printed, surrounding it with the heavy black border of mourning, a dirge in memory of "Fitz-James O'Brien;"[52] and on the same date the *Leader* announced that Thomas A. Davis and Frank Wood were making arrangements to collect and publish O'Brien's works. On April 26 appeared the oft-referred-to obituary of "Lieut. Fitz-James O'Brien, U. S. Volunteers" in *Harper's Weekly*.

Aldrich himself had written an article on O'Brien and had sent it to *Harper's Weekly*; but the article was returned, and Aldrich comments: "I distinctly remember my disgust. The manuscript, which lay in a drawer of my work-table for two or three years afterward, was either lost or destroyed at the time (1865) I moved to Boston."[53] Nevertheless, years later, in 1897, while he was editor of *The Atlantic Monthly*, Aldrich wrote a letter containing a passing tribute to the literary importance of his old comrade.

> I am sorry that the *Atlantic* did not put in its claim to being the father of the short story. Of course there were excellent short stories before the *Atlantic* was born—Poe's and Hawthorne's—but the magazine gave the short story a place which it had never before reached. It began with "The Diamond Lens" of Fitz-James O'Brien, and ended with—well, it has not ended yet.[54]

On May 3, an elegiac poem was printed in the *Leader*, sent by M. D. Urner of Cincinnati, an acquaintance of O'Brien's and an admirer of his work; and finally, on June 19, at the annual convention of the Theta Delta Chi fraternity, held in New York, William H. Merriam pronounced an elaborate eulogy, which was printed in its entirety in the *Times* of June 21.

The news of O'Brien's death reached his mother through a chance meeting—a striking coincidence. Bayard Taylor set sail for Liverpool on his way to Russia on May 7, 1862. He crossed England, going via Paris and Gotha to St. Petersburg, where he arrived on June 15.[55] It must have been, then, during the last week in May or the first in June that the sad encounter thus recorded in the diary of Mrs. James T. Fields took place:

> When Bayard Taylor and his wife were dining in a hotel restaurant at Dover, I believe,—it was one of the south of England towns,—they saw themselves closely

[52] *Vanity Fair*, V, 190 (Apr. 19, 1862). Winter names Charles Dawson Shanly as the author, and prints it with different line arrangement in Winter, 1881, p. xiv.

[53] Winter, *Old Friends*, p. 101.

[54] M. A. DeWolfe Howe, *The Atlantic Monthly and its Makers*, Boston, 1919, p. 86.

[55] See Hansen-Taylor and Scudder, *op. cit.*, I, 386–387.

observed by a lady and gentleman sitting near them. Finally the gentleman arose and came to speak to Taylor, said he observed they were Americans, and asked if he had ever heard of F. J. O'Brien. "Oh, yes," said Taylor, "I knew him very well. He was killed in our war." Then the lady burst into tears and the gentleman said: "She is his mother!"[56]

By this startling and unexpected news of her son's death the overflowing abundance of the mother's love received a sharp check, and in a letter written a year later an unidentified "B.M.C." clearly shows how great the shock had been.

In April 1863.

Dear Sir:

Whilst on a vessel going from Genoa to Civita Vecchia, I met a nice middle aged gentleman. During the evening what I thought was a very old and feeble lady approached him several times, very nervous and anxious about the weather and everything else—

Next morning I asked the gentleman "how his mother was"—He said she was not his mother but his wife—That when he married her a few years before, she was a fine-looking, well-preserved woman but since the death of her son, by a former marriage, she had become a complete wreck—He was travelling for her health and after spending Holy Week in Rome, expected to go to Egypt. Her son was FitzJames O'Brien. Since then I read everything I can find by him or about him with the greatest interest and never can I forget the sad, sad look of the dear old lady.

Respectfully
B.M.C.[57]

Thomas E. Davis, whom O'Brien on his deathbed named as one of his two literary executors, met Mrs. DeCourcy O'Grady in Europe still later, "and she expressed great affection for her lost boy, and deep interest in the idea of publishing his works. I intimated to her . . . that, in case the book should succeed, a suitable monument would be erected over O'Brien's grave."[58]

O'Brien's body was for a long time held in the receiving vault at Greenwood, but on November 27, 1874, it was removed, to be buried in a grave

[56] Howe, *Memories of a Hostess,* p. 228, entry under date of Nov. 9, 1865.

[57] MS in Romm collection.

[58] Winter, 1881, p. xxxii.

near the southwest corner of the Cemetery.[59] A small marble headstone was set up and on it was carved, "Fitz-James O'Brien. Here lies the body of that brilliant poet and writer who, whatever his faults may have been, had the saving graces of genius and high principle, as shown by his disinterested devotion to the land of his adoption." This was seen by William Sidney Hillyer when he visited the grave in 1898;[60] but when the writer of the present study sought out Grave 1,183, in Public Lot 17,263, on the twelfth of September, 1925, this was not what he found. At the peak of the rise in Maple Avenue, as he approached from the Western Entrance, he came to a flight of five stone steps. These he climbed, to the top of the terrace. To the left almost at his feet an American flag was stuck in the sod; beyond it was a white marble headstone two feet high. From the top an unrolling scroll seemed to run down over the front of the stone. Below the topmost bulge of the scroll, protected somewhat from the weather, was cut the word O'BRIEN. Below it the marble was perfectly smooth. Above, it seemed so too; but the searcher of a nearly obliterated fame approached more closely and was with difficulty able to trace the marks of the all-but-obliterated name—FITZ-JAMES.

[59] See *ibid.*, p. xxvii, n; and D. H. McCoy to W. Winter, Oct. 8, 1880. In Romm collection.

[60] See *N. Y. Times*, July 2, 1898. Here the name is given as "Fitzjames,"—evidently in the interests of consistency, for the present writer feels sure that he was following the actual marks and not inventing, when he records the inscription as "Fitz-James."

Bibliography

I. Collected Editions

The Poems and Stories of Fitz-James O'Brien. Collected and edited, with a Sketch of the Author, by William Winter. Boston: James R. Osgood and Company. 1881. [Contains Sketch of O'Brien, by William Winter; Dirge for O'Brien, by C. D. Shanly; and Recollections of O'Brien, by Thomas E. Davis, Frank Wood, George Arnold, Stephen Fiske, and Louis H. Stephens. The forty-three O'Brien Poems included are:—Sir Brasil's Falcon, Kane, The Lost Steamship, A Fallen Star, The Ballad of the Shamrock, Amazon, The Man at the Door, The Enchanted Titan, Loss, Our Christmas Tree, The Pot of Gold, Minot's Ledge, The Legend of Easter Eggs, Down in the Glen at Idlewild, Wanted—Saint Patrick, The Prize Fight, The Song of the Locomotive, Irish Castles, Loch Ine, An April Day, Johnny, The Skaters, The Demon of the Gibbet, The Wharf Rat, The Havelock, The Countersign, The Zouaves, A Soldier's Letter, The Prisoner of War, Winter, The Sewing Bird, A Summer Idyl, By the Passaic, The Three Gannets, The Sea, Willy and I, The Challenge, When I Came Back from Sea, An Old Story, Helen Lee, Strawberries, Battledores, The Finishing School. The thirteen Stories included are:—The Diamond Lens, The Wondersmith, Tommatoo, Mother of Pearl, The Bohemian, The Lost Room, The Pot of Tulips, The Golden Ingot, My Wife's Tempter, What Was It?, Duke Humphrey's Dinner, Milly Dove, The Dragon Fang.]

The Diamond Lens with Other Stories by Fitz-James O'Brien. Collected and Edited, with a Sketch of the Author, By William Winter. A new edition. New York, Charles Scribner's Sons, 1885. [Thirteen Stories as above.] Reissued, 1893.

The Diamond Lens and Other Stories. London, Ward and Downey. 1887. [Same as 1885 edition.]

What Was It? and Other Stories. By Fitzjames O'Brien. London: Ward and Downey. 1889. [Last eight of the above thirteen stories, with What Was It? placed first.]

The Golden Ingot, The Diamond Lens, A Terrible Night, What Was It? A Mystery. Reynolds Publishing Company, Inc., New York. [1921.] Reissued, 1923, in "Famous Authors' Handy Library."

Collected Stories by Fitz-James O'Brien. Edited with an Introduction by Edward J. O'Brien. Albert and Charles Boni, New York, 1925. [Contains eight of the thirteen stories of Winter's collection—The Diamond Lens, The Wondersmith, The Lost Room, The Pot of Tulips, The Golden Ingot, My Wife's Temper (*sic*), What Was It?, The Dragon Fang Possessed by the Conjurer Piou-Lu.]

The Diamond Lens and Other Stories by Fitz-James O'Brien with an introduction by Gilbert Seldes. Illustrations by Ferdinand Huszti Howath. New York. William Edwin Rudge. 1932. [Contains The Diamond Lens, The Wondersmith, The Pot of Tulips, The Golden Ingot, What Was It?, Duke Humphrey's Dinner, The Dragon Fang Possessed by the Conjurer Piou-Lu.]

II. Poems

A. The Nation (Dublin)

Oh! Give a Desert Life to Me. (Mar. 15, 1845).

Epigram on hearing a Young Lady Regret her Eyes being Bloodshot. (Mar. 29, 1845). Reprinted, revised, with title Impromptu to a Lady, in The Cork Magazine, I, 663 (September, 1848); in The Parlour Magazine, I, 215 (June 21, 1851).

Loch Ina, A Beautiful Salt-Water Lake, in the County of Cork, Near Baltimore. (July 26, 1845). Reprinted in The Family Friend, IV, 197 (Apr. 1, 1851), as Lough Ina, combining half-lines to make regular quatrains; in Hayes, Edward, The Ballads of Ireland, London, Edinburgh, and Dublin, 1855, I, 21–22; in Hayes, ibid., Boston, 1856, I, 58–59; in Winter, 1881, pp. 65–66, as Loch Ine; in McCarthy, Justin, Irish Literature, Philadelphia, 1904, VII, 2603; and in Welsh, Charles, The Golden Treasury of Irish Songs and Lyrics, 1907, II, 198–199.

Irish Hurra for Past Heroism. Commented on Nov. 8, 1845; not printed.

The Famine. (Mar. 7, 1846).

The Boatmen of Kerry. (Mar. 14, 1846). Reprinted in Hayes, The Ballads of Ireland, 1855, pp. 15–17.

Excelsior. (Mar. 13, 1847).

B. The Cork Magazine

An Ode to the Divinest of Liquors. I, 564–565 (July, 1848); Reprinted in The Parlour Magazine, I, 119 (May 24, 1851).

My Childhood's Prayer. I, 592 (August, 1848).

Una of Lough-Ine; A Ballad. I, 639–640 (August, 1848).

Serenade. I, 653 (September, 1848).

Impromptu to a Lady, on her Complaining at Breakfast that her Eyes were Blood-shot. I, 663 (September, 1848).

The Loves and the Fate of the Dragon-Fly and the Water-Lily. I, 681–683 (September, 1848). Reprinted in The Family Friend, III, 77 (Aug. 1, 1850).

The Fisher's Lay. I, 720 (October, 1848).

Where Shall We Dwell? I, 741 (October, 1848).

The Epicurean. II, 31 (November, 1848).

Forest Thoughts. II, 99–100 (December, 1848). Reprinted in The Metropolitan Magazine, LIV, 395–396 (April, 1849); and in The Parlour Magazine, I, 95 (May 17, 1851).

C. THE IRISHMAN (Dublin)

"Say sacred Clarseac." (Feb. 3, 1849).

D. THE FAMILY FRIEND

Lines Addressed to a Young Lady about to Depart for India. III, 45 (July 15, 1850).

A Lyric of Life. III, 106 (Aug. 15, 1850).

E. THE PARLOUR MAGAZINE

To a Captive Sea-Gull. I, 23 (May 3, 1851). Reprinted in The American Whig Review, XVI, 364 (October, 1852).

Our Old Garden Chair. I, 215 (June 21, 1851).

Impromptu On Hearing a Young Lady Complain that her Eyes were Bloodshot. I, 215 (June 21, 1851).

The Lonely Oak. I, 287 (July 12, 1851).

Dawn.—A Sonnet. I, 359 (Aug. 2, 1851). Reprinted in The Dublin University Magazine, XLI, 299 (March, 1853).

To an Infant. I, 431 (Aug. 23, 1851).

Hateful Spring. I, 449 (Aug. 30, 1851).

Fortune in the Fire. II, 69 (Sept. 20, 1851). Reprinted as Irish Castles with an added stanza in Hayes, The Ballads of Ireland, 1855, II, 355–356; in Winter, 1881, pp. 63–64; and in Connolly, The Household Library of Ireland's Poets, 1887, p. 70.

F. THE DUBLIN UNIVERSITY MAGAZINE

The Wish; or, the Fall of the Star. XXXVIII, 140–141 (August, 1851).

G. HOUSEHOLD WORDS

An Abiding Dream. IV, 182–183 (Nov. 15, 1851).

A Child's Prayer. IV, 277 (Dec. 13, 1851).

H. THE LANTERN

A Legend of the Olden Time. Part I. I, 70–71 (Feb. 21, 1852).
A Legend of the Olden Time. Part II. I, 90–91 (Mar. 6, 1852).
The Ballad of Sir Brown. I, 99 (Mar. 13, 1852). Reprinted in The New York Picayune, X, 6 (Mar. 27, 1858).
The Demon Tie, I, 130–131 (Apr. 3, 1852). Reprinted in N. Y. Picayune, X, 50 (May 8, 1858).
An Old Story. I, 143 (Apr. 17, 1852). Reprinted in N. Y. Picayune, X, 5 (Mar. 27, 1858); and in Winter, 1881, p. 110.
To April. I, 144 (Apr. 17, 1852). Reprinted in N. Y. Picayune, X, 9 (Apr. 3, 1858).
The Shirt Fiend, A Christian Carol. I, 154 (Apr. 24, 1852).
Street Lyrics. The Beggar Child. I, 166 (May 1, 1852).
Wine! I, 174 (May 8, 1852).
Street Lyrics. The Crossing Sweeper. I, 186 (May 15, 1852).
The Spectral Shirt. I, 219 (June 5, 1852).
Fifth Avenue Legends. The Doctor, the Lawyer, and the Lady. I, 250–251 (June 19, 1852).
Street Lyrics. The Street Monkey. II, 8 (July 10, 1852).
He Writes for Bread. II, 47 (July 31, 1852).
Pauline. As Seen by Diogenes. III, 156–158 (Mar. 19, 1853).

I. THE AMERICAN WHIG REVIEW

Madness. XVI, 126 (August, 1852).
Pallida. XVI, 264 (September, 1852).
The Song of the Immortal Gods. Written at their Express Desire. XVI, 268–269 (September, 1852).
The Old Knight's Wassail. XVI, 272 (September, 1852).
The Shadow by the Tree. XVI, 364–365 (October, 1852).
Oinea. XVI, 566–567 (December, 1852).

J. NEW-YORK DAILY TIMES

The Prophecy of Christmas. (Jan. 15, 1853).
Gebhold. (June 8, 1853).
A Storm. (July 19, 1853).
The May Wind and the Poet. (July 29, 1853).
The Seventh. (May 2, 1861). Reprinted in N. Y. Leader (May 4, 1861); in Moore, The Civil War in Song and Story, 1882, (1st ed. 1865), p. 231; in White, Poetry Lyrical, Narrative, and Satirical of the Civil War, 1866, pp. 14–16; in Moore, Frank, The Rebellion Record, 1861, I, 17–18.

K. SHEET MUSIC

Beginning the World—Bleak House Ballads No. 1. Words by Fitz-James O'Brien. Music by Thomas Baker. New York. Published by Horace Waters, 333 Broadway (1853).

Once a Year. Ballad. The Words by Fitz James O'Brien Esq. The Music by Thomas Baker. New York. Published by Horace Waters, 333 Broadway (1853).

L. UNITED STATES MAGAZINE AND DEMOCRATIC REVIEW

Sir Brasil's Falcon. XXXIII, 248–257 (September, 1853). Offprints as paper-covered pamphlet (10 pp.):—Sir Brasil's Falcon, / A Poem / by Fitz-James O'Brien. / Published in September No. of the United States Review. / 1853. Reprinted in Winter, 1881, pp. 3–16.

M. PUTNAM'S MONTHLY MAGAZINE

The Garden Walk. III, 582 (June, 1854).

The Three Gannets. IV, 536 (November, 1854). Reprinted in Winter, 1881, p. 104; and in Connolly, Household Library of Ireland's Poets, 1887, p. 585.

Sea. IV, 666 (December, 1854). Reprinted as The Sea in Winter, 1881, p. 105; and in Connolly, Household Library of Ireland's Poets, 1887, p. 166.

Winter. V, 11 (January, 1855). Reprinted with verbal changes in Winter, 1881, pp. 89–90.

Willy and I. V, 40 (January, 1855). Reprinted in Winter, 1881, p. 106.

The Challenge. V, 504 (May, 1855). Reprinted in Winter, 1881, p. 107; in Stedman, E. C., and Hutchinson, E. M., A Library of American Literature, 1889, VIII, 397; and, with verbal differences as The Helmet, in New-York Daily Tribune, Mar. 6, 1881; same in Hansen-Taylor and Scudder, Life and Letters of Bayard Taylor, 1885, p. 286.

N. THE EVENING POST

The Song of the Bacchante. (Oct. 10, 1855).

The Heath. (Oct. 19, 1855).

Sing, Linnet, Sing. (Oct. 20, 1855).

To —. (Oct. 22, 1855).

An Episode. (May 1, 1856).

The Lake. (May 6, 1856).

O. HARPER'S NEW MONTHLY MAGAZINE

When We Husked the Corn. XIII, 382–383 (August, 1856).

How It Happened. XIV, 56 (December, 1856).

What Santa Claus Brought Me. XIV, 196 (January, 1857). Reprinted in The Saturday Press, Dec. 25, 1858.

My Valentine. XIV, 505–506 (March, 1857).

By the Passaic. XIV, 767 (May, 1857). Reprinted in Winter, 1881, pp. 102–103; as On the Passaic, in Matthews, American Familiar Verse, 1904, pp. 173–174; and in Pattee, Century Readings for a Course in American Literature, Third Edition, 1926, p. 651.

A Summer Idyl. XV, 219–220 (July, 1857). Reprinted in Winter, 1881, pp. 99–101.

Helen Lee. XV, 809–810 (November, 1857). Reprinted in Winter, 1881, pp. 111–117.

Amazon. XVI, 793–794 (May, 1858). Reprinted in Winter, 1881, pp. 32–35.

The Finishing School. XVII, 433–447 (September, 1858). Reprinted with twelve original illustrations in Winter, 1881, pp. 121–142.

Love at a Lattice. XVIII, 58–60 (December, 1858).

The Prize-Fight. XVIII, 84–86 (December, 1858). Reprinted in The Saturday Press, Nov. 20, 1858, and Oct. 1, 1859; in Winter, 1881, pp. 57–61; in Connolly, The Household Library of Ireland's Poets, 1887, p. 251.

Wanted—St. Patrick. XVIII, 525 (March, 1859). Reprinted in Winter, 1881, 54–56.

My First of April. XVIII, 661–662 (April, 1859). Reprinted in N. Y. Saturday Press, Apr. 2, 1859; in Winter, 1881, pp. 66–68, with title An April Day.

The Meeting by the Hemlocks. XIX, 512 (September, 1859).

The Enchanted Titan. XX, 52–53 (December, 1859). Reprinted in Winter, 1881, pp. 37–39.

Our Christmas Tree. XX, 513–514 (March, 1860). In MS form, ten stanzas shorter, called Our Christmas Eve. Reprinted in Winter, 1881, pp. 42–45.

The Lost Steamship. XX, 678–679 (April, 1860). Reprinted in N. Y. Saturday Press, Mar. 24, 1860; in Winter, 1881, pp. 20–22; in Connolly, Household Library of Ireland's Poets, 1887, p. 583; in Warner, Library of the World's Best Literature, 1896, XVIII, 10743–10744; in Peck, The World's Great Masterpieces, 1898, XVI, 8556–8558; in Stedman, An American Anthology, 1900, pp. 303–304, with title The Second Mate.

When I Came Back from Sea. XXI, 237–238 (July, 1860). Reprinted in Winter, 1881, pp. 107–109.

The Sewing Bird. XXI, 433–442 (September, 1860). Reprinted in Winter, 1881, pp. 90–99; in Pattee, The Feminine Fifties, 1940, pp. 298–299.

My Johnny. XXI, 518 (September, 1860). Reprinted in Winter, 1881, pp. 68–70, with title Johnny.

A Fallen Star. XXI, 834–835 (November, 1860). Reprinted in N. Y. Saturday Press, Oct. 27, 1860; 5 stanzas in Harper's Weekly, Apr. 26, 1862; in Winter, 1881, pp. 23–27; in Connolly, Household Library of Ireland's Poets, 1887, p. 228.

The Skaters. XXII, 350 (February, 1861). Reprinted in Winter, 1881, pp. 71–73; in Stedman and Hutchinson, A Library of American Literature, 1889, VIII, 389–390.

The Ballad of the Shamrock. XXII, 433–436 (March, 1861). Reprinted in Winter, 1881, pp. 28–31.

The Legend of Easter Eggs. XXII, 637–638 (April, 1861). Reprinted in Winter, 1881, pp. 50–52; in Connolly, Household Library of Ireland's Poets, 1887, p. 721.

Minot's Ledge. XXII, 660 (April, 1861). Reprinted in Winter, 1881, pp. 48–50.

The Countersign. XXIII, 396 (August, 1861). Reprinted in N. Y. Leader, Nov. 30, 1861; in Hayward, Poetical Pen-Pictures of The War, 1863, pp. 255–256; in Winter, 1881, pp. 78–80; in Connolly, Household Library of Ireland's Poets, 1887, p. 261.

The Pot of Gold. XXIII, 397 (August, 1861). Reprinted in Winter, 1881, pp. 45–48.

The Havelock. XXIII, 512–513 (September, 1861). Reprinted in Winter, 1881, pp. 75–77.

Of Loss. XXIII, 650 (October, 1861). Reprinted in Winter, 1881, pp. 39–42, with title, Loss; in Peck, The World's Great Masterpieces, 1898, XVI, 8559–8561.

The Tenement House. XXIII, 732–734 (November, 1861). Reprinted in N. Y. Leader, Oct. 26, 1861.

The Prisoner of War. XXIV, 348 (February, 1862). Reprinted in N. Y. Leader, Feb. 1, 1862; in Winter, 1881, pp. 86–88.

A Soldier's Letter. XXIV, 508 (March, 1862). Reprinted in N. Y. Leader, Mar. 1, 1862; in Winter, 1881, pp. 83–85.

Down in the Glen at Idlewild. XXV, 236 (July, 1862). Reprinted in N. Y. Leader, June 28, 1862; in Winter, 1881, pp. 53–54.

P. THE HOME JOURNAL

What Befell. Oct. 18, 1856. Reprinted as The Demon of the Gibbet in Winter, 1881, pp. 73–74; and in Connolly, The Household Library of Ireland's Poets, 1887, p. 336.

By the Alders. Oct. 25, 1856.

Q. HARPER'S WEEKLY

The Little Maid I Lost Long Ago. I, 125 (Feb. 21, 1857).

Kane. I, 161 (Mar. 14, 1857). Reprinted in Bryant, William Cullen, ed., The Family Library of Poetry and Song, 1870, pp. 933–934; in Beers, Henry A., ed., A Century of American Literature, 1776–1876, 1878, pp. 372–375; in Coates, The Fireside Encyclopaedia of Poetry, 1878, pp. 276–277; in Winter, 1881, pp. 16–19; in Connolly, The Household Library of Ireland's Poets, 1887, p. 643; in Peck, The World's Great Masterpieces, 1898, XVI, pp. 8561–8563, with full-page illustration; in Stevenson, Burton Egbert, Poems of American History, 1908, p. 379; and in Pattee, The Feminine Fifties, 1940, pp. 297–298.

How the Bell Rang, July 4th, 1776. I, 418 (July 4, 1857). Reprinted in N. Y. Saturday Press, July 7, 1860. Appears many times later under title Independence Bell—July 4th, 1776, e. g., in Swinton's Fourth Reader, 1883, pp. 337–340; in Baldwin, James, School Reading by Grades, Fourth Year, 1897, pp. 71–73; in Wade and Sylvester, Fourth Reader, 1907, pp. 258–261; in Bolenius, Emma M., Fourth Reader, 1919, pp. 110–113; in Gathany, J. Madison, American Patriotism in Prose and Verse, 1919, pp. 203–205.

A Storm in Summer. I, 419 (July 4, 1857),—in The Man about Town.

Bacchus. I, 735 (Nov. 14, 1857). Reprinted in Evening Post, Nov. 11, 1857.

The Wonders of Santa Claus. I, 820 (Dec. 26, 1857).

The Zouaves. IV, 469 (July 28, 1860). Reprinted in N. Y. Saturday Press, July 28, 1860; in Winter, 1881, pp. 80–82.

Amy Scudder. VI, 122 (Feb. 22, 1862). Reprinted from MS (lacking last eight stanzas) by Horace Parker Chandler in The Sword and the Pen, published during the ten days of the Soldiers' Home Bazaar held in Boston, Dec. 7–17, 1881; same in The Shield—ΘΔΧ—February, 1924.

R. THE KNICKERBOCKER, OR NEW-YORK MONTHLY MAGAZINE

The Boatman of Whitehall. LII, 145–148 (August, 1858).

Homeless. LII, 587 (December, 1858).

The Ghosts. LIII, 40 (January, 1859).

The Man at the Door. LVII, 71–72 (January, 1861). Reprinted in N. Y. Saturday Press, Dec. 15, 1860; in Winter, 1881, pp. 35–37.

Jack's Valentine. LVII, 149 (February, 1861).

Treachery. LVII, 285 (March, 1861).

S. THE SATURDAY PRESS

January. Jan. 8, 1859.

T. VANITY FAIR

Song of the Locomotive. I, 20 (Jan. 7, 1860). Reprinted in Winter, 1881, pp. 61–63.

Pemberton Mills. I, 52 (Jan. 21, 1860).

Death, the Builder. I, 70 (Jan. 28, 1860).

No One to Blame. I, 85 (Feb. 4, 1860).

Song of the Shirtless. I, 91 (Feb. 4, 1860).

Lines to Zoyara. I, 101 (Feb. 11, 1860).

Opening-Day (After Tennyson). I, 120 (Feb. 18, 1860).

Twenty Per Cent. I, 142 (Feb. 25, 1860).

Counter-Jumps. I, 183 (Mar. 17, 1860).

The Counter-Jumper Swell. I, 263 (Apr. 21, 1860).

A Sermon to Organ Grinders. II, 53 (July 28, 1860).

Meriam's Address to the Great Meteor. II, 65 (Aug. 4, 1860).

The Song of the Beggar. II, 87 (Aug. 18, 1860).

The Strawberries. A Summer Picture. III, 143 (Mar. 23, 1861). Reprinted in Winter, 1881, pp. 118–119, with title Strawberries.

The Wharf Rat. III, 172 (Apr. 13, 1861). Reprinted in N. Y. Leader, Apr. 20, 1861; in Winter, 1881, pp. 74–75.

Whom This Cap Fits Let Him Wear It. IV, 10 (July 6, 1861).

U. THE HOUSEHOLD JOURNAL

of Information, Amusement, and Domestic Economy.

(First no. pub. Oct. 6, 1860).

Battledores, FitzJames O'Brien. I, 1 (Oct. 6, 1860). Reprinted in N. Y. Saturday Press, Sept. 22, 1860; in Winter, 1881, pp. 119–120.

V. HISTORY OF THE SEVENTH REGIMENT

By Colonel Emmons Clark.

2 vols. N. Y. 1890.

The Midnight March. II, 3 (certainly written in 1861).

W. THE CONTINENTAL MONTHLY

devoted to Literature and National Policy.

Watching the Stag. II, 105 (July, 1862).

X. UNLOCATED

The Ornithorhyncus (c. 1853). Referred to in Winter, Old Friends, p. 310, and in conversation with A. D. Shattuck. Also in Winter's list for Second Vol.

The Cave of Silver. Referred to in Chas. A. Whittier to Fitz-James O'Brien, March 20, 1862. Reprinted in Tiffany, Rev. O. H., ed., Gems for the Fireside, 1882, pp. 362–363 (Mentioned in Winter's MS list as The Silver Seeker).

Carrier's New Years Address for New York Times. Mentioned by Augustus Maverick and A. D. Shattuck.

Address to Donati's Comet. Summer of 1858. Referred to by Mrs. M. E. W. Sherwood.

Y. MSS

Our Christmas Eve. In collection of Capt. F. L. Pleadwell, Bureau of Medicine and Surgery, Washington, D. C.

"Down the hills and over the bay." About a gull; A. F. Goldsmith.

Rose de Mai. A. F. Goldsmith.

A Fragment. (Amy Scudder lacking the last eight stanzas) sent to Horace Parker Chandler by Winter in 1881 to be sold at the Soldiers' Home Bazaar in Boston, Dec. 7–17, 1881.

Living Too Fast by FitzJames O'Brien. Facsimile in Winter, 1881, pasted in between pp. 24 and 25.

An Episode. FitzJames O'Brien; New York Public Library.

The Wharf Rat. In Historical Society of Pennsylvania.

Persia. In Historical Society of Pennsylvania.

Meriam's Address to the Great Meteor. In Historical Society of Pennsylvania. Also in Romm collection.

Pemberton Mills. Romm collection.

Whom This Cap Fits, Let Him Wear It. Romm collection.

Nemesis. Idea for a poem. New York Public Library.

III. Stories

A. HOUSEHOLD WORDS

An Arabian Night-mare. IV, 166–168 (Nov. 8, 1851).

B. THE HOME COMPANION

The Phantom Light: A Christmas Story. I, 5–6 (Jan. 3, 1852); 21–22 (Jan. 10); 37–39 (Jan. 17); 53–55 (Jan. 24); 68–70 (Jan. 31); 84–85 (Feb. 7); 101–102 (Feb. 14); 117–118 (Feb. 21); 131–133 (Feb. 28).

C. THE LANTERN

The Wonderful Adventures of Mr. Papplewick. I, 94–95 (Mar. 13, 1852); 120–121 (Mar. 27); 133 (Apr. 10); 150–151 (Apr. 17); 163 (May 1); 180 (May 8).

D. THE AMERICAN WHIG REVIEW

A Voyage in My Bed. XVI, 264–268 (September, 1852).
Carrying Weight. XVI, 269–272 (September, 1852).
One Event. XVI, 351–362 (October, 1852).
The King of Nodland and his Dwarf. XVI, 554–566 (December, 1852).

E. HARPER'S NEW MONTHLY MAGAZINE

Celeste Bertin. VII, 499–504 (September, 1853).
A Dead Secret. VII, 806–815 (November, 1853).
A Peep Behind the Scenes. VIII, 509–510 (March, 1854).
Belladonna. IX, 78–83 (June, 1854).
The Fiddler. IX, 536–539 (September, 1854).
My Son, Sir. X, 246–251 (January, 1855).
Baby Bloom. X, 503–508 (March, 1855).
The Beauty. XI, 193–196 (July, 1855).
The Bohemian. XI, 233–242 (July, 1855). Reprinted in Winter, 1881, pp. 281–308; in 1885, 1887, pp. 139–166; in Hawthorne, Library of the World's Best Mystery and Detective Stories, English-Irish, 1907, pp. 24–48.
Duke Humphrey's Dinner. XI, 352–357 (August, 1855). Reprinted in Winter, 1881, pp. 408–425; in 1885, 1887, pp. 266–283; in Seldes, 1932, pp. 215–238.
A Drawing-Room Drama. XI, 397–398 (August, 1855).
Milly Dove. XI, 535–543 (September, 1855). Reprinted in Winter, 1881, pp. 426–453; in 1885, 1887, pp. 284–311.
The Duel. XI, 649–653 (October, 1855).
The Pot of Tulips. XI, 807–814 (Novmber, 1855) Reprinted in Winter, 1881, pp. 332–354; in 1885, 1887, pp. 190–212; in E. J. O'Brien, Collected Stories, 1925, pp. 122–148; in Seldes, 1932, pp. 133–163.
Sister Anne. XII, 91–96 (December, 1855).
Babie Bertie's Christmas. XII, 208–216 (January, 1856).
The Dragon Fang Possessed by the Conjuror Piou-Lu. XII, 519–526 (March, 1856). Reprinted in Winter, 1881, pp. 454–479; in 1885, 1887, pp. 312–337; in E. J. O'Brien, Collected Stories, 1925, pp. 210–240; in Seldes, 1932, pp. 239–275.
Milicent. XIII, 67–75 (June, 1856).
Twice in Love. XIII, 367–374 (August, 1856).
How Nellie Lee Was Pawned. XIII, 500–504 (September, 1856).
A Terrible Night. XIII, 639–642 (October, 1856). Reprinted in Hawthorne, Library of the World's Best Mystery and Detective Stories, English-Irish, 1907, pp. 48–55; in Fitz-James O'Brien, The Golden Ingot, The Diamond Lens, A Terrible Night, What Was It? A Mystery, 1921, pp. 73–85; in O'Brien, Famous Authors' Handy Library, 1923, pp. 73–85.

Mary Burnie of the Mill. XIII, 782–784 (November, 1856).
The Crystal Bell. XIV, 88–91 (December, 1856).
Dora Dee. XIV, 369–371 (February, 1857).
Uncle and Nephew. XIV, 518–526 (March, 1857).
Seeing the World. XV, 542–546 (September, 1857).
A Screw Loose. XV, 629–634 (October, 1857).
The Lost Room. XVII, 494–500 (September, 1858). Reprinted in Winter, 1881, pp. 309–331; in 1885, 1887, pp. 167–189; in French, Masterpieces of Mystery, 1920 (reprinted 1937), Riddle Stories, pp. 232–258; in E. J. O'Brien, Collected Stories, 1925, pp. 95–121.
What Was It? A Mystery. XVIII, 504–509 (March, 1859). Reprinted in Winter, 1881, pp. 390–407; in 1885, 1887, pp. 248–265; in De Berard, Classic Tales by Famous Authors, 1902, XV, 87–103; in Matthews, The Short Story, 1907, pp. 229–246; in Baldwin, American Short Stories, 1904, pp. 211–228; in Trent and Henneman, The Best American Tales, 1907, pp. 285–307; in Ashmun, Modern Short Stories, 1914, pp. 179–197; in French, Great Ghost Stories, 1918, pp. 346–365; in Fitz-James O'Brien, The Golden Ingot, The Diamond Lens, A Terrible Night, What Was It? A Mystery, 1921, pp. 87–96 (abridged); in Scarborough, Famous Modern Ghost Stories, 1921, pp. 253–273; in O'Brien, Famous Authors' Handy Library, 1923, pp. 87–96; in E. J. O'Brien, Collected Stories, 1925, pp. 190–209; in Smith, Literary Contrasts, 1925, pp. 131–145; in French, Tales of Terror, 1925, pp. 74–94; in Wells, American Mystery Stories, 1927, pp. 93–108; in Harper, C. A., American Ghost Stories, 1928, pp. 53–70; in Rhys and Scott, Tales of Mystery, 1928, pp. 177–185; in Seldes, 1932, pp. 191–214; in Wise and Fraser, Great Tales of Terror and the Supernatural, 1944, pp. 403–416.
Mother of Pearl. XX, 392–399 (February, 1860). Reprinted in Winter, 1881, pp. 257–280; in 1885, 1887, pp. 115–138.
The Child That Loved a Grave. XXII, 682–684 (April, 1861).
Captain Alicant. XXIII, 105–108 (June, 1861).
Mrs. Jujube at Home. XXIII, 378–381 (August, 1861).
Tommatoo. XXV, 325–335 (August, 1862). Reprinted in Winter, 1881, pp. 224–256; in 1885, 1887, pp. 82–114.
How I Overcame My Gravity. XXVIII, 779–781 (May, 1864).

F. PUTNAM'S MONTHLY MAGAZINE

Elegant Tom Dillar. I, 525–530 (May, 1853).
Hard Up. IV, 50–63 (July, 1854).
Mrs. Macsimum's Bill. IV, 660–665 (December, 1854).
The Spider's Eye. VIII, 11–18 (July, 1856). Reprinted in Stories by American Authors, 1884, III, 5–29, with O'Brien's name as author; same book reprinted 1898 with Lucretia P. Hale's name as author.

G. HARPER'S WEEKLY

My Wife's Tempter. I, 795–796 (Dec. 12, 1857). Reprinted in Winter, 1881, pp. 374–389; in 1885, 1887, pp. 232–247; in Hawthorne, Library of the World's Best Mystery and Detective Stories, English-Irish, 1907, pp. 56–69; in Hawthorne, The Lock and Key Library, American Stories, 1912 (Reprinted 1915), pp. 321–332; in E. J. O'Brien, Collected Stories, 1925, pp. 171–189 (title appears as My Wife's Temper).

H. THE ATLANTIC MONTHLY

The Diamond Lens. I, 354–367 (January, 1858). Reprinted in Atlantic Tales, 1866, pp. 21–49; last two sections in Beers, A Century of American Literature, 1878, pp. 375–385; complete in Winter, 1881, pp. 145–176; and in 1885, 1887, 1893, pp. 3–34; last two sections in Stedman and Hutchinson, A Library of American Literature, 1889, VIII, 389–397; complete in Warner, Library of the World's Best Literature, 1896, XVIII, 10733–10743; section five in Peck, The World's Great Masterpieces, 1898, XVI, 8549–8556; parts of sections four and five in McCarthy, Irish Literature, 1904, VII, 2594–2603; complete in Patten, Short Story Classics (American), 1905, I, 127–162; in Hale and Dawson, The Elements of the Short Story, 1915, pp. 209–239; in Fitz James O'Brien, The Diamond Lens, The Happy Hour Library, Inc., n. d. [c. 1919], pp. 7–47; in French, Masterpieces of Mystery, 1920, Mystic-Humorous Stories, pp. 38–76 (reprinted 1925 and 1937); in Pattee, Century Readings in American Literature, 1920, pp. 537–549; in Fitz-James O'Brien, The Golden Ingot, The Diamond Lens, A Terrible Night, What Was It? A Mystery, 1921, pp. 29–72; in Jessup, Representative American Short Stories, 1923, pp. 281–298; in O'Brien, Famous Authors' Handy Library, 1923, pp. 29–72; in E. J. O'Brien, Collected Stories, 1925, pp. 1–38; in Seldes, 1932, pp. 21–65.

The Wondersmith, IV, 463–482 (October, 1859). Reprinted in Winter, 1881, pp. 177–223; in 1885, 1887, pp. 35–81; in De Berard, Classic Tales by Famous Authors, 1902, V, 203–247; in E. J. O'Brien, Collected Stories, 1925, pp. 39–94; in Seldes, 1932, pp. 67–132.

I. THE NEW YORK PICAYUNE

From Hand to Mouth. X, 2–3 (Mar. 27, 1858); X, 10 (Apr. 3); X, 18 (Apr. 10); X, 26–27 (Apr. 17); X, 34 (Apr. 24); X, 42 (May 1); X, 50 (May 8); X, 58 (May 15, 1858): last instalment by Bellew. Reprinted in Good Stories, Part IV, 1868, pp. 3–49; and in Famous Stories, [1879?], pp. 173–219.

J. THE KNICKERBOCKER, OR NEW-YORK MONTHLY MAGAZINE

The Golden Ingot. LII, 176–186 (August, 1858). Reprinted in Winter, 1881, pp. 355–373; in 1885, 1887, pp. 213–231; in Hawthorne, Library of the World's

Best Mystery and Detective Stories, English-Irish, 1907, pp. 9–24; in Hawthorne, The Lock and Key Library, American Stories, 1912 (reprinted 1915), pp. 305–320; in Fitz-James O'Brien, The Golden Ingot, The Diamond Lens, A Terrible Night, What Was It? A Mystery, 1921, pp. 3–28; in O'Brien, Famous Authors' Handy Library, 1923, pp. 3–28; in E. J. O'Brien, Collected Stories, 1925, pp. 149–170; in Seldes, 1932, pp. 165–190.

Jubal, the Ringer. LII, 230–234 (September, 1858).

Bob O'Link. LVII, 253–257 (March, 1861).

The Bullfinch. LVIII, 29–40 (July, 1861).

K. THE SATURDAY PRESS

Three of a Trade; or, Red Little Kriss Kringle. Dec. 25, 1858. Reprinted in same, Dec. 19, 1859; in Good Stories, Part III, 1868, pp. 119–125; and in Famous Stories, [?1879], pp. 119–125.

L. FRANK LESLIE'S ILLUSTRATED NEWSPAPER

December 11, 1858.

The Red Petticoat: A Tale of the Great Panic. Is announced for the first number of Frank Leslie's, The Stars and Stripes. Announcement repeated on Dec. 18 and 25; but it never appeared.

M. UNLOCATED

Lost. On O'Brien's list of twenty stories to be collected and published.

N. MSS

Violina, the Birth of a Poet. 6 pp. folio, unfinished. Francis Wolle, University of Colorado, Boulder, Colo.

On a Rock. 4 pp. folio, unfinished. Romm collection.

IV. PLAYS

My Christmas Dinner. A Farce. Dec. 25, 1852. (Wallack's Lyceum). Repeated on Dec. 27 and 28, and on Jan. 4, 1853.

A Gentleman from Ireland. A Comedy, in Two Acts. Dec. 11, 1854 (Wallack's Theatre). Published in The Minor Drama. The Acting Edition. No. CLVI. As Performed at Wallack's Theatre. New York. Samuel French, Publisher. [1858]. Ran Dec. 11–21, 25–26, 29–30, and intermittently to Jan. 13, 1855. Revived c. Apr. 14, and Nov. 17, 1855; and c. Nov. 13, 1858. Also at Boston Theatre, Boston, 1860; Brougham's Theatre, Feb. 22 to Mar. 1, 1869; Mar. 15; Theatre Francais, May 19; Academy of Music, Cleveland, Ohio, Dec. 6; Wallack's Theatre, Apr. 20, 1870; Brooklyn Theatre,

Dec. 12, 1871; Academy of Music, Apr. 29, 1875. All these performances with John Brougham in the part of Gerald Fitzmaurice. Also played by W. R. Floyd at Varieties Theatre, New Orleans (before 1880), and by Frank Winter at National Theatre, Washington, D. C. (as late as 1893).

The Sisters. A drama in two acts adapted from the French, Ange ou Diable. Dec. 27, 1854 (Wallack's Theatre). (Listed in Ireland, Records of the New York Stage, p. 635, as "Like and Unlike, or the Sisters"). Ran Dec. 27, 1854 to Jan. 13, 1855.

Duke Humphrey's Dinner. A dramatic sketch. Feb. 4, 1856. (Wallack's Theatre). Repeated on Feb. 5, 6, and 7.

The Cup and the Lip. A three act play. No performance. (Noticed on Dec. 27, 1856, as "about to be brought out at Wallack's").

The Tycoon, or Young America in Japan. A burlesque. July 2, 1860 (Laura Keene's Theatre). Produced by Joseph Jefferson. Ran until July 21. Written in collaboration with Charles G. Rosenberg.

Blood Will Tell. Not produced. MS left with Thomas E. Davis.

The Two Ophelias. Not produced.

?Samson. Not produced. (Louis H. Stephens).

?Rosedale, or The Rifle Ball by Lester Wallack. Sept. 30, 1863.

V. Miscellaneous

A. The Family Friend

The Council of Friends. Busybody, I, 206 (July, 1849); Debt, Freedom, Gambling, Hunger, 207; Nobody, 208. Bachelor, I, 248–249 (September, 1849); Jealousy, 249.

Council of Observation. A Star, A Withered Flower, I, 315 (November, 1849); A Feather, 316.

Philosophy in Disguise. I, 294–295 (November, 1849).

The Council of Friends. Economy, Envy, Money, Newspaper, II, 147 (Mar. 1, 1850); Peace, 148.

Family Conversation. III, 131–134 (Sept. 1, 1850).

Home. III, 282–285 (Nov. 15, 1850).

On Ostentation. IV, 9–11 (Jan. 1, 1851).

Babies! IV, 73–75 (Feb. 1, 1851).

Children. A Vindication. IV, 170–174 (Mar. 15, 1851).

The Simple History of a Family Friend. V, 3–6 (July 1, 1851).

B. The Parlour Magazine

The Sunbeam, the Dew-Drop, and the Rose. From the Persian. I, 94 (May 17, 1851).

C. THE LANTERN

The Gory Gnome: or the Lurid Lamp of the Volcano! A Model Melo-Drama, In Three Acts. I, 73 (Feb. 28, 1852).
The Physiology of Pantomimes Un-"ravelled." I, 112 (Mar. 20, 1852).
Lantern Slides. No. I. The Comic Artist. I, 257 (June 26, 1852).
Lantern Slides. No. II. Joke Makers. II, 23 (July 17, 1852).
Lantern Slides. No. III. The Poet. II, 44 (July 31, 1852).
The Man Without a Shadow. A New Version. II, 91 (Sept. 4, 1852).

D. THE LEISURE HOUR

?Aladdin at the Crystal Palace; or, Science versus Fairy-Land. I, 261–262 (Apr. 22, 1852).

E. THE AMERICAN WHIG REVIEW

Fragments from an Unpublished Magazine. XVI, 262–272. (September, 1852); 350–365 (October); 552–568 (December).
Odds and Ends. XVI, 272 (September, 1852).
The Woes of a Literary Partner. XVI, 567–568 (December, 1852).

F. THE NEW YORK DAILY TIMES

Literature as a Profession—Difficulties of Writers. (Nov. 13, 1852).
Art and Art Critics. (Nov. 27, 1852).
A Learned Doctor. (Dec. 2, 1852).
Literary Parties. (Mar. 9, 1853).
The Way to Get Buried. (Mar. 19, 1853).
Sixpence Too Little. (Apr. 16, 1853).
A Sick Bachelor. (May 13, 1853).
Ecume de Mer. (June 15, 1853; June 24; July 13; July 19).
Alfred Tennyson. (Nov. 13, 1855). (A review of Maud and Other Poems.)
The Seventh Regiment. (May 2, 1861). Reprinted in Moore, Rebellion Record, 1861, I, D. 148–154; The Civil War in Song and Story, 1882 (1st Edition, 1865), pp. 228–233, with title The March of the Seventh Regiment; extracts in Swinton, History of the Seventh Regiment, 1870, pp. 37, 42, 96, 106, 153; and in Clark, History of the Seventh Regiment of New York, 1806–1889, 2 vols., 1890, I, 474 ff.

G. THE EVENING POST

From an Unpublished Manuscript. On Social Manners in America. Dec. 24, 1852.

H. PUTNAM'S MONTHLY MAGAZINE

Our Young Authors—Mitchell. I, 74–78 (January, 1853).
Our Young Authors—Melville. I, 155–164 (February, 1853).
The Last Poet Out. IV, 213–217 (August, 1854). (A review of Lyrics by the Letter H).
The Editor at Large. IV, 331–337 (September, 1854); IV, 434–442 (October, 1854).
Our Authors and Authorship. Melville and Curtis. XI, 384–393 (April, 1857).

I. HARPER'S NEW MONTHLY MAGAZINE

The Two Skulls. VI, 343–344 (February, 1853).
Your Health! XI, 531–535 (September, 1855). (Review of Letters to the People on Health and Happiness, by Catherine E. Beecher).
Bird Gossip. XI, 820–825 (November, 1855).
A Paper of All Sorts. XVI, 507–515 (March, 1858).
A Nest of Nightingales. XVIII, 520–522 (March, 1859).

J. YOUNG AMERICA

(Title changed to Yankee Doodle: or Young America with Vol. II, No. 1, on July 5, 1856).

The Green Curtain. I, 42 (Jan. 26, 1856); I, 149 (Mar. 29, 1856).
Bachelor Buttons. By Benedick. I, 95 (Mar. 1, 1856).
Brown Studies. I, 99–100 (Mar. 1, 1856); 111–112 (Mar. 8); 123–124 (Mar. 15); 135–136 (Mar. 22); 147–148 (Mar. 29); 159–160 (Apr. 5); 171–172 (Apr. 12); 183–184 (Apr. 19); 195–196 (Apr. 26); 207–208 (May 3); 219 (May 10); 231 (May 17); 243 (May 24); 255–256 (May 31); 267 (June 7); 279–280 (June 14, 1856).
Fashionable Lexicon. I, 144 (Mar. 22, 1856).
The Spring Fashions. After the Manner of the "Daily Times." I, 154 (Mar. 29, 1856).
Beauties of the Vernal Season. In the Style of an eloquent Morning Paper. I, 161 (Apr. 5, 1856).

K. HARPER'S WEEKLY

The Man about Town. I, 66–67 (Jan. 31, 1857); 82–83 (Feb. 7, 1857); 99 (Feb. 14); 114–115 (Feb. 21); 130–131 (Feb. 28); 147 (Mar. 7); 163 (Mar. 14); 179 (Mar. 21); 195–196 (Mar. 28); 211–212 (Apr. 4); 227 (Apr. 11); 242 (Apr. 18); 259 (Apr. 25); 274 (May 2); 290–291 (May 9); 307 (May 16); 323 (May 23); 339 (May 30); 355 (June 6); 387 (June 20); 403 (June 27); 419 (July 4); 435 (July 11); 451 (July 18); 499 (Aug. 8); 515 (Aug. 15); 531

(Aug. 22); 547 (Aug. 29); 563 (Sept. 5); 579 (Sept. 12); 595 (Sept. 19); 611 (Sept. 26, 1857).

L. THE NEW YORK PICAYUNE

The Man about Town. pp. 241–242 (Nov. 21, 1857); pp. 252–253 (Nov. 28); pp. 262–263 (Dec. 5, 1857).

M. THE SATURDAY PRESS

(Oct. 23, 1858–Nov. 27, 1858; The New York Saturday Press, Dec. 4–Dec. 25; The New-York Saturday Press, Jan. 1, 1859 on).

Dramatic Feuilleton. Oct. 23, 30, 1858; Nov. 13, Review of his own A Gentleman from Ireland; Nov. 20, 27; Dec. 4, 11, 18, 25; Jan. 1, 8, 29, 1859.

N. ATLANTIC MONTHLY

Review of Mothers and Infants, Nurses and Nursing by Dr. Al. Donné. III, 645–646 (May, 1859).

O. BOSTON COURIER

Advertisements and notices of Geraldine. Sept. 17, 1859, and Sept. 19, 21, 23, 29, and Oct. 3, 6, 8, 10, 12, and 13.

Advertisements and notices of Matilda Heron in Medea and Camille. Oct. 14 and 15, 1859.

P. THE ATLAS AND DAILY BEE, BOSTON, MASS.

Advertisements and notices of Geraldine. Sept. 19, 1859, and Sept. 20, and Oct. 6, and 12.

Q. VANITY FAIR

The Sybarites of the Shop. I, 72 (Jan. 28, 1860).

Here and There. I, 108 (Feb. 11, 1860); 125 (Feb. 18); 150 (Mar. 3); 189 (Mar. 17); 204 (Mar. 24); 214 (Mar. 31); 238 (Apr. 7); 324 (May 19); 391 (June 16); II, 22 (July 7, 1860).

The Sorrows of a Dead-Head. I, 116 (Feb. 18, 1860).

Set a T— to Catch a T—. I, 294 (May 5, 1860).

Those Little Bills. II, 53 (July 28, 1860).

R. WILKES' SPIRIT OF THE TIMES

Synopsis and analysis of Geraldine by Mrs. Sidney F. Bateman. May 24, 1862.

S. MSS

Requisition for supplies for McClellan Rifles, Aug. 24, 1861. F. J. O'Brien Capt.
Note book—Details of Guard, F. J. O'Brien.
Note book—Picket Stations. F. J. O'Brien.
Scrap of paper—Parole Prescott Countersign Bunker Hill.
The Diamond Lens and other tales—& poems by Fitz James O'Brien. (A list of twenty stories). Alfred F. Goldsmith.

VI. Letters

(Items in this list followed by R were seen in and copied from the collection of the late Charles Romm of 110 Fourth Ave., New York City.)

A. BY FITZ-JAMES O'BRIEN

F. J. O'Brien to Dr Sir. Bath [?1849–1851]. In Historical Society of Pennsylvania.
Fitz James O'Brien to Dear Sir (Editor of Putnam's). Oct. 20th [?1855]. In Historical Society of Pennsylvania.
Fitz-James DeCourcy O'Brien to Dear Sir (?Thomas Bailey Aldrich) September, 1856. In Winter, Old Friends.
FitzJames O'Brien to Messrs. Phillips Sampson and Co. Nov. 28th [1857]. In Yale Library.
FitzJames O'Brien to Messrs. Phillips Sampson & Co. Dec. 1st [1857]. In Yale Library.
The Author of "The Diamond Lens" to the Editors of the Evening Post. Jan. 18, 1858. Printed Jan. 20, 1858.
Fitz-James O'Brien to the Editors of the Evening Post. Feb. 19, 1858. Printed Feb. 20, 1858.
F. J. O'Brien to Dear Sir (?James Russell Lowell). Oct. 10, 1859. In N. Y. Public Library.
O'Brien to Charles H. Nordhoff. [?December, 1859]. Owned by Capt. F. L. Pleadwell (MC), U. S. Navy (Ret.).
F. J. O'Brien to [John E. Owens]. Nov. 21, 1860. In Winter, Old Friends.
FitzJames O'Brien to Sir. June 10, 1861. R.
FitzJames O'Brien to Dr Sir. July 17, 1861. Owned by Francis Wolle.
O'Brien to Thomas E. Davis. Jan. 21, 1862. In Winter, 1881.
FitzJames O'Brien to [?Frank Wood]. In The New York Leader, Mar. 8, 1862.
O'Brien to Frank [Wood]. In The New York Leader, Mar. 29, 1862.
F. O'B. to Mrs. M. E. W. Sherwood [March, 1862]. In The New York Times, July 2, 1898.
O'Brien to Thomas E. Davis [Apr. 1, 1862]. R.

B. TO FITZ-JAMES O'BRIEN

(All of these in the Romm collection).

P. F. Leavens to FitzJames O'Brien, Esq. June 3, 1861.
Orson H. Bester to FitzJames O'Brien, Esq. June 4, 1861.
Jenny [Danforth] to Mon Cher Baron. [?1861].
Eliza O'Grady (his mother) to Fitzjames. Oct. 25, 1861.
Jos. W. Harper, Jr. to FitzJames O'Brien, Esq. Jan. 13, 1862.
Frank Wood to Fitz. Jan. 14, 1862.
Frank Wood to Capt. F. J. O'Brien. Feb. 1, 1862.
Tom Davis to Fitz. Feb. 8, 1862.
Tom to Fitz. Feb. 24, 1862.
Frank Wood to Lieut. F. J. O'Brien. Mar. 7, 1862.
Frank Wood to Fitz. Mar. 16, 1862.
Chas. A. Whittier to Fitz. Mar. 20, 1862.

C. ABOUT FITZ-JAMES O'BRIEN

Bayard Taylor to George H. Boker. Sept. 15, 1854. In N. Y. Tribune, Mar. 6, 1881.
Bayard Taylor to Richard Henry Stoddard. November, 1854. In Life and Letters of Bayard Taylor.
Guy to the Editors of the Evening Post. Jan. 14, 1858.
Thomas E. Davis to Hon. A. W. Van Wyck. Dec. 12, 1861. R.
F. W. Lander (Brigadier-General, U. S. A.) to Bierstadt. Dec. 31, 1861. R.
Thos. E. Davis, Jr. to Brig. Genl. Shields. Jan. 8, 1862. R.
[General] George B. McClellan to General Lander. Feb. 17, 1862. In Winter, 1881.
S. F. Barstow to Dr. Salter. Feb. 28, 1862. R.
George A. Thurston to Thomas E. Davis. Apr. 1, 1862. In Winter, 1881.
Frank Wood to L. H. Stephens. Apr. 6, 1862. R.
W. P. to Mrs. M. E. W. Sherwood. n. d. [1862]. In N. Y. Times, July 2, 1898; reprinted in The Shield—ΘΔΧ—December, 1898.
B. M. C. to Dear Sir. April 1863. R.
Louis H. Stephens to William Winter. Aug. 3, 1880. In Winter, 1881.
Louis H. Stephens to William Winter. Aug. 18, 1880. R.
F. H. Bellew to William Winter. Oct. 7, 1880. R.
D. H. McCoy to W. Winter. Oct. 8, 1880. R.
Stephen Fiske to William Winter. Oct. 8, 1880. In Winter, 1881.
R. Shelton Mackenzie to William Winter. Oct. 9, 1880. R.
W. R. Floyd to William Winter. Oct. 16, 1880. R.

Thomas Bailey Aldrich to William Winter. Oct. 20, 1880. In Winter, Old Friends.

Thomas E. Davis to William Winter. Oct. 22, 1880. In Winter, 1881.

William Winter to B. H. Ticknor, Esq. Oct. 26, 1880. Yale.

Geo. Haven Putnam to William Winter. Oct. 27, 1880. R.

G. W. S. McClellan to William Winter. Nov. 1, 1880. Owned by Alfred F. Goldsmith.

William Winter to Osgood. Nov. 10, 1880. Yale.

William Winter to Ticknor. Nov. 13, 1880. Yale.

Col. Emmons Clark to William Winter. n. d. [1880]. Owned by Alfred F. Goldsmith.

A. R. Waud to W. Winter, Esq. Dec. 7, 1880. R.

William Winter to Ticknor. Dec. 22, 1880. In Winter, 1881, in Library of Yale University.

William Winter to Ticknor. Jan. 6, 1881. In Winter, 1881, in Library of Yale University.

Lester Wallack to William Winter. Mar. 27, 1881. R.

VII. Miscellaneous MS. Sources

Admission Papers of Solicitors' Apprentices. In the King's Inn, Dublin.

Entrance Book, Trinity College, Dublin.

Index to Prerogative Wills, 1811–1858. In Public Record Office of Ireland, Dublin.

Primary Valuation of Tenements, 1851. In Valuation Office, Ely Place, Dublin.

Original Manuscript Office Book of Household Words. In possession of Elkin Matthews Ltd., Booksellers, 33 Conduit Street, London, W. 1.

A copy of testimony given by Frank Opeltt, taken before the Court Martial in the case of O'Brien,—tried for the shooting of Serg't Davenport. In Romm collection.

Certificate, State of New-York, Depot of Volunteers, (Division Armory, co. White and Elm Streets.) New-York. Oct. 16th 1861. FitzJames O'Brien qualified to serve as a Company Officer. In Romm collection.

Envelope postmarked New York, Jan. 14, addressed Capt. F. J. O'Brien A. D. C. Care of Stephen Mirzan Willards Hotel Washington D. C. In Romm collection.

Copy of General Order 111, Camp Kelley, Jan. 22, 1862, appointing O'Brien as Aide de Camp to Brig. Genl Lander. R.

Winter, William. Marginal notes, briefly characterizing some of the O'Brien poems and stories—in Romm collection.

Winter, William. Note-book, O'Brien—List of things for Volume 2. Inside, Material for Second Vol. of O'Brien's Works. In Romm collection.
Winter, William. His own copy of 1881. Marginal corrections.

VIII. Reviews, Criticisms, and Other Articles Relating to O'Brien in Magazines

A. THE FAMILY FRIEND

IV, Appendix, p. 9 (Feb. 15 or Mar. 1, 1851). Description of O'Brien.

B. THE AMERICAN WHIG REVIEW

XVI, 12–20 (July, 1852). A Letter to the Proprietors of Harper's Magazine. Pay to contributors.

C. THE LANTERN

II, 137 (Oct. 2, 1852). Criticism of Fragments from an Unpublished Magazine in The Whig Review. Probably by William North.

D. PUTNAM'S MONTHLY MAGAZINE

I, 1 (January, 1853). Policy.

E. THE NEW YORK PICAYUNE

Jan. 15, 1853. My Christmas Dinner.
Dec. 23, 1854. A Gentleman from Ireland.
Jan. 13, 1855. The Sisters and A Gentleman from Ireland.
Jan. 20, 1855. The Sisters and A Gentleman from Ireland.
Apr. 21, 1855. A Gentleman from Ireland revived.
Nov. 24, 1855. A Gentleman from Ireland revived.
Dec. 22, 1855. Duke Humphrey's Dinner in rehearsal.
Feb. 16, 1856. Review of Duke Humphrey's Dinner.
Sept. 20, 1856. Cartoon, "Effect of Dramatic Copyright Law."
Nov. 13, 1858. A Gentleman from Ireland revived.
Feb. 5, 1859. O'Brien as a dramatic critic.
Mar. 12, 1859. Cartoon, O'Brien wearing coronet.
Mar. 26, 1859. Notice of Wilkins's Bohemian Walks and Talks in Harper's Weekly.

F. THE HOME JOURNAL

Aug. 4, 1855. Notice of Duke Humphrey's Dinner.
Dec. 29, 1855. Comment on Babie Bertie's Christmas.
Dec. 27, 1856. Notice of The Cup and the Lip.

G. FRANK LESLIE'S ILLUSTRATED NEWSPAPER

Feb. 16, 1856. Review of Duke Humphrey's Dinner.
Dec. 11, 1858. Advertisement of The Red Petticoat.
Dec. 18, 1858. Advertisement of the Red Petticoat.
Dec. 25, 1858. Notice of The Red Petticoat.

H. HARPER'S WEEKLY

I, 707 (Nov. 7, 1857) to II, 211 (Apr. 3, 1858). Bohemian Walks and Talks, column by E. G. P. Wilkins.
VI, 165–166 (Mar. 15, 1862). Lander's death.
VI, 267 (Apr. 26, 1862). Lieut. Fitz James O'Brien.
XXV, 163 (Mar. 12, 1881). Review of Winter, 1881.

I. THE SATURDAY PRESS

(Oct. 23, 1858–Nov. 27, 1858; The New York Saturday Press, Dec. 4, 1858–Dec. 25, 1858; The New-York Saturday Press, Jan. 1, 1859 on).

Nov. 13, 1858. Review of A Gentleman from Ireland by O'Brien.
Nov. 20, 1858. Reprint of The Prize-Fight. Editorial, Literary Pay.
Mar. 12, 1859. O'Brien attacked in last no. of the Constellation.
July 2, 1859. Reference to The Cup and the Lip.
Nov. 12, 1859. "M. le Baron" and the actresses.
Jan. 21, 1860. Review of Mother of Pearl.
Mar. 3, 1860. Pfaff's and Bohemians.
Mar. 24, 1860. Review of The Lost Steamship, and reprint.
Apr. 28, 1860. Brougham in A Gentleman from Ireland.
June 16, 1860. Bohemia defended.
June 30, 1860. Announcement of The Tycoon.
July 7, 1860. Review of The Tycoon; reprint of Independence Bell.
July 28, 1860. Reference to the Chicago Zouaves and reprint of O'Brien's poem.
Sept. 22, 1860. Reprint of Battledores.
Oct. 27, 1860. Reprint of A Fallen Star.
Dec. 15, 1860. Reprint of The Man at the Door.
Aug. 5, 1865. Advertisement of Pfaff's.

J. VANITY FAIR

I, 12 (Dec. 31, 1859). At the Café by T. B. A.
I, 172 (Mar. 10, 1860). Ages of American Authors.
II, 45 (July 21, 1860). O'Brien listed among playwrights.
II, 183–185 and 195–197 (Oct. 13 and Oct. 20, 1860). The Prince's Ball by Edmund C. Stedman.

II, 205 (Oct. 20, 1860). Mentions Fitz James O'Inchiquin's "Mother of Pearl."
III, 282 (June 15, 1861). Return of the Seventh.
IV, 211 (Nov. 9, 1861). Cartoon by Mullen, O'Brien recruiting.
V, 190 (Apr. 19, 1862). "Fitz-James O'Brien. Wounded, February 16, 1862. Died, April 6, 1862." A dirge by C. D. Shanly.

K. WILKES' SPIRIT OF THE TIMES

May 24, 1862. Review of Geraldine, quoting a synopsis and analysis of the play by O'Brien.

L. THE ROUND TABLE

I, 43 (Jan. 2, 1864). Dramatic Critics in New York.
I, 80 (Feb. 6, 1864). Bohemianism.
I, 250 (Apr. 2, 1864). Frank Wood obituary.
III, 245 (Apr. 21, 1866). Literariana,—Contrast between O'Brien and William North.
III, 308 (May 19, 1866). Review of Ada Clare's Only a Woman's Heart.
III, 326 (May 26, 1866). Literariana.—O'Brien as O'Bouncer.
III, 467 (July 28, 1866). The Characteristics of Our Later Poetry.
VII, 365 (June 6, 1868). List of O'Brien's writings contributed to Notes and Queries by L. H. B., West Springfield, Mass., May 23, 1868.
VII, 413 (June 27, 1868). More O'Brien stories.
VIII, 159 (Sept. 5, 1868). Reference to Babie Bertie's Christmas.
VIII, 233 (Oct. 3, 1868). Two more O'Brien poems.
IX, 187 (Mar. 20, 1869). A Gentleman from Ireland revived.

M. THE NEW YORK CITIZEN

Sept. 30, 1865. Account of E. G. P. Wilkins and O'Brien by George Arnold. Reprinted in Winter, 1881.

N. HARPER'S NEW MONTHLY MAGAZINE, AN INDEX TO

Volumes I. to L.: From June, 1850, to May, 1875. New York: Harper & Brothers, Publishers, Franklin Square. 1875.

O. THE ATLANTIC MONTHLY

XLIII, 242–252 (February, 1879). Stoddard, R. H., Reminiscences of Bayard Taylor.

P. THE CATHOLIC WORLD

XXXIII, 138 (April, 1881). Review of Winter, 1881.
CX, 751–762 (March, 1920). A Keltic Poe by Joseph J. Reilly (Ph. D.).

Q. SCRIBNER'S MONTHLY

XXII, 469–472 (July, 1881). Review of Winter, 1881.

R. THE CRITIC

III, 208 (May 2, 1885). Review of Winter, 1885.
IV, 34 (July 18, 1885). "A Manufacturer of Cold Creeps," quoted from The Saturday Review, July 11, 1885.

S. THE LITERARY WORLD

June 13, 1885. Review of Winter, 1885.

T. THE ATHENAEUM

No. 3138, pp. 821–822 (Dec. 17, 1887). Review of Winter, 1887.

U. JOURNAL OF THE CORK HISTORICAL AND ARCHAEOLOGICAL SOCIETY

II, 201 (October, 1893). Quotes from Cork Almanack, 1823.

V. THE SHIELD

A Magazine Published Quarterly in the Interests of Theta: Delta: Chi. Founded in 1869. Revived in 1884. (The Elmira Advertiser Association, Printers, Elmira, N. Y.).

XIV, 325 (September, 1898). "The Bees." (Quoted from II, 9).
XIV, 411 (December, 1898). Quotes Hillyer and "W. P." from N. Y. Times.
XIV, 418 (December, 1898). Lambda Graduate Association.
XL, 231–235 (February, 1924). MS. of Amy Scudder.

W. JOHN O'LONDON'S WEEKLY

p. 258. (Nov. 15, 1924). Genius and Dandy. A Forgotten Master of the Short Story. By Prof. Emery Barnes.

IX. Reviews, Criticisms, and Other Articles Relating to O'Brien in Newspapers

A. THE NATION. (DUBLIN)

Oct. 4, 1845. "Heremon" declined.
Nov. 8, 1845. Uncomplimentary reference to "Heremon."
Nov. 15, 1845. Objections to "Heremon."
Feb. 7, 1846. Similar reference.

B. THE LIMERICK CHRONICLE

May 13, 1848. Irish emigration.

C. THE ADVOCATE: OR, IRISH INDUSTRIAL JOURNAL (DUBLIN)

Dec. 16, 1848. Quotes from The Cork Examiner. Famine conditions.

D. THE SATIRIST (LONDON)

May 12, 1850. Irish emigration.

E. NEW YORK DAILY TIMES

Apr. 14, 1852. Rights of Labor.
Apr. 15, 1852. Editorial on sewing women.
June 14, 1853. Reference to My Christmas Dinner.
Dec. 12, 1854. Review of A Gentleman from Ireland.
Dec. 28, 1854. Review of The Sisters.
June 30, 1855. Comment on The Bohemian and on The Beauty.
July 30, 1855. Comment on A Drawing-Room Drama.
Feb. 4, 1856. Announcement of Duke Humphrey's Dinner.
Feb. 5, 1856. Review of Duke Humphrey's Dinner.
Apr. 30, 1857. ΘΔΧ Convention.
July 4, 1860. Review of The Tycoon.
Apr. 7, 1862. Editorial, announcing O'Brien's death.
Apr. 9, 1862. Funeral notice.
Apr. 10, 1862. Obituary notice.
June 21, 1862. Theta Delta Chi Society.
Mar. 12, 1881. Review of Winter, 1881.
Apr. 26, 1890. Obituary of Charles Pfaff.
July 2, 1898. (Saturday Review of Books and Art, pp. 444–5) Fitzjames O'Brien by Mrs. M. E. W. Sherwood; Facts in O'Brien's Brilliant Career by William Sidney Hillyer. (Largely reprinted in The Shield—ΘΔΧ—December, 1898).

F. THE NEW YORK HERALD

Dec. 2, 1852. Advertisement of My Christmas Dinner. Also on Dec. 28, 29, and 30, 1852, and on Jan. 4, 1853.
Dec. 27, 1852. Review of My Christmas Dinner.
Dec. 12, 1854. Review of A Gentleman from Ireland.
Dec. 28, 1854. Review of The Sisters.
Feb. 4, 1856. Advertisement of Duke Humphrey's Dinner. Also on Feb. 5, 6, and 7.

Feb. 5, 1856. Review of Duke Humphrey's Dinner.
July 1, 1860. Announcement of The Tycoon.
July 3, 1860. Review of The Tycoon.
Aug. 9, 1861. The McClellan Rifles.
Aug. 10, 1861. The Clinton Rifles.
Aug. 14, 1861. The McClellan Rifles.
Aug. 18, 1861. O'Brien elected Capt. of Co. A.
Sept. 18, 1861. McClellan Rifles on Staten Island.
Apr. 7, 1862. O'Brien's death.
Apr. 9, 1862. Funeral announcement.
Apr. 10, 1862. O'Brien's funeral.

G. THE EVENING POST (NEW YORK)

Dec. 21, 1852. Mention of "a criticism of Ik Marvel" in Putnam's.
Jan. 4, 1853. Advertisement of My Christmas Dinner.
Feb. 6, 1857. Harper's Weekly features The Man about Town.
Jan. 14, 1858. Dispute about the author of The Diamond Lens.
Jan. 20, 1858. Letter denying North's authorship, by the author of The Diamond Lens.
Feb. 20, 1858. O'Brien reiterates claim to authorship of The Diamond Lens.
Feb. 23, 1858. Biographical facts about O'Brien and announcement of the publication of a volume of his poems and tales.
Mar. 4, 1859. What Was It? like Bulwer's Zanoni, quoted from Boston Courier.
Mar. 25, 1859. O'Brien worthy contributor to Harper's Monthly.
Apr. 29, 1859. A review by O'Brien in the May Atlantic.
Aug. 25, 1859. O'Brien author of The Meeting By the Hemlocks in September Harper's. My Double and How he Undid Me in September Atlantic has been attributed to writer of the Diamond Lens.
Sept. 20, 1859. Mention of The Wondersmith by O'Brien in the October Atlantic.
Sept. 21, 1859. Story by O'Brien praised as 'enough to give distinction to the magazine.'
Aug. 9, 1861. The McClellan Rifles. Officers, gentlemen with former service.
Sept. 20, 1861. Consolidation of McClellan Guard and Hancock Guard.
Nov. 7, 1861. 'Fitz-James O'Brien Under Arrest.' Account of shooting Sgt. Davenport.
Nov. 8, 1861. 'Mr. O'Brien's Case.' Not under arrest. Acted in self-defense.
Feb. 17, 1862. Official report of Gen'l. Lander about Blooming Gap raid.
Apr. 7, 1862. Editorial on death of Fitz-James O'Brien.

H. NEW-YORK DAILY TRIBUNE

Dec. 25, 1852. Notice of new Putnam's Magazine.
Dec. 28, 1852. Notice of My Christmas Dinner.
July 2, 1860. Announcement of The Tycoon.
July 3, 1860. Review of The Tycoon.
Sept. 30, 1861. McClellan Rifles.
Feb. 17, 1862. Capture of Bloomery Gap.
Feb. 18, 1862. Praise of Lander.
Feb. 20, 1862. The Skirmish at Blooming Gap.
Feb. 25, 1862. From Gen'l. Lander's Division.
Mar. 3, 1862. Death of Gen'l. Lander, Mar. 2, 1862.
Apr. 9, 1862. Funeral notice.
Apr. 10, 1862. O'Brien's funeral.
Mar. 6, 1881. Fitz-James O'Brien.—Review of Winter, 1881, by Richard Henry Stoddard.
Apr. 25, 1890. Charles Pfaff of "Bohemia" Fame Dead.

I. NEW ORLEANS DELTA

Feb. 7, 1858. Account of O'Brien's steal from North for The Diamond Lens.

J. THE BOSTON COURIER

Mar. 2, 1859. What Was It? not original—imitated from scene in Bulwer's Zanoni.
Sept. 15, 1859. Gayler's play.
Sept. 19, 1859. Miss Heron opens.
Oct. 15, 1859. Henry Squires in Boston. Heron in Camille.

K. THE NEW YORK LEADER

July 7, 1860. Review of The Tycoon.
July 14, 1860. O'Brien contrasted with Brougham.
Apr. 20, 1861. O'Brien to war.
Aug. 3, 1861. "A Regiment of Beaux."
Aug. 10, 1861. The Beaux in a Bad Way.
Aug. 24, 1861. Notice of The Havelock, of McClellan Rifles, and of Clinton Rifles.
Nov. 30, 1861. Reprint of The Countersign and emphasis of O'Brien's authorship.
Dec. 7, 1861. O'Brien withdrew from McClellan Rifles.
Jan. 4, 1862. New Year's Eve at Pfaff's.

Mar. 1, 1862. Bloomery Gap.
Mar. 8, 1862. Letter from O'Brien.
Mar. 15, 1862. O'Brien returning to recuperate.
Mar. 22, 1862. O'Brien's condition.
Mar. 29, 1862. Letter of O'Brien to Wood.
Apr. 12, 1862. Obituary notice, and Editorial.
Apr. 19, 1862. Wood and Davis literary executors.
Apr. 26, 1862. Review of Harper's Weekly obituary.
May 3, 1862. Fitz-James O'Brien by M. D. Urner.
June 21, 1862. Notice of Merriam's eulogy.

L. STAPLETON (STATEN ISLAND) GAZETTE

Nov. 4(?), 1861. Story of O'Brien's shooting of Sgt. Davenport.

M. THE ALBION

Apr. 12, 1862. Drama—Tribute to O'Brien by "Mercutio" (William Winter).

N. THE SWORD AND THE PEN

Published during the ten days of the Soldiers' Home Bazaar held in Boston, Dec. 7–17, 1881. Horace Parker Chandler, ed. Printed MS. of Amy Scudder.

O. THE BROOKLYN EAGLE

July 11, 1886. Interview with Walt Whitman about Pfaff's.

P. THE BOSTON HERALD

Apr. 28, 1924. "As the World Wags"—O'Brien in Boston by Philip Hale.

X. General Bibliography

Actors as They Are; a Series of Sketches of the Most Eminent Performers Now on the Stage. New York: O. A. Roorbach, Jr., 18 Ann Street. 1856.

Allibone's Dictionary of English Literature and British and American Authors. Supplement, by John Foster Kirk. Philadelphia. 1891.

Appleton, D. Cyclopediae of American Biography. D. Appleton and Co. New York, 1888.

Ashmun, Margaret. Modern Short Stories. Edited with an introduction and with Biographies and Bibliographies. Macmillan Company. New York. 1914. (See What Was It?).

Atlantic Tales. A Collection of Stories from the Atlantic Monthly. Boston. Ticknor and Fields. 1866. (See The Diamond Lens).

Baldwin, Charles Sears, ed. American Short Stories. Selected and Edited with an Introductory Essay on the Short Story. Longmans, Green and Co. New York & London. 1904. (New impression, 1916). (See What Was It?).

Baldwin, James. School Reading by Grades. Fourth Year. American Book Company. 1897. (See How the Bell Rang).

Barnes, Prof. Emery. Genius and Dandy. A Forgotten Master of the Short Story. In John O'London's Weekly, p. 258 (Nov. 15, 1924).

Barrus, Clara, M. D. John Burroughs—Boy and Man. Garden City, N. Y., and Toronto. Doubleday, Page & Company, 1922.

Bazalgette, Léon. Walt Whitman The Man and His Work. Translated from the French by Ellen FitzGerald. Garden City, New York. Doubleday, Page & Company, 1920.

Beaty, John O. John Esten Cooke, Virginian. New York. Columbia University Press. New York. 1922.

Beers, Henry A., ed. A Century of American Literature, 1776–1876. New York. Henry Holt & Co. 1878. Leisure Hour Series.—No. 100. (See Kane and The Diamond Lens.)

Bleyer, Willard Grosvenor, Ph. D. Main Currents in the History of American Journalism. Houghton Mifflin Company. Boston, New York, Chicago, San Francisco. The Riverside Press, Cambridge, 1927.

Bolenius, Emma Miller. Fourth Reader. (The Boys' and Girls' Readers). Houghton Mifflin Company. 1919. (See How the Bell Rang).

Botta, Anne C. L., Memoirs of, written by her friends. New York. Continental Publishing Co. 1894.

Brown, Stephen J., S. J. Ireland in Fiction. A Guide to Irish Novels, Tales, Romances, & Folk-Lore. Maunsel & Co. Limited, Dublin and London. 1916.

Brown, T. Allston. A History of the New York Stage from the First Performance in 1732 to 1901. 3 v. New York. Dodd, Mead and Company. 1903.

Bryant, William Cullen, ed. The Family Library of Poetry and Song. Being Choice Selections from the Best Poets, etc. New York: Fords, Howard, and Hulbert. Copyright 1870. (See Kane).

Burke, Sir Barnard, C. B., LL. D. A Genealogical and Heraldic History of the Landed Gentry of Ireland. London. Harrison & Sons, 45, Pall Mall, S. W., Booksellers to His Majesty The King. 1912.

Canby, Henry Seidel. The Short Story in English. New York. Henry Holt and Co. 1909.

A Study of the Short Story. New York. Henry Holt and Co. 1913.

City of Cork Election [1820].

City of Cork Election. Lists of the Freemen and Freeholders, Alphabetically arranged, who voted at the Cork Election, December, 1826. Printed by J. Connor, 35, Grand-Parade.

Clark, Colonel Emmons. History of the Seventh Regiment of New York 1806–1889. 2 v. New York. Published by the Seventh Regiment. 1890.

Coates, Henry T., comp. and ed. The Fireside Encyclopaedia of Poetry. Comprising The Best Poems of the Most Famous Writers, English and American. Porter & Coates, Philadelphia. 1878. (See Kane).

Condon, Peter, "The Irish in the United States," The Catholic Encyclopedia, 1910, VIII, 132–145.

Congdon, Charles Tabor. Reminiscences of a Journalist. Boston, James R. Osgood and Company, 1880.

Connolly, Daniel, ed., The Household Library of Ireland's Poets, with full and choice selections from the Irish-American Poets, and a complete department of Authentic Biographical Notes. Published by the Editor, 28 Union Square, New York. 1887.

Connor's Cork Directory for the year 1830. Cork: Printed by J. Connor, 14, Tuckey-Street.

Conwell, Russell H. The Life, Travels, and Literary Career of Bayard Taylor. Boston. B. B. Russell, 57 Cornhill, 1879.

Cook, Dutton. A Book of the Play: Studies and Illustrations of Histrionic Story, Life, and Character. In Two Volumes. London: Sampson, Low, Marston, Searle, & Rivington. Crown Buildings, Fleet Street. 1876.

The Cork Almanac, 1823. Calculated by Thomas Holt, published by King and Company, Patrick Street, and printed by John Hennessy, Frenchchurch Street. Quoted in Journal of the Cork Archaeological Society. Cork: Published by Guy & Co. Ltd., 70, Patrick Street, 1893, II, 201.

Crimmins, John D. Irish-American Historical Miscellany. Relating largely to New York City and Vicinity, together with much interesting material relative to other parts of the Country. New York City, Published by the Author, 1905.

Davis, Elmer. History of The New York Times 1851–1921. New York, The New York Times, 1921.

De Berard, Frederick B., ed. Classic Tales by Famous Authors. With a General Introduction by Rossiter Johnson, LL.D. Story Tellers Edition. 20

vols. Published by The Bodleian Society. New York. 1902. (See What Was It? and The Wondersmith).

Derby, J.(ames) C. Fifty Years among Authors, Books and Publishers. New York: Copyright, 1884, by G. W. Carleton & Co., Publishers. London: S. Low, Son & Co. 1884.

Disher, M. Willson, ed. The Cowells in America. Being The Diary of Mrs. Sam Cowell During Her Husband's Concert Tour in the Years 1860–1861. London. Oxford University Press, Humphrey Milford. 1934.

Donaldson, Thomas. Walt Whitman the Man. New York, Francis P. Harper. 1896.

Ellet, Mrs. The Queens of American Society. New York: Charles Scribner & Company, 654 Broadway. 1868.

Emerson, Ralph Waldo. Letters and Social Aims. New and Revised Edition. Boston. Houghton Mifflin Company. The Riverside Press, Cambridge. 1884.

Esenwein, J. Berg. Studying the Short-Story. The Writer's Library. The Home Correspondence School, Springfield, Mass. Publishers. 1912.

Famous Stories by DeQuincey, Hawthorne, Thackeray, Zschökke, Winthrop, Hood, Macnish, Lee, and others. Illustrated by Nast, Hennessy, Hoppin, Meadows, Perkins, Ehninger, Eytinge, Jr., Lumley, Davenport, and others. Boston: DeWolfe, Fiske and Company, 365 Washington Street. [1879?]. (See From Hand to Mouth and Three of a Trade).

Faxon, Frederick Winthrop. A Check-List of American and English Periodicals. Boston. 1908.

Firkins, Ina Ten Eyck. Index to Short Stories. The H. W. Wilson Company. White Plains, N. Y. 1915. (Second and Enlarged Edition. N. Y. 1923).

Fitzgerald, Percy. The World Behind the Scenes. London. Chatto and Windus, Piccadilly. 1881.

Fitzgerald, Thos. W. H., ed. Ireland and her People. A Library of Irish Biography together with a Popular History of Ancient and Modern Erin to which is added an Appendix of Copious Notes and Useful Tables supplemented with A Dictionary of Proper Names in Irish Mythology, Geography, Genealogy, etc., Embracing a Period of Forty Centuries of Legend, Tradition and History; with Numerous Illustrations. Fitzgerald Book Company. Chicago. n. d.

Ford, James L. Forty-Odd Years in the Literary Shop. New York. E. P. Dutton & Company, 681 Fifth Avenue. (Copyright 1921).

French, Joseph Lewis, ed. Masterpieces of Mystery. 4 vols. Doubleday, Page & Co. 1920. (See The Lost Room and The Diamond Lens). Reprinted 1937.

ed. Tales of Terror. (See What Was It?).

ed. Great Ghost Stories. New York. Dodd, Mead and Company. 1918. (See What Was It?).

Gathany, J. Madison, ed., American Patriotism in Prose and Verse, 1775–1918. New York. The Macmillan Company. 1919.

Good Stories. Part III. Price, 50 cents. Boston: Ticknor and Fields. 1868. (See Three of a Trade).

Part IV. Boston. Ticknor and Fields, 1868. (See From Hand to Mouth). (Illustrated by S. Eytinge, Jr.).

Greenslet, Ferris. The Life of Thomas Bailey Aldrich. Boston and New York. Houghton Mifflin Company. 1908.

Gregory, Winifred, ed. American Newspapers 1821–1936. A Union List of Files Available in the United States and Canada. New York. The H. W. Wilson Company. 1937.

ed. Union List of Serials in Libraries of The United States and Canada. New York. The H. W. Wilson Company. 1927. (Second edition, 1943).

Guy's Topographical Directory of County Cork: comprising the Several Parishes, Townlands, Towns, Villages; etc. Cork: Guy & Co. Ltd. Printers & Publishers, 70, Patrick Street. 1888.

Hale, Edward Everett, and Dawson, Fredrick T. Elements of the Short Story. H. Holt and Co. New York. 1915. (See The Diamond Lens).

Hale, Philip. "As the World Wags." In The Boston Herald, Apr. 28, 1924.

Harper, C. Armitage, ed. American Ghost Stories. Boston and New York. Houghton Mifflin Company. 1928. (See What Was It?).

Harper, J. Henry. The House of Harper. A Century of Publishing in Franklin Square. New York and London. 1912.

Harper's New Monthly Magazine, An Index to. Volumes I. to L.: From June, 1850, to May, 1875. New York: Harper & Brothers, Publishers, Franklin Square. 1875.

Hawthorne, Julian, ed. Library of The World's Best Mystery and Detective Stories. 6 vols. English-Irish. The Review of Reviews Co. New York. 1907. (See The Bohemian, A Terrible Night, My Wife's Tempter, and The Golden Ingot).

The Lock and Key Library. 1912. 10 v. (Same as above, expanded from 6 to 10 vols.). Reprinted 1915.

Hayes, Edward, col. and ed. The Ballads of Ireland. 2 v. A. Fullarton & Co. London, Edinburgh, and Dublin. 1855. Reprinted in Boston, 1856.

Hayward, J. Henry. Poetical Pen-Pictures of The War: Selected from our Union Poets. Published for the purpose of founding a Building Fund for the "Union Home and School," established for the Education and Maintenance of our Volunteers' Children who may be left unprovided for. Organized May, 1861. Chartered by Act of Legislature, April, 1862. New York: Published by the Editor. 13 Park Row. 1863. (See The Countersign).

Hemstreet, Charles. Literary New York Its Landmarks and Associations. With 65 Illustrations. G. P. Putnam's Sons. New York & London. The Knickerbocker Press. 1903.

Hennessy, Michael Edmund. Men of Irish Blood Who Have Attained Distinction in American Journalism. In The Journal of the American-Irish Historical Society. Volume III. Boston, Mass. Published by the Society. 1900.

Hillyer, William Sidney. Facts in O'Brien's Brilliant Career. In N. Y. Times, July 2, 1898. (Largely reprinted in The Shield—ΘΔΧ—December, 1898).

Holland, M. The Cork Magazine and its Writers. In Journal of the Ivernian Society, VII, 142–146 (April–June, 1915).

Holloway, Emory. The Uncollected Poetry and Prose of Walt Whitman. Much of which has been But Recently Discovered with Various Early Manuscripts now first published. 2 vols. Garden City, N. Y., and Toronto. Doubleday, Page, & Company. 1921.

Whitman. An Interpretation in Narrative. New York & London. Alfred A. Knopf. 1926.

Howe, M. A. DeWolfe. The Atlantic Monthly and its Makers. Boston. The Atlantic Monthly Press, Inc. 1919.

Memories of a Hostess A Chronicle of Eminent Friendships drawn chiefly from the diaries of Mrs. James T. Fields. Atlantic Monthly Press. Boston. 1922.

Howells, William Dean. Literary Friends and Acquaintances, A Personal Retrospect of American Authorship, Harper and Brothers Publishers; New York and London, 1911. (First edition 1900).

Hudson, Frederic. Journalism in the United States, from 1690 to 1872. New York: Harper & Brothers, Publishers, Franklin Square. 1873.

Hutton, Laurence. Curiosities of the American Stage. Illustrated. New York. Harper & Brothers, Franklin Square. 1891.

Ireland, Joseph N. Records of the New York Stage from 1750 to 1860. 2 v. New York: T. H. Morrell, Publisher. 1867.

Irish Celts. A Cyclopedia of Race History, containing biographical Sketches of more than fifteen hundred Distinguished Irish Celts, with a chronological index. By A Member of the Michigan Bar. Illustrated. Detroit: Published by L. F. Kilroy and Company. 1884.

The Autobiography of Joseph Jefferson. The Century Co., New York. 1889.

Jessup, Alexander, and Canby, Henry Seidel, eds. The Book of the Short Story. New York and London. D. Appleton and Company. 1904.

Jessup, Alexander, ed. Representative American Short Stories. Allyn and Bacon. Boston New York Chicago Atlanta San Francisco. [1923]. (See The Diamond Lens).

Journal of the American-Irish Historical Society, The. Boston, Mass. Published by the Society. 1900. III, 71–72.

Journal of the Ivernian Society, VII, 142–146 (April–June, 1915).

Keese, William L. William E. Burton Actor, Author, and Manager. A Sketch of his Career with Recollections of his Performances. Illustrated. New York & London. G. P. Putnam's Sons. The Knickerbocker Press. 1885.

Lamb, James H. Biographical Dictionary of the United States. James H. Lamb and Co. Boston. 1900.

Lee, Sidney, ed. Dictionary of National Biography. London. Smith, Elder, & Co., 15 Waterloo Place. 1909. XV, 1111–1112.

Maps for 1841–2 Ordnance Survey of Ireland, 6 in. to 1 mile.

Matthews, Brander, ed. American Familiar Verse. Vers de Société. Longmans, Green, and Co. 91 and 93 Fifth Avenue, New York. London and Bombay. 1904. (See By the Passaic).

The Short Story. Specimens Illustrating Its Development. New York—Cincinnati—Chicago. American Book Company. 1907. (See What Was It?).

Matthews, Brander. Inquiries and Opinions. New York. Charles Scribner's Sons. 1907.

Maurice, Arthur Bartlett. The New York of the Novelists. New York. Dodd, Mead & Co. 1916.

Maverick, Augustus. Henry J. Raymond and The New York Press, for Thirty Years. Progress of American Journalism from 1840 to 1870. With Portrait, Illustrations, and Appendix. Published by Subscription only. Hartford, Conn.: A. S. Hale and Company. Chicago: Geo. W. Rogers. 1870.

McCarthy, Justin, M. P., ed., Irish Literature. 10 vols. John D. Morris & Co. Philadelphia. 1904. (See Loch Ina and The Diamond Lens).

Moore, Frank, ed. The Rebellion Record: A Diary of American Events, with Documents, Narratives, Illustrative Incidents, Poetry, etc. 4 v. New York: G. P. Putnam. 1861. (See The Seventh Regiment).

Moore, Frank. The Civil War in Song and Story. 1860–1865. Collected and arranged. New York. Peter Fenelon Collier. 1882. (1st edition in 1865). (See The Seventh Regiment).

Mott, Frank Luther. A History of American Magazines 1741–1850. New York London. D. Appleton and Company. 1930.

A History of American Magazines 1850–1865. Cambridge, Massachusetts. Harvard University Press. 1938.

A History of American Magazines 1865–1885. Cambridge, Massachusetts. Harvard University Press. 1938.

American Journalism, A History of Newspapers in the United States through 250 Years 1690 to 1940. New York. The Macmillan Company. 1941.

Mumford, Lewis. Herman Melville. Harcourt, Brace and Company. New York. 1929.

Murger, Henry. The Latin Quarter ("Scènes de la Vie de Bohème"). Translated by Ellen Marriage and John Selwyn. With an Introduction by Arthur Symons. New York. Doubleday Page and Company. 1901.

Nevins, Allan. The Evening Post A Century of Journalism. Boni and Liveright Publishers: New York. 1922.

North, William. The / Slave of the Lamp / A Posthumous Novel. / By William North, / Author of Anti-Coningsby, Etc. / "Who Will Exchange Old Lamps for New?" / Arabian Nights' Entertainments / New York: / H. Long & Brother, 121 Nassau Street / 1855. Republished as—The Man of the World. A Novel. Philadelphia. 1877. Peterson's Dollar Series.

Oberholtzer, Ellis Paxson. The Literary History of Philadelphia. George W. Jacobs & Co., Publishers. 1906.

O'Brien, Edward J. The Advance of the American Short Story. New York. Dodd, Mead & Co. 1923.

O'Brien, Fitz James. The Diamond Lens. The Happy Hour Library, Inc. New York, N. Y. n. d. [c. 1919]. (Contains The Diamond Lens, q. v., and Friend Eli's Daughter By Bayard Taylor).

The Diamond Lens and Other Stories. With an Introduction by Gilbert Seldes. New York. William Edwin Rudge. 1932. (See Collected Editions).

O'Brien, Frank M. The Story of The Sun. New York, 1833–1918. With an introduction by Edward Page Mitchell, Editor of "The Sun." New York: George H. Doran Company. 1918.

O'Brien, Michael J. (Historiographer, American Irish Historical Society). The Irish in the United States. Reprinted from "The Glories of Ireland." Phoenix Limited, Washington, D. C. 1914.

O'Brien, W. P. (C. B.) The Great Famine in Ireland and A Retrospect of the Fifty Years 1845–95 with A Sketch of the Present Condition and Future Prospects of The Congested Districts. Downey & Co. Limited. 12 York Street, Covent Garden, London. 1896.

Odell, George C. D. Annals of the New York Stage, Columbia University Press, New York, 1931, vols. VI and VII.

O'Donoghue, D. J. (Librarian, University College, Dublin). The Poets of Ireland. A Biographical and Bibliographical Dictionary of Irish Writers of English Verse. Dublin. Hodges Figgis & Co., Ltd. London. Henry Froude, Oxford University Press. 1912.

O'Donovan, John, Esq., ed. Miscellany of the Celtic Society. Dublin: Printed for the Celtic Society. 1849.

O'Reilly, John Boyle. In Bohemia. Boston. The Pilot Publishing Co. 1886.

Parry, Albert. Garrets and Pretenders. New York. Covici, Friede. 1933.

Pattee, Fred Lewis. The Development of the American Short Story An Historical Survey. Harper & Brothers Publishers. New York & London. 1923.

The Feminine Fifties. D. Appleton-Century Company. New York London. 1940.

ed. Century Readings for a Course in American Literature. New York. The Century Co. 1920. Revised ed. 1922. Third Edition, 1926. (See By the Passaic and The Diamond Lens).

In Cambridge History of American Literature, II, 373–374. New York: G. P. Putnam's Sons. Cambridge, England: University Press. 1918.

Patten, William, ed. Short Story Classics (American). P. F. Collier & Son. New York. 1905. (See The Diamond Lens).

Payne, George Henry. History of Journalism in the United States. D. Appleton and Company. New York, London. 1926.

Peck, Harry Thurston, Editor-in-Chief. The World's Great Masterpieces. 20 vols. American Literary Society. New York Chicago. 1898. (See The Diamond Lens, The Lost Steamship, Of Loss, and Kane).

Perry, Bliss. Walt Whitman. (American Men of Letters). Boston and New York. Houghton Mifflin Company. The Riverside Press Cambridge. 1906.

Phillips, Henry Albert. The Plot of the Short Story. An exhaustive study, both synthetical and analytical, with copious examples, making the work A Practical Treatise. Introduction by Matthew White, Jr. (The Authors' Handbook Series). The Stanhope-Dodge Publishing Co. Larchmont, N. Y. 1912.

Platt, Isaac Hull. Walt Whitman. (The Beacon Biographies edited by M. A. DeWolfe Howe.) Boston. Small, Maynard & Company. 1904.

Quinn, Arthur Hobson. A History of the American Drama From the Beginning to the Civil War. Harper & Brothers. New York and London. 1923.

Reilly, Joseph J. A Keltic Poe. In The Catholic World, CX, 751–762 (March, 1920).

Rhys, Ernest, and Scott, C. A. Dawson, eds. Tales of Mystery (Startling stories of the supernatural). Hutchinson & Co. (Publishers), Ltd. Paternoster Row, London, E. C. 4. 1928. (See What Was It?).

Richardson, Charles F. American Literature 1607–1885. 2 v. G. P. Putnam's Sons. Copyright 1888.

Rider's New York City. A Guide-Book for Travelers. New York. Henry Holt and Company. 1923.

Rogers, Cameron. The Magnificent Idler, The Story of Walt Whitman. Doubleday, Page and Company, Garden City, N. Y. 1926.

Sanborn, Kate. My Favorite Lectures of Long Ago For Friends who Remember. Boston. 1898.

Scarborough, Dorothy. The Supernatural in Modern English Fiction. G. P. Putnam's Sons. New York and London. 1917.

Famous Modern Ghost Stories. Selected, with an introduction. G. P. Putnam's Sons. New York and London. 1921. (See What Was It?).

Schedule of the Population of each Superintendent Registrar's District or Poor Law Union in 1841, 1851, 1861, 1871, and 1881. Published for the office of Registration of Marriages, Births, and Deaths in Ireland. Dublin. 1883.

Seldes, Gilbert, ed. The Diamond Lens and Other Stories by Fitz-James O'Brien. New York. William Edwin Rudge. 1932. (See Collected Editions).

Sherman, Rev. Andrew M., of Morristown, N. J. The O'Briens of Machias, Me., Patriots of American Revolution: Their Services to the Cause of Liberty. Together with A Sketch of the Clan O'Brien by Thomas Hamilton Murray. Boston, Published for the Society [The American Irish Historical Society], 1904.

Sherwood, Mrs. M. E. W. An Epistle to Posterity Being Rambling Recollections of Many Years of My Life. New York and London. Harper and Brothers, Publishers. 1898.

Fitzjames O'Brien. In N. Y. Times, July 2, 1898. (Largely reprinted in The Shield—ΘΔΧ—December, 1898).

Smith, Dr. C. Alphonso. Die Amerikanische Literature. Vorlesungen, gehalten an der Königlichen Friedrich-Wilhelms-Universität zu Berlin. Berlin. Weidmannsche Buchhandlung. 1912.

ed. Literary Contrasts. Ginn and Company. Boston, etc. 1925. (See What Was It?).

Smyth, Albert H. Bayard Taylor (American Men of Letters). Boston and New York. Houghton Mifflin Company. The Riverside Press, Cambridge. 1896.

Stedman, Edmund Clarence. Poets of America. Boston and New York. Houghton Mifflin Company. The Riverside Press, Cambridge. 1885.

ed. An American Anthology 1787–1900. Selections Illustrating the Editor's Critical Review of American Poetry in the Nineteenth Century. Boston and New York. Houghton Mifflin Company. The Riverside Press, Cambridge. Copyright, 1900. (See The Lost Steamship).

and Hutchinson, E. M., comp. and ed. A Library of American Literature from the Earliest Settlement to the Present Time. 11 vols. New York, Charles L. Webster & Company. 1889–1890. (See The Diamond Lens, The Challenge, and The Skaters).

Stedman, Laura, and Gould, George M., M. D. Life and Letters of Edmund Clarence Stedman. 2 vols. New York. Moffat, Yard and Company. 1910.

Stevenson, Burton Egbert, col. and ed. Poems of American History. Boston and New York. Houghton Mifflin Co. 1908. (See Kane).

Stoddard, Richard Henry. Recollections, Personal and Literary, Edited by Ripley Hitchcock. With an Introduction by Edmund Clarence Stedman. New York. A. S. Barnes & Company. 1903.

Stories by American Authors. New York. Chas. Scribner's Sons. 1884. (See The Spider's Eye).

Swinton, Frank. Swinton's Fourth Reader. Copyright, 1883, Ivison, Blakeman, Taylor, and Company Publishers. New York and Chicago. (See How the Bell Rang).

Swinton, William. History of the Seventh Regiment, National Guard, State of New York, During the War of the Rebellion; with a preliminary chapter on the origin and early history of the regiment, a summary of its history since the war, and a Roll of Honor, comprising brief sketches of the services rendered by members of the regiment in the Army and Navy of the United States. Illustrated by Thomas Nast. New York and Boston. Fields, Osgood, & Co. 1870.

Tassin, Algernon. The Magazine in America. New York. Dodd, Mead and Company. 1916.

Taylor, Bayard. The Echo Club, and Other Literary Diversions. Boston: James R. Osgood and Company, Late Ticknor & Fields, and Fields, Osgood & Co. 1876.

John Godfrey's Fortunes: Related by Himself. A Story of American Life. Household Edition, New York, G. P. Putnam's Sons, 27 and 29 West 23d Street, 1889. (First edition, 1864).

Taylor, Bayard, Life and Letters of, edited by Marie Hansen-Taylor and Horace E. Scudder. In two volumes. Boston. Houghton Mifflin Company. New York: 11 East Seventeenth Street. The Riverside Press, Cambridge. 1885.

Thackeray, William Makepeace. The Snobs of England, by one of themselves. In Punch, Feb. 28, 1846–Feb. 27, 1847. Published as The Book of Snobs. Chaps. XVII–XXIII first restored in Library edition, 1867–9, Vol. XXIII.

Ticknor, Caroline. Glimpses of Authors. Boston and New York. Houghton Mifflin Company. The Riverside Press, Cambridge. 1922.

Tiffany, Rev. O. H., D.D., ed. Gems for the Fireside, Russell and Hederson, Boston. 1882. (See The Cave of Silver).

Tompkins, Eugene. The History of the Boston Theatre 1854–1901. Compiled with the assistance of Quincy Kilby. Boston and New York. Houghton Mifflin Company. The Riverside Press, Cambridge. 1908.

Townsend, Horatio, the Rev., M. A. Statistical Survey of the County of Cork. Dublin: Printed by Graisberry and Campbell, 10, Back-lane, Printers to the Dublin Society. 1810.

Trent, William Peterfield. A History of American Literature. D. Appleton and Co. New York. 1920. (1st edition. 1901).

and John B. Henneman, eds. The Best American Tales. New York. Thomas Y. Crowell & Co. 1907. (See What Was It?).

Triggs, Oscar Lovell. Selections from The Prose and Poetry of Walt Whitman. Boston. Small, Maynard & Company. 1898.

Tuckey, Francis H. The County and City of Cork Remembrancer; or Annals of the County and City of Cork. With an Introductory Essay. Cork: Osborne Savage and Son, Patrick Street. 1837.

Vedder, Elihu. The Digressions of V. Written for his own Fun and that of his Friends. Boston and New York. Houghton Mifflin Company. 1910.

Wade, Joseph H., and Sylvester, Emma. Fourth Reader. (The Language Readers). Ginn & Company. 1907. (See How the Bell Rang).

Wallack, Lester. Memories of Fifty Years. With an introduction by Laurence Hutton. New York. Charles Scribner's Sons. 1889.

War of the Rebellion, The: A Compilation of the Official Records of the Union and Confederate Armies. Washington: Government Printing Office. 1881. Series I—Volume V. p. 388. Gen. Lander moves to Romney, W. Va.; pp. 405–407. Reports of Affair at Bloomery Gap, W. Va. by Brigadier-General F. W. Lander and by Colonel J. Sencendiver.

Warner, Charles Dudley, ed. Library of the World's Best Literature. R. S. Peale and J. A. Hill. New York. 1896. (See The Diamond Lens and The Lost Steamship).

Wells, Carolyn. The Technique of the Mystery Story. Introduction by J. Berg Esenwein. The Writer's Library. The Home Correspondence School, Springfield, Mass. Publishers. 1913.

ed. American Mystery Stories: The Oxford University Press, American Branch. 1927. (See What Was It?).

Welsh, Charles, ed. The Golden Treasury of Irish Songs and Lyrics. 2 vols. New York. Dodge Publishing Company, 40–42 East 19th Street. 1907.

West, Will. A Directory, and Picture, of Cork and its Environs. Cork; Printed by and for the Editor. 1810.

White, Richard Grant, select. and ed. Poetry Lyrical, Narrative, and Satirical of the Civil War. New York. The American News Company. 119 & 121 Nassau Street. 1866. (See The Seventh).

Whitman, Walt, Selections from the Prose and Poetry of, Edited with an Introduction by Oscar Lovell Triggs, Ph.D. (The University of Chicago). Boston. Small, Maynard & Company. 1898.

Wickham, Joseph Francis. Fitz-James O'Brien: A Chapter in the History of the Short Story in America. Sept. 22, 1908. Master's thesis: Columbia University.

Willis, N. P., The Prose Works of. Philadelphia: Henry C. Baird, 1852.

Willis, N. P., and Coyne, J. Stirling, Esqrs. The Scenery and Antiquities of Ireland, illustrated from drawings by W. H. Bartlett. London:—George Virtue. [1842]. 2 v.

Wilson, James Grant. Bryant and His Friends: Some Reminiscences of the Knickerbocker Writers. New York. Fords, Howard, and Hulbert, 1886.

Wilson, Rufus Rockwell. New York, Old and New. 2 vols. J. B. Lippincott. Phila. and London. 1909 (3rd edition).

Winter, William. Brown Heath and Blue Bells. Being Sketches of Scotland with other Papers. New York. Macmillan. 1895. ("Fitz-James O'Brien. 1881,"—the Sketch from Winter, 1881, with style concentrated).

The Jeffersons. (American Actor Series). With Illustrations. Boston. James R. Osgood and Company. 1881.

The Library of the late William Winter Sold by Order of his Son Jefferson Winter. To be sold at Auction Friday Afternoon, April 28, 1922 at 2:30 o'clock. The Walpole Galleries, 12 West 48th Street, New York, N. Y.

Life and Art of Joseph Jefferson together with some account of his Ancestry and of the Jefferson family of actors. New York & London. Macmillan & Co. 1894.

ed. Life, Stories, and Poems of John Brougham. James R. Osgood & Co. Boston. 1881.

Marginal notes, briefly characterizing some of the O'Brien poems and stories,—in Romm collection.

Note-book, O'Brien—List of things for Volume 2. Inside, "Material for Second Vol. of O'Brien's Works." In Romm collection.

Old Friends Being Literary Recollections of Other Days. New York. Moffat, Yard and Company. 1909.

Other Days being Chronicles and Memories of the Stage. New York. Moffat, Yard & Co. 1908.

The Poems and Stories of Fitz-James O'Brien. Collected and Edited, with a Sketch of the Author. Boston: James R. Osgood and Company. 1881.

Shadows of the Stage. Macmillan & Co. New York and London. 1892.

Vagrant Memories; being further recollections of other days. New York. Geo. H. Doran & Co. 1915.

Wise, Herbert A., and Fraser, Phyllis, eds. Great Tales of Terror and the Supernatural. Random House. New York, 1944. (See What Was It?).

INDEX

UNIVERSITY OF COLORADO STUDIES

Numbers of the University of Colorado Studies are issued from time to time as suitable contributions are received from members of the Faculty, preference being given to articles which may be: (1) Too long for publication in the usual journals; (2) Not quite suited to any other journal; (3) Concerned especially with Colorado; (4) Belonging to a group representing the activity of a university department or division.

Beginning with the academic year 1938–1939 most numbers of the *Studies* limit their contents to articles in some broad field of knowledge, as the humanities, social studies, physical sciences, or the biological sciences.

Departments or divisions of the University wishing to furnish material for an issue of the *Studies* should appoint some one person to interview the faculty members who might be able to contribute papers. This same person should consult the editor many months in advance of the proposed publication. Authors are asked to follow as nearly as possible the "suggestions" on the third page of the cover of this number.

The autumn issue of each year prints, as in the past, the abstracts of students' theses accepted toward advanced degrees. These autumn issues now constitute the General Series, known as Series A. Other series are devoted to Humanities (B), Social Sciences (C), Physical and Biological Sciences (D). See fourth page of cover for list of publications to date.

It is requested that all exchanges be addressed to the *Library of the University of Colorado, Boulder, Colorado*—not to the Editor.

Educational institutions, libraries, and societies desiring to be placed on the exchange list should make request to the *Editor of University of Colorado Studies, Boulder, Colorado.* Business communications also should be sent to the Editor.

Suggestions to Contributors

1. Manuscript is to be typewritten on one side of paper $8\frac{1}{2}$ x 11 inches, double spaced and with ample margins; carbon copies are not acceptable.

2. Do not underline any words in the typewritten sheets except titles of books or magazines.

3. Certain words with variable spellings may be standardized as follows: co-author co-operate, death rate, guinea-pig, high school (noun), high-school (adjective), man-like, per cent, percentage, program, so-called, subclass, text-book, theater, today, X-rays zoology.

4. If in doubt as to beginning a word with a capital, use a small letter; the editor can easily change it if change is needed. Capitals are less used now than formerly.

5. Punctuation should follow approved English usage. Among other points this requires a comma before *and* in a series of words and a comma before *and* or *but* introducing part of a compound sentence. The colon is seldom used except just before a series of nouns, adjectives, or phrases. Use the dash only as follows: (1) to set off parenthetical expressions too long and emphatic for commas, but not grammatically independent; (2) to precede an explanation appended as an appositive at the end of a sentence, e.g., This was the practice of the tribe—a practice established for many centuries. Distinguish by double length a dash from a hyphen.

6. Do not put a period after the title of your article or after any of the centered subtitles.

7. Save expense of footnotes by putting footnote material, if possible, into the text. When footnotes are used, they are to be numbered consecutively through an entire article or entire chapter. Footnotes should be typed one after the other on a separate sheet, not interspersed with text or put at the bottoms of the manuscript pages. The first line of a footnote is always indented.

8. References, whether in literature cited, bibliography, or footnotes should all be made consistent as to order of author's name, subject, name of publication, volume number, page, and date. See recent numbers of *Studies* for acceptable styles to employ.

9. The *Studies* does not indent quoted paragraphs; hence in the manuscript they should be full width. Never indent anything in prose except the first line of a paragraph.

10. Tables are to be without ruled lines. They should be typed on sheets separate from the text. Please reduce tables to a minimum.

11. Since printing is expensive, avoid unnecessary material, especially tables and long lists which are of little interest except to the author.

12. If it is desired to use line drawings or photographs, consult the editor before preparing them.

13. If the article is one for which a summary can be prepared it is highly desirable to make a summary, having it somewhat less than one page in length.

UNIVERSITY OF COLORADO STUDIES

Volume 1, Number 1 of the Studies was issued in January, 1902. Volumes thus far published have consisted of four numbers with the following exceptions: Volume 12 (one number), Volume 13 (two numbers), Volume 14 (two numbers). A complete subject and author index of Volumes 1-25 is printed in No. 1 of Volume 26, and is available on request.

Beginning with the academic year 1938-1939 there is, as heretofore, the General Series (A), and two or more issues in other series.

Publication to Date

General Series (A): Volumes 1-26 complete; Vol. 27, No. 1, October, 1942; Vol. 27, No. 2, December, 1943.

Series B: Studies in the Humanities: Vol. 1 complete; Vol. 2, No. 1, May, 1943; No. 2, May, 1944.

Series C: Studies in the Social Sciences: Vol. 1, No. 1, July, 1939; No. 2, May, 1941; No. 3, May, 1942.

Series D: Physical and Biological Sciences: Vol. 1 complete. Vol. 2, No. 1, August, 1943.

The price of single numbers of the *Studies* is usually $1.00. Libraries on the exchange list will be supplied *gratis* with *desiderata* if these are still available. It is requested that any duplicate copies be returned. All correspondence is to be addressed to the Editor, as indicated on page 2 of the cover of this number.

University of Colorado Semicentennial Series (1927)

Vol. I. *Geology and Natural Resources of Colorado*, by Russell D. George (out of print).

Vol. II. *Colorado Plant Life*, by Francis Ramaley.

Vol. III. *Zoology of Colorado*, by Theodore D. A. Cockerell.

Vol. IV. *Colorado: Short Studies of its Past and Present*, by George Norlin, Junius Henderson, Etienne B. Renaud, Colin B. Goodykoontz, Joe Mills, James F. Willard, Harry M. Barrett, and Irene P. McKeehan.

Vol. V. *Creative Intelligence and Modern Life*, by Francis J. McConnell, Frederick J. E. Woodbridge, Roscoe Pound, Robert A. Millikan, Lorado Taft, and Paul Shorey.

The University of Colorado Semicentennial publications (except Vol. I) are on sale to individuals at $1.00 per volume. Address, *University of Colorado Book Store, Macky Building, Boulder, Colorado.*

Libraries will be supplied with the available volumes of the Semicentennial Series as long as the supply lasts, the books (in cloth-bound edition) being sent by parcel post. Librarians are asked to furnish 15 cents in stamps to defray cost of packing and postage on each volume desired. Address the Editor, as indicated on page 2 of the cover of this number.